Authorship and authority: the writings of James VI and I

MANCHESTER
1824

Manchester University Press

# Authorship and authority: the writings of James VI and I

## Jane Rickard

Manchester University Press
Manchester and New York
*distributed exclusively in the USA by Palgrave*

*Published by* Manchester University Press
Oxford Road, Manchester M13 9NR, UK
*and* Room 400, 175 Fifth Avenue, New York, NY 10010, USA
www.manchesteruniversitypress.co.uk

*Distributed exclusively in the USA by*
Palgrave, 175 Fifth Avenue, New York,
NY 10010, USA

*Distributed exclusively in Canada by*
UBC Press, University of British Columbia, 2029 West Mall,
Vancouver, BC, Canada V6T 1Z2

*British Library Cataloguing-in-Publication Data*
A catalogue record for this book is available from the British Library

*Library of Congress Cataloging-in-Publication Data applied for*

ISBN 978 0 7190 7486 8 *hardback*

First published 2007

16 15 14 13 12 11 10 09 08 07    10 9 8 7 6 5 4 3 2 1

Typeset in 10.5/12.5 Centaur
by Servis Filmsetting Ltd, Manchester
Printed in Great Britain
by The Cromwell Press Ltd, Trowbridge

# Contents

# Figures

# Acknowledgements

It is my pleasure to thank the many individuals and institutions who assisted in the production of this book. The doctoral research that opened up my interest in James as an author was undertaken at the University of Warwick and, while the book develops what was only one part of the thesis, I remain grateful to those whose comments on that earlier work helped me to develop as a scholar: in particular, Bernard Capp, Carol Rutter, James Mardock, and my PhD examiners, Jonathan Bate and Kevin Sharpe. Kevin Sharpe, through his own work, through conversation, and through his reading of my work remains a major source of guidance, and his professional support has been of incalculable value. After leaving Warwick I had the opportunity to teach for a short while at the University of Wisconsin-Madison, where I was privileged to work with Heather Dubrow. She has been a valued colleague and friend ever since, offering careful readings of my work and unfailing professional support and encouragement. As a rigorous scholar, dedicated teacher, and generous colleague she has also been an inspiration.

This book has benefited immeasurably from the three months I spent at each of the Huntington and Folger Shakespeare Libraries, and I am extremely grateful for the fellowships from both libraries that made this possible. I would like to thank all of the reading room staff and the curators at both libraries, and to give particular thanks to Susi Krasnoo at the Huntington and Georgianna Zweigler at the Folger for general guidance and practical help, and to Stephen Tabor at the Huntington for his generous help and expertise in dealing with bibliographical enquiries during and since my fellowship. I would also like to thank my fellow readers at both libraries for helping to make all of those months so intellectually stimulating and rewarding, and memorably fun. I was especially pleased to have the opportunity to give a research paper at the Huntington, and would like to thank everyone who attended and made the discussion afterwards so useful.

Many people have assisted me in the development of my research. Michael Greaney and Hilary Hinds at Lancaster University offered professional advice in the early stages, while Richard Wilson provided enthusiastic support and encouragement. Marcus Nevitt at the University of Sheffield commented in detail on an early chapter draft. At the Folger I had the good fortune to meet Steven W. May, who generously showed me some of his own work prior to publication, discussed James VI and I's poetry at some length with me, and has subsequently read and carefully commented upon considerable portions of the manuscript. I owe much to his expertise in the field of the manuscript circulation of poetry. I also met Bernice W. Kliman who, in our very first conversation, agreed to read and comment on a chapter, subsequently providing useful, kind, and encouraging comments. I am grateful to those who provided opportunities to present my research and those who responded to my papers with helpful questions and comments, particularly at the universities of Reading, Hull, Stirling, and Aberdeen. I wish also to thank the staff of the other libraries in which I have worked, particularly the British Library, the National Library of Scotland, the Bodleian, and the Brotherton.

I would like to thank the Leverhulme Trust and the University of Leeds for supporting me in the final stages of the project. Leeds School of English is a stimulating, exciting, and convivial department, and I feel privileged to be part of it. My colleagues here have been a valuable source of support, inspiration and empathy. Particular thanks are due to my Renaissance colleagues. Michael Brennan helped with some difficult Sidney questions. Paul Hammond has offered professional advice, and lent his expertise on textual and bibliographical matters. Martin Butler has generously read and commented in detail on portions of the manuscript, and offered support and encouragement, as well as having long inspired me with his own work. I also wish to thank the Folger Shakespeare Library and the British Museum for providing the images, Helen Litton for generously and expertly preparing the index, and all of the staff at Manchester University Press.

I would like to thank my family and friends for the less definable but much appreciated help that has been given in the form of listening, sympathising, reassuring, sometimes teasing, and always believing in me. My final thank-you is to Richard Meek: for all of those after-dinner conversations in which so much of this book took shape; for not only reading and commenting thoughtfully on numerous drafts, but for doing so with enthusiasm every time; for sustaining me with endless patience, understanding and care, and unshakeable faith in me; and for always saying that thanks were not necessary, thank you.

Some of the material here has previously appeared in other versions: parts of Chapters 2 and 3 were published as 'The Word of God and the Word of the King: The Scriptural Exegeses of James VI and I and the King James Bible' in Ralph Houlbrooke (ed.), *James VI and I: Ideas, Authority, and Government* (Aldershot: Ashgate, 2006), pp. 134–49; and parts of Chapters 1 and 5 were published as 'From Scotland to England: The Poetic Strategies of James VI and I' in *Renaissance Forum*, 7 (2004). I am grateful for permission to reprint.

# A note on texts

Early editions of James's writings are used throughout, and original spellings are retained. All references to his prose works in the first three chapters are to first and second editions of these works. All references to his prose works in the fourth and fifth chapters are to his collected edition of prose, *The Workes* (1616). James's printed poems are cited from the original editions in which they appear. The poems that were not printed in his lifetime but appear in the royal manuscript collection, 'All the Kings short poesis that ar not printed' (British Library, Additional MS 24195), are cited from this manuscript. Poems that were neither printed nor collected in his lifetime are cited from James Craigie (ed.), *The Poems of James VI of Scotland*, 2 vols (Edinburgh and London: William Blackwood & Sons, 1955–1958), and various manuscripts are cited in considering the manuscript circulation of his poems in Chapter 5.

Readers wishing to consult these works in modern editions will find most of James's prose works in Charles Howard McIlwain (ed.), *The Political Works of James I*, reprinted from the 1616 edition (Cambridge, Mass.: Harvard University Press, 1918; reprinted, New York: Russell and Russell, 1965), and Johann P. Sommerville (ed.), *King James VI and I: Political Writings* (Cambridge: Cambridge University Press, 1994), but we still lack modern editions of his early scriptural works. All of James's poems may be found in Craigie (ed.), *Poems*.

# Introduction: reading James VI and I

Since thought is free, thinke what thou will
O troubled hart to ease thy paine
Thought vnreuealed can doe no euill
Bot wordes past out, cummes not againe.

So begins 'Song. the first verses that euer the King made', a poem by James VI of
Scotland that was probably written in 1582, when he was fifteen or sixteen years old.[1]
Some two decades later he would become James I of England and rule for a further
twenty-two years, a total reign that spans some of the most important literary and cultural developments of the Renaissance. Literature was growing in prestige and authority during this period, and the role of the author was acquiring increasing distinction.
To a degree unprecedented amongst his royal predecessors in Scotland and England,
James recognised and sought to exploit through his own practice the power not only of
writing, not only of printing, but of literary forms, conventions, and associations. His
writing career was long and varied, and began, as indeed it would end, not with the
political treatises that we might expect from a monarch interested in writing, but with
poetry.

'Song. the first verses that euer the King made' points towards many of the issues at
the heart of this book. Most obviously, the poem exhibits some of the authorial ten-
dencies and strategies that would feature in James's subsequent writings. Here we see a
writer concerned to foreclose interpretation and debate: the opening phrase – 'Since
thought is free' – presents questionable claim as given fact; and, in addressing the poem
to his own 'troubled hart', James proposes a circular model of interpretation, whereby

---

1 The poem is quoted as it appears in 'All the Kings short poesis that ar not printed'
(British Library, Additional MS 24195, fol. 51r–v), a manuscript collection that seems to
have been prepared by James, Prince Charles, and Thomas Carey between 1616 and 1618.
This collection will be discussed further in Chapter 4, below. The poem also appears in
a Scottish manuscript compiled before 1586 (the Maitland quarto), that indicates James
wrote it when he was fifteen. James Craigie reproduces both versions (*The Poems of James VI
of Scotland*, 2 vols (Edinburgh and London: William Blackwood & Sons, 1955–1958),
II, 132–3).

he is both author and audience of the text. This particular poem was not published in the King's lifetime, but even in the later writings that were widely circulated his desire to control not only the creation of a text but also its interpretation would persist. Moreover, this poem demonstrates James's capacity to write about the conditions and constraints of his public role as king at a certain remove – to be both subject and object in his own writing. This capacity would be most fully explored in his anonymously published works.

At the same time these lines highlight both the King's anxieties about the problems that would persist through his poetic and political career, and the contradictions of his response: the poem suggests that thinking is safe while 'wordes past out' are dangerous – but it does so *in writing*. This written acknowledgement that words once uttered cannot be retracted ('cummes not againe') highlights his awareness of the difficulties to which his proclivity for writing could lead, and draws attention to his persistence in writing nevertheless. The poem, written during the period 1582–3 when he was physically imprisoned (see below), suggests that thought, and by extension writing, is a means of escape – a realm of freedom in contrast to his present physical circumstances. But how far does this poem mark the beginning of James entrapping himself – creating written records by which he could be judged and to which he could be held accountable? Even this poem reached an opponent of the King, David Calderwood, who included a copy in the draft manuscript of his controversial *Historie of the Kirk of Scotland*, alongside an 'Antithesis' that rewrites the poem to question and oppose its author. This 'Antithesis' begins 'Since thought is thrall to thy ill will, / O troubled heart, great is thy pain!'[2] James's poem, then, despite its self-consciousness about the dangers of public utterance, was itself susceptible to hostile appropriation and response, highlighting the risk that his writings would always involve.

Most importantly, this poem raises the theoretical question of how we should approach the writings of a monarch, a figure central to the history of the age in which he lives. In its confessional and personal tone, the poem seems to invite the kind of straightforward biographical reading to which James's writings – if considered at all – have tended to be subjected. Yet the poem itself also offers a salutary warning against just such a reading. It hints at the tantalising prospect of the King's private self, but also suggests that this may be 'vnreuealed' within public utterance. Indeed the poem's suggestion of a discrepancy between thought and expression is at the same time an attempt to claim a space for this poem outside of the King's actual lived experience. James would further imply that this poem transcended the immediate circumstances of its composition by including it in a manuscript collection of his poems more than

2  It is not clear how or when Calderwood (1575–1650) obtained his copy of the poem, nor even when this part of his history was written. His copy of James's poem and the 'Antithesis' are reproduced in David Calderwood, *The History of the Kirk of Scotland*, ed. Thomas Thomson, 8 vols (Edinburgh: Wodrow Society, 1843), III, 784–5.

three decades later, in an anglicised version.[3] Any such ideal of literary transcendence was, however, already compromised by the circulation and reception the poem met in the Scottish context in which it was written. While the poem is ostensibly private, James may himself have allowed some circulation, giving a copy to a senior government official, Sir Richard Maitland, who compiled the Maitland quarto in which the poem appears.[4] We may, then, see the poem as an act of constructing the idea of the King's private self for specific readers. But even if the King had intended it to be read only by a select few, Calderwood returns it to an explicitly political and oppositional forum.

As the poem itself is not as free from immediate political embroilment as it claims, so too is its bold assertion that 'thought is free' a deluded one. The degree to which anyone is the originator of their own thoughts and writings, 'author of himself' as Shakespeare's Coriolanus has it, is a question which has been at the centre of critical and theoretical debate. We might feel that a king, whose status and role is shaped by tradition, convention, the expectations of his subjects, political and religious theory and exigency, is even less likely than many of his subjects to be capable of 'free thought'. Certainly this claim seems particularly ironic from the pen of one crowned as a baby, and since then subjected to the influence of various regents and guardians and the strict teachings of his tutor, George Buchanan. James also read widely, and the engagement of his writings with other writers, texts, and conventions further calls into question his claim of self-determination. Even his use of poetry as a vehicle for ostensibly private self-exploration is itself a conventional gesture.

What this early poem emphasises, then, is that while James's writings do not exist within some kind of transcendent literary realm, it is equally the case that they are not reducible to straightforward political autobiography. Royal thought is neither completely free nor completely isolable within his texts. Rather, his texts construct the King as much as they reveal him, and not even James himself has complete control over these processes of construction and revelation, and the meanings thereby generated. These writings engage in and with their political, religious, social, literary, and cultural contexts in varied and complex ways as the King himself seems to find a range of answers to the key question his writings force us to reconsider: what is the relationship between literature and politics and how far can each be used in the service of the other? Within these royal writings, the literary and the political variously combine, overlap and collide. It is this territory that the present book seeks to chart.

This interrelationship between literature and politics, and between text and context, has indeed been at the centre of much late twentieth- and early twenty-first-century

---

3　See note 1, above.

4　Steven W. May, 'The Circulation in Manuscript of Poems by King James VI and I', in James Dutcher and Anne Lake Prescott (eds), *Renaissance Historicisms: Essays in Honor of Arthur F. Kinney* (Newark: University of Delaware Press, forthcoming). I am grateful to Steve May for the opportunity to read this work before publication.

scholarship, particularly within New Historicist criticism.[5] Many New Historicist critics have called into question the separation of text and context and argued for the complex interplay between the two. Yet one of the problems with much New Historicist work that Jean E. Howard identifies in her insightful early critique is 'its failure to reflect on itself. Taking the form of the reading, a good deal of this criticism suppresses any discussion of its own methodology and assumptions.'[6] Accordingly, some of these critics have tended to maintain a rigid sense of what belongs in these two categories of 'text' and 'context' (however these categories are named); the terms on which texts are allocated to either category have rarely been made explicit; and canonical literary texts continue to be given primacy. The work of Stephen Greenblatt, for example, emphasises interplay and exchange, but he employs oppositions such as 'works of art' and 'the world' without fully defining each category or establishing the grounds on which he is distinguishing between them, while the wide range of texts he addresses tend to remain subservient to the analysis of Shakespeare's works.[7] In these ways such New Historicist work has not entirely broken down the text/context divide, and has continued to relegate the writings of figures such as James to a largely secondary position. As such the analyses James's writings have received have often done little to illuminate them.

Given the interests of New Historicist critics, and the continuing influence of New Historicism on early modern studies, the lack of attention paid to royal writing is curious.[8] The exception to this lack of attention amongst New Historicist critics is, of

5 Even before the development of a New Historicist approach to literary studies in the early 1980s, however, the political historians Quentin Skinner and J. G. A. Pocock had begun to question traditional divisions between canonical and non-canonical texts and to direct attention to the ways in which all texts should be understood in a broad context. In a preface of 1978, for example, Skinner explains his approach thus: 'I regard it as . . . essential to consider the intellectual context in which the major texts were conceived – the context of earlier writings and inherited assumptions about political society, and of more ephemeral contemporary contributions to social and political thought' (*The Foundations of Modern Political Thought*, 2 vols (Cambridge: Cambridge University Press, 1978), I, xi). See also Pocock, *Politics, Language and Time: Essays on Political Thought and History* (London: Methuen, 1972).

6 Jean E. Howard, 'The New Historicism in Renaissance Studies', *English Literary Renaissance*, 16 (1986), 13–46 (p. 31). This problem may result in part from the insistence of Stephen Greenblatt and other leading New Historicist critics that New Historicism is not a coherent doctrine or programme. See Greenblatt, 'Introduction', *Learning to Curse: Essays in Early Modern Culture* (New York and London: Routledge, 1990), pp. 1–15 (p. 3); and Louis Montrose, 'New Historicisms' in Stephen Greenblatt and Giles Gunn (eds), *Redrawing the Boundaries: The Transformation of English and American Literary Studies* (New York: Modern Language Association of America, 1992), pp. 392–418 (p. 407).

7 See, for example, Stephen Greenblatt, *Shakespearean Negotiations: The Circulation of Social Energy in Renaissance England* (Oxford: Oxford University Press, 1988).

8 In recent years some critics have continued to see New Historicism as the major influence on literary criticism (see Dympna C. Callaghan, 'Recent Studies in Tudor and Stuart Drama',

course, Jonathan Goldberg's *James I and the Politics of Literature* (1983). Goldberg is more concerned with exploring points of connection between the texts he considers than with interrogating the historical evidence with which he contextualises them, and, as Jenny Wormald has emphasised, is even historically inaccurate at times.[9] He maintains his overall thesis – that 'in writing, authority is established' – by quoting from James's writings very selectively, not considering what contemporary responses they met, and assuming that propagandistic accounts of Jacobean absolutist power reflected the actuality of the Jacobean state.[10] Goldberg's practice is to locate the King's writing as a fixed source of meaning, authority, and influence that forms a backdrop against which other (more canonical) texts can be read. His account thus does not fully engage with the complexity and instability of James's writings; in order to exploit these writings as a source of illumination for other texts, he and other critics have attempted to fix their meaning. By contrast the present book argues that, far from providing a stable framework or fixed point of reference, the King's writings have complexity and instability in common with the texts they have been used to illuminate, and constantly escape any attempts to fix their meaning, even the attempts of the King himself. My reading of James's *Daemonologie* (1597), for example, exemplifies both the limitations of critical approaches that attempt to use such texts as this to illuminate other texts, such as *Macbeth*, and the highly mediated, constructed, and calculated nature of James's writings.

*Studies in English Literature, 1500–1900*, 44 (2004), 405–44; and Ruth Morse, 'The Year's Contributions to Shakespeare Studies: 1. Critical Studies', *Shakespeare Survey*, 56 (2003), 300–31). Others have suggested that it has been institutionalised and popularised to the extent that we appear, particularly in Shakespeare studies, to be at a crossroads awaiting its replacement. See Hugh Grady, 'Shakespeare Studies, 2005: A Situated Overview', *Shakespeare*, 1 (2005), 102–20; and Douglas Bruster, *Shakespeare and the Question of Culture: Early Modern Literature and the Critical Turn* (New York: Palgrave, 2003). Grady advocates a shift towards a 'presentist criticism', which is in fact largely a return to the self-consciousness evident in Greenblatt's early work about the impact of the present on critical constructions of the past, but does not address how and why New Historicism prioritises certain kinds of texts. For an early critique of New Historicism that does focus on its prioritisation of canonical texts see James Holstun, 'Ranting at the New Historicism', *English Literary Renaissance*, 19 (1989), 189–225.

9  Jenny Wormald, Review of Jonathan Goldberg, *James I and the Politics of Literature*, *History*, 70 (1985), 128–30. See also Richard Helgerson's review, which suggests that Goldberg reduces literature and the social and political order to 'an undifferentiated mass of disembodied discourse' (*Renaissance Quarterly*, 38 (1985), 180–3 (182)).

10  Jonathan Goldberg, *James I and the Politics of Literature: Jonson, Shakespeare, Donne, and Their Contemporaries* (Baltimore and London: Johns Hopkins University Press, 1983), quotation from p. 56. For a discussion of the ways in which Goldberg's account overestimates the extent of Jacobean absolutism and oversimplifies the relationship between power and ideology see Alan Sinfield, *Faultlines: Cultural Materialism and the Politics of Dissident Reading* (Oxford: Oxford University Press, 1992), pp. 81–5.

These writings call into question some of the premises of New Historicist criticism in ways that have not been fully acknowledged even in work that itself challenges those premises. For example, in his influential reading of the *Henriad*, 'Invisible Bullets', Greenblatt provocatively argues that art is complicit with power and excludes the possibility of genuine subversion, suggesting that power produces and contains its own subversion to further itself.[11] David Scott Kastan responds thus: 'Representation is powerful and dangerous and its subversions are not, I think, as easily contained or co-opted as the New Historicists would suggest.'[12] His discussion of the Elizabethan theatre argues persuasively for its subversive and demystifying potential. He moves from the Elizabethan period to the execution of Charles I, and notably skips the monarch who was even more self-conscious and explicit than his predecessor or successor about being '*as it were set . . . vpon a publique stage*'.[13] Kastan suggests that theatre 'enacts, not necessarily on stage, but in its fundamental transaction with the audience, the exact shift in the conception of authority that brings a king to trial and ultimately locates sovereignty in the common will of its subjects'. Yet this is precisely what James's published writings also enact as he repeatedly does even more directly what Kastan suggests theatre does: he makes kingship 'the subject of the attention and judgement of an audience of subjects'.[14]

These royal writings thus reveal instances when power and representation, authorship and authority, literature and politics do not comfortably co-exist but undermine each other. James's royal power does not necessarily enable him to create effective representations, and his self-representations do not simply affirm his power. Rather, his writings, as we shall see, at times fail to achieve their aim of reinforcing royal authority, instead exposing the contradictions of the claims that underlie kingship and generating potentially subversive readings.[15] The extent to which James strives to prevent such readings – employing such means as instructive prefaces and marginalia – suggests that power is not in itself enough to guarantee that subversion will be contained, but rather that authority and opposition are in constant and unpredictable struggle, even within the writings of a king. These writings, while far from canonical and indeed on the edges of what is being studied even by scholars who have reacted against canonicity, reveal, then, a real king engaging in the very debates about which much New

11    Greenblatt, 'Invisible Bullets', in *Shakespearean Negotiations* ('Invisible Bullets' first published 1981), pp. 21–65 (see esp. pp. 30, 37).
12    David Scott Kastan, 'Proud Majesty Made a Subject: Shakespeare and the Spectacle of Rule', *Shakespeare Quarterly*, 37 (1986), 459–75 (p. 472).
13    James I, *Basilikon Doron* (London: Felix Kyngston for John Norton, 1603), preface, sig. A1v.
14    Kastan, 'Proud Majesty', pp. 474, 461.
15    In challenging the New Historicist model of containment and exploring the possibility of subversive readings, my approach shares some common ground with the Cultural Materialist approach of 'dissident reading', developed, for example, in Sinfield's *Faultlines*. Cultural Materialist critics have not, however, tended to share New Historicism's focus on the representation of royalty or to focus on monarchical writing specifically.

Historicist work speculates. For as both author and authority, a central political figure with a keen interest in literature, James straddles both the political and literary spheres, thereby crystallising the relationship between them. Study of James's writings thus furthers the project of New Historicism and of those who have responded to it, and clarifies many issues currently at the core of early modern studies.

Underlying much New Historicist work is the question Michel Foucault provocatively poses in 'What Is an Author?' (1969): 'what matter who's speaking?'[16] Foucault's contention that the 'author' is constituted by and the function of larger social forces and discourses is a response to Roland Barthes's 'The Death of the Author' (1968), which focuses on the 'author' as mere vehicle for pre-existing linguistic codes.[17] James's writings sit in an interesting relation to both of these post-structuralist challenges to the notion of the individual agency of the author. As other commentators have also noted, these writings suggest the limitations of Foucault's question.[18] That the *Lepanto* (1591), an epic poem celebrating a Catholic victory over the Turks, for example, was written by the King of Scotland, not by a subject nor by the Queen of England, does and should matter. This poem, which carefully presents James's religious allegiances, could function as a tool of international diplomacy precisely because of the identity of its author. To a large extent, then, James wants his readers to take exactly the approach that Barthes argues against: Barthes proposes that 'to give a text an Author is to impose a limit on that text, to furnish it with a final signified, to close the writing', and James printed, for example, an edition of *Basilikon Doron* in 1603 under his name with a preface that explains the text to come then states '*that this is the onely meaning of my booke*'.[19] In such instances James wants to close his texts and to be the final signified — he wants his readers to believe that the text represents his views and opinions, to think they can know him through the text, and to limit their readings to his instructions. Indeed it is notable that Barthes uses the phrase 'Author-God': 'a text is not a line of words releasing a single "theological" meaning (the "message" of the Author-God)'.[20] This is just how James constructs himself in some of his texts, in

---

16  Michel Foucault, 'What Is an Author?', in *Language, Counter-Memory, Practice: Selected Essays and Interviews*, ed. Donald F. Bouchard and trans. Bouchard and Sherry Simon (Oxford: Blackwell, 1977), pp. 113–38 (p. 138).

17  Roland Barthes, 'The Death of the Author', in *Image Music Text*, ed. and trans. Stephen Heath (London: Fontana Press, 1977), pp. 42–8.

18  Peter C. Herman challenges Foucault's question by pointing out that royal authors 'wrote from an entirely different subject-position', creating a subgenre in which 'nothing matters more than who is speaking' for 'The meaning of the verse *derives* from the speaker's identity' (' "Best of Poets, Best of Kings": King James and the Scene of Monarchic Verse', in Daniel Fischlin and Mark Fortier (eds), *Royal Subjects: Essays on the Writings of James VI and I* (Detroit: Wayne State University Press, 2002), pp. 61–103 (p. 70)). This perhaps underplays, however, the role of the reader and his or her expectations in constructing meaning.

19  Barthes, 'Death of the Author', p. 147; James, *Basilikon Doron* (1603), preface, sigs A3r–6v.

20  Barthes, 'Death of the Author', p. 146.

terms both of his emphasis on royal proximity and comparability to the divine, and of his occasionally dictatorial authorial style. Barthes's use of the phrase suggests that such ambition is not limited to a royal writer, but that literature offers all authors the promise of God-like power; this provides one possible explanation for how drawn James is to writing.

While James emphasises his royal presence in such texts as the *Lepanto* and *Basilikon Doron*, at other times he tries to deny or conceal his presence or to write fiction from which he appears detached. His presence is concealed, for example, in the first version of his *Apologie for the Oath of Allegiance* (1607), not only by virtue of anonymous publication but also through the construction of a fictional persona (a loyal subject). In such cases James himself seems to have realised that it matters whom the reader thinks is speaking, and to have believed in his ability to manipulate that perception. Elsewhere James wrote fictions under his own name. His most explicitly fictional writing is found in his early poetry; in one sonnet, for example, the persona proclaims 'I sung of sorrows neuer felt by me'.[21] But even when James himself denies the autobiographical import of his writing, he is still likely to be read as its primary referent by both his contemporaries and, as we shall consider more below, modern critics. Who is speaking thus matters in James's case, but what matters even more is who the reader thinks is speaking.

James elsewhere shapes his authorial presence by claiming – most explicitly in his scriptural exegeses – that God is speaking through him. In this regard he is subscribing to a medieval view of authorship that Sean Burke summarises as maintaining that 'the author (or *auctor*) was the scriptor through whom the Divine script was performed'. Burke points out that this view is effectively reproduced by Barthes in 'The Death of the Author', but with 'language' substituted for 'God'.[22] We might read this insight back on to James: what he presented as the divine, we may see as merely a series of linguistic codes that authorised kingship. Yet James was not merely the vehicle for the divine script – whether we understand that in religious or in linguistic terms – but shaped and exploited it to justify and reinforce his authority. While he was limited by the language and the conceptualisation of authority available to him, he was not, then, the passive vehicle either of the claims he makes in his scriptural exegeses or of the claims of Foucault and Barthes. Even for James himself the degree of his own agency and of his presence in his texts were vexed questions that might be answered differently according to the occasion.

The very term 'author' had a wide range of meanings in the Renaissance, and James seems to have had a particularly broad sense of what constituted royal authorship. 'Author', 'authority', and 'authorise' all share, of course, the same etymology. The Latin root 'auctor' means not only 'writer', but also one who authorises or has authority, as

---

21  BL Add. MS 24195, fol. 13r.
22  Sean Burke (ed.), *Authorship from Plato to the Postmodern: A Reader* (Edinburgh: Edinburgh University Press, 1995), pp. xvi–xvii.

well as a teacher, a creator, an originator, a prime mover or agent.[23] The word 'author' continued to carry this range of meanings in the Renaissance, and therefore to be intertwined – and even in some instances interchangeable – with 'authority'.[24] The first definition of 'authority' listed in the *Oxford English Dictionary* is 'Power to enforce obedience', but it also offers the following definitions: 'Power to influence the conduct and actions of others' (4); 'Power over, or title to influence, the opinions of others' (5); and 'Power to inspire belief . . .; authoritative statement; weight of testimony. Sometimes weakened to: Authorship, testimony' (6). Even 'authority' then, could mean either the power to enforce or the power to influence or inspire, and it is in this second 'weakened' sense that it is closest to 'author'. James not only is both an author and a source of authority but also seeks to realise and to blur the etymological link between the two. This means that, for him, his writing was a means of expressing and enacting his political power (of influencing conduct and opinion and inspiring belief), while his political power was a means of controlling interpretation of his writing. This link also means that he could count himself as 'authoring' – in the sense of authorising – texts that he had not actually written. As Curtis Perry also notes, 'James may have had a broader sense of his authorial function than have subsequent critics', and this is most evident in his sponsorship of the King James Bible (1611).[25] The Bible's epistle identifies the King as 'the principall moouer', one of the definitions of 'auctor', and as 'Author of the Worke', ensuring that the Bible implies not only his authority but also his creative, originatory force.[26]

The blurring between authoring and authorising that the King James Bible epitomises also illuminates other areas of James's writings. Back in the 1940s D. H. Willson proposed that many of the King's claims of authorship were essentially false: James

---

23 P. G. W. Glare *et al.* (eds), *The Oxford Latin Dictionary* (Oxford: Oxford University Press, 1968–82), includes the following definitions: 'One who approves, sanctions or authorizes' (3); 'A person who has weight or authority' (4); 'One who persuades, teaches or advises, esp. authoritatively' (6); 'An acknowledged expert (in a subject), esp. when serving as a precedent or model, an authority' (8); 'The originator, source, author (of information, etc.) (10); 'The person or thing responsible or principally responsible . . ., the prime mover or agent, originator, initiator, cause' (12); creator, artist, author, 'original author (as distinct from imitator, adaptor, etc.)', giver, source (13); 'the originator or founder of a family, race, etc.' (15).

24 For a discussion of the intersection of the words 'author' and 'authority' see Jeffrey Masten, *Textual Intercourse: Collaboration, Authorship, and Sexualities in Renaissance Drama* (Cambridge: Cambridge University Press, 1997), esp. p. 66.

25 Curtis Perry, 'Royal Authorship and Problems of Manuscript Attribution in the Poems of King James VI and I', *Notes and Queries*, n.s. 46 (1999), 243–6. Kevin Sharpe further suggests that the terms 'authoring' and 'authorising' 'were used virtually indiscriminately' in the period ('Foreword', Fischlin and Fortier (eds), *Royal Subjects*, pp. 15–36 (p. 17)). Such linguistic indeterminacy would have facilitated James's project of extending the scope of his 'authorship'.

26 *The Holy Bible, Conteyning the Old Testament and the New* (London: Robert Barker, 1611), sig. A2v.

'accepted far more assistance than was compatible with normal standards of authorship, and published several pieces under his name which he had not written. His own accounts of how his works came into being are utterly untrustworthy.'[27] Willson does not, however, attempt to clarify what 'normal standards of authorship' were in the Renaissance, and the work of later critics suggests the anachronistic nature of his account.[28] The recognition that a considerable amount of Renaissance writing was the product of various kinds of collaborative practices would suggest that James's approach to writing – accepting assistance, working with other writers – was far from unusual. Yet what is distinctive in his case is that his authority – as both symbolic justification and actual political force – enables him to take full credit as author for collaboratively produced texts. The King never shares his title pages with other authors.

The picture is further complicated by the fact that some contemporary readers seem to have valued singular authorship more than collaborative production, at least with regard to works associated with the King. In a letter of March 1623 John Chamberlain wrote that 'For want of better matter I send you here certain verses made upon Jacke and Toms journy . . . They were fathered at first upon the King but I learne since they were only corrected and amended by him.'[29] The verses in question are a pastoral poem recounting a trip to Spain by Prince Charles and the Duke of Buckingham, 'Off Jacke and Tom', which was not printed in James's lifetime but attributed to him in various contemporary manuscript collections.[30] By writing that the verses were after all *'only corrected and amended'* by the King, Chamberlain implies a preference for a model of authorship that posits the author as the father or originator of a text. This is a model that modern theorists have discredited, arguing that any literary work, even simply any use of language, is necessarily 'unoriginal' – that any author is to some extent simply

27  D. H. Willson, 'James I and His Literary Assistants', *Huntington Library Quarterly*, 8 (1944–5), 35–57 (p. 57).

28  Recent critics have acknowledged the role of collaboration in Renaissance literature, though they have disagreed as to how widespread deliberate collaborative practices were. Arthur F. Marotti, among others, has suggested that manuscript poems were often 'socially produced'. See *Manuscript, Print and the English Renaissance Lyric* (Ithaca: Cornell University Press, 1995). Steven W. May has, however, called into question some aspects of this claim. See 'Renaissance Manuscript Anthologies: Editing the Social Editors', *English Manuscript Studies, 1100–1700*, 11 (2002), 203–16. Perhaps the boldest claims are those made by Jeffrey Masten in his study of Renaissance theatre: Masten proposes that 'collaboration was a prevalent mode of textual production in the sixteenth and seventeenth centuries, only eventually displaced by the mode of singular authorship with which we are more familiar' (*Textual Intercourse*, p. 4). For a response to Masten see Jeffrey Knapp, 'What Is a Co-Author?', *Representations*, 89 (2005), 1–29.

29  Norman Egbert McClure (ed.), *The Letters of John Chamberlain*, 2 vols (Lancaster: Lancaster Press, 1939), II, 484.

30  Craigie (ed.), *Poems*, II, 192–3.

combining pre-existing materials.[31] Correcting a poem that someone else has written is obviously not the same as singlehandedly writing a poem that inevitably, perhaps unconsciously, draws on other texts and common linguistic currency. Nevertheless, Chamberlain's terms remind us that James's broad conception of himself as author may not be as readily distinguishable from other forms of authorship for us as for some of his contemporaries.

James was thus writing in accordance with a culture in which collaborative textual production was widespread and royal singular authorship valued. The whole project of kingship was in many ways collaborative: royal rule was largely dependent upon the co-operation of the political elite and the obedience of the subject. But such collaboration was submerged within the myth of the monarch as authorised by God and accountable only to God. In the same way James might seek assistance from others for his writings but conceal the extent of their interventions in order that the representation of his authorship reflect the myth of his authority. Notably, however, he did not entirely conceal the fact that a king might seek such assistance: in 1599 he advised his son '*Flatter not your selfe in your laboures, but before they be set foorth, let them firste bee priuelye censured by some of the best skilled men in that craft, that in these workes ye mell with*'.[32] This advice suggests James's awareness of his own fallibility as an author and recognition that he can benefit from the skills of others. Whether or not he originally intended these comments to be widely published is, as we shall see in Chapter 3, a vexed question.

That other people are rarely given credit for contributions to works attributed to the King makes it difficult to ascertain exactly how much assistance he received. As we shall see, he was highly concerned to control the ways in which he was represented and interpreted: this may have meant he was willing to seek advice and assistance in some cases, but it also meant that he carefully corrected and revised his works himself. This degree of concern and care makes it seem unlikely that he would have accepted assistance from other people without directing, checking, and approving their contributions, and suggests that he would thus have been at the very least a shaping influence on all of the works to which he put his name. Moreover, whether he authored, part-authored, or authorised a text – wrote it singlehandedly, wrote it with assistance, or commissioned others to write for him – that text was still associated with his authority and could contribute to shaping public perception of him.[33] The present book addresses texts which

---

31 Barthes, for example, describes a text as 'a multi-dimensional space in which a variety of writings, none of them original, blend and clash . . . a tissue of quotations' ('Death of the Author', p. 146). More recently, Masten has suggested that 'if we accept that language is a socially produced (and producing) system, then collaboration is more the condition of discourse than its exception' (*Textual Intercourse*, p. 20).

32 James VI, *Basilikon Doron* (Edinburgh: Robert Waldegrave, 1599), p. 140.

33 Curtis Perry similarly suggests that whether or not the manuscript poems he is discussing were 'literally produced by the hand and heart of the king' they 'speak for the crown' ('"If Proclamations Will Not Serve": The Late Manuscript Poetry of James I and the Culture of Libel', in Fischlin and Fortier (eds), *Royal Subjects*, pp. 205–32 (p. 212)).

circulated under James's name, including those which may have been written collaboratively, engaging with what seems to have been his broad definition of authorship, considering the role of collaboration in his self-presentation, and arguing that all of these
texts are shaped by and help to construct him. Particularly in his early Scottish reign,
the King engaged in reciprocal and collaborative ways with other writers and here, as
we shall see in the first chapter, the collaborative nature not only of royal authorship
but of royal authority remains visible.

James's attempts to blur the distinction between authorship and authority were in
keeping with an age in which, as scholars such as Kevin Sharpe have emphasised, 'language represented power' and 'rhetoric and governance could not be dissociated'.[34]
Lacking even a standing army or police force, early modern monarchs depended upon
representation to realise their power.[35] Any act of representing monarchical authority
is to some extent, then, an admission that it needs to be represented, and therefore that
it is not absolute. This forms a political corollary to Edward Said's suggestion that 'one
aspect of authorship is its contingent authority . . . any absolute truth cannot be
expressed in words, for only diminished, flawed versions of the truth are available to
language. This is as much as to say that *fiction alone speaks or is written* – for truth has no
need of words.'[36] In these terms, every time James writes he tacitly admits that he does
not possess absolute authority, nor absolute truth. Paradoxically, however, he writes in
the attempt to convince his subjects otherwise. Jacqueline Miller responds to Said by
asking 'Does silence signify the perfection of authority, or the complete loss of it for
the author whose medium is language?', and this suggests something of the complexity of James's position.[37] His authority partly lies in and is constituted by his textual
representation, but such representation might also expose the limits of that authority.

James seems to have been keen to reach a wide readership. While some of his writings circulated only in exclusive court circles, others, most notably *Basilikon Doron*, were
published on a mass scale and in different languages. The King himself seems to have
written consciously for different readerships, one of which was broad and unspecific:
he would reflect in 1620 that some of his books were dedicated to particular individuals, but others 'which treated of matters belonging to euery qualitie of persons, [were] therefore indef-
initely dedicated to the Reader in generall'.[38] His readers ranged, as we shall see in the course

34  Kevin Sharpe and Steven N. Zwicker, 'Politics of Discourse: Introduction', in Sharpe and
    Zwicker (eds), *Politics of Discourse: The Literature and History of Seventeenth-Century England* (Berkeley,
    Los Angeles and London: University of California Press, 1987), pp. 1–20 (pp. 7–8).
35  Cf. Greenblatt, 'Invisible Bullets', p. 64. For a general discussion of the importance of public
    display and performance in the age of personal monarchy see John Adamson (ed.), *The
    Princely Courts of Europe, 1500–1750* (London: Weidenfeld and Nicolson, 1999).
36  Edward Said, *Beginnings: Intention and Method* (New York: Basic, 1975), p. 86.
37  Jacqueline T. Miller, *Poetic License: Authority and Authorship in Medieval and Renaissance Contexts*
    (Oxford: Oxford University Press, 1986), p. 30.
38  James I, *A Meditation vpon the Lords Prayer*, in *The Workes of the Most High and Mighty Prince, Iames*
    (London: Robert Barker and John Bill, 1620), p. 572.

of this book, from John Chamberlain to Elizabeth I, from Scottish Catholic earls to the English scholar Gabriel Harvey, from Catholic controversialists on the continent to Scottish and English poets.

Yet James's writings risked empowering his numerous and varied readers. J. G. A. Pocock suggests that 'to speak at all is to give some other power over us', for any utterance is available for interpretation and, even if the author of a statement intends to be ambiguous, 'his statement may convey meaning to others . . . outside any range of ambiguity he may have intended'.[39] Annabel Patterson has qualified such a view by arguing for a 'theory of *functional* ambiguity in which the indeterminacy of language was fully and knowingly exploited by authors and readers alike' as they protected and liberated themselves by transferring interpretative responsibility on to external authorities, such as the censor.[40] Yet James represents a distinctive case that Patterson does not consider: he cannot transfer interpretative authority elsewhere because he is both author and authority. He tries in some of his writings to exploit ambiguity and in others to dictate meaning, but in either case the responsibility for their interpretation can be shared only between author and reader.

The transaction between authors and readers is, for many recent critics, one in which the latter has more authority than the former.[41] Stephen B. Dobranski has, however, given a more nuanced view of the relationship between authorial and readerly authority, suggesting that the two are reciprocal and proportional, meaning that gestures that seek to authorise the author paradoxically also authorise the reader.[42] Again the particular case of royal writing is not considered, but Dobranski's model captures the complex double bind in which James places himself: as an author he is authorised by and authorises his readers; and, in his unique case, this also represents the King being authorised by and authorising his subjects. What authorship and authority have in common, then, is dependence upon the recipient – the reader or subject.[43]

One of the most complex aspects of the relation between authorship and authority is the question of how far and in what ways James's writings can be considered 'literary'. As far back as 1975 G. P. V. Akrigg defended James as 'a literary man . . . of no mean competence or achievement'. He does not define the term 'literary', and the

39 Pocock, *Politics, Language and Time*, pp. 23–4.

40 Annabel Patterson, *Censorship and Interpretation* (Wisconsin and London: University of Wisconsin Press, 1984), p. 18.

41 Kevin Sharpe and Steven N. Zwicker, for example, make it clear in the introduction to their *Reading, Society and Politics in Early Modern England* (Cambridge: Cambridge University Press, 2003) that 'what we want to stress is the power and centrality of the reader in all the commerce of the book' (pp. 1–37 (p. 3)).

42 Stephen B. Dobranski, *Readers and Authorship in Early Modern England* (Cambridge: Cambridge University Press, 2005), esp. pp. 12, 17, 22.

43 In this regard James's writings sit in an interesting relationship with Greenblatt's argument in 'Invisible Bullets' that *Henry V* exposes the parallel reliance of stagecraft and kingcraft upon the imagination of its audience/subjects. See Chapter 1, below.

evaluative nature of his article seems outdated now, but he emphasises the clarity and pithiness of James's writings and his 'sensitivity to words', and suggests that 'like a poet, he thinks in terms of images'.[44] But Akrigg's evaluation seems to have had little impact. While modern critics are unlikely to go so far as proclaiming with Akrigg's precursors that, of the wide range of James's prose writings, 'the only one that seems worthy of perusal at the present day is the "Basilicon Doron" ',[45] or describing his *Meditation vpon St. Matthew* (1620) as 'this strange affair, a product of premature senility',[46] James's writings have rarely been considered worthy of literary analysis. As we shall consider further below, a growing number of literary critics are now, however, addressing royal writing, and their work is concerned to emphasise its literariness.[47]

The tradition of resistance to the notion that James's writing be considered 'literary' may derive in part from the preconception that the writings of a political figure can only be of historical interest.[48] It may be to some extent a product of a lack of awareness of what James actually wrote, which itself relates to a lack of availability – we still lack modern editions of some of his output (see below). It may also relate to the King's avoidance of certain literary styles that have become markers of literary ability.[49] But there may also be more complex explanations. The present book argues that any attempt

44  G. P. V. Akrigg, 'The Literary Achievement of King James I', *The University of Toronto Quarterly*, 44 (1975), 116–29 (p. 128).

45  James VI and I, *Basilikon Doron*, ed. Charles Butler (London, 1887), preface, p. xii.

46  Willson, 'James I and His Literary Assistants', p. 55.

47  Daniel Fischlin, for example, emphasises that James's commentaries on Revelation – one of the areas of his writing to have attracted least critical comment – have both a 'literary and political function' (' "To Eate the Flesh of Kings": James VI and I, Apocalyse, Nation and Sovereignty', in Fischlin and Fortier (eds), *Royal Subjects*, pp. 388–420 (p. 390)).

48  The same preconception also extends, of course, to the writings of other political figures, such as Elizabeth I. Leah S. Marcus, Janel Mueller, and Mary Beth Rose point out in their recent edition of her letters, poems, prayers, and speeches that these writings have received only piecemeal consideration and require further study (*Elizabeth I: Collected Works* (Chicago and London: University of Chicago Press, 2000), p. xi).

49  Michael R. G. Spiller argues that James's 'A Sonett: On Sir William Alexanders harshe vearses after the Inglishe fasone' was written in 1604 and records James's response to English poetry. The poem warns 'Bewray there harsh hard trotting tumbling wayne / Such hamringe hard the mettalls hard require / Our songs ar fil'd with smoothly flowing fire' (Craigie (ed.), *Poems*, II, 114–15). Spiller suggests James is responding to the ability, evident by this point in the work of Sidney, to convey the impression of a mind spontaneously speaking, which for someone rhetorically trained like James would seem harsh and disordered ('The Scottish Court and the Scottish Sonnet at the Union of the Crowns', in Sally Mapstone and Juliette Wood (eds), *The Rose and the Thistle: Essays on the Culture of Late Medieval and Renaissance Scotland* (East Linton: Tuckwell Press, 1998), pp. 101–15 (pp. 104–7)). This aspect of Renaissance poetry has, of course, subsequently been considered a great achievement, and, if James was indeed consciously rejecting it in favour of an older poetic style, this was, ironically, detrimental to his later poetic reputation.

to define James's writings as either straightforwardly literary or non-literary simplifies the complex relation between the literary and the political that informs these writings. His interests and ambitions were both political and literary: his writings were constructed not merely to achieve immediate and specific political ends in a direct and straightforward way but also to bolster the royal image in more general and cultural terms, and to bequeath to posterity James as an author. This concern with what we might term cultural capital is evident in the extent to which he situates himself within literary traditions and writes according to literary codes and conventions (in the late 1580s and early 1590s he wrote, for example, Petrarchan love lyrics). His desire to monumentalise his writings was most fully expressed in his decision to produce a prestigious folio edition of his *Workes*. And his contemporaries recognised his literary identity: most famously, Ben Jonson proclaimed 'How, best of kings, dost thou a sceptre bear! / How, best of poets, dost thou laurel wear!'[50] Yet the literary and the political are always difficult to disentangle and at times pull against each other, leaving James's writings falling short of certain definitions of literariness, particularly with regard to issues of fictionality and referentiality. These definitions are themselves, however, the subject of on-going debate.

Catherine Gallagher and Stephen Greenblatt, for example, define 'texts that have been regarded as nonliterary' as 'lacking the aesthetic polish, the self-conscious use of rhetorical figures, the aura of distance from the everyday world'.[51] This attempt to summarise a standard definition of 'nonliterary' is inevitably imprecise; what, for example, does 'aesthetic polish' mean, and would it be recognised as such by every reader? Nevertheless, we can observe that James, a skilled and self-conscious rhetorician with an interest in aesthetics, wrote works that are 'literary' according to the first two criteria. But these works may not appear 'literary' according to the third criterion: the writings of a king seem inevitably embroiled in *his* 'everyday world', even if this is a world that is remote from that of his ordinary subjects. Further, fiction has been defined by the fact that, as Peggy Kamuf puts it, 'it refers, but to nothing in existence'.[52] James's writings always seem to have a referent: the King himself. For his unique identity as king is public, to a large extent owned and constructed by his subjects, and it pre-exists his writings, even his life. This makes available to his readers a range of ideas, expectations, and associations to which his writings can be related.

We need to make some important distinctions here, however. An 'aura of distance from the everyday world' is a quality not necessarily inherent in a text, but created

---

50 Ben Jonson, Epigram IV, 'To King James', in Ian Donaldson (ed.), *Ben Jonson* (Oxford: Oxford University Press, 1985), p. 223, lines 1–2.

51 Catherine Gallagher and Stephen Greenblatt, *Practicing New Historicism* (Chicago and London: University of Chicago Press, 2000), p. 9.

52 Peggy Kamuf, ' "Fiction" and the Experience of the Other', in Elizabeth Beaumont Bissell (ed.), *The Question of Literature: The Place of the Literary in Contemporary Theory* (Manchester: Manchester University Press, 2002), pp. 156–73 (p. 157), quoted in Andrew Bennett, *The Author* (London and New York: Routledge, 2005), p. 118.

according to the perspective of the reader. James's readers – both his contemporaries and subsequent critics – may have refused to read his writings in terms of an 'aura of distance' from his 'everyday world' of political responsibility, even as the King himself is, somewhat like a literary text, distant from their own everyday world. James, however, at times desired and attempted to create an 'aura of distance' not between King and subject but between his writings and his political concerns. This is most evident in his poetry's employment of mythological tropes; in a sonnet of 1621, for example, he refers to sitting 'vpon Parnassus forked hill'.[53] In some cases, he tried to write 'fictions' in which he is not the referent, which refer to 'nothing in existence', as in the admission in the poem quoted above that he has written of sorrows he has never experienced. But even the sequence of which this poem forms part has attracted simplistic biographical readings.[54] The ways in which James's writings fall short of certain definitions of literariness are, then, in large part the result of how he was and is *read*, not entirely of how he wrote. Of course, 'literature' may be defined purely in terms of how it is perceived – Terry Eagleton suggests that it is entirely constituted by historically variable value-judgements – but this does not necessarily mean that the aims and concerns of the author should be entirely overlooked.[55]

Acknowledging the potential for discrepancies between intention and reception complicates our sense of James's authorial identity. Critics of his poetry have attempted to produce a single definition of that identity; Peter C. Herman, for example, argues that 'James always writes *as a monarch* and never as a mere poet'.[56] Yet his roles as king and poet are in a complex, shifting and often contradictory relationship. While he is always likely to be *read 'as a monarch* and never as a mere poet', this is not how he 'always writes' or wants to be read. There is no single, fixed, identifiable relationship between James the king and James the poet. James's attempts to manipulate and exploit the relationship between politics and poetry involve implying *either* analogy or separation between them according to the occasion. To take two examples from the same period: in 1622 James wrote a poem advising people to leave London, which explicitly supports his proclamation to the same effect of the same year; in the summer of 1621 he wrote a sonnet in praise of his favourite, Buckingham, that strikingly avoids any reference to the political controversies of these months, in which the favourite was embroiled.[57] In the first instance, poetic and political statement are rendered equivalent. In the second, the poem is apparently separated from its political moment, though even this apparent separation serves the purpose of extricating Buckingham from

---

53  Craigie (ed.), *Poems*, II, 177.
54  See Chapter 1, below.
55  Terry Eagleton, *Literary Theory: An Introduction*, second edition (Oxford: Blackwell, 1996), p. 14. Eagleton also writes that 'literature' might mean 'any kind of writing which for some reason or another somebody values highly' (p. 8), but does not consider the implications of that somebody being the author rather than a reader.
56  Herman, ' "Best of Poets, Best of Kings" ', p. 61.
57  Craigie (ed.), *Poems*, II, 178–81, 177.

political controversy. This poem nevertheless, as we shall see in Chapter 5, attracted considerable negative comment. In such cases, then, James requires a mode of reading that allows for a significant degree of separation between poetics and politics, but at the same time his writing has political implications that both accord with, and exceed, his political purposes.

More complexly, James at times, as we have noted, fictionalises 'the King's' experiences or represents 'the King' from the perspective of a fictional persona. Such instances suggest that 'the King' is the product rather than the agent of representation – that James writes the monarch as much as he 'writes as a monarch'. In this regard his writings complicate the theory of the King's two bodies; the fallible, mortal 'body natural' writes and that writing helps to construct the supposedly unerring 'body politic'.[58] In so far as this act of construction is apparent, it reveals that the 'body politic' does not after all transcend historical contingency. But the distinction between the 'two bodies' of the monarch is blurred, just as the relationship between James's poetics and politics, between his authorial identity and his political identity, is not always readily determinable. This very indeterminacy, in turn, increases the susceptibility of his writings to being read in ways contrary to his intentions.

James's writings vary greatly, of course, in terms of their style, genre, and purpose, and, consequently, in terms of the extent and nature of their relationship to notions of literariness, and some broad developments in his writing career may be traced. His early poetry (of the 1580s and early 1590s) is the aspect of his oeuvre most readily defined as 'literary'. These verses playfully admit their own deceptiveness, but we might note that they also hint at the tensions between such forms of writing and James's political concerns. When he reflects 'My Muse hath made a willfull lye I grante / I sung of sorrows neuer felt by me' he presents artifice as dishonesty. He cannot go so far as Sidney who, in claiming that the poet 'nothing affirms, and therefore never lieth', situates poetry outside the realms of truth versus falsehood, because elsewhere he writes poetry with a political import that he wants his subjects to accept as 'truth'.[59] Moreover, for a king to admit his capacity to deceive is politically problematic, but at least, in the poem quoted, the 'lye' is acknowledged and deflected on to his muse. For royal poetry both to exploit the cultural capital of poetic feigning and to be capable of acting as political vehicle, that which is entirely feigned must be clearly demarcated. Yet this is a compromise that to a degree undermines both goals, diminishing the complexity of the poetry by identifying feigning simply as lying, *and* diminishing its political efficacy by raising the possibility of royal falsity.

58  For discussion of this theory and its contemporary currency see Ernst H. Kantorowicz, *The King's Two Bodies: A Study in Mediaeval Political Theology* (Princeton: Princeton University Press, 1957), and Marie Axton, *The Queen's Two Bodies: Drama and the Elizabethan Succession* (London: Royal Historical Society, 1977).

59  Sir Philip Sidney, *The Defence of Poesy*, in Richard Dutton (ed.), *Sir Philip Sidney: Selected Writings* (Manchester: Carcanet Press, 1987), p. 130.

The playfulness and openness to interpretation often evident in this early poetry was largely replaced by an increasing concern to dictate how his texts should be interpreted, as James turned to writing explicitly religious and political prose. While these works participated in the theological, social, and political debates of James's 'everyday world', and refer to issues and people very much 'in existence', the King himself made a striking bid for their transcendence of these concerns, Chapter 4 argues, by including them all in his *Workes* of 1616. In the last years of his reign James returned to more explicitly literary forms of writing, even composing, as noted above, a sonnet in 1621, and this emphasises that he continued to be interested in and to value literature throughout his long career.

The present book argues that all of James's writings, including his religious and political prose works, are to a large extent the product of his interest in the ability of art to manipulate and deceive, and of his self-consciousness about the relationship between authors, texts, and readers. While these issues arise not only in relation to literature but also in relation to other rhetorical uses of language, James seems to have developed this interest and self-consciousness through his early experience with poetry in particular. For though in the 1580s he was also reading and beginning to write in other genres, he was especially concerned with reading, translating, collaborating, and writing within the arena of poetry, and this is the period in which his authorial aims and concerns began to take shape. He seems to have become acutely aware of the power of art, of writing as a central means of establishing his authority, and perhaps even of the extent to which his authority depended upon effective representation. He was likewise aware that others might use this power against him, and was therefore concerned to guide, respond to, or censor other writers.[60] At the same time he shared the awareness of many of his contemporaries that the reader too has agency in determining meaning – he even translated from the French poet Du Bartas the observation that the Poet 'Doeth graue so viue [lifelike] in vs his passions strange, / As maks the reader, halfe in author change'.[61] It is this awareness that leads him to close his texts – to try to dictate their meaning – and that is in tension with his desire to exploit the power of

60  We might here note that James was an avid reader and collector of books throughout his life, and would become 'the first English monarch systematically to keep printed dossiers on subjects that interested him', but his particular concern was to 'collect all the books written by everyone who wrote against him' (T. A. Birrell, *English Monarchs and Their Books* (London: British Library, 1987), pp. 26, 27).

61  James VI, *Essayes of a Prentise, in the Diuine Art of Poesie* (Edinburgh: Thomas Vautroullier, 1584), sig. E2r. A number of recent studies have emphasised that reading was – and was understood to be – an active process in the early modern period. See, for example, Lisa Jardine and Anthony Grafton, ' "Studied for Action": How Gabriel Harvey Read His Livy', *Past and Present*, 129 (1990), 30–78; Roger Chartier, *The Order of Books: Readers, Authors, and Libraries in Europe between the Fourteenth and Eighteenth Centuries*, trans. Lydia G. Cochrane (Cambridge: Polity Press, 1994 (first published in France in 1992)); Kevin Sharpe, *Reading Revolutions: The Politics of Reading in Early Modern England* (New Haven and London: Yale

art. As he thus writes with a sophisticated – and anxious – understanding of literature, so, then, do all of his writings repay literary analysis.

The aims and the limitations of James's engagement with literature are partly explicable in terms of the broader cultural and literary contexts of his reign. Many authors in the early modern period turned to external sources of authority, such as patrons, as a means of authorising their works.[62] As King, James could not turn to earthly patrons – he indeed was that source of authority for others. But his kingship was dependent upon the notion of divine right, and throughout his writings he draws on divine authority in much the same way that other contemporary writers draw on other external sources of authority. Literary authorship itself was, however, growing in prestige in the late sixteenth and early seventeenth centuries.[63] In his 1603 panegyric to the King, Thomas Greene claims that the laurel wreath 'is the richest Crowne a King can haue', and that 'To be a Prince it is an honour'd thing, / Yet eu'ry Poet to himselfe's a King'.[64] This neatly captures the appeal to James of writing poetry; Greene suggests it brings its own form of authority and adds lustre to kingship. As Herman also notes, James accordingly seeks to authorise his own writing not only by emphasising the royal authority he derives from God but by drawing on 'the growing authority of poetic authorship itself'.[65] Greene's poem also reveals, however, tensions between poetic and royal authority. The assertion that 'eu'ry Poet to himselfe's a King' suggests that poetry is a sphere in which everyone assumes authority, and which, therefore, fails to reflect – and might even offer a challenge to – the notion of the monarch's unique status. The poem seems to propose that poetry is more important than kingship, the laurel wreath richer than the crown – rather a double-edged compliment to pay a poet–king.

While literary authorship was evidently attractive to James, so too was the press. His desire to reach a mass audience within and beyond his own kingdom – evident from the beginning of his writing career in, as we shall see, the anglicisation of works composed in Scots – was realised through the printed book, a mass commodity.[66] But the nature of print, and of the values with which it was associated, was problematic for the

University Press, 2000); Sharpe and Zwicker, *Reading, Society and Politics*; and Dobranski, *Readers and Authorship*.

62  For further discussion of this point see, for example, Evelyn B. Tribble, *Margins and Marginality: The Printed Page in Early Modern England* (Charlottesville and London: University Press of Virginia, 1993).

63  See, in particular, Richard Helgerson, *Self-Crowned Laureates: Spenser, Jonson, Milton, and the Literary System* (Berkeley, Los Angeles, and London: University of California Press, 1983).

64  Thomas Greene, *A Poets Vision, and a Princes Glorie* (London: William Leake, 1603), sigs B4v–C1r.

65  Herman, '"Best of Poets, Best of Kings"', p. 83.

66  David Zaret notes that print culture 'might fairly be described as a mass culture' (*Origins of Democratic Culture: Printing, Petitions, and the Public Sphere in Early-Modern England* (Princeton: Princeton University Press, 2000), p. 136). See also Joseph Loewenstein, 'The Script in the Marketplace', *Representations*, 12 (1985), 101–14.

King in a number of ways. Firstly, the printed book created a 'literary marketplace' – a largely commerce-driven arena that in part replaced an old-style patronage economy.[67] The association with commerce led to the so-called 'stigma of print', which meant that, through most of the sixteenth century and much of the seventeenth, many men of rank either deliberately avoided print or tried to maintain the illusion that they had only reluctantly allowed their work to be printed.[68] As it was entirely incompatible with the prestige of monarchy to write for a patron, neither could a monarch be seen to write for commercial gain.

Secondly, the nature of the printing process left the printed book as a less than ideal reflection of royal authority. While some critics have emphasised the fixity of print, Adrian Johns's monumental study has suggested print's lack of authority:

> early modern printing was not joined by any obvious or necessary bond to enhanced fidelity, reliability, and truth . . . If an early modern reader picked up a printed book . . . then he or she could not be immediately certain that it was what it claimed to be, and its proper use might not be so self-evident. Piracy was again one reason: illicit uses of the press threatened the credibility of all printed products.[69]

Such problems, evident even in some of the King's own writings, suggest that his attempts to exploit print as a means of disseminating a royally authorised image of royalty are to some extent at odds with the nature of the medium. He was greatly concerned, as we shall see throughout this study, with the final form of his works, but this concern is frequently rendered ironic by the reality of the finished product. For the printing process involved various participants who might not act entirely in accordance with the desires of the author. Here Martin Butler's comments on Jonson's *Workes* are instructive: he suggests that this collection represents not, as critics have previously suggested, a 'prodigious collaboration between an imperiously single-minded dramatist and his compliant printer' but 'a complex, many-layered negotiation between a number of participants: author, compositors, corrector and other printing house employees'.[70]

67  See Loewenstein, 'The Script in the Marketplace'. We should also note, however, that, as Chartier points out, 'patronage and the market were . . . not mutually exclusive' (*The Order of Books*, p. 46).

68  Marotti, *Manuscript*, p. 228. See also J. W. Saunders, 'The Stigma of Print: A Note on the Social Bases of Tudor Poetry', *Essays in Criticism*, 1 (1951), 139–64.

69  Adrian Johns, *The Nature of the Book: Print and Knowledge in the Making* (Chicago and London: University of Chicago Press, 1998), p. 5. Johns is reacting in particular against the arguments of Elizabeth L. Eisenstein, *The Printing Press as an Agent of Change: Communications and Cultural Transformations in Early Modern Europe*, 2 vols (Cambridge: Cambridge University Press, 1979). His emphasis on the instability of print has been developed by, for example, David McKitterick in *Print, Manuscript and the Search for Order, 1450–1830* (Cambridge: Cambridge University Press, 2003).

70  Martin Butler, 'Introduction: From *Workes* to Texts', in Butler (ed.), *Re-Presenting Ben Jonson: Text, History, Performance* (London: Macmillan Press, 1999), pp. 1–19 (p. 10).

A printer may have been more likely to be 'compliant' when dealing with the work of a monarch, but the unauthorised publication of an edition of James's *Apologie for the Oath of Allegiance* in 1609 suggests that the compliance of all participants was not always guaranteed.[71]

Third, there was growing concern that the press was open to all comers, however unlearned, and that printing thereby tarnished other writers by association. Printing presses were established later in Scotland than in England, and secular literature in Scotland was, Sarah M. Dunnigan suggests, relatively confined within a manuscript culture until the end of the sixteenth century.[72] By this time in England, conversely, there was already a sense that the press was being excessively and badly used. In 1601 Samuel Daniel felt the need to write 'Musophilus: Containing, A generall Defence of Learning', a verse dialogue presenting arguments for and against learning and writing. One of the arguments against reflects concern as to how the press is being used:

> Do you not see these Pamphlets, Libels and Rymes,
> These strange confused tumults of the minde
> Are growne to be the sickenesse of these times,
> The great disease inflicted on mankinde?[73]

While the dialogue as a whole is a defence of learning, this is a compelling account of a culture in which learning has degenerated and the press is used for mass production of cheap and damaging publications.[74]

71 See Chapter 3, below.

72 Sarah M. Dunnigan, *Eros and Poetry at the Courts of Mary Queen of Scots and James VI* (Basingstoke: Palgrave Macmillan, 2002), p. 50. Printing was introduced in Scotland after James IV issued his patent in 1507. Jonquil Bevan notes that the press in Scotland was then for a long time 'relatively small (and sometimes contentious)', and suggests that its size may have been the result not only of economic and political factors but also of the fact that the Scots were accustomed to buying books printed on the continent ('Scotland' in John Barnard and D. F. McKenzie (eds), *The Cambridge History of the Book in Britain, Volume IV, 1557–1695* (Cambridge: Cambridge University Press, 2002), pp. 687–700 (pp. 688, 692, 689)). For further discussion of printing in Scotland see Alastair Mann, *The Scottish Book Trade 1500–1720: Print Commerce and Print Control in Early Modern Scotland* (East Linton: Tuckwell Press, 2000). *A History of the Book in Scotland* is to be published in four volumes by Edinburgh University Press (gen. eds Bill Bell and Jonquil Bevan).

73 Samuel Daniel, *The Works of Samuel Daniel* (London: Simon Waterson, 1601), sig. B4r (second count).

74 For further discussion of print culture in late sixteenth- and early seventeenth-century England see H. S. Bennett, *English Books and Readers, 1558–1603* (Cambridge: Cambridge University Press, 1965) and *English Books and Readers, 1603 to 1640* (Cambridge: Cambridge University Press, 1970); Chartier, *The Order of Books*; Joseph Loewenstein, *Ben Jonson and Possessive Authorship* (Cambridge: Cambridge University Press, 2002); and Barnard and McKenzie (eds), *Cambridge History of the Book, Volume IV, 1557–1695*.

When James acceded to the throne of England, some of the panegyrics with which he was greeted addressed these concerns to him. Greene's *A Poets Vision, and a Princes Glorie*, for example, claims that poetry has fallen into decline and disrepute, and reflects explicitly on the relatively democratic nature of print, suggesting that 'throngs' of learned and inspired poets would write if it were not that 'eu'rie Cuckowe [has] accesse, / And bring[s] vnsau'rie writings to the Presse'. His poem looks to James to renew poetry, proclaiming 'Now commeth in our long-detained Spring, / Reduced back by a victorious King'.[75] While Greene is evidently trying to maintain a distinction between good and bad poetry, he reveals that getting into print is no mark of quality, and that the press has become so cheapened that poets may avoid being associated with it. Indeed he implicitly calls into question James's printing of his writings, suggesting that he has entered a degraded forum that learned and inspired poets would rather avoid. Although he is looking to James to renew poetry, he has identified a problem of access to the press that the King, however he might try to dignify writing and printing by example, cannot rectify, at least not without major social and economic changes. In the event, James was not able entirely to dispel negative views of writing books through his own practice. Even thirteen years into his English reign, when he printed his prestigious folio *Workes*, there remained a perception – according to the preface contributed by Bishop Montague – that '*since that Booke-writing is growen into a Trade; It is as dishonorable for a King to write bookes; as it is for him to be a Practitioner in a* Profession'.[76]

Writing and printing so extensively was, then, a risky strategy for the King. It enabled him to construct and disseminate his image throughout his realm and beyond, but by its very nature it risked not only reinforcing but also undermining his authority. He began to prioritise writing and printing in Scotland, but even there he had no real precedent. This is true of his books on political theory: as Jenny Wormald notes, 'not only was it highly unusual for a king to write books. It was remarkable in the extreme for a Scottish king to do so . . . because before the sixteenth century there had been, in sharp distinction to England, virtually no tradition of political theorizing'.[77] But it is also true of his engagement with literature more broadly: 'to a degree unprecedented for a Scottish monarch (even given the literary reputations of James I, IV, and V, as well as Mary), James had a literary identity'.[78] His Scottish predecessors may have written, but the key difference is the extent to which James printed his writings, entering the 'literary marketplace' and developing a public authorial identity.

75  Greene, *A Poets Vision*, sigs C2v, B4v.
76  James I, *The Workes of the Most High and Mighty Prince, Iames* (London: Robert Barker and John Bill, 1616), sig. B2v.
77  Jenny Wormald, 'James VI and I, *Basilikon Doron* and *The Trew Law of Free Monarchies:* The Scottish Context and the English Translation', in Linda Levy Peck (ed.), *The Mental World of the Jacobean Court* (Cambridge: Cambridge University Press, 1991), pp. 36–54 (p. 38).
78  Carolyn Ives and David J. Parkinson, ' "The Fountain and Very Being of Truth": James VI, Poetic Invention, and National Identity', in Fischlin and Fortier (eds), *Royal Subjects*, pp. 104–23 (p. 105).

More crucially, given the extent to which James's reputation has been based on his English reign, his style of self-representation had no real precedent in England; as in Scotland, previous monarchs had written but not to the extent or in the manner of James.[79] Over the course of Elizabeth's long reign (1558–1603) she had met and shaped English expectations of monarchical display and been remarkably successful in her representational strategies.[80] Like James, Elizabeth wrote – she was indeed 'an immensely productive writer' – but, again, the key difference is that she did not publish widely in any area; there is even 'recurrent evidence that Elizabeth made efforts to keep most of her verses out of general circulation'.[81] The reprinting of a number of James's works in England at the time of his accession made it clear that the Scottish King was not going to adapt his style according to that of his predecessor and the expectations she might have shaped. After acceding to the English throne, James did not entirely neglect other traditional means of royal self-representation, such as portraiture and architecture.[82] He was not, I argue in Chapter 3, as unwilling to engage in public

79 For brief selections and analyses of the poetry of James's predecessors alongside his poetry see Peter C. Herman (ed.), *Reading Monarchs Writing: The Poetry of Henry VIII, Mary Stuart, Elizabeth I, and James VI/I* (Tempe, Arizona: Arizona Center for Medieval and Renaissance Studies, 2002).

80 There are a vast number of studies of Elizabeth's public presentation. See, amongst others, Jean Wilson, *Entertainments for Elizabeth I* (Woodbridge: Brewer, 1980); Roy Strong, *Gloriana: The Portraits of Queen Elizabeth I* (London: Thames and Hudson, 1987); Susan Frye, *Elizabeth: The Competition for Representation* (Oxford: Oxford University Press, 1993); John Guy (ed.), *The Reign of Elizabeth I: Court and Culture in the Last Decade* (Cambridge: Cambridge University Press, 1995); David Howarth, *Images of Rule: Art and Politics in the English Renaissance, 1485–1649* (Basingstoke and London: Macmillan, 1997); Mary Hill Cole, *The Portable Queen: Elizabeth I and the Politics of Ceremony* (Amherst: University of Massachusetts Press, 1999); and Lisa Hopkins, *Writing Renaissance Queens: Texts by and about Elizabeth I and Mary, Queen of Scots* (Newark: University of Delaware Press; London: Associated University Presses, 2002). For a digestible overview of Elizabeth's reign see Christopher Haigh, *Elizabeth I*, second edition (London: Longman, 1998), which includes a bibliographical essay (pp. 182–90).

81 Marcus, Mueller, and Rose (eds), *Elizabeth I: Collected Works*, pp. xi, xx. See also Steven W. May (ed.), *Queen Elizabeth I: Selected Works* (New York: Washington Square Press, 2004), which notes that some of Elizabeth's poems did experience limited manuscript circulation (p. xxii).

82 On portraiture and material culture see Antony Griffiths, *The Print in Stuart Britain, 1603–1689* (London: British Museum, 1998), esp. pp. 39, 45–68; and R. Malcolm Smuts, 'Art and the Material Culture of Majesty in Early Stuart England', in Smuts (ed.), *The Stuart Court and Europe: Essays in Politics and Political Culture* (Cambridge: Cambridge University Press, 1996), pp. 86–112. On architecture see James Robertson, 'Stuart London and the Idea of a Royal Capital City', *Renaissance Studies*, 15 (2001), 37–58; Colin Platt, *The Great Rebuildings of Tudor and Stuart England* (London: UCL Press, 1994); and J. Newman, 'Inigo Jones and the Politics of Architecture', in Kevin Sharpe and Peter Lake (eds), *Culture and Politics in Early Stuart England*

performance as has been supposed. He did employ court writers, most notably Ben Jonson, though he was not surrounded by court writers creating a national cult to the extent that Elizabeth had been.[83] And the very year after his accession he took the significant step of assuming patronage of Shakespeare's playing company, suggesting he recognised the growing power and influence of the theatre.[84] However, he did not exploit any of these other means of royal representation to the extent that he exploited writing which, uniquely, enabled him to attempt to take charge of his own public relations.

Despite James's (often overlooked) concern with public relations, he was not to be treated kindly by the early historians of his reign. Arthur Wilson's *History of Great Britain, Being the Life and Reign of King James the First* (1653) and *The Court and Character of King James* (1650), attributed to Anthony Weldon, have been particularly influential, but both represent sustained attempts to discredit James in accordance with the larger need of the commonwealth period to discredit the Stuart monarchy. One of Wilson's most lasting contributions to James's historiography has been his emphasis on the King's dislike of being 'looked on' and disdain for his subjects, which, according to Wilson, led James to regard even his Royal Entry into London of 1604 as nothing more than a 'brunt' to be 'endured'.[85] This view of James has become such an orthodoxy that Goldberg is able to reproduce it – 'James did display an unmovingness even as he moved through London; indeed, his responses, insofar as he registered any, were negative, drawing back

Footnote no. 82 (*cont.*)

> (Stanford: Stanford University Press, 1993), pp. 229–56. For an overview of James's self-representation through a range of means in England see Linda Levy Peck, 'The Mental World of the Jacobean Court: An Introduction', in Peck (ed.), *Mental World*, pp. 1–20. On James's engagement with ceremony and display in Scotland, see, amongst others, Julian Goodare and Michael Lynch (eds), *The Reign of James VI* (East Lintin: Tuckwell Press, 2000), esp. Lynch, 'Court Ceremony and Ritual during the Personal Reign of James VI', pp. 71–92, and Aonghus Mackechnie, 'James VI's Architects and Their Architecture', pp. 154–69; David Stevenson, *Scotland's Last Royal Wedding* (Edinburgh: John Donald, 1997); and Mapstone and Wood (eds), *The Rose and the Thistle*.

83 Curtis Perry suggests this difference was precisely because it was so difficult for poets to respond to James's self-styling as a poet. See *The Making of Jacobean Culture* (Cambridge: Cambridge University Press, 1997).

84 For the text of this 1604 Act see E. K. Chambers, *The Elizabethan Stage*, 4 vols (Oxford: Oxford University Press, 1923), II, 208–9. For further discussion of the Act, and of James's attitude to the theatre more generally, see Janet Clare, '*Art made tongue-tied by authority': Elizabethan and Jacobean Dramatic Censorship* (Manchester: Manchester University Press, 1990), esp. pp. 98–100. For a discussion that questions whether James took a personal interest in theatre, and whether it was he who instigated the patenting of the King's men, see Leeds Barroll, 'A New History for Shakespeare and His Time', *Shakespeare Quarterly*, 39 (1988), 441–64, esp. pp. 454–61.

85 Arthur Wilson, *The History of Great Britain, Being the Life and Reign of King James the First* (London: Richard Lownds, 1653), pp. 12–13.

from his people . . . displaying boredom and fatigue' – without even citing a source.[86] Wilson, however, is writing not only from a position of bias but forty-nine years after an event that took place when he was just nine years old. Weldon's attack on James is even more damaging; Wormald describes it as a 'brilliant and deeply biased character sketch [which] has never quite failed to influence later attitudes to James I, even for those who have never even heard of Weldon'.[87] Weldon launches a personal assault on the King's whole bearing – his dress, his gait, his speech, and so on – as well as accusing him of excessive liberality, corruption, weakness, and cowardice, and coining the lasting epithet 'the wisest foole in Christendome'.[88]

These early accounts have been effectively challenged by revisionist historians who have emphasised the immense religious, political, and economic difficulties James faced in Scotland and England. These difficulties may be summarised as follows. James was crowned (in 1567, aged thirteen months) as the result of the forced deposition of his mother, Mary Queen of Scots. The Kirk had helped to authorise the action of the confederate lords against Mary, forcefully demonstrating the hold of the Scottish Church over the Scottish monarchy.[89] Civil War between the followers of the 'godly' prince and the supporters of the Catholic queen ensued, from 1568 to 1573. Even beyond this, James was surrounded by faction and violence as various regents and guardians sought and lost power, and his own life was several times at risk.[90] As far into his reign as 1582, he was kidnapped by leading Presbyterian nobles. These 'Ruthven Raiders' ruled for ten months against his will, before he escaped from their custody, and were subsequently upheld for their actions by the Kirk, indicating its continuing opposition to the Crown.[91] In 1587 Mary was executed in England, an act that simultaneously emphasised the power of the English monarchy and the vulnerability of the Scottish. Elizabeth had a considerable hold over James because he was anxious to safeguard his hoped-for accession to the English throne, while his extreme financial difficulties enabled the English Queen further to manipulate him by offering or withholding financial support.[92] Prior to the execution James

---

86  Goldberg, *James I*, p. 32.

87  Jenny Wormald, 'James VI and I: Two Kings or One?', *History*, 68 (1983), 187–209 (pp. 191–2).

88  Sir A. W., *The Court and Character of King James* (London: R.I., 1650), pp. 177–89.

89  For a discussion of the Reformation in Scotland see Jenny Wormald, *Court, Kirk and Community: Scotland 1470–1625* (Edinburgh: Edinburgh University Press, 1981), pp. 75–139.

90  See Michael Lynch, *Scotland: A New History* (London: Pimlico, 1991), pp. 219–26; Wormald, *Court, Kirk and Community*, esp. pp. 145–6; Willson, *King James*, esp. pp. 28–30, 33–5; and Maurice Lee, *John Maitland of Thirlestane and the Foundation of the Stewart Despotism in Scotland* (Princeton: Princeton University Press, 1959).

91  Wormald, *Court, Kirk, and Community*, p. 128; Julian Goodare, 'Scottish Politics in the Reign of James VI', in Goodare and Lynch (eds), *The Reign of James VI*, pp. 32–54 (pp. 35–6).

92  The Scottish Crown's financial resources were very limited and James increasingly depended 'on unprecedented, regular taxation and massive credit' (Lynch, *Scotland*, pp. 234–5). For a

indicated to Elizabeth that, while he opposed it, he would not avenge it, which brought him into conflict with those of his subjects who argued for vengeance against England.[93]

In addition to these events, James faced theoretical challenges to royal authority from various quarters. During the 1570s theories of resistance to royal authority were developing throughout Europe, and the most important advocate of such theories in Scotland was James's own tutor, George Buchanan. His *De Iure Regni apud Scotos* (published in Edinburgh in 1579 but written around twelve years earlier, just after Mary's forced abdication) justified the treatment of Mary and supported the contractual theories advanced by Huguenot writers of the 1570s.[94] This threat was overtaken in the 1580s by the claims of the counter-Reformation papacy for the right of popes to depose rulers, leading to the fear amongst Protestant monarchs that this might be put into practice by assassins.[95] Further opposition came from the extreme Presbyterians, led by Andrew Melville, in the late 1590s.[96] Notoriously, in an encounter of 1596 Melville grabbed the King's sleeve and told him that he was not head of the church but 'God's silly vassal'.[97] James himself would reflect in 1599 that '*vnto one faulte is all the common people of this Lande subjecte . . . which is, to judge and speake rashelie of their Prince*'.[98]

After he became King of England James no longer faced many of the threats of his Scottish reign, but the Gunpowder plot of 1605 demonstrated his continued vulnerability. He came into conflict with the English parliament over the related issues of the Common Law, the Royal Prerogative and freedom of speech.[99] He continued

Footnote no. 92 (*cont.*)

    discussion of the subsidy James received from Elizabeth from 1586 onwards see Julian Goodare, 'James VI's English Subsidy', in Goodare and Lynch (eds), *The Reign of James VI*, pp. 110–25.

93  Willson, *King James*, pp. 78–80.

94  Wormald, 'James VI and I, *Basilikon Doron* and *The Trew Law*', p. 41. See also Jimmy H. Burns, *The True Law of Kingship: Concepts of Monarchy in Early Modern Scotland* (Oxford: Oxford University Press, 1996), pp. 196, 185; and I. D. McFarlane, *Buchanan* (London: Duckworth, 1981).

95  Wormald, *Court, Kirk, and Community*, p. 148.

96  Wormald, 'Two Kings or One?', p. 196.

97  For a contemporary account see extract from James Melville's diary included in Robert Ashton (ed.), *James I by His Contemporaries* (London: Hutchinson, 1969), pp. 174–5. For further discussion see Stephen King, ' "Your Best and Maist Faithfull Subjects": Andrew and James Melville as James VI and I's "Loyal Opposition" ', *Renaissance and Reformation*, 24 (2000), 17–30.

98  James, *Basilikon Doron* (1599), p. 62.

99  For Jacobean parliamentary history see, amongst others, Kevin Sharpe (ed.), *Faction and Parliament: Essays in Early Stuart History* (Oxford: Oxford University Press, 1978); Conrad Russell, *Parliaments and English Politics, 1621–1629* (Oxford: Oxford University Press, 1979), and *The Addled Parliament of 1614: The Limits of Revisionism* (Reading: University of Reading,

to struggle financially and to be unable to persuade parliament to grant him as much in subsidies as he wanted.[100] Other perceived aspects of his governance also attracted criticism: his favouritism towards the Scots; his fondness for individual favourites (Robert Carr and later George Villiers); and the extravagance and corruption of court life.[101] James's pacifistic approach to foreign affairs was also unpopular, and his major project of the last years of his reign highlighted a significant divergence between his priorities and those of many of his subjects. The King may have hoped that a marriage between his heir, Prince Charles, and the Spanish Habsburg Princess would be a move towards European peace and unity. For the majority of his subjects, however, the Habsburgs were the popish enemy and the match was unacceptable. James had been negotiating for the Spanish match for some time, but the outbreak of war in 1618–19 between the Catholic Habsburgs and his daughter Elizabeth and Protestant son-in-law Frederick V increased opposition to his policy. Many of James's subjects believed that, far from marrying into the Catholic Habsburg dynasty, England had a responsibility to intervene in the war. The King maintained a pacifist stance and a determination to conclude the marriage negotiations, but met increasing opposition and criticism.[102]

1992); Thomas Cogswell, 'A Low Road to Extinction? Supply and Redress of Grievances in the Parliaments of the 1620s', *Historical Journal*, 33 (1990), 283–303; and Andrew Thrush, 'The Personal Rule of James I, 1611–1620', in Thomas Cogswell, Richard Cust, and Peter Lake (eds), *Politics, Religion and Popularity in Early Stuart Britain: Essays in Honour of Conrad Russell* (Cambridge: Cambridge University Press, 2002), pp. 84–101.

100   The parliament of 1610 saw particularly extended debates over royal expenditure and the level of parliamentary subsidy. Robert Cecil, the Lord Treasurer, presented to parliament a proposal 'for a one-time subsidy to pay off the King's debts and a "contract" to commute some prerogative rights into an annual tax on land worth £200,000'. After five months of debate the Commons granted a subsidy worth only £100,000 and royal debt went on to rise. By 1618 royal debt had risen to £900,000, the largest peacetime debt in English history (Mark A. Kishlansky, *A Monarchy Transformed: Britain, 1603–1714* (London: Allen Lane, 1996), pp. 86–8).

101   See Alastair Bellany, *The Politics of Court Scandal in Early Modern England: News Culture and the Overbury Affair, 1603–1660* (Cambridge: Cambridge University Press, 2002); Linda Levy Peck, ' "For a King not to be bountiful were a fault": Perspectives on Court Patronage in Early Stuart England', *Journal of British Studies*, 25 (1986), 31–61; R. Malcolm Smuts, 'Cultural Diversity and Cultural Change at the Court of James I', in Peck (ed.), *Mental World*, pp. 99–112; and Wormald, 'Two Kings or One?'.

102   For further detail see Thomas Cogswell, 'England and the Spanish Match', in Richard Cust and Ann Hughes (eds), *Conflict in Early Stuart England* (London and New York, Longman, 1989), pp. 107–33, and *The Blessed Revolution: English Politics and the Coming of War, 1621–1624* (Cambridge, Cambridge University Press, 1989); and Glyn Redworth, *The Prince and the Infanta: The Cultural Politics of the Spanish Match* (New Haven, Conn. and London: Yale University Press, 2003).

Where these problems reflected James's failings in the accounts of earlier historians, revisionist historians have proposed various ways in which these problems were not entirely of his own making, and emphasised his considerable achievements in dealing with them. Wormald's seminal article of 1983, 'James VI and I: Two Kings or One?' stresses that, in contrast to the traditional picture of James I put forward by Wilson, Weldon, and others, James VI was a successful and popular king according not only to later historians but to his contemporaries. She argues that James did not suddenly become a less effective ruler in 1603, but rather that the English viewed him negatively because he failed to live up to their expectations. She also re-evaluates James's relationship with the English parliament and concludes that he succeeded in defusing 'problems within the church and the state, and thereby presided over a kingdom probably more stable than his predecessor had left, and certainly than his successor was to rule'.[103] More recently other studies have re-examined further aspects of James's perceived failings. For example, Mark Kishlansky has pointed out that, while he undoubtedly made financial mistakes, the financial problems he faced were in large part the result of the debt he inherited from Elizabeth, the extent of his necessary expenses, and deep-seated problems with seventeenth-century fiscal theory and practice.[104] W. B. Patterson has given a sympathetic account of the pacifistic approach to foreign policy for which James was criticised by his contemporaries, emphasising his laudable pursuit of religious reconciliation throughout Europe.[105] Leeds Barroll has questioned the long-lived view of James as a self-indulgent and politically inept king, concentrating on events surrounding the accession to demonstrate his 'political acumen and decisiveness'.[106] Following such work, the most recent scholarly biography of the King, Pauline Croft's *King James*, offers 'an authoritative analysis of his remarkable, though flawed, achievements'.[107]

The present book contributes to this reassessment of King James by examining the ways in which his writings were simultaneously a response to, a strategy for dealing with, and a factor in the problems and criticisms he faced. His writings are shaped according to his sense of context and audience as he tries to counter and forestall threat

103  Wormald, 'Two Kings or One?', pp. 204, 208–9.
104  Kishlansky, *A Monarchy Transformed*, pp. 83–6.
105  W. B. Patterson, *King James VI and I and the Reunion of Christendom* (Cambridge: Cambridge University Press, 1997).
106  Leeds Barroll, 'Assessing "Cultural Influence": James I as Patron of the Arts', *Shakespeare Studies*, 29 (2001), 132–62 (133). For further defences of James see, among others, Peck, ' "For a King not to be bountiful were a fault" '; Maurice Lee, *Great Britain's Solomon: James VI and I in His Three Kingdoms* (Urbana and Chicago: University of Illinois Press, 1990); Malcolm Smuts, 'The Making of *Rex Pacificus*: James VI and I and the Problem of Peace in an Age of Religious War', in Fischlin and Fortier (eds), *Royal Subjects*, pp. 371–87; and Diana Newton, *The Making of the Jacobean Regime: James VI and I and the Government of England, 1603–1605* (Woodbridge: Boydell, 2005).
107  Pauline Croft, *King James* (Basingstoke: Palgrave Macmillan, 2003), blurb.

and criticism, and to lend his authority much needed reinforcement. Yet his preoccupation with writing attracted criticism, and in various ways his writing undermines his claims of authority. These texts are not, then, the stable historical documents of traditional approaches to the writing of history.[108] They are volatile interventions into early modern culture that signify both more and less than their author intended, but that are nevertheless central to understanding James as monarch and historical figure. The picture that emerges is of a king who was perceptive, calculating, opportunistic, reactive, and adaptable, but put too much store by his own ability to control representation and interpretation. In particular this book offers a corrective to the still prevalent view of James as aloof and unconcerned with courting the populace. My analysis of his writings reveals a king sensitive to the competing demands of the multiple audiences he faced, consciously adjusting his register according to his sense of his audience, and even engaging with his ordinary subjects on their linguistic terms. But in this regard, as in others, James's writings often achieved the opposite of their intended effect.

The intertwined literary and historical significance of James's writings was for a long time neglected almost entirely. On the one hand, his explicitly political writings were treated only as providing direct access to his political views and the views of his culture, and not subjected to literary analysis. The standard edition, Charles Howard McIlwain's *The Political Works of James I* (1918, reprinted in 1965), gives a typically narrow view of its own value: McIlwain hopes it will provide a 'service to present-day students of the history of political thought and institutions'.[109] On the other hand, the political, as well as the literary, significance of the full range of James's writings was often overlooked. Thus McIlwain's edition omits the scriptural exegeses with which James began his 1616 *Workes*. We still lack a modern edition containing all five of his scriptural exegeses. Similarly, his poetry continued to receive, as Sharpe pointed out in 1993, 'no historical and little critical evaluation'.[110] The only complete edition of his poetry remains that of James Craigie, which was published in the 1950s and which misleadingly implies that all of the poetry belongs to James's Scottish reign: *The Poems of King James VI of Scotland*. This may have furthered the neglect of the poetry amongst scholars of James I.

Goldberg's *James I and the Politics of Literature* was one of the first literary studies to consider James's writings and continues to be highly influential, but, as noted above, he overlooks much of the complexity of James's writings. Since the mid-1990s a number

---

108   Sharpe and Zwicker suggest that 'historical method has been premised on the stable text as vehicle of authorial intention and coherent meaning. Even now most historians remain fixed in notions of textual stability' (*Reading, Society and Politics*, p. 25).

109   Charles Howard McIlwain (ed.), *The Political Works of James I* (Cambridge, Mass.: Harvard University Press, 1918), preface, p. vii.

110   Kevin Sharpe, 'The King's Writ: Royal Authors and Royal Authority in Early Modern England' in Sharpe and Lake (eds), *Culture and Politics*, pp. 117–38 (p. 127).

of articles, chapters, and editions have reflected and furthered interest in, and understanding of, James as an author.[111] It was not until 2002, however, that the first book-length study of James's writings was produced. *Royal Subjects: Essays on the Writings of James VI and I*, a collection of essays by different contributors edited by Daniel Fischlin and Mark Fortier, reflects some of the interest and complexity of its topic. The present book, the first monograph devoted to James's writings, builds on and extends this important work.

Given the volume of James's output and the vast array of political, religious, and literary contexts in which his works were produced and received, a single book cannot hope to offer a comprehensive or definitive account. What the present book highlights, however, is the development of his aims and concerns as an author across the media in which he wrote. Beginning with his poetry of the early 1580s, it moves through his early scriptural exegeses and contemporaneous correspondence with Elizabeth; his first prose treatises, including *Daemonologie* (perhaps the most conspicuous omission of Fischlin and Fortier's collection); his *Apologie for the Oath of Allegiance*; his printed speeches to his English parliament; the King James Bible; his *Workes*; and his late manuscript poetry. By examining this range of works, the circumstances of their publication, their material form, and the interaction between writing and reception, this book illuminates the trajectory of James's writing career. It reveals that he was flexible and willing to experiment as an author and highlights his prioritisation of different genres in different periods and contexts. But it also reveals that similar concerns and anxieties preoccupied him throughout his career, and that his writings never entirely overcame but often exacerbated the difficulties he faced.

The first chapter examines the construction of James as an author in the political and cultural contexts of 1580s and early 1590s Scotland, focusing on his printed and manuscript poetry of this period. It emphasises the extent to which the King's literary image was, like his political authority, a collaborative construction, produced collectively by James and the other poets with whom he interacted. The discussion suggests that poetry could be for James both a vehicle for subtly and indirectly reinforcing his (especially in this period rather fragile) authority, and a forum for literary playfulness. It also shows, however, James's increasing concern with controlling the

---

111   See Sharpe, 'The King's Writ'; Johann P. Sommerville (ed.), *King James VI and I: Political Writings* (Cambridge: Cambridge University Press, 1994); Daniel Fischlin and Mark Fortier (eds), *The True Law of Free Monarchies and Basilikon Doron* (Toronto: Centre for Reformation and Renaissance Studies, 1996); Daniel Fischlin, '"Counterfeiting God": James VI (I) and the Politics of *Daemonologie* (1597)', *The Journal of Narrative Technique*, 26 (1996), 1–29; Sandra J. Bell, 'Writing the Monarch: King James VI and *Lepanto*', in Mary Silcox, Helen Ostovich, and Graham Roebuck (eds), *Other Voices, Other Views: Expanding the Canon in English Renaissance Studies* (Newark: University of Delaware Press, 1999), pp. 193–208; Herman (ed.), *Reading Monarchs Writing*; and Neil Rhodes, Jennifer Richards, and Joseph Marshall (eds), *King James VI and I: Selected Writings* (Aldershot: Ashgate, 2003).

interpretation of his writing, and his growing sense of a conflict between aesthetics and politics. Addressing a similar chronological period to that of the first chapter, the second examines James's scriptural exegeses of the mid- to late 1580s. It argues that these were politically engaged texts and that the King consciously exploited them as such, even as he maintained that he was merely reproducing the word of God. These works prepare for the major political treatises that he would write in the 1590s by emphasising a link between royal and divine authorship and authority. They also reveal, however, the contradictions inherent in the claims James would be increasingly anxious to make that control over the meaning of a text lies with its author – contradictions that also emerge in his correspondence with Elizabeth of the second half of the 1580s.

The third chapter turns to the King's major prose works of the last years of the sixteenth century and first decade of the seventeenth, and the King James Bible. These publications variously demonstrate James's growing concern to respond explicitly to opposition and misinterpretation, and his keenness to exploit the potential of the press. Despite the care he evidently took with these works, however, he could not always prevent unauthorised or inaccurate publication, and his attempts to manipulate the reader expose the illusions and deceptions that underlie kingship. His writings remain susceptible to misinterpretation and criticism, which they seem increasingly to have met in England. These works highlight, then, the ambivalent and contradictory nature of James's relationship with print. All of the prose works by James considered in Chapters 2 and 3 were included in his folio edition of *Workes* in 1616, and this collection's monumentalisation of the royal author is the focus of the fourth chapter. The chapter argues that, by re-presenting his works in this format, James was implying that their interest and value extended beyond the immediate and political into the realm of literary posterity. The *Workes* extends, however, the tensions between the King's political and literary aims as it responds to the concerns and resistance of his readers, and inadvertently invites precisely the kind of readings and reappropriations that he was so anxious to avoid. This collection is, nevertheless, a significant intervention in contemporary literary culture and, in particular, sits in a complex relationship with the folio collection of *Workes* Ben Jonson published in the same year.

The final chapter turns to James's writings of 1618–24, focusing in particular on the poems he produced and circulated in manuscript in this period. While there are a number of significant differences between this late poetry and that of the 1580s and early 1590s, it is striking that in a climate of considerable opposition and criticism he again responded with poetry, as well as with two new scriptural exegeses. James's late poetry highlights not only his belief in the political force of poetry, but also – given the increasing importance of manuscript verse as a means of shaping public opinion in this period – his responsiveness to cultural developments. Yet these poems, to an even greater extent than any of his other writings, involve him in empowering, and acknowledging his dependence upon, the reader/subject. And as James was struggling to contain opposition with further writing, some of his earlier writings were, ironically enough, being used as fuel for that very opposition. This emphasises the fundamental irreconcilability of his project for his writing with actual processes of reading and interpretation. This chapter shows, then, the culmination of the tensions and contradictions between authorship and authority, literature and politics, that James struggled to reconcile over the course of more than forty years; ultimately, his authorship contributed less to the reinforcement of his authority than to its deconstruction.

# Constructing the writer–king: the early poetry

In 1584 the eighteen-year old King of Scotland printed his first work, *The Essayes of a Prentise, in the Diuine Art of Poesie*, a collection of original poems, poetic translations, and poetic theory. This was a remarkable act, especially given the tendency in this period of men of rank to avoid print, and the relative confinement of secular literature within manuscript culture in Scotland in particular.[1] The collection makes only a slight concession to such sensibilities; it was not printed under James's name, but includes such clues to the author's identity as an acrostic dedicatory poem that spells out IACOBVS SEXTVS.[2] And it had no precedent; as Peter C. Herman notes, 'no monarch before James had their verses printed in a book for circulation as a commodity in the market-place'.[3] Yet he not only *had* his verses printed in a book, but was evidently personally involved in the printing process.[4] In 1584, then, when the Scottish King published his quarto volume he was doing something very new (see figure 1).

This collection was reprinted a year later, and followed by another in 1591, *His Maiesties Poeticall Exercises at Vacant Houres*. In the intervening years the King wrote a considerable number of poems that were not printed in his lifetime, including a sequence of love lyrics and a court masque. He also surrounded himself with a group of court poets, who have subsequently become known as the 'Castalian Band'.[5] These were in

---

1  See the Introduction, above.

2  James VI, *Essayes of a Prentise, in the Diuine Art of Poesie* (Edinburgh: Thomas Vautroullier, 1584), sig. A1r. All subsequent references are to this edition and are given in parentheses in the text.

3  Herman, ' "Best of Poets, Best of Kings" ', p. 83.

4  At the very end of *Essayes of a Prentise*, James makes an addition with a note explaining that it is 'for the filling out of thir vacand pageis' (sig. P4r). This suggests that the rest of the collection must have been set and seen by him before he decided to make this addition.

5  The term 'Castalian' comes from the name of a spring on Mount Parnassus that was sacred to the Muses, and the phrase 'Castalian band' has become widely used by critics and historians to describe the Scottish court poets of the 1580s and early 1590s, largely on the basis of James's reference to 'ye sacred brethren of Castalian band' in his epitaph on Montgomerie (Craigie (ed.), *Poems*, II, 107–8, line 2). Priscilla Bawcutt has persuasively argued, however, that this term was not employed by this circle to describe themselves, and

# THE ESSAYES OF
## A PRENTISE, IN THE
### DIVINE ART OF
#### POESIE.

Imprinted at Edinbrugh, by Thomas
Vautroullier.
1584.

CVM PRIVILEGIO

REGALI.

1 Title page of *The Essayes of a Prentise, in the Diuine Art of Poesie*
(Edinburgh: Thomas Vautroullier, 1584)

the main men for whom poetry was an extension of their involvement in other aspects of courtly and political life, such as William Fowler, who participated in wedding negotiations for James, accompanied him to Denmark, and became Queen Anne's secretary, and Thomas and Robert Hudson, who were musicians in the royal household. The other key members of this circle have been identified as William Alexander, Robert Ayton, John Burel, Alexander Hume, Alexander Montgomerie, and John Stewart.[6] James's interaction with these men reflects the relatively informal nature of his Scottish court.[7] Even beyond this circle, poetry, politics, and religion were interconnected for the young King: for example, the Archbishop Patrick Adamson contributed two Latin verses to *Essayes of a Prentise* (sig. A1r–v); and James wrote a sonnet to his Secretary of State from 1584 to 1592, John Maitland.[8] Poetry was, then, a central part of James's early reign and the medium in which he began to explore and represent the relationship between authorship and authority. Yet this was also a medium in which James's voice could only be one among many.

This chapter will trace the development of James's poetic aims and concerns in the course of his Scottish reign, beginning by establishing the broad political and poetic contexts in which he began to write and print. It argues that he was constructed as a writer—king within a context of exchange and collaboration with other poets, and explores the intersection of his role as patron with his own poetic practice within this context. The chapter then looks more closely at the relationship between James's poetics and politics, suggesting both that his poetry reveals his self-consciousness about the complexities of this relationship, and that – despite this self-consciousness – poetics and politics collide in ways that remained beyond his control. It concludes with a consideration of the relationship between James's attempt to control the interpretation of one of his major poems, the approach to his poetry of a contemporary reader, and the authority the King himself assumes as a reader of poetry.

Footnote 5 *(cont.)*
> that this epitaph, written around 1598, more likely refers to poets in general, or to poets present at court in the late 1590s, than to the poets of the earlier period ('James VI's Castalian Band: A Modern Myth', *Scottish Historical Review*, 80 (2001), 251–9). Nevertheless, I will, given the prevalence of the term in discussions of Scottish court poetry, continue to use it for ease of reference.

6 For a discussion of each of these figures see R. D. S. Jack, 'Poetry under James VI', in Jack (ed.), *The History of Scottish Literature*, 4 vols (Aberdeen: Aberdeen University Press, 1988), I, 125–40.

7 See Wormald, 'Two Kings or One?', who suggests that Scottish kingship had a 'peculiarly personal quality' (p. 189). For a contemporary account that emphasises how familiar James was with his domestics and gentlemen of the bedchamber see Sir Henry Wotton's letter of 1601/2, extracted in Ashton (ed.), *James I*, pp. 4–5.

8 Craigie (ed.), *Poems*, II, 107. Maitland also wrote poetry (Lee, *Maitland*, p. 41).

## Poetry, politics, and print

James's first publication raises the related questions of why he prioritised print, and why he prioritised poetry. His early education involved access to a substantial library that was up to date with current publication, even though the value of such a collection was not agreed upon by all; according to his librarian, Peter Young, in a letter of circa 1575, 'the fascioun of the maist part' is to ask 'quhat [what] neidis his Majestie sa mony Buikis'.[9] This library involved James in having, during his formative years, direct experience of print as a major forum in which royal authority could be both disputed and validated. An example close to home was the circulation in print of the works of his tutor, George Buchanan, including his influential *De Iure Regni apud Scotos*, dedicated to the young King. As noted in the Introduction, above, this work advocates resistance theory and justifies the treatment of James's mother. James also, however, had access to printed works advocating absolutist theories of kingship, such as Jean Bodin's *Six Livres de la Republique* (Paris, 1576) and Guillaume Budé's *L'Institution du Prince* (Paris, 1547).[10] Given such examples of the different ways in which print could be employed, it seems no coincidence that James's first publication appeared in the same year as an act of parliament 'Anent slanderers of the King, his progenitours, Estait and Realme', the first such act of his reign.[11] One of the specific concerns of this act was to censor Buchanan's *De Iure Regni*, even though it had already been in circulation for five years and Buchanan dead for two. The timing suggests that James's first publication was part of a concerted attempt to control the representation of royalty; Buchanan's anti-monarchical writing would not only be removed, but would be replaced with a representation of the King produced by the King.

If James thus had a strong sense of the importance of print as a medium to be controlled and exploited, so too does he seem to have been aware of the importance of poetry as a genre in which political debates were being played out in Scotland in this period. As Sandra Bell observes, 'poetical satire had long questioned the role of the monarch, and the flood of Reformation satires from 1560 to 1584 – verse which directly questioned the monarchy – further politicised poetry'. Many of the satires are directed at James's mother, but a number question Scotland's need for a monarchy at all.[12]

9  Letter quoted in T. W. Baldwin, *William Shakspere's Small Latine & Lesse Greeke*, 2 vols (Urbana: University of Illinois Press, 1944–50), I, 536; see pp. 532–56 for a discussion of James's education.

10 See George F. Warner (ed.), *The Library of James VI, 1573–1583, from a manuscript in the hand of Peter Young, his tutor* (Edinburgh: Edinburgh University Press, 1893).

11 *The Laws and Actes of Parliament Maid be King James the First and His Successours* (Edinburgh: Waldegrave, 1597), pp. 59v–60r (this act is also reproduced in T. Thomson (ed.), *The Acts of the Parliaments of Scotland*, 12 vols (Edinburgh, 1844), III, 296). This was also the year of the 'Black Acts', which sought to assert royal power over the Kirk (see Alan R. MacDonald, *The Jacobean Kirk, 1567–1625* (Aldershot: Ashgate, 1998), pp. 26–8).

12 Bell, 'Writing the Monarch', pp. 198–9, 205. The main collection of Scottish Reformation satires is James Cranstoun (ed.), *Satirical Poems of the Time of the Reformation* (Edinburgh:

Moreover, poems that Mary herself had allegedly written, the so-called 'casket sonnets', discovered in 1567, were perceived as an indictment of her as an adulterous and corrupt queen, and used as evidence in the English commission into the murder of her husband and James's father, Henry, Lord Darnley. Buchanan, who had earlier written panegyrics for the Queen, played a central role in the exposure and damning interpretation of these poems.[13] The fate of the 'casket sonnets' indicates the political potency of literary writing in this context, and the susceptibility of royal poetry to being read as though it were not literary or fictional at all. Poetry was thus being used to satirise and condemn the monarchy, but there was also a wave of royalist literature by the mid-1560s and a tradition of court poetry, which, Michael Lynch proposes, 'had tangible political effects'.[14] James had the opportunity to see, then, the potential of poetry both to undermine and to uphold the monarchy.

Shortly after taking up residence in Edinburgh in 1579 he began to attempt to channel that potential to serve his own ends, bringing Scottish poets into the orbit of the court and endeavouring to ensure that Scottish poetry would be predominantly royalist. His poetic treatise of 1584, *Ane Schort Treatise conteining some Reulis and Cautelis* [rules and warnings] *to be obseruit and eschewit* [avoided] *in Scottis Poesie* (hereafter referred to as *Reulis and Cautelis*), is the most explicit attempt of which we have record to guide this Scottish poetic Renaissance. One of its concerns is to reinforce the 1584 act of parliament against slanderous writings. The act ordains that no subject shall 'meddle in the affaires of his Hienes' and *Reulis and Cautelis* similarly asserts:

> ze man [you may] also be war of wryting any thing of materis of comoun weill, or vther sic graue sene subiectis [subjects taken from books] (except Metaphorically, of manifest treuth opinly knawin, zit [yet] nochtwithstanding vsing it very seindil [seldom]) because nocht onely ze essay nocht zour awin *Inventioun*, as I spak before, bot lykewayis they are to graue materis, for a Poet to mell [meddle] in. (*Essayes*, sigs M2v–3r)

This is the only section in which James departs from the purely literary and technical aspects of poetry, and its placement at the end of the treatise, which itself comes late in *Essayes of a Prentise*, suggests the extent of his concern to provide a poetic framework for this politically motivated instruction. The value of 'Inventioun' is emphasised throughout the treatise and this may likewise be designed to give this instruction further poetic justification.

Blackwood, 1891–3; reprint, New York: AMS, 1974). See also J. E. Phillips, *Images of a Queen: Mary Stuart in Sixteenth-Century Literature* (Berkeley and Los Angeles: University of California Press, 1964).

13  Dunnigan, *Eros and Poetry*, pp. 15, 17. The sonnets appear in Buchanan's anti-Marian tract *De Maria Scotorum Regina* (1571), which was quickly translated into English and reprinted (p. 174n). See Dunnigan, pp. 15–45, for further discussion of anti-Marian readings of the sonnets, and for a reading of the sonnets themselves.

14  Lynch, *Scotland*, p. 213.

James none the less here concedes that a poet can write about state affairs 'Metaphorically', and this may be in part an attempt to justify another poem in the collection, *Ane Metaphoricall Inuention of a Tragedie Called Phoenix*. This allegorical poem appears to be in large part a response to the treatment of, and a defence of, Esmé Stuart, a favourite of the King whose Catholicism and perceived influence over James caused concern in Scotland and England, and led to his forced exile after the Ruthven Raid of 1582.[15] The King himself thus seems to have resorted to metaphor to write about politically sensitive issues. His anxiety and uncertainty about such use of metaphor is, however, suggested by the rather odd qualification in the passage from *Reulis and Cautelis* quoted above ('of manifest treuth opinly knawin'), and in the prefacing of the *Phoenix* with an acrostic verse that spells out the favourite's name (*Essayes*, sig. G3r). James seems to have wanted his poem to be neither completely explicit nor entirely ambiguous. Perhaps it was more ambiguous than he intended, however: the acrostic verse did not prevent at least one contemporary reader interpreting the Phoenix of the poem in terms James could not have intended or accepted, as we shall see below. The King's attitude towards and use of metaphor thus begins to suggest conflict between his desire to exploit poetry and his concern to control the representation and interpretation of political matters.

As James sought to censor poetry that might undermine his authority, so he wrote and patronised the kinds of poetry that might reinforce it. In the years immediately after his 1583 escape from the custody of the Ruthven Raiders, he was just beginning to take control of his government and his position continued to be fragile. He did not reach his majority until 1587, and, Jimmy H. Burns suggests, between 1583 and 1585 the ascendancy of James Stewart, Earl of Arran, precludes our regarding the King as being in full control of the government.[16] James was not yet, therefore, politically secure enough to make bold and controversial assertions about his authority as he would years later in his major political treatises, *The True Lawe of Free Monarchies* (1598) and *Basilikon Doron* (1599). In these treatises he would respond explicitly to all the opposition he faced by asserting that a king is chosen by God and accountable only to God, and that the deposition of a king is never lawful. In the 1580s and early 1590s, however, he used poetry, and, as we shall consider in the next chapter, scriptural exegeses, to represent and reinforce his royal image and authority in less direct, less inflammatory ways.[17]

15  For readings of the *Phoenix* in the light of these events see Simon Wortham, ' "Pairt of My Taill Is Yet Untolde": James VI and I, the *Phoenix*, and the Royal Gift', in Fischlin and Fortier (eds), *Royal Subjects*, pp. 182–204; David Bergeron, *James I and Letters of Homoerotic Desire* (Iowa City: University of Iowa Press, 1999), pp. 32–64; and Dunnigan, *Eros and Poetry*, pp. 97–104.

16  Burns, *True Law of Kingship*, p. 223. See also Lee, *Maitland*, p. 75.

17  This is not to suggest that James maintained a consistent identification between prose and direct political assertion, poetry and subtle political implication: even *Basilikon Doron* begins with a sonnet and ends with a quotation from Virgil. As this example emphasises, the King believed in the authority of the poet over and beyond specific political circumstance.

Arran himself seems to have approved of James's first publication: in the year it was printed he sent a copy to Lord Burghley, along with a letter suggesting that in reading the collection Burghley 'will persaue a gude Inclinatioun in his majestie to do weill'.[18] This suggests that those with political power over James did not perceive his early printed poetry as a threat.

Nevertheless the King's poetry presents some politically important ideas to his subjects, and subtly prepares for his gradual assumption of greater political power. This poetry forms an image of royal cultural centrality; a microcosm of a state in which the King directs and is served by his subjects. A hint as to the relationship between monarch and subject James desired may be perceived in the term he uses to address the readers of *Reulis and Cautelis*: '*the docile bairns of knawledge*' (*Essayes*, sig. K1v). More specifically, in telling people how to write this treatise presents an image of king as law-maker, source of authority to be followed, paving the way for the role he would gradually assume in the government of Scotland.[19] In the preface he justifies writing the treatise on the basis that although there are other treatises already, many were written a long time ago and 'lyke as the tyme is changeit sensyne [since], sa is the ordour of Poesie changeit' (sig. K2r). This sense of bringing Scottish poetic discourse up to date parallels, and perhaps indirectly suggests, James's desire to bring Scottish political culture out of its turbulent past. He is thus using poetry to begin to assert the basis and implications of his royal authority.

The poetry James wrote and patronised sought not only to control and shape poetic – and to some extent political – culture within Scotland but also to bring Scotland into the mainstream of European culture, and to bolster the image of Scottish cultural achievement abroad. This attempt is most evident in the self-conscious move in *Reulis and Cautelis* away from the style of older Scots poetry towards that of contemporary French poetry, in which the King evidently read widely. His promotion of Scottish poetry involves both differentiation and imitation. He suggests its specificity and uniqueness, arguing that other recent poetic treatises are inadequate to serve the purposes of Scots poets because 'there hes neuer ane of thame written in our language' (*Essayes*, sig. K2v). At the same time he draws extensively on Du Bellay's *Deffense de la Langue Françoyse*, as well as a range of other French and Latin sources, though he is, as Jack puts it, 'no servile imitator'.[20] He also employed a Frenchman, Thomas

18  George Stevenson (ed.), *Poems of Alexander Montgomerie: Supplementary Volume* (Edinburgh and London: William Blackwood and Sons, 1910), pp. xlvi–xlvii. The copy of *Essayes of a Prentise* held in the Folger Shakespeare Library has Burghley's name on the cover and is likely the copy he was sent in 1584 (shelfmark RB HH121/23).

19  See also Rebecca Bushnell, 'George Buchanan, James VI and Neo-classicism', in Roger A. Mason (ed.), *Scots and Britons: Scottish Political Thought and the Union of 1603* (Cambridge: Cambridge University Press, 1994), pp. 91–111 (esp. pp. 105–11). Bushnell suggests that *Reulis and Cautelis* reveals the King 'working out his sense of himself as a "free" lawmaker and a Scot' (p. 106), rather than constructing and promoting himself as such.

20  R. D. S. Jack, 'James VI and Renaissance Poetic Theory', *English*, 16 (1967), 208–11 (p. 209). See Craigie (ed), *Poems*, I, xv–xxv for a survey of French influences on James's poetry.

Vautroullier, to print *Essayes of a Prentise*. Following the interests of *Reulis and Cautelis*, James and his circle sought to introduce new poetic forms into Scotland. The King himself wrote, for example, a court masque in 1588 that is comparable to contemporary French and English court entertainments, and is, according to Allan F. Westcott, 'the sole extant example of its type in Scottish literature'.[21] The group produced translations and imitations of some of the great works of the European Renaissance, such as William Fowler's translation of Petrarch's *Trionfi* and John Stewart's abridgement of Ariosto's *Orlando Furioso*. This focus on continental poetry shifted the emphasis of poetry away from the local Scottish traditions that included a strong vein of political satire; presented an image of Scottish cultural achievement in the international terms likely to impress an international audience; and drew on the literary authority of recognised poets to legitimise writing and publishing poetry at home.

James's relationship to English literary culture in the 1580s is more complex. *Reulis and Cautelis* may draw upon some English sources, but critics have disagreed as to whether he was even exposed to any at this point.[22] His treatise comments, however, that 'we differ from [the English] in sindrie reulis of Poesie' (*Essayes*, sig. K2v), suggesting both some awareness of the nature of English poetry and a desire for Scottish poetry to be differentiated from it. It therefore seems likely that James at this point was not entirely isolated from English influence, but choosing to pursue a strategy of aligning Scottish poetry with France rather than England (mirroring Scotland's traditional political allegiances), and presenting it as contending with rather than bowing to English cultural standards. This stance towards England is further suggested by James's choice of printers. Having employed the Frenchman Vautroullier to print his first collection of poetry, he would employ an Englishman, Robert Waldegrave, to print his second in 1591 and his treatises of the late 1590s. What both printers have in common is that they began their printing careers in London and were involved in printing controversies there (Vautroullier printed the writings of a heretic and Waldegrave was involved in the production of the infamous Marprelate tracts).[23] That James employed both men to print for him shortly after they fled to Scotland may represent not only a desire to draw upon the latest London printing practices. It may also represent a subtle assertion that the King of Scotland was superior to the Queen of England in his capacity to control the press and harness it to serve his own purposes.

21  Allan F. Westcott (ed.), *New Poems of James I of England* (New York: Columbia University Press, 1911), p. lviii. This masque will be considered further below.

22  R. D. S. Jack and P. A. T. Rozendaal suggest that George Gascoigne's *Certayne Notes of Instruction* (1575) is an important English source ((eds), *The Mercat Anthology of Early Scottish Literature 1375–1707* (Edinburgh: Mercat Press, 1997), p. 471n). Richard M. Clewett argues, conversely, that James was isolated from English influence in 1584 ('James VI of Scotland and His Literary Circle', *Aevum*, 47 (1973), 441–54).

23  Harry Aldis, *A List of Books Printed in Scotland before 1700* (Edinburgh: Edinburgh Bibliographical Society, 1904), pp. 122–3; Bevan, 'Scotland' pp. 694–5.

All of this would suggest that James wanted even his earliest publication to reach an English audience, and this is further indicated in the work itself. His preface to his translation of Du Bartas's *L'Vranie* reflects not only his belief in the power of print, but also what he expected the market of his book to be: he explains that he desires 'to set forth [Du Bartas's] praise . . . Which I thought, I could not do so well, as by publishing some worke of his, to this yle of *Brittain*' (*Essayes*, sig. C3r). This desire to reach English readers required, however, some anglicisation of James's native late Middle Scots – a concession in potential conflict with his attempt to promote his own nation. Most of *Essayes of a Prentise* reveals at least a degree of anglicisation; tellingly, given English concerns about Esmé Stuart, particular care seem to have been taken with anglicising the poem in which he is defended.[24] The language of *Reulis and Cautelis*, however, is much more Scots in grammar and orthography than is that of the poems.[25] Some editors have suggested this is simply because 'there would have been little point in using English to formulate the rules for composition in Scots'.[26] I would suggest that it has more to do with James balancing competing needs: within a collection partially anglicised for English readers, he reserves a space for promoting the specificity and importance of certain aspects of Scottish culture. James was thus trying to use print to communicate the cultural sophistication of Scotland, its language, its poetry, and, above all, its King to an audience extending beyond its borders. This was a politically and diplomatically valuable act of communication for a Scotsman with a claim to the English throne.

James made a further bid for visibility within English literary culture in 1587 when he contributed a sonnet to a volume of Latin poems marking the death of Sir Philip Sidney.[27] That James contributed to the collection and Elizabeth did not, despite her far closer relation to Sidney, emphasises their very different approach to poetry and public relations, and further suggests that James was trying to exploit poetry and print as an arena in which he might outdo the English Queen. Herman proposes that James's poem was motivated by diplomatic considerations: by praising a prominent Protestant courtier, he could discreetly imply that he continued to support England despite the

---

24  The *Phoenix* appears in Bodleian Library, MS 165, along with *The Furies* and *Lepanto*, which would both be included in James's second collection of poetry. Comparing the manuscript and printed versions reveals that a considerable degree of anglicisation has taken place in all three cases (see Craigie (ed.), *Poems*, I, 292–5). Craigie acknowledges that this anglicisation is inconsistent and incomplete, but suggests that in many cases 'the governing principle of the change seems to have been to remove from the text words which might be unfamiliar or appear provincial to a southern reader' (p. 293). It is not clear who carried out this anglicisation, but it was presumably done on James's authority.

25  Craigie, *Poems*, I, 306.

26  Rhodes, Richards, and Marshall (eds), *King James VI and I*, p. 2.

27  *Academiae Cantabrigiensis Lachrymae Tumulo Philippi Sidneii Sacratae* (London: Ioannis Windet, 1587), sig. K1r. James's poem, uniquely in the volume, appears in both English and Latin. Again, it is difficult to determine who is responsible for the anglicisation.

execution in this year of his mother. [28] This may not, however, have been his sole motivation. Given that Sidney's political and literary circle were sympathetic to Buchanan's
*De Iure Regni*, James's sonnet may have been another attempt to replace Buchanan's influence with his own.[29] His sonnet concludes with the claim that 'euermore of him shall
liue the best', which might be read as echoing the engagement of Sidney's writings with
the trope of immortality, and implying that those writings – 'the best' of Sidney – will
indeed live for ever. It is possible but by no means certain that James was familiar with
Sidney's writings, which were not to be printed until the 1590s, in 1587.[30] But if he was
indeed eulogising Sidney as, amongst other things, a writer, this poem provides an early
example of the King's interest in, and sophisticated engagement with, English poetry.
More certainly, James is here promoting himself; this line reflects the immortality conferred on him by the publication of his poem.

Beyond the political, diplomatic, and self-promotional considerations so far out-
lined, James also wrote some poetry for private consumption. For example, when he
prepared *Essayes of a Prentise* for publication he chose to exclude 'Ane Admonitoun to the
Maister Poet', a poem to Alexander Montgomerie, but he uses quotations from it as
illustrative examples in *Reulis and Cautelis*.[31] This indicates that he thought the poem fit
for public consumption in terms of form, but not in terms of content. In being written
to or for a specific individual known personally to the King, the poem to Montgomerie
is of a kind with others written before 1618 that James chose not to print.[32] Most of
these poems were excluded not only from the two printed collections but also from
manuscript circulation; until the late 1610s when, as we shall see in Chapter 5, James's
priorities shift, his manuscript poems seem usually to have been passed on to specific

28   Herman, ' "Best of Poets, Best of Kings" ', pp. 73–7.
29   According to James E. Phillips, Sidney himself said of the young King in a 1579 letter to
     Buchanan 'God prosper him and mak him lerne be yow' ('George Buchanan and the Sidney
     Circle', *Huntington Library Quarterly*, 12 (1948–9), 23–55 (pp. 36, 41, 33)).
30   Michael G. Brennan notes that the Sidneys, aware that James was Elizabeth's likely succes-
     sor, were keen to cultivate his favour from the early 1580s onwards, and that Philip Sidney
     acted as a go-between for James at the English court, canvassing in 1585 for an English
     pension for him (*The Sidneys of Penshurst and the Monarchy, 1500–1700* (Aldershot: Ashgate,
     2006), pp. 88, 91, 64). If Sidney was aware of James's interests in poetry, he may well have
     introduced him to some of his writings during these exchanges as a way of reinforcing the
     standing of the Sidney family with him.
31   For example, the quotation 'Into the Sea then Lucifer vpsprang' (*Essayes*, sig. L2r) is from this
     poem. For the poem itself see Craigie (ed.), *Poems*, II, 120–9.
32   Examples of poems of this type include 'A Sonnet to Chanceller Maitland' and 'A Sonett:
     on Sir William Alexanders harshe vearses after the Inglishe fasone'. Another kind of poem
     that James chose not to print in this period is the explicitly political and autobiographical,
     such as 'Song. the first verses that euer the King made'. These poems appear in BL Additional
     MS 24195, fols 37r, 43r, 51r–v. They may also be found in Craigie (ed.), *Poems*, II, 107, 114, 132.
     For a discussion of the latter poem see the Introduction, above.

individuals connected with the court without going any further.[33] This lack of manuscript circulation may be a reflection of his wishes and of the terms on which poems were given to specific individuals.[34] His manuscript poems were not entirely confined within the Scottish court, however; when the English political agent and poet Henry Constable visited the Scottish court in 1589, James showed him the first sonnet of the *Amatoria*, a sequence of love lyrics.[35] James may not have printed certain poems simply because they were not part of the public image that he was trying to cultivate. But these apparently private exchanges might also serve the political purposes of demonstrating the favour of the King or the loyalty of those entrusted with his 'private' poems, and of thus identifying, and strengthening the bonds between, a circle of intimates. Moreover, privately showing Constable a poem led, as we shall see, to Constable helping to promote James as a poet in England.

James also seems to have taken a genuine interest in aesthetics, but politics and aesthetics are always difficult to disentangle. For example, the degree of technical detail in *Reulis and Cautelis*, including lengthy discussions of how to place syllables and what kinds of words to rhyme, and of its concern with rhythm and music, suggest his interest in poetry as art form, not just as political vehicle. Yet this could also be read as a strategy for making the political implications of the treatise more subtle. In a printed dedication to James, Thomas Hudson refers to the 'delite your Maiest. tooke in the Hautie stile of the most famous Writers' and explains how the King encouraged and helped him to write.[36] We might read this as an example of James's aesthetic interest in, and selfless support of, other poets, or in terms of Hudson helping to construct the King as a source of cultural sophistication and wisdom. James's decision to entitle the last piece in *Essayes of a Prentise* not 'Sonnet of the King' but 'Sonnet of the Authour' (sig. P3r) may be indicative of a desire to be an author as distinct from being King, but it may equally be the case that the emphasis on the literary nature of the collection is a means of rendering more subtle and insidious its political implications. James's royal identity makes politics inseparable from his writings, at least in the eyes of his readers, and, as we shall see, he is not fully in control of the ways in which the two might appear to interrelate.

33  May, 'Circulation in Manuscript'.

34  This corresponds with James's decision to print only seven copies of the first edition of *Basilikon Doron* (1599), which were, according to the preface he added to the version printed in 1603, '*dispersed amongst some of my trustiest seruants, to be keeped closelie by them*', and with his angry reaction to what he alleges was the unofficial circulation of one of these copies beyond this select group (*Basilikon Doron* (London: Felix Kyngston for John Norton, 1603), sig. A2v). See Chapter 3, below.

35  Joan Grundy (ed.), *The Poems of Henry Constable* (Liverpool: Liverpool University Press, 1960), 'Introduction', pp. 15–104 (pp. 21, 27–30). That Constable saw James's poem is evident in his response, 'To the K: of Scots vpon occasion of a sonet the K: wrote in complaint of a contrarie winde which hindred the arriuall of the Quene oute of Denmark. Sonet' (p. 142).

36  Thomas Hudson, *The Historie of Judith* (Edinburgh: Thomas Vautrouillier, 1584), sig. A2r.

James's programme for poetry seems to have met a degree of success. His court poets reinforced the relationship between monarch and subject he was trying to establish. For example, in dedicating a manuscript collection of verse to the King in the mid-1580s, John Stewart wrote: 'Sir, haising [having] red zour [your] maiesteis maist prudent Precepts in the deuyn art of poesie, I haif assayit my Sempill spreit [have tried my simple spirit] to becum zour hienes scholler.'[37] Hudson's dedication to James describes the text it precedes as a 'litle worke at your owne commandement enterprised [undertaken]'.[38] This was exactly the image of royal authority and wisdom, and of dutiful obedience amongst his subjects, that it was in James's political interests to promote. Sandra Bell's claims that the poetry of the 'Castalian Band' mythologised James in the Scottish cultural consciousness, while his own verse helped 'to establish him – within and without Scotland – as a powerful Scottish king ruling over a civilised nation', may be overstated.[39] But other critics have agreed that 'in his desire to quell the printed, polemical debate about the monarch, James (at least in his reign as king of Scotland) was successful, escaping the literary denunciations inflicted upon Mary'.[40]

James also seems to have had some impact upon – and some visibility within – English literary culture by the 1590s. Craigie suggests that his *Lepanto* and his translation of Du Bartas's *Les Furies*, both included in *His Maiesties Poeticall Exercises* in 1591, 'set the seal on the reputation of King James as a poet within Great Britain'.[41] James's endorsement of printing poetry may even have helped to legitimise the printing of poetry for others.[42] Certainly other poets drew upon his poetry. For example, Sir John Harington included James's epitaph on Sidney in his 1591 translation of Ariosto, *Orlando Furioso*, and Sidney's sister, Mary Sidney Herbert, Countess of Pembroke, seems to have drawn

37  Thomas Crockett (ed.), *Poems of John Stewart of Baldynneis*, 2 vols (Edinburgh and London: Blackwood, 1913), II, 3.

38  Hudson, *Judith*, sig. A3r.

39  Bell, 'Writing the Monarch', pp. 199, 204. Bell's claims about the rather generalised notion of 'Scottish cultural consciousness' are not fully substantiated. That the English suddenly began to perceive Scotland as a 'civilised nation' seems unlikely; even after James's accession to the English throne, many English continued to view the Scots as greedy, lawless, and uncivilised (see Wormald, 'Two Kings or One?', pp. 190–1, 193).

40  Dunnigan, *Eros and Poetry*, pp. 6–7. See also Jack, who concurs that this escape from literary attack was due not only to James's religious policies but also to his literary role ('Poetry Under James VI', p. 136).

41  Craigie (ed.), *Poems*, I, xlvii. Craigie includes in this volume a list of contemporary references to James as a poet, further indicating how widely his poetry was known. See appendix A, pp. 274–80.

42  While Marotti argues that the publication of Sir Philip Sidney's verse in the 1590s began to provide the necessary sociocultural legitimation for printing verse (*Manuscript*, pp. 228–9), Steven W. May suggests that the publication of *Essayes of a Prentise* had already set a precedent ('Tudor Aristocrats and the Mythical "Stigma of Print"', in A. Leigh Deneef and M. Thomas Hester (eds), *Renaissance Papers 1980* (Durham, NC: The Southeastern Renaissance Conference, 1981), 11–18 (pp. 16–17)).

on *Essayes of a Prentise* for the forms in which she cast her translation of the psalms.[43] Constable celebrated James's poetry in his printed sonnet sequence *Diana* (1592). The first of the four sonnets to James that appear in the middle of this sequence focuses (unlike the preceding sonnets to Elizabeth) on the monarch as writer:

> Thy scepter no thy pen I honoure more
> More deare to me then crowne thy garland is
> . . .
> That laurell garland which (if hope say true)
> To thee for deeds of prowesse shall belong
> And now allreadie vnto thee is due
> As to a Dauid for a kinglie songe.[44]

Constable enjoyed considerable reputation and influence amongst his contemporaries.[45] He therefore – as James perhaps realised he would – provided a useful conduit in England for James's image as a David-like poet–king, successfully combining ruling and writing, achieving great fame and promising more.

Poetry, then, played a major and relatively successful role in James's early Scottish reign. Yet we should not see the King as singlehandedly bringing about these developments through his royal authority. The view of the King as the source from which all power and influence flows, epitomised in Jonathan Goldberg's *James I and the Politics of Literature*, requires qualification. For, despite James's royal status, he engaged with other poets not only as a patron but also as a fellow poet. This meant combining the power of the patron with the humility of the poet, and blurring the distinction between his roles as writer and king, even as these identities were still being constructed. Moreover, as Herman has suggested, James was less legitimising authorship than seeking to appropriate for himself what, as we noted in the Introduction, was the increasing authority and prestige of authorship in this period. Herman's suggestion that 'the king does not confer authority on authorship; rather, authorship confers authority on the king' assumes a greater degree of complementarity between royal authorship and authority than the present book reveals.[46] Nevertheless, James himself evidently believed in the authority of the poet, and this is reflected in the extent of his personal engagement with other poets.

It is difficult to determine how far this engagement extended into collaborative poetic production. Curtis Perry has suggested that manuscript poems circulated by James as his own may have been produced collaboratively or by others, and that he may

43  Craigie (ed.), *Poems*, II, 234; Steven W. May, *The Elizabethan Courtier Poets: The Poems and Their Contexts* (Columbia and London: University of Missouri Press, 1991), p. 209.

44  Grundy (ed.), *The Poems of Henry Constable*, p. 140, lines 6–12. The sequence also includes a commendatory sonnet that Constable contributed to *His Maiesties Poeticall Exercises*, and the response that, as noted above, he made to a poem by James.

45  See Grundy (ed.), *The Poems of Henry Constable*, pp. 59–60.

46  Herman, ' "Best of Poets, Best of Kings" ', p. 85.

in some cases have merely corrected and amended verses others had written.[47] This accords with the work of a number of critics who have argued that meaning was often collaboratively constructed in Renaissance poetic manuscripts.[48] James's early printed collections of poetry may also involve some collaboration, but, here as well as in his manuscript poetry of the same period, 'collaboration' represents something more significant and complex than a king simply commissioning others to write particular passages or poems for him. His first collection suggests that a coterie model of poetic production, more usually associated with manuscript poetry, lies behind both his printed and manuscript poetry of this period. Across both media James participated in a complex process of exchange with other poets, and it was this process that produced this Scottish poetic Renaissance and the image of the poet–king.

### 'The mouse did helpe the lion on a daye': poetic influence and exchange

James himself seems to have been aware that his relationship to other poets was one of reciprocality, and, further, that the roles he and other poets could play for each other were interchangeable. In 'Ane Admonitoun to the Maister Poet', he defers to Montgomerie as 'maistre of our art' and excuses offering him advice by reminding him that 'The mouse did helpe the lion on a daye'.[49] In identifying himself with the humble mouse and Montgomerie with the mighty lion, James recognises that he is the less senior poet of the two. His use of 'lion', an image conventionally associated with royalty, suggests his self-consciousness about the fact that this poetic order is a reversal of the political order in which he has the greater authority. The line thus implies that even figures of authority need the help of their inferiors, and that the King might play for others the roles he needs them to play for him. It also suggests he believed that a poet such as Montgomerie enjoyed a form of authority distinct from, but comparable to, political authority. Here we might note that the title of James's first collection (*Essayes of a Prentise, in the Diuine Art of Poesie*) attributes proximity to the divine, and the authority thence derived, to poetry itself rather than to the King exclusively.[50]

47  Perry, 'Royal Authorship and Problems of Manuscript Attribution', 243–6.

48  See in particular J. W. Saunders, 'From Manuscript to Print: A Note on the Circulation of Poetic MSS in the Sixteenth Century', *Proceedings of the Leeds Philosophical and Literary Society* (1951), 507–28; Marotti, *Manuscript*; and Wendy Wall, *The Imprint of Gender: Authorship and Publication in the English Renaissance* (Ithaca and New York: Cornell University Press, 1993), pp. 23–109.

49  BL Add. MS 24195, fols 46r–49v. This poem may also be found in Craigie (ed.), *Poems*, II, 120–9.

50  The belief that the poet was divinely inspired was widespread in the Renaissance and went back to the *Ion* of Plato, which proposes that 'These lovely poems are not of man or human workmanship, but are divine and from the gods, and . . . the poets are nothing but the interpreters of the gods, each one possessed by the divinity to whom he is in bondage' (quoted in Burke (ed.), *Authorship from Plato to the Postmodern*, p. 16).

The humble role that James thus assumes in the poetic arena reflects, and perhaps acknowledges, his subordination to figures such as Arran in the political arena at this time, but with the crucial difference that in his poetry he has more choice in the role he plays.

The poet with whom James seems to have been most keen to develop a reciprocal relationship was Guillaume de Salluste Sieur Du Bartas (1544–90). Du Bartas began publishing his explicitly scriptural poetry in the late 1570s, and was so popular with his Protestant contemporaries that no fewer than two hundred editions of his poems were published in the half-century after they first appeared.[51] Having acquired a copy of Du Bartas's *La Sepmaine, ou Creation du Monde* (Paris, 1578) by 1583, James was responsible for the translation of several works from this and subsequent collections over the next few years.[52] The French poet reciprocated by translating James's epic poem, the *Lepanto*, and exploited this association with royalty by including his translation in collections of his own works, and seeking to include James's translation of *L'Vranie*.[53] The two also exchanged a series of letters and met in person when the former took up James's invitation to visit the Scottish court.[54] The first two publications of the 'Castalian Band' – the King's own *Essayes of a Prentise* and Thomas Hudson's *The Historie of Judith*, also printed in 1584 – both offer translations of Du Bartas's poetry, and these were the first translations into another contemporary language of any of his poetry.[55] These two publications reflect some of James's poetic concerns, and some of the contradictions of his attempt to be both poet and king.

51  Craigie (ed.), *Poems*, I, liv.

52  A catalogue of the King's library which runs to 1583 indicates that a copy was given to the young king by his nurse, Helena Little or Gray (Warner, *The Library of James VI*, p. xxvi). In addition to his translations of *L'Vranie* and *Les Furies*, included in his printed collections, we have fragments of two further translations by James that were not printed and seem never to have been completed (see Craigie (ed.), *Poems*, II, 148–58).

53  The first appearance of Du Bartas's *La Lepanthe* in France, as part of an expanded version of *La Seconde Sepmaine*, was in 1591, the same year that it appeared in James's collection. Du Bartas signed a contract in 1585 for an edition of his poems that was also to have included James's translation of *L'Vranie*, but publication of this edition did not take place (Urban Tignier Holmes, John Coriden Lyons, and Robert White Linker (eds), *The Works of Guillaume de Salluste Sieur Du Bartas*, 3 vols (Chapel Hill: University of North Carolina Press, 1935–40), I, 19).

54  Henry of Navarre appears to have tried to exploit James's admiration for Du Bartas by turning the visit into an informal diplomatic mission to explore the possibility of a marriage between James and Henry's sister. In this regard the visit was unsuccessful, but Du Bartas and his company were treated lavishly by the King, who tried to persuade Du Bartas to stay in his service (Holmes, Lyons, and Linker (eds), *Works of Du Bartas*, I, 20–2; see also Lee, *Maitland*, p. 116; and A. Francis Steuart (ed.), *Memoirs of Sir James Melville of Halhill, 1535–1617* (London: Routledge, 1929), p. 321).

55  James Craigie (ed.), *Thomas Hudson's History of Judith* (Edinburgh and London: William Blackwood & Sons, 1941), p. xxvi.

As King, James was clearly in a position of authority over Du Bartas, but as poet he defers to what he considers the Frenchman's poetic greatness. His first major work in his *Essayes of a Prentise* is his translation of Du Bartas's *L'Vranie*. In the preface to the reader he refers to Du Bartas as a 'deuine and Illuster Poete'. He describes being moved by reading his work 'to preas to attaine to the like vertue', then explains that, realising he lacks 'the like lofty and quick ingyne, . . . skill and learning', he has decided that the best he can do is to translate his work instead (sig. C3r). He further lays himself bare, and gives the reader the opportunity to evaluate him in relation to Du Bartas, by including the original as a parallel text, 'noght thereby to giue proofe of my iust translating, but by the contrair, to let appeare more plainly to the foresaid reader, wherin I haue erred' (sig. C3v).[56] Whether all of this is mere conventional employment of the trope of poetic humility or a reflection of genuine admiration, James is thus publicly admitting his fallibility, and establishing between himself and Du Bartas a poetic hierarchy that reverses the political order, placing him in a secondary and junior position.

While James is clearly not seeking political or economic advancement from Du Bartas, the relationship he establishes with him equates to the relationship between a poet and a patron, with James as the humble panegyrist seeking to elevate his subject. He even affirms his intention 'to doe what lay in me, to set forth his praise, sen I could not merite the lyke my self' (*Essayes*, sig. C3r), positioning himself as a mere conduit for the praise Du Bartas deserves and suggesting his own inadequacy in comparison. The association thereby established between James and a panegyrist is intensified by the nature of the poetry he translates; in this poetry Du Bartas is writing as a court poet who has experience of writing for royal patrons. For example, James's translation of *L'Vranie* includes the following:

> Whiles thought I to set foorth with flattring pen:
> The praise vntrewe of Kings and noble men,
> And that I might both golde and honours haue,
> With courage base I made my Muse a slaue.

> (*Essayes*, sigs D1r and D2r)

Here the King is ventriloquising a poet viewing the position of king from an explicitly external perspective. He is thereby simultaneously acknowledging the possibilities that as king he is susceptible to being flattered with 'praise vntrewe' and that as a writer he has the potential to write 'with flattring pen'. These lines suggest, then, that James was remarkably self-aware as regards both the false glorification his royal position invites, and the temptations and difficulties involved in writing about one's superiors. He is indirectly exploring both his own relationship to other figures of authority and how his panegyrists might consider their relationship to him. Indeed these lines anticipate the lament of the writer who would become one of James's most important panegyrists in

---

56  James's translation is faithful to the original, but for a list of minor errors, omissions, and additions see Craigie (ed.), *Poems*, I, 301–4.

England, Ben Jonson: 'I have too oft preferred / Men past their terms, and praised some names too much.'[57] James was evidently far more aware of the complexities of pane-gyric than critics have tended to acknowledge.[58]

There is, then, a certain doubleness here; James seems to be exploring the perspec-tives of both patron and poet. The position of humble poet in which he places himself is clearly in tension with the notion of the supremacy of the monarch, and, although these admissions of inadequacy and fallibility are made in a poetic arena, in a wider arena they might imply his limitations as ruler. Yet, as has become a critical common-place, the relationship between poet and patron tends to be symbiotic, with the poetic praise offered to the patron serving also to further the career of the poet, and this can be seen here. James benefits from his relationship with Du Bartas, and not only because Du Bartas's translations made possible the wider international dissemination of his work. The King evidently saw Du Bartas as representing a kind of literary authority that he wanted to appropriate to himself. James indeed hints at this in the invocation to his translation of *Les Furies* when he asks God to grant that

> as [Du Bartas] his subject faire
> Doth (liberall) to me len [lend],
> That so he len his loftie stile,
> His golden draughts, his grace.[59]

As James is borrowing subject and style from Du Bartas, so too he is borrowing liter-ary authority. Indeed, his strategy of translating Du Bartas is comparable to his strat-egy of paraphrasing the Bible, which we will consider in the next chapter; in both cases he draws authority to himself by reproducing in his own words a text that he perceives to have its own authority. But while James is thus drawing on Du Bartas's literary authority, Du Bartas in turn, by including his translation of James's poetry in one of his collections, is drawing on royal authority as a means of authorising his own work. This begins to suggest that 'authority' itself has no fixed point of origin.

At the same time as translating *L'Vranie*, James also commissioned Thomas Hudson to translate *La Judith*, another minor work by Du Bartas that originally appeared along-side *L'Vranie*.[60] Hudson's *Historie of Judith* and James's own *Essayes of a Prentise* mirror each

57  Jonson, 'An Epistle to Master John Selden', in Donaldson (ed.), *Ben Jonson*, pp. 331–3, lines 20–1. See also Epigram 65, 'To My Muse', pp. 243–4.

58  See, for example, Goldberg, who speculates that, in receiving Jonson's 'Panegyre' on his arrival in England in 1603, James may have been so flattered by its recognition of his poetic talents that he did not notice that Jonson was in fact affirming his own status as a poet, concluding that 'James's rhetoric assured his blindness' (*James I*, p. 122).

59  James VI, *His Maiesties Poeticall Exercises at Vacant Houres* (Edinburgh: Robert Waldegrave, 1591), sig. A4v. All subsequent references are to this edition and given in parentheses in the text. As with his *Vranie*, James's translation of *Les Furies* is faithful to the original, but for a list of minor errors, omissions, and additions see Craigie (ed.), *Poems*, I, 317–26.

60  See Craigie (ed.), *Hudson's Judith*, p. xxvi.

other: not only do they both offer translations of Du Bartas's verse but they were also published by the same printer in the same year. It appears James and Hudson were embarking on a joint project of disseminating Du Bartas's work. The relationship between these two contemporaneous publications is intensified by the fact that each author contributes a commendatory sonnet to the other's work, and in both cases this is the first poem in the text. While James, as both dedicatee and commissioner of *Judith*, is a more significant presence in this work than Hudson is in *Essayes of a Prentise*, the parallel placement of commendatory sonnets emphasises the sense of exchange, reciprocation, and even equivalence between the royal poet and other poets.[61]

The relationship between James's role as patron and his role as poet is further complicated by *Judith*'s invocation of another royal patron, the Queen of Navarre, to whom Du Bartas dedicated the original poem. Hudson includes a translation of Du Bartas's preface to the reader in which Du Bartas describes having been commanded by the Queen of Navarre to turn the history of Judith into an epic poem, and is 'the first in Fraunce, who in a iust Poeme hath treated in our toung of sacred things'.[62] This is replicated in the situation described in Hudson's dedication to James: like the Queen of Navarre, James has commanded a poet to turn one text into another; like Du Bartas, Hudson is leading the way in translating a work into his own tongue. James thus instigated through Hudson a situation in which he effectively plays the part of the Queen of Navarre, a grand patron receiving the poetic offerings of her lowly subject. At the same time, however, he also seems to want to play the part of Du Bartas, not only in writing and translating poetry in his own contemporaneous publication but in apparently contributing to the writing of Hudson's *Judith* itself. Hudson's dedication publicises this involvement, referring to his 'assured confidence which I ankred on your highnesse helpe and correction', and to the work as indeed being 'corrected by your Maiest. owne hande'.[63] This emphasis on James's involvement serves to promote him as a poet, but it rather detracts from any notion of him as a powerful patron being courted.

The process of members of the 'Castalian Band' contributing to each other's work that *Judith*'s dedication advertises also underlies James's own contemporaneous publication. *Essayes of a Prentise* seems to have been discussed within the circle prior to being printed. For example, in *Reulis and Cautelis* James offers the following advice: 'For compendious praysing of any bukes, or the authouris thairof, or ony argumentis of vther historeis, . . . vse *Sonet* verse, of fourtene lynis, and ten fete in euery lyne' (sig. M4r–v). This advice must have been transferred in advance to the five poets who provide introductory sonnets prais-

---

61  This was not the only instance of James reciprocating in kind the commendatory sonnets that other poets provided for him. For example he contributed a sonnet to a translation of Petrarch's *Trionfi* of 1587 by William Fowler, who had provided a sonnet for the King's first collection of poetry and would do so again for his second (for James's sonnet see Henry W. Meikle (ed.), *The Works of William Fowler*, 3 vols (Edinburgh and London: William Blackwood & Sons, 1914–1940), I, 18).

62  Hudson, *Judith*, sig. A5r.

63  Hudson, *Judith*, sig. A3r.

ing this book and its author.[64] All of these sonnets, and all twelve of James's sonnets of invocation, employ the same interlacing rhyme scheme.[65] There are also specific echoes between them: for example, Robert Hudson's sonnet refers to 'Parnassis forked topp' (sig. *2v, line 6); M. W.'s sonnet to 'Parnassus hill' (sig. *3r, line 2); and James's twelfth sonnet of invocation to 'Parnass hill' (sig. C1r, line 7).[66] These indications of discussion raise in turn the possibility that other poets may have helped to write parts of the work attributed to the King. One editor of Montgomerie has suggested that he may have inspired or helped in the production of *Reulis and Cautelis*.[67] The treatise contains several quotations from poems by both James and Montgomerie, none of which is attributed, indicating James's willingness to draw upon Montgomerie's expertise without giving him public credit, and his sense that their respective works form a single resource.

In addition to any such concealed collaboration, the commendatory sonnets these other poets contributed play a major part in the collection's construction of James as poet and King. These sonnets would have provided, for the majority of readers, their first perception of the King as a poet. The first sonnet, by Hudson, ends by proclaiming:

> The *Monarks* all to thee shall quite their place:
> Thy endles fame shall all the world fulfill.
> And after thee, none worthier shalbe seene,
> To sway the *Sword*, and gaine the *Laurell* greene.
>
> (*Essayes*, sig. *2r, lines 11–14)

These claims for poetic fame and posterity, which may suggest something of James's belief in the power of print, are interlaced with political claims; James is worthy not only to gain poetic recognition but to rule, and to be treated with deference even by other rulers. From the very start of the volume, then, poetic achievement is being presented as part of – and evidence for – political worth. Yet there is an uneasy tension between the poem's attempt to construct the King as a great poet and figure of authority and the fact that its very presence indicates his reliance upon others.

The commendatory sonnets try to defuse this tension by denying or effacing the role of other poets in constructing the royal image. The second sonnet, by Robert Hudson, ends with a continuation of the theme of poetic fame:

> But since I know, none was, nor is, nor shall,
> Can rightly ring the fame that he hath wonne,

---

64 Noted in Jack and Rozendaal (eds), *Mercat Anthology*, p. 473n.
65 This rhyme scheme has subsequently become known as 'Spenserian'. It is not clear which figure within the group first adopted this form, but it is evident that Spenser, who did not publish any sonnets until the dedicatory verses at the opening of *The Faerie Queene* (1590), could have been drawing on *Essayes of a Prentise*. For further discussion see Jack, 'Introduction', in Jack and Rozendaal (eds), *Mercat Anthology*, p. xxviii; Craigie (ed.), *Poems*, I, xxvi; and Westcott (ed.), *New Poems of James I*, pp. l–li.
66 'M. W.' has not been identified.
67 See Stevenson (ed.), *Poems of Alexander Montgomerie*, p. 268.

Then stay your trauels, lay your pennis adowne,
For *Caesars* works, shall iustly *Caesar* crowne.

(Essayes, sig. *2v, lines 11–14)

This is, however, disingenuous. Hudson suggests James has already won poetic fame, but this is the King's first publication and he did not yet have such fame beyond court circles. The poem is in fact performative in its intention, constructing the idea of James's poetic fame even as it presents it as a *fait accompli*. In other words, this sonnet reveals that his poetic fame is dependent upon the words of other poets even as it proposes that his own works are sufficient.

While these opening sonnets try to set the King apart from other poets, James himself tends to collapse the distinction by adopting a humble poetic stance, not only in his presentation of his relationship to Du Bartas but also in his addresses to the reader. For example, the collection ends with James asking 'Therefore, good Reader, when as thow dois reid / These my first fruictis, dispyse them not at all' (*Essayes*, sig. P3r). There is a marked contrast between this humility and the stance of reverence towards him adopted by the other poets, and this suggests the conventionality, the constructedness, and the expediency of both stances. Indeed the comment on poetic flattery that James translates from Du Bartas ironises the opening sonnets, suggesting that they too may represent mere 'praise vntrewe of Kings'. The collection thus simultaneously reveres the King as his royal status demanded, calls into question the sincerity of such praise, and presents James as a humble poet in a reciprocal relationship with other humble poets.

We have seen, then, that James's early poetry grows out of a context in which the lines between poetry and patronage, influence and exchange, authorship and collaboration, are significantly blurred. His poetry and the related work of Du Bartas and Hudson reveal that literary 'authority' is a collaborative construction. Given the analogy between political and literary authority that this material begins to establish, and that James would try to maintain throughout his reign, this implies what indeed was the case – that his political authority was likewise constructed in part by those around him. To the extent that *Essayes of a Prentise* attempts to construct him as an autonomous author and to conceal or downplay others' contributions, it is an apt comment on the nature of royal authority: the myth of divine right kingship works to conceal the reality of the collaborations and negotiations involved in rule. But the very presence of other poets in the collection risks exposing the degree of illusion in the claims of political autonomy and unique status that James would be increasingly concerned to make. He may have tried, as we shall consider below, to maintain an apparent separation between poetics and politics where such damaging implications might be perceived, but he was reliant upon his readers doing the same.

### 'My Muse hath made a willfull lye I grante': playing the court poet

Critics of James's poetry have suggested that his authorial identity is consistent and easily definable, Herman arguing that he 'always writes *as a monarch* and never as a mere poet', yet this simplifies the complex relationship between his poetic and royal identities.[68] James's poetry of the 1580s and early 1590s reflects on this relationship as it engages with questions of poetic feigning, artifice, and deception. This section will examine more closely the relationship between James's poetics and politics by considering three different instances: his sonnets of invocation in *Essayes of a Prentise*; his masque for the 1588 marriage of his favourite, the Earl of Huntly, which was not printed; and his poetic sequence, the *Amatoria*, also not printed. In the first instance, desire for political control seems to underlie his stated poetic desires, but the implications of this analogy are potentially damaging, and here James seems to acknowledge his dependence on his readers. In the second, he seems to make a more conscious attempt to maintain an apparent separation between poetics and politics as part of a larger political strategy. The third and most extended example reveals James exploring and reflecting upon the nature of poetic representation and the relationship between writer and text, but also shows that the less he writes explicitly 'as a monarch' the more his poetic persona is susceptible to constructions and appropriations beyond his control.

The twelve sonnets of invocation to the Gods, the first poems ostensibly by James in *Essayes of a Prentise*, express a desire for poetic description to be so vivid that readers believe they are actually experiencing that which is being described. The fourth ends with the King asking that all his readers' senses be 'so bereaued, / As eyes and earis, and all may be deceaued' (sig. B1r). This acknowledgement of art as deception has potentially damaging implications for a king. As James lays bare the mechanics of poetry, he also may be read as laying bare the mechanics of kingship, pointing towards a Machiavellian model of rulers as needing to employ cunning and fraud.[69] His expression of a desire to affect the senses of his readers may indeed reflect a deeper desire to control his subjects. The awareness of the affective power of language evident in these sonnets goes some way towards explaining the extent of James's prioritisation of verbal representation. Yet for those readers who discern this connection between poetics and politics, the acknowledgement that he has the capacity to use language to deceive might call into question his political integrity.

This expression of a desire to deceive the reader is also an acknowledgement of the reliance of art upon the imagination of its consumer. James indeed acknowledges the role of the reader: in discussing how to represent a beloved in *Reulis and Cautelis*, he advocates 'remitting alwayis to the Reider to iudge of hir' (*Essayes*, sig. M2v). This notion of 'remitting' to the reader is, however, in conflict with the notion of deceiving the reader, and rather ironised by the fact that it appears in a treatise in which James is being prescriptive to his readers. He seems to be struggling to reconcile his

68  See the Introduction, above.
69  James and his poetic circle may indeed have been familiar with Machiavelli's *Il Principe*; Fowler had produced a translation of this work by the end of the sixteenth century, though this was not printed (see Meikle (ed.), *Works of William Fowler*, I, xxx–xxxi).

understanding of art with his position as king. For while it might be acceptable, and even conventional, for a poet to admit to wanting to deceive his readers, or to defer to them, for a king to assume such attitudes towards his subjects might undermine his political integrity and authority. Moreover, this acknowledgement of how art works may also be read as an acknowledgement that the King is likewise reliant upon the perceptions of his subjects. In this regard James's own writings prefigure what Stephen Greenblatt has suggested is *Henry V's* exposure of the parallel reliance of stagecraft and kingcraft upon the imagination of its audience/subjects. For Greenblatt this reliance upon the imagination of the onlooker always works to the King's advantage: 'all kings are "decked" out by the imaginary forces of the spectators, and a sense of the limitations of king or theater only excites a more compelling exercise of those forces'.[70] Yet James was, as we will see increasingly throughout this book, so anxious about how his writings might be read, and so keen to control the imaginations of his subjects, as to suggest that the recipients of royal representation were not always as receptive and cooperative as Greenblatt proposes.[71] James's very first publication thus both reflects upon and, as a representation of the King for the consumption of his subjects, enacts the royal dependency upon public perception that Shakespeare was later to dramatise. This exemplifies the fact that the relationship between his writings and those of his contemporaries is much more complex than even New Historicist critics have tended to recognise.

The image of the royal poet offered in these sonnets would be recalled four years later in James's masque, but here he tries to use the relationship between poetics and politics in more sophisticated ways than in 1584. The masque begins:

> If euer I ô mightie Gods haue done yow seruice true
> In setting furth by painefull pen your glorious praises due
> If one [sic] the forked hill I tredd, if euer I did preasse
> To drinke of the Pegasian spring, that flowes without releasse
> If euer I on Pindus dwell'd, and from that sacred hill
> The eares of euerie liuing thing did with your fame fullfill
> Which by the trumpett of my verse I made for to resounde
> From pole to pole through euerie where of this immoble rounde
> Then graunte to me who patrone am of Hymens triumphe here
> That all your graces may vpon this Hymens band appeare.

This first section having appealed to the gods to bless the wedding in return for the poetic praise the speaker has rendered them, the speaker asks the gods for a sign of their blessing. Mercury then enters and announces 'I messenger of Gods aboue am here vnto

---

70  Greenblatt, 'Invisible Bullets', pp. 63–5.
71  Greenblatt's view of theatre has been challenged by, for example, Kastan, who argues for its subversive and demystifying potential ('Proud Majesty Made a Subject'). See the Introduction, above.

yow sent / To showe by proofe your tyme into there seruice well is spent'.[72] While the repeated 'if' in the opening lines suggests that James is still maintaining a stance of poetic humility, he has displaced on to the figure of Mercury a confirmation that he has succeeded in pleasing the gods with his poetry. The masque thus suggests that what James had earlier claimed in his sonnets of invocation he would do – the last affirms that by singing the names of the gods he will make 'with your names the world to ring' (*Essayes*, sig. C1r, lines 6–8) – he has now achieved. James is here self-mythologising, suggesting that four years on he is no longer a mere 'prentise', and may even have delivered the first thirty-four lines of his masque himself.[73] He was casting himself in a role he wanted to play: the role of poet.[74]

The masque's strategy of presenting James as a poet, through both reference and demonstration, and of not explicitly referring to his royal identity or to current political affairs, serves specific political ends. At this time the Spanish Armada was on its way northwards. In the preceding years, James had been in negotiations with Catholic allies in Europe as well as with England, and in the summer of 1588 was 'still refusing to make clear his support for England until his political and financial demands were met'.[75] Although Huntly, a leading Catholic noble, had converted to Protestantism for

72  BL Add. MS 24195, fols 52r–55v. Note that in this manuscript there is a degree of editorial revision independent of James, and the language of the poems has been substantially anglicised. For further discussion of this manuscript see Chapter 4, below. The masque also appears, written in the King's hand, in Bodleian Library, MS 165 (fols 60r–64v), but in both manuscripts it is only a fragment. Both versions may also be found in Craigie (ed.), *Poems*, II, 134–45.

73  Here I concur with Rhodes Dunlap, who states that the opening speech 'is unmistakably intended for James himself to recite' ('King James's Own Masque', *Philological Quarterly*, 41 (1962), 249–56 (pp. 250–1)); Craigie (*Poems*, II, 246); and Sarah Carpenter ('Early Scottish Drama', in Jack (ed.), *History of Scottish Literature*, I, 199–212 (p. 203)). The strongest evidence is line 9, which refers to the King in the first person: 'Then graunte to me who patrone am of Hymens triumphe here'. For James to have performed these lines was entirely in keeping with his performance of some verses to a later favourite, Buckingham, thirty-three years later. See Chapter 5, below.

74  Without any surviving contemporary comment on the occasion of the 1588 masque, we cannot be certain that the manner of James's participation was not perceived as a breach of decorum. Yet, according to Clare McManus, James's court did not share 'the English masque embargo on the effacement of aristocratic identity in disguise' ('Marriage and the Performance of the Romance Quest: Anne of Denmark and the Stirling Baptismal Celebrations for Prince Henry', in L. A. J. R. Houwen, A. A. Macdonald, and S. Mapstone (eds), *A Palace in the Wild* (Leuven: Peeters, 2000), pp. 177–98 (p. 191)). This acceptance of disguise may have extended into an acceptance of James's poetic role-playing.

75  Roderick J. Lyall, 'James VI and the Sixteenth-Century Cultural Crisis', in Goodare and Lynch (eds), *The Reign of James VI*, pp. 55–70 (p. 67). See also Willson, *King James VI and I*, pp. 78–84. These circumstances will be discussed in more detail in Chapter 2, below, in the context of James's scriptural works of this period.

the marriage, many viewed his 'conversion' with suspicion, and in 1588 he was already involved in Catholic intrigue.[76] Demonstrating favouritism to Huntly at this time thus had the potential to disrupt the delicate diplomacy with England that was obviously important to James, as it also had the potential to damage his relations with the Kirk. It is possible that he simply wanted to write a masque for a favourite who happened to be a Catholic, despite the political context. It seems more likely that he hoped that this court occasion would encourage England to meet his demands by serving as a subtle warning that he had the potential to give his support to Catholics instead. Either way, his strategy of appearing to distance his poetry from his kingship enables him to show support for Huntly without implicating himself too deeply, thereby maintaining the delicate balance of his diplomacy. By presenting his poetry in mythological terms (referring, for example, to 'the forked hill' of Parnassus (line 3)), he further appears to disengage his poetry from immediate political concerns. Indeed, by emphasising the sanctity of poetry (referring to Parnassus as 'that sacred hill' (line 5)), he implies that it transcends the world of political debate. This masque thus maintains a degree of ambiguity as to the relationship between text and context, working towards particular political purposes while, or even by, appearing to be apolitical. It thus depends upon those who saw or heard about the masque not being certain that James 'always writes as a monarch' – a difficult strategy for a king to pursue.

Written around the time of his own 1589 marriage, James's *Amatoria* also engage with a specific literary genre – erotic poetry – in ways that veil their political resonance; these are ostensibly private poems addressed to James's beloved, but his marriage to Anne of Denmark was a crucial dynastic match that was inevitably of international interest.[77] Unlike the masque, however, these poems are less concerned to maintain an ambiguous relationship between poetics and politics than self-consciously to explore the relationship between self-representation and self-fictionalisation. They are playful literary exercises produced within and for an exclusive poetic circle, for which Anne, who probably was not even able to read them, was largely a pretext.[78] As such, they illuminate James's view of poetry. They also highlight, however, the impossibility of controlling all of the ways in which the literary and the political collide.

All of the *Amatoria* appear in the royally authorised manuscript 'All the Kings short poesis', but this does not in itself mean that James was their sole author; as we have seen, even his printed work may have involved collaboration.[79] The picture has been

76  See Lyall, 'James VI and the Sixteenth-Century Cultural Crisis', p. 67; Craigie (ed.), *Poems*, II, 245; and Lee, *Maitland*, p. 177.

77  While the exact date of composition of every piece in the *Amatoria* is not known, topical references suggest that most were written in the months before and after James's marriage. For notes on dating see Craigie (ed.), *Poems*, II, 225–30.

78  McManus suggests that at this point Anne spoke no Scots ('Marriage and the Performance of the Romance Quest', p. 181).

79  For some specific examples of echoes between lines in the *Amatoria* and lines in Montgomerie's poetry, which may suggest his direct involvement in this sequence, see Morna

further complicated by Curtis Perry's discovery of a manuscript collection of circa 1603 that attributes some of these poems to James's lifelong friend Sir Thomas Erskine, later Earl of Kelie (British Library, Additional MS 22601). Perry argues that the most likely explanation of this is that at least some of the *Amatoria* were produced in collaboration.[80] Steven W. May, however, proposes that it is more plausible that MS 22601 simply represents copies of the King's poems that Erskine had obtained.[81] It seems to me impossible, but also unnecessary, to determine exactly the 'authorship' of these pieces; their inclusion in 'All the Kings short poesis' indicates that, as far as James was concerned, he had 'authored' them, however generous his definition of that term. As we have seen, his identity as a poet–king was itself a collaborative construction and these poems extend this process. The sequence's exploration of different poetic personas and literary conventions works as a metaphor for the circumstances in which the poems themselves seem to have been produced and circulated.

The *Amatoria*, like other of James's works, construct a notion of the writer's 'private' self, but they do so in the self-aware manner that was a part of the literary conventions with which James was engaging.[82] For example, one sonnet ends with an appeal to the beloved to 'restore me to my selfe againe', and 'Constant Loue in all Conditions' refers to the persona's 'inward flame'.[83] This 'self', however, is not consistently identified as the King, and some of the poems, such as 'Two Sonnets to her M: tie to show the difference of stiles', proclaim themselves as literary exercises (fols 6r–v). Morna F. Fleming suggests that the two styles represented in this pair of sonnets are 'honesty and artificiality' and reads the first 'honest' sonnet biographically: 'James is admitting that he was never a poet first and foremost, but a monarch . . . and now very much a king oppressed by the petty quarrels continually arising in court'.[84] This poem's assertion that 'Long since forsooth my Muse begunne to tire / Through daylie fascherie of my oun affaires' (lines 5–6) does indeed invite such a reading, particularly since it is consistent with the claim in James's preface to *His Maiesties Poeticall Exercises* that he is unable to correct his own texts because '*my burden is so great and continuall, . . . my affaires and fasherie will not permit mee*' (sig. 2v). Yet this reading does not pay sufficient attention to the nature of the exercise: the first sonnet is constructed to give the impression that it is giving us a glimpse into reality, just as the second is constructed to give an impression

R. Fleming, 'The *Amatoria* of James VI: Loving by the *Reulis*', in Fischlin and Fortier (eds), *Royal Subjects*, pp. 124–48 (pp. 139–40), and Dunnigan, *Eros and Poetry*, p. 204n.

80  Perry, 'Royal Authorship and Problems of Manuscript Attribution'. Two of the *Amatoria* pieces also appear in Bodleian Library, MS 165.

81  May, 'Circulation in Manuscript'.

82  For a discussion of a range of *Amatoria* poems in the context of *Reulis and Cautelis* and contemporary European poetic theory and convention see Fleming, 'The *Amatoria* of James VI'.

83  BL Add. MS 24195, fol. 7v, line 14; fol. 10v, line 21. Subsequent references to the *Amatoria* are to this manuscript and are given in parentheses in the text, but these poems may also be found in Craigie (ed.), *Poems*, II, 68–98.

84  Fleming, 'The *Amatoria* of James VI', p. 140.

of conventionality; neither is straightforwardly autobiographical. And the first sonnet
is disingenuous in the same way as are many of the great Elizabethan sonnets, such as
the first sonnet of Sidney's *Astrophil and Stella*: the poet claims that he is unable to write
poetry but he does so in a poem.

Similarly, 'A Dier at her M: ties desyer', a lament about unrequited love, is followed by
a sonnet claiming that this lament is not a representation of personal experience but a
mere literary exercise: 'My Muse hath made a willfull lye I grante / I sung of sorrows
neuer felt by me' (fol. 13r). This claim is borne out by Steven May's suggestion that the
lament is an imitation of a popular and widely circulated Elizabethan poem, Sir Edward
Dyer's 'He that his mirth hath lost'.[85] The importance to James of the explanatory sonnet
is evident in the fact that in 'All the Kings short poesis' it appears on a sheet inserted after
a page on which he has written 'the sonnett lakkis heere quhiche [which] interprettis all
the matter' (fol. 12v). It would appear that this sonnet was originally excluded, then added
according to the King's instructions after he had examined the manuscript. For James,
then, this was an important interpretative sonnet. Its defence of poetic feigning is,
according to Dunnigan, a strategy for avoiding the implications of the anti-feminism of
the preceding pieces and the incrimination of Anne.[86] This may be part of its motivation, but I would suggest that it has a much broader significance. This sonnet highlights
James's understanding of literary expression as distinct from autobiography, and, particularly in terms of recent Scottish history, this has a crucial political dimension. James
must have been aware that part of his mother's downfall was that the 'casket sonnets' were
read not as literary exercises but as straightforward evidence of her beliefs and actions.
No wonder, then, that he should be concerned to help his readers avoid such hermeneu-
tic errors. This makes it all the more ironic that straightforward biographical readings of
his writings, such as that considered above, are still being produced by modern critics.

James's explicit defence of poetic feigning resonates with such contemporary English
comments as Sidney's affirmation in *The Defence of Poesy* that the poet 'nothing affirms,
and therefore never lieth'.[87] Yet most, if not all, of the *Amatoria* seems to have been
written before the publication of the works of Sidney (his treatise was printed in 1595
and his *Astrophil and Stella* in 1591), and of the other major sonnet sequences of the 1590s
(Daniel's *Delia* was printed in 1592 and Spenser's *Amoretti* in 1595). This may simply indicate shared sources and influences, or it may reflect the manuscript circulation of
Sidney's works in the Scottish court.[88] Either way, that the King employed this topos

85  James's version does not stay as close to the original as some of the other surviving imita-
    tions of this poem, but uses it as a model (May, *The Elizabethan Courtier Poets*, pp. 66–7). Again
    we see James engaging with contemporary Elizabethan literary culture, but without being a
    'slavish imitator'.

86  Dunnigan, *Eros and Poetry*, p. 89.

87  Sidney, *Defence of Poesy*, in Dutton (ed.), *Sidney: Selected Writings*, p. 130. See also Introduction,
    above.

88  Stevenson suggests that there can be 'no question of the king's familiarity with [Sidney's]
    poems', and cites him commending Sidney 'for the best and sweetest writer that ever he

in his verses suggests that he was responding to contemporary attitudes that poetic feigning was an appropriate mode for amorous, Petrarchan verse, and indeed believed it had a degree of cultural capital in which he wanted to partake.

Yet James's engagement with contemporary literary culture was in some ways in tension with his royal status. Other poets – even Sidney who was a nobleman and prominent courtier – did not face the same degree of public exposure and scrutiny as a king. James was the most public of figures (and his marriage a public event). He was evidently separating the literary identity represented in the *Amatoria* from his public, political identity, but he was reliant on his readers doing the same. For any reader who makes interpolations about James as king on the basis of these poems, the admission of 'lying' is even more problematic than the expression of the desire to deceive his readers considered above. It raises the question of how a subject can trust the King's word, and proposes a model of reading the King that calls into question the claims of truthfulness he was concerned to make elsewhere. Perhaps it was in part because of these potential problems that James did not publish the *Amatoria*. He does seem to have allowed some manuscript circulation, but it is notable that those people beyond the court to whom he seems to have shown these poems were also poets (Henry Constable and, as we shall see below, Nicholas Breton) – the people most likely to understand and appreciate them for the non-autobiographical literary exercises they were.

'My Muse hath made a willfull lye I grant' is one of the poems also attributed to Sir Thomas Erskine. If the King was indeed claiming as his own a poem written by Erskine, this adds a further level to the poem's 'feigning'. Yet 'the King' is anyway not merely the author to whom the *Amatoria* is attributed but the object it constructs. One sonnet early in the sequence, 'To the Queen, Anonimos', represents the King in the third person, referring, for example, to the 'happie Monarch sprung of Ferguse race / That talkes with wise Minerue when pleaseth thee' (fol. 5v, lines 9–10). This use of the third person reflects a separation between the King and the literary persona representing the King. This would suggest that the 'I' of the sequence is not 'the King' in any straightforward sense, but rather that the 'I' is a subject-position, which could be assumed by poets other than James, and 'the King' a set of ideas to be represented. Within the terms of

knew', but does not give specific dates (*Poems of Alexander Montgomerie*, pp. lix–lxi, liv–lvi). As noted above, it is possible that James was familiar with Sidney's writings as early as 1587, and the following years provided more opportunities for his exposure to them. Brennan notes that Sidney's younger brother, Robert, 'worked assiduously from the late 1580s to cultivate the personal friendship of James', and made a successful visit to the Scottish court in August 1588 (*The Sidneys of Penshurst*, pp. 40, 101). Robert could have introduced the King to his brother's writings during his visit. Another possible source is William Fowler, who obtained a manuscript of *Astrophil and Stella*, which he could well have shown his king, but, according to Henry Woudhuysen, this was probably not until 1591. As Woudhuysen notes, 'it is not easy to come to many definite conclusions about' the circulation of Sidney's work before the early prints (*Sir Philip Sidney and the Circulation of Manuscripts, 1558–1640* (Oxford: Oxford University Press, 1996), pp. 358, 214–15, 293).

the collection itself, then, there is no contradiction between the collaborations that may have been involved in its production and its attribution to a single author, because the 'royal author' is itself just a subject-position. In other words James may be only one of several poets constructing 'the King' to whom the collection is attributed, in which case the question of whether the King really wrote all the poems in the collection seems somewhat redundant.

Beyond the collection, however, the notion that the 'royal author' is merely a subject-position that can be assumed by others has radical implications. A contemporary English commonplace book reveals one instance of someone writing poetry as the King. It contains a sonnet by Nicholas Breton, 'In Sunny beames the skye doth shewe her sweete', that seems to be an imitation of the sonnet by James that Constable also saw, 'A complaint against the contrary Wyndes'. Breton's poem is attributed to James as 'A passionate Sonnet made by the Kinge of Scots uppon difficulties ariseing to crosse his proceedinge in love & marriage with his most worthie to be esteemed Queene'. Stephen Powle, the compiler of the commonplace book, has added the following note: 'Geaven me by Master Britton who had been (as he sayed) in Scotland with the Kinges Majesty: but I rather thinke they weare made by him in the person of the Kinge.'[89] The telling phrase 'in the person of the Kinge' reveals the problem for James of writing poetry in terms that were not specific to his status as king; this was an era in which contemporary monarchs could not be impersonated on the stage, but James's poetry created a literary identity that could be assumed by others. And this in turn might raise the question of whether his royal identity really was unique and inherent, or whether it too was merely a reproducable performance. Little wonder, then, that James's poetry would increasingly emphasise his royal identity in an attempt to control interpretation.

### 'Misconstrued by sundry': the question of interpretation

In this chapter so far we have seen James's involvement with writing that emphasises his identity an author more than his identity as king, that is playful, and that is willing to admit its own deceptiveness. His later writings, by contrast, tend to be more concerned to emphasise his authorial identity and authority, and to dictate the ways in which he should be interpreted. His epic poem the *Lepanto*, included in *His Maiesties Poeticall Exercises* in 1591, marks a point at which we can glimpse this shift. The anxious desire to control interpretation that begins to emerge explicitly in this poem is, of course, an unrealisable desire, as is highlighted by considering a specific reader of James's printed poetry, Gabriel Harvey. Moreover, it is a notion that James himself contradicts in his own reading of Edmund Spenser's *The Faerie Queene*.

*His Maiesties Poeticall Exercises* makes a far more confident assertion of royal authorship than *Essayes of a Prentise*. James is no longer a 'prentise' but 'his maiestie' (there is no longer any pretence of anonymity), who no longer produces 'essayes' but 'poeticall exercises',

89  Bodleian Library, MS Tanner 169, fol. 43r, cited in Marotti, *Manuscript*, p. 14.

while poetry itself is relegated from a 'diuine art' to an activity for 'vacant houres'. The earlier title subordinates James to the art of poetry but here the King is the focus. While *Essayes of a Prentise* begins with a sequence of commendatory sonnets, *His Maiesties Poeticall Exercises* begins with a direct address from James, 'The Authour to the Reader', and the commendatory sonnets that follow are thereby rendered less prominent. The title of this address contrasts suggestively with that of his only address to the reader in the earlier collection (the preface to *The Vranie*), which is 'To the Fauourable Reader'. James no longer appeals to his readers to be 'fauourable' and his authorial presence is firmly stated.

'The Authour to the Reader' reflects explicitly on this progression and suggests that James's relationship to poetry has changed:

> *And in case thou find aswel in this work . . . many incorrect errours, both in the dytement and orthography, I must pray thee to accept this my reasonable excuse, which is this. Thou considers, I doubt not, that vpon the one part, I composed these things in my verie young and tender yeares: wherein nature, (except shee were a monster) can admit no perfection. And nowe on the other parte, being of riper yeares, my burden is so great and continuall, without anie intermission, that when my ingyne and age could, my affaires and fasherie will not permit mee, to re-mark the wrong orthography committed by the copiars of my vnlegible and ragged hand, far les to amend my proper errours. (Poeticall Exercises, sig. 2r–v)*

There is a strong sense here that James is separating his present self from his poems, almost disowning them as juvenilia, while emphasising his present maturity and responsibility. His claims about how busy he is are rather undermined by the fact that he has found the time to prepare the collection and write the preface, and we should perhaps not take these claims – any more than the similar claims voiced in the *Amatoria* poem discussed above – too literally. The fact that he makes them may primarily reflect a growing awareness of an expectation that a king should be prioritising state affairs over poetry. Yet he still reveals that he would have liked to check the copy of his text before it was printed – the kind of basic work one might expect a king to consider beneath him. This emphasises the extent of his desire to maintain control over the form in which his poetry circulated. At the same time this preface provides for James to dismiss any minor details that caused controversy as mere orthographic error. In each of these ways the presentation of this collection provides an apt frame for the most important poem it contains.

Although it was not printed until 1591, the *Lepanto* seems to have been written before July 1585.[90] The poem praises the Catholic victory against the Turks in 1571, and emphasises that the hero is Spanish, perhaps as a deliberate attempt to compliment the Spanish.[91] At the same time, in its references to election and the certainty of salvation

90  As noted above, at this point Du Bartas signed a contract regarding the edition of his earlier poems that never took place, but which was to have included his translation of the *Lepanto*. The contract certifies that he had placed copies of all these with the publishers (Holmes, Lyons, and Linker (eds), *Works of Du Bartas*, I, 19).

91  Herman, ' "Best of Poets, Best of Kings" ', p. 78. My concern here is with James's anxiety about interpretation, but for a detailed reading of the poem as 'a sophisticated expression

it is protestantised throughout, and it carefully avoids denominational tags.[92] This ambiguity may be a deliberate strategy for enabling readings amenable to both the Protestant and Catholic sides that James was negotiating with in the mid-1580s. By 1591, however, political circumstances had changed and James, keen to placate the Kirk and to keep favour with England, had moved more decisively towards Protestantism.[93] At this point he printed the *Lepanto* with a preface claiming that it had been '*set out to the publick view of many, by a great sort of stoln Copies, purchast (in truth) without my knowledge and consent*', and '*misconstrued by sundry*'. The preface strengthens the Protestantism of the poem, even referring to its Spanish hero as a '*forraine papist bastard*' (*Poeticall Exercises*, sig. G4r). The anglicisation of the poem for publication, noted above, emphasises the importance to James of its English readership.[94] Notably, however, Du Bartas's translation of the *Lepanto*, which appeared in collections of his works from 1591 onwards, and which, according to Craigie, 'established James's fame on the continent',[95] does not include the preface, which was therefore lacking in all the other versions made from his translation. This may be simply because he first translated the work before James added the preface, but it may also be further evidence of the King's careful manipulation of different audiences; James may have preferred that the work be left open to a more pro-Catholic reading for his continental audience.

Whether the misinterpretation James describes had actually occurred, or whether this was simply a strategy to legitimise printing the poem with the preface, he had evidently realised the danger of leaving his writing open to different interpretations.[96] In the preface he explains his original approach to the text:

> it hath for lack of a Praeface, bene in some things misconstrued by sundry, which I of verie purpose thinking to haue omitted, for that the writing thereof, might haue tended in my opinion, to some reproach of the skilfull learnedness of the Reader, as if his braines could not haue conceaued so vncurious a worke, without some maner

Footnote 91 *(contd)*

    of James's functional coupling of poetics and politics to achieve, however partially, discursive self-empowerment' see Daniel Fischlin, ' "Like a Mercenary Poet": The Politics and Poetics of James VI's *Lepanto*', in Sally Mapstone (ed.), *Older Scots Literature* (Edinburgh: John Donald, 2005), pp. 540–59 (p. 555).

92 Sharpe, 'The King's Writ', p. 129. Sharpe further suggests that 'the poem gestures to an ecumenical hope for a unified *respublica Christiana* which James cherished throughout his life'.

93 See Chapter 2, below.

94 Cf. Jack, 'Introduction', in Jack and Rozendaal (eds), *Mercat Anthology*, p. xv. Jack also notes that James nevertheless retains the sound of Scots when no English equivalent is available, so, for example, even in the 1603 London edition, 'the Archangel Gabriel imitates a Scots wind, which "From hilles can hurle *ore heugh*", gaining "speed *aneugh*" to clinch a Scots rhyme'. Even in this politically significant work, James still shows some concern with poetry as poetry and is unwilling entirely to sacrifice style and aesthetics for the sake of his English readers.

95 Craigie (ed.), *Poems*, I, xlvii.

96 No copies of the unauthorised version to which James refers are known to exist (Craigie (ed.), *Poems*, I, 326).

*of Commentarie, and so haue made the worke more displeasant vnto him: it hath by the contrary falen out.*
(*Poeticall Exercises*, sig. G4r)

This explanation maintains the King's authorial integrity, claiming that the original lack of a commentary was a deliberate choice, which was partly motivated by aesthetic considerations (a desire not to make the text 'displeasant'). He goes on to justify his poem in terms of poetic models and rules: he set *'furth the ground of a true History, (as* VIRGIL *or* HOMER *did) like a painter shadowing with vmbers a portrait els drawne in grosse, for giuing it greter viuenes* [vividness], *so I eike* [add] *or paire to the circumstances of the actions, as the rules of the poeticke arte will permit'* (sig. G4v). Yet – whether such aesthetic considerations really were central to the original composition of the poem, or simply provide an excuse for the poem's ambiguities – this preface reflects a tension between aesthetic considerations and political efficacy. It suggests that it is because James followed the *'rules of the poeticke arte'* that he left his poem open to readings he now finds politically undesirable. Attributing the readings that he terms misinterpretations to the lack of a commentary, he goes on to explain *'the nature . . . of this Poeme'* (sigs G4v–H1r).

What we see in the preface, then, is James attempting to close the text, to shift the responsibility for interpretation from the reader back to the writer.[97] This attempt involves emphasising his royal authority: he claims that, without the preface he is now adding, the poem has been read as James *'far contrary to my degree and Religion, like a Mercenary Poet'* writing *'in praise of a forraine Papist bastard'* (*Poeticall Exercises*, sig. G4r). Towards the end of the preface he reaffirms that *'it becomes not the honour of my estate, like an hireling, to pen the praise of any man'* (sig. H1r). The terms he uses suggest the extent to which he now wants his poetry to be seen not as the output of an ordinary poet but as poetry appropriate to, and invested with the authority of, a king. He is also thereby revealing his anxiety that this may not be the case, and indeed, contradicting himself – elsewhere he certainly pens the praise of Du Bartas. The preface is concerned to emphasise James's status, making not only these references to his *'degree'* and *'estate'*, but also to *'the highnes of my rancke and calling'* (sig. H1r). James is thus trying to use his royal authority to authorise his poem – to justify how he has written it and to control how it should be read.

This desire to control interpretation was not coupled with a desire to limit circulation; on the contrary, the King was evidently willing for the authorised version of his poem to circulate widely at home and abroad. As well as being translated into French by Du Bartas, the *Lepanto* was translated into Dutch in 1593 and into Latin in 1604. It would also be the only one of James's poems to be reprinted in London in 1603, and indeed the only one printed in his English reign.[98] A model of the kind of circulation

97  This is, of course, a conventional usage of prefatory material; as Gérard Genette notes, 'The original assumptive authorial preface . . . has as its chief function *to ensure that the text is read properly'* (*Paratexts: Thresholds of Interpretation*, trans. Jane E. Lewin (Cambridge: Cambridge University Press, 1997; originally published in French as *Seuils*, 1987), p. 197). See this study for further discussion of such conventions.

98  For a full bibliography see Craigie (ed.), *Poems*, II, lxxxv–cii.

he seems to have wanted is in fact embedded in the poem itself. A figure of authority, Gabriel, delivers a speech that circulates from the ordinary people to their superiors:

> And so from hand to hand
> It spreads and goes, and all that heard
> It, necessare it fand.
> And last of all, it comes vnto
> The Duke and Senates eare,
> Who found it good . . .

(Poeticall Exercises, sig. H4r)

As people approve of Gabriel's speech and reproduce it without changing it, so James wanted the *Lepanto* to be widely circulated – perhaps even reaching the ears of influential figures in England or on the continent – and 'found . . . good' rather than 'misconstrued'. The preface, then, renders explicit an already present desire for authorial control.

The case of the *Lepanto* may have been a major factor in leading James to believe it was important to impose his royal authority on his texts in an explicit manner, and to provide guidance as to how his texts should be read, particularly when he was engaging with sensitive political matters and would be read by a wide audience. These, as we will see in later chapters, would be dominant features of many of his later writings, as he increasingly struggled to reconcile the openness to interpretation of literary writing with the political demands of his position. Yet while the *Lepanto* tries to impose authorial control over interpretation, readers in this period were also asserting their jurisdiction over the texts they read. In 1584 Gabriel Harvey, who has been used to exemplify the highly politicised nature that reading might assume in this period, added a note to his copy of Conrad Gesner's *Bibliotheca* advising 'Read what you can then rightly call your own'.[99] Harvey bought and annotated copies of both of James's collections of poetry in the years immediately following their publication. These copies still exist, providing one of the most concrete examples we have of a contemporary response to James's poetry.[100]

Harvey's annotations in both of James's collections, which he had bound together with an edition of some of Du Bartas's works, indicate his admiration for them. For example, in *Essayes of a Prentise*, on the page introducing the twelve sonnets of invocation, he writes 'the souerain grace of A perfect Oratour, & diuine Poet, to expresse all thinges as sensibly, & liuely, as may be deuised' (sig. A3r). His vocabulary here – 'souerain', 'diuine', 'liuely' – reflects the terms in which the collection itself represents James and his poetry, suggesting the extent to which Harvey has absorbed that representation. His praise of Du Bartas is, however, even more hyperbolic, and, when he reaches the

---

99  Jardine and Grafton, ' "Studied for Action" ', p. 76.
100  These copies are held in the Old Library of Magdalene College, Cambridge (shelfmark Lect 26). See Virginia F. Stern, *Gabriel Harvey: His Life, Marginalia and Library* (Oxford: Oxford University Press, 1979) for discussion of Harvey's biography, his habits in annotating, and the nature and extent of his library.

beginning of James's translation of *L'Vranie*, his praise is for the poem's originator, whom he terms 'in a manner the only Poet of Diuines', not for its translator (sig. C4r). We might also here note that, of the ten quotations from James's poetry in Robert Allot's *Englands Parnassus* (1600), nine are from his translation of *L'Vranie*.[101] This would suggest that James was right to think that incorporating the work of Du Bartas into his canon might add lustre to his own reputation as a poet.

In his *Pierces Supererogation* (London, 1593) Harvey translates his private comments into public praise, and singles out James's two translations of Du Bartas and his *Lepanto* for particular commendation. Like Constable's *Diana* of the previous year, this publication must have furthered James's poetic reputation in England. We might note, however, that Harvey's description of James as 'a Homer to himselfe'[102] suggests that the King may be a greater poet in his own eyes than in anyone else's. Moreover, Harvey is not so reverent towards the King's works as to be unwilling to annotate his copies with corrections and notes on points where he disagrees. In his notes on *Reulis and Cautelis*, for example, he suggests a better structure for the treatise, improves on the punctuation, and disagrees with some of James's comments on imitation.[103] Moreover, where James would increasingly insist that his texts dictate their meaning to their reader, Harvey imposes his own allegorical meaning. His notes on James's *Phoenix* identify the dead Phoenix as 'The Queen executed' and the new Phoenix as James himself (*Essayes*, sigs I1v–2r). Given that the poem was printed three years before Mary's execution, James could not possibly have intended this reading. The Phoenix that Harvey identifies as Mary comes to the poem's speaker 'For sauing her from these, which her opprest, / Whose hot pursute, her suffred not to rest' (sig. H3v). At a time when James was seeking to maintain favour in England and ensure that Mary's downfall would not endanger his chance of succeeding to the English throne, he would no doubt have been appalled by a reading that suggests he tried to shelter her and viewed Elizabeth and her government as oppressors. Harvey thus exemplifies just how far even a sympathetic reader might exceed the bounds of authorially approved interpretations.

The resistance to readers imposing their own interpretations figured in the preface to the *Lepanto* was contradicted not only by such readers as Harvey, however; it was also contradicted by James himself only five years after the publication of the *Lepanto*, and again the point at issue concerns his mother. James's response to the publication in 1596 of the extended version of *The Faerie Queene* was reported by the English ambassador Robert Bowes as follows:

> The K[ing] hath *conceaved* great offence against Edward [*sic*] Spencer publishing in prynte in the second book p[art] of the Fairy Queene and ixth chapter some dishonourable

101   Westcott (ed.), *New Poems of James I*, p. lvi.

102   Quoted in Eleanor Relle, 'Some New Marginalia and Poems of Gabriel Harvey', *Review of English Studies*, 23 (1972), pp. 401–16 (p. 409).

103   See Relle, 'Some New Marginalia and Poems of Gabriel Harvey', pp. 405–6, for further detail.

effects (as the k. *demeth* therof) against himself and his mother deceassed. He alledged that this booke was passed with priviledge of her mats [majesty's] Commission[er]s . . . he still desyreth that Edward Spencer for faulte, may be dewly tried and punished. (italics mine)[104]

This reveals the significance James attached to poetry; his reaction contrasts with his tacit acceptance of Mary's fate in 1587, perhaps hinting that representation and perception matter more to him than actual events. It reflects the belief that poetry is, or should be, in the control of the monarch – a situation that, as we have seen, he worked hard to create in Scotland. Spenser may indeed have intended to represent Mary through the figure of Duessa, and contemporary commentators certainly made this connection.[105] Yet James's reading of the text as an attack against *himself* is, as Bowes's language suggests ('conceaved', 'demeth'), a subjective construction (and, ironically, by complaining James draws attention to this possible reading). His certainty that this is *the* meaning of the work is a simplistic view of such a complex work of literature, but it reflects the way in which he would increasingly maintain that his own works have only single fixed meanings.

The contradictions of James's position are highlighted by the connections between Spenser's work and his own. The 1590 edition of *The Faerie Queene*, like the *Lepanto*, contains an extra-textual attempt to explain the text's '*general intention and meaning*' and avoid '*jealous opinions and misconstructions*'.[106] James, however, does not read the extended version of the poem in the light of this attempt (as he wanted his readers to read his *Lepanto* in the light of its preface), but imposes a reading that exceeds the author's stated intentions. As Goldberg points out, Spenser even figures in the canto in question the poet (Bonfont/Malfont) being subjected to monarchical authority, his tongue nailed to a post as punishment for his bold speeches and lewd poems.[107] This might be read as Spenser appealing against the censorship of his work. Yet James does not identify with Spenser as a poet, nor read his work according to '*the rules of the poeticke arte*' that he had so recently espoused. Rather he tries, as he had in the preface to the *Lepanto*, to impose

---

104  Report quoted in Frederick Ives Carpenter, *A Reference Guide to Edmund Spenser* (Chicago: University of Chicago Press, 1923), pp. 41–2. Elizabeth did not respond to James's request.

105  See Richard A. McCabe, 'The Masks of Duessa: Spenser, Mary Queen of Scots, and James VI', *English Literary Renaissance*, 17 (1987), 224–42. Florence Sandler suggests that the representation of Duessa in Book V accords with the representation of Mary in officially condoned Protestant literature of around 1587 ('*The Faerie Queene*: An Elizabethan Apocalypse', in C. A. Patrides and Joseph Wittreich (eds), *The Apocalypse in English Renaissance Thought and Literature: Patterns, Antecedents, Repercussions* (Manchester: Manchester University Press, 1984), pp. 148–74 (p. 163)).

106  Edmund Spenser, 'Letter to Raleigh', in *The Faerie Queene*, ed. A. C. Hamilton, second edition (Harlow: Longman, 2001), pp. 714–18. All subsequent references are to this edition.

107  Goldberg, *James I*, p. 2. Oddly enough, Spenser's description of the 'Poet bad' as having spread 'rayling rhymes' (V.ix.25) echoes in James's 'The wiper of the Peoples teares' (1622/3), which is a poetic attack against 'railing rymes and vaunting verse' (see Chapter 5, below). This suggests James did absorb Spenser's definition of the 'Poet bad'.

his royal authority on the text. By assuming that he can determine the meaning of the text when he is in the position of reader, however, he contradicts the claims he makes in the *Lepanto* that it is the writer who controls the meaning of a text. He thus inadvertently acknowledges that other readers – like Harvey – might 'conceave' meanings in his work he has not intended. Here, then, we see the incompatibility of '*the rules of the poeticke arte*' and the rules of the art of politics.

Finally, James's concern with *The Faerie Queene* may relate not only to its alleged attack on him and his mother but also to his own poetic ambitions, expressed, for example, in the 'Sonnet Decifring the Perfyte Poete' prefaced to *Reulis and Cautelis*, which ends '*Goddis, grant I may obteine the Laurell trie*' (*Essayes*, sig. K4r). Perhaps he viewed Spenser's epic poem as competing with his *Lepanto* for the admiration of the Elizabethan audience he was evidently keen to court, and wanted to attach to himself the kind of literary authority Spenser had gained. Herman suggests that 'at some level James wanted to replace *The Faerie Queene*, which glorifies his predecessor and casts his mother as a whore, with the *Lepanto*, the king's own Protestant epic. The 1603 *Lepanto*, in sum, announces to his new kingdom that James, not Spenser, deserves the title of England's Protestant Virgil.'[108] This argument is given further plausibility by the parallel between this scenario and events in 1584 considered above. In the Scotland of James's youth, Buchanan had been a famous and anti-Stuart writer, and, two years after his death, James censored Buchanan's work and published his own. These actions began to place James in the ideological and literary centre Buchanan had occupied. Similarly, Spenser was one of the most successful writers in late Elizabethan England, and, according to James, anti-Stuart; the King therefore tried to censor him and perhaps to replace him, as though hoping that he could in England, as he had in Scotland, assume a position of centrality, not only as King but also as writer.

We have seen, then, the extent of James's literary aspirations both within and beyond Scotland, but this discussion has also suggested the tensions and contradictions between such aspirations and the political demands of his position. As a writer he engages with literary tropes, stances and rules, but such tropes, stances, and rules are in some ways in conflict with his royal status, and this conflict is brought to the surface when James is in the position of reading other literature. His awareness of the ability of literature to persuade, manipulate, even deceive the reader feeds into both his prioritisation of writing as a means of self-representation and his anxieties about representations produced by other writers. This leaves him in the contradictory position of trying to assume the authority to control meaning both when he is in the position of writer *and* when he is in the position of reader. This is a contradiction that would also emerge, as we shall see in the next chapter, in his attempts to turn his own reading of the Bible into writing.

This chapter has also shown how a figure like James complicates the relationship between patron and poet. That he plays both parts interchangeably may suggest he

108 Herman, ' "Best of Poets, Best of Kings" ', p. 93.

perceived that both roles have a certain authority and status, and, indeed, that the literary authorisation gained from being associated with such figures as Du Bartas is not so different whether he contributes to their work or they contribute to his, nor so different from the political authorisation he lends them. The process of exchange in which James engages with other writers thus mirrors the exchange between James the king and James the poet, as both borrow from, authorise, and interpret each other. All of this emphasises the proximity of the roles of patron and poet, and indeed of politics and literature more generally. Further, if even the ultimate source of authority and patronage in the realm also needs to be authorised by other poets, it suggests that authority has no fixed source, but rather is created through a fluid and complex process of exchange; a process that forms a textual version of Foucault's suggestion that 'power is exercised rather than possessed'.[109] Any time a poet reflects or draws upon authority, then, he is also contributing to a continual process of constructing that authority, and this is as true of James's poetry as it is of the poetry of those who wrote for him.

109  Michel Foucault, *Discipline and Punish: The Birth of the Prison*, trans. Alan Sheridan (Harmondsworth: Penguin, 1977 (first published as *Surveiller et punir*, 1975)), p. 26.

# The word of God and the word of the King:
# the early scriptural exegeses

In the 1580s and 1590s an identity was being forged for James as not only a great writer but also an important reader. He seems to have been acutely aware that not only the production of his own writing but also the interpretation of the writings of others might serve to reinforce his authority. The most important text of all for James was, of course, the Bible. His desire to control the meaning of this vital source of political as well as spiritual authority was a desire he shared with his royal predecessors. Elizabeth, for example, supported the production of a new official version of the Bible, the Bishops' Bible, in 1568.[1] What was distinctive in James's case, however, was the extent to which he used not only his political authority but also textual authority to achieve this end. His first publication, *Essayes of a Prentise* (1584), contained a translation of Psalm 104. This seems to have been part of a major project, never completed, of translating all of the psalms.[2] But while James's publishing career began with poetry, Scottish printers in the late sixteenth century were, according to A. A. MacDonald, mainly publishing religious works, the exceptions being Vautroullier and Waldegrave who were printing the poetry of James and his circle.[3] The King's next two publications, both with Henry Charteris (one of the printers MacDonald cites), tap into this market. In 1588 he printed *Ane Fruitfull Meditatioun, Contening ane Plane and Facil Expositioun*, a commentary on Revelation 20: 8–10 (hereafter referred to as *Ane Fruitfull Meditatioun*), and in 1589 *Ane Meditatioun vpon the First Buke of the Chronicles of the Kingis*, on 1 Kings 15: 25–9

---

1 For a discussion of how both Henry VIII and Elizabeth tried to use their political authority to control reading of Scripture see Robert Weimann, *Authority and Representation in Early Modern Discourse*, ed. David Hillman (Baltimore and London: Johns Hopkins University Press, 1996).

2 James's preface to *His Maiesties Poeticall Exercises* (1591) proposes that if this work is well accepted, it 'will moue me to hast the presenting vnto thee, of . . . such nomber of the PSALMES, as I haue perfited: & incourage mee to the ending out of the rest' (sig. 2v). The early manuscript held in the British Library, Royal MS 18 B.16, contains thirty psalms (see James Doelman, 'The Reception of King James's Psalter', in Fischlin and Fortier (eds), *Royal Subjects*, pp. 454–75 (p. 469, n. 5) for further detail).

3 A. A. MacDonald, 'Early Modern Scottish Literature and the Parameters of Culture', in Mapstone and Wood (eds), *The Rose and the Thistle*, pp. 77–100 (pp. 93–4).

(hereafter referred to as *Ane Meditatioun*). These were the first works he printed under his name, though their title pages do not give his name prominence and assert that these meditations are merely 'set doun be [by]' the King, emphasising that they are in a different category to original writing such as poetry.[4] In the 1580s James also wrote *A Paraphrase vpon the Reuelation of the Apostle S. Iohn* (hereafter referred to as *A Paraphrase vpon the Reuelation*), though this would not be published until 1616. Thus he tried, as he did with poetry, to stamp his authority on scriptural exegesis through direct participation in the genre.

These scriptural exegeses continue to receive little critical analysis and have been excluded from the canon of James's 'political works'.[5] Yet this was an age in which not only were language and power intimately related, but, more specifically, 'the authority of Protestant exegesis was ever more widely being appropriated by the public' and 'questions of textual exegesis and the issue of political power were inextricably entwined'.[6] Scriptural exegeses written by a king crystallise and extend these complex interrelations between political authority and exegesis: far from existing outside the realm of politics, they were inevitably politically engaged and potentially powerful texts, and James sought to exploit them as such, while maintaining that they merely reproduce the word of God.[7] What these works also extend, however, is the contradictions inherent in his representation of the relationship between writer and reader that we began to see emerging in the last chapter.

This chapter begins with a consideration of the ways in which scriptural exegesis accords with James's aims and concerns as king and writer, and the specific purposes it served both in the immediate domestic context and in an international context. It then examines the larger claims about the relationship between authorship and authority, and

---

4  James VI, *Ane Fruitfull Meditatioun* (Edinburgh: Henry Charteris, 1588) and *Ane Meditatioun vpon the First Buke of the Chronicles of the Kingis* (Edinburgh: Henry Charteris, 1589). Subsequent references are to these editions and given in parentheses in the text.

5  The standard text of James's writings, McIlwain (ed.), *The Political Works of James I*, does not include any scriptural exegeses. Sommerville's *King James VI and I: Political Writings* largely follows McIlwain's lead by excluding all of the scriptural exegeses except *A Meditation vpon St. Matthew* (1619), as does the more recent Rhodes, Richards, and Marshall (eds), *King James VI and I: Selected Writings*. As noted in the Introduction, above, we still lack modern editions of the others. Fischlin has recently produced the first chapter-length study of James's *Paraphrase vpon the Reuelation* and *Fruitfull Meditatioun* (' "To Eate the Flesh of Kings" '). Fischlin is more concerned with analysing these texts as part of James's overall 'literary strategy of self-empowerment' than with examining the specific circumstances in which they were written and ways in which they were read.

6  Weimann, *Authority and Representation*, pp. 63, 79.

7  Sharpe suggests it is precisely because these texts claim a space above polemical exchange that McIlwain excluded them from James's *Political Works* ('The King's Writ', p. 127). Such willingness to accept these texts as what on the surface they claim to be, and consequent failure to recognise their political motivation, may have been quite what James wanted.

between the royal and the divine, that interpreting Scripture enables him to make. As the discussion goes on to show, however, his exegeses also expose the contradictions in, and limitations of, these very claims. The chapter then turns to the series of letters exchanged between James and Elizabeth in this period, which provide a context for James's use of his exegeses as tools of his international diplomacy, and further complicate the writer–reader relationship he is trying to establish. It ends by pointing towards the role his exegeses would play in his later Scottish and English reigns, both in terms of their relationship to some of his later writings and in terms of some of the responses they met. Even apparently supportive responses highlight that once in the public domain these exegeses were susceptible to being used in ways the King had not intended.

## Constructing the King as biblical interpreter in the Scottish context

James's desire to control the meaning of the Bible was twofold. Firstly, he wanted to assert royal authority over a text that had been, and could be again, interpreted in ways that undermined his authority.[8] Secondly, both as a king and as a writer he required external authorisation in the form of the Bible. For his political authority lay in maintaining he was God's Elect, king by divine right, while his authority as a writer also derived in large part from his relationship with the divine. Even though, as we saw in the last chapter, James to some extent blurred the boundaries between poet and patron, no other mortal could fully play the part of patron for him: as the ultimate authority on earth, a Protestant king could address only God as an explicit source of external authority for his writing. Nevertheless, as James had drawn on other poets to help authorise his published poetry, so his two scriptural exegeses of the late 1580s are, as we shall see, lent additional authority by Patrick Galloway, a minister of the Scottish Church, who contributes a preface to both.

James's choice of a psalm as his first exercise in religious writing to be printed was apt in a number of ways. King David was, as we began to see in the first chapter, important as a model for the poet–king, but he also afforded 'an Old Testament precedent for royal authorisation of Bible translation'.[9] Translating the psalms provided a way for James to intensify his association with this biblical figure; as King David reproduced the word of God for his people, so King James reproduces the word of God for his. James would later describe David as a 'propheticall King', and his own scriptural

8  As noted in the Introduction, above, James faced a number of theoretical challenges to his authority at this time, and each of these positions was supported by scriptural interpretation. Buchanan, for example, was concerned to demonstrate in *De Iure Regni* that the resistance theory he advocates is entirely consistent with scripture (Burns, *The True Law of Kingship*, p. 231).

9  John N. King, 'James I and King David: Jacobean Iconography and its Legacy', in Fischlin and Fortier (eds), *Royal Subjects*, pp. 421–53 (p. 430). See this chapter for a discussion of King David as the foremost scriptural model for Jacobean iconography.

writings suggest that he also wished to draw to himself some of the spiritual authority of the prophet.[10] Had he completed a Psalter for use in churches, it would have been
a major assertion of royal control over worship, entailing 'the participation of every
voice in every parish of the church'.[11] But his project of translating the psalms was
unsuccessful in that he did not complete it, and those psalms he did complete were not,
with the exception of 104, printed in his lifetime.[12]

James's rendering of Psalm 104 begins 'O Lord inspyre my spreit and pen, to praise
/ Thy name, whose greatnes farr surpassis all: / That syne [thereafter], I may thy gloir
and honour blaise', and ends promising 'To *Iehoua* I all my lyfe shall sing' (*Essayes*, sig.
N3r–v). The King is using the scriptural text to imply not only his own piety, but also
his role as divinely inspired poet. Moreover, these lines clearly echo his twelve sonnets
of invocation at the beginning of the collection, which appeal to the gods 'that thou
my veine Poetique so inspyre' and promise 'I shall your names eternall euer sing' (*Essayes*,
sigs A3v, C1r). While the very presence of the psalm helps to suggest that this largely
secular collection is not divorced from the religious, this echoing goes further in implying equivalence between the King's own poetry and the divine poetry he translates.
Moreover, 104 just happens to be a psalm of which Buchanan had produced a Latin
version that was famous across Europe.[13] James's inclusion of his own version of this
psalm thus extends his project, of 1584 and beyond, of replacing his tutor's influence
with his own.

In the late 1580s James's literary engagement with the Bible began to serve clearer
political purposes. Though he now was more established at the centre of government
than he had been in 1584, his hold on political power was still insecure, and the Kirk
remained a source of opposition to the Crown. Lee suggests that by 1587 James was per-
suaded of 'the distasteful necessity of securing the active co-operation of the kirk', and
that in the years 1587–8 he was succeeding in winning the Kirk's favour.[14] One of the
main functions of James's two published scriptural exegeses of 1588 and 1589 was to
support this attempt to placate the Kirk by emphasising his support of the 'true' religion and rejection of Catholicism. His choice of Revelation for his first exegesis was a
politically charged one: as Bernard Capp emphasises, 'politics and apocalyptic thought

10   James makes this comment in *The True Lawe of Free Monarchies* (Edinburgh: Robert Waldegrave,
     1598), sig. B3r. All subsequent references to this work are to this edition and given in paren-
     theses in the text. Esther Gilman Richey quotes William Kerrigan's observation that in the
     Renaissance the term 'prophet' could mean 'teacher, preacher, poet, or inspired interpreter
     of the bible' (*The Politics of Revelation in the English Renaissance* (Columbia: University of Missouri
     Press, 1998), p. 1). James placed himself in all of these roles, and the ambivalence of the term
     'prophet' made it easier for him to blur the boundaries between them.
11   Doelman, 'The Reception of King James's Psalter', p. 454.
12   We shall briefly consider below the edition of the psalms published under James's name
     in 1631.
13   Doelman, 'The Reception of King James's Psalter', p. 455.
14   Lee, *Maitland*, pp. 121, 156.

were bound closely together in early modern Europe' as Protestant propagandists exploited Revelation as a means of defending the Reformation.[15] This involved identifying the Pope with the Antichrist, an identification that gained widespread acceptance during the first half of Elizabeth's reign.[16] James emphasises this identification. In *Ane Fruitfull Meditatioun*, for example, he unequivocally summarises his argument with a marginal note that asserts 'The Pape is Antichrist, & Paperie ye lowsing [loosing] of Satan, fra quhom [from whom] proceidis fals doctrine, and crueltie to subuert ye kingdome of Christ' (sig. B2r).

James's choice of Patrick Galloway as the contributor of prefaces was also significant. In 1584 Galloway, minister of Perth, had been denounced as a rebel because of his alleged links with the pro-English and anti-Catholic Ruthven Raiders. In 1588 the general assembly appointed him to a delegation that in February exhorted James to purge Scotland of Catholics, and in August thanked him for his concern with the defence of Protestantism.[17] For James to respond by quickly inviting, or at least allowing, Galloway to write him a preface (the preface, dated 1 October 1588, claims that Galloway received the work on 5 September) was to make the statement that he accepted the general assembly's encouragement and thanks. It suggests that the period of conflict between the King and Protestant 'rebels' is forgotten, and that James is now willing to embrace even the more extreme Protestant elements amongst his clergy. It is a shrewd move that lends credibility to the claims the meditations themselves make, and the praise the prefaces inevitably offer.

In this first preface Galloway describes the text as 'ane worke worthie of all praise . . . and ane testimonie of his hienes maist vnfeinzeit [unfeigned] loue toward trew religioun' (*Ane Fruitfull Meditatioun*, sig. A2r). In the preface to *Ane Meditatioun* the following year, by which time he had become one of James's household ministers, he asserts that James is 'most earnestlie and zealouslie bent in the eis [eyes] of the haill warld [whole world], to offer with himself to the King of Kinges and Lord of Lordes his gift and present, as ane witnes of his vpricht meaning in the caus of Christ, and anefauld [honest or simple] coniunctioun in him with the haill reformed christiane Kirkes in the earth' (sig. A2r). Galloway's concern to emphasise that James's support of Protestantism is unfeigned, upright, and honest suggests an anxiety that people might doubt his sincerity; a doubt that was not without foundation, as we shall see later. His prefaces make

15  Bernard Capp, 'The Political Dimension of Apocalyptic Thought' in Patrides and Wittreich (eds), *The Apocalypse in English Renaissance Thought and Literature*, pp. 93–124 (pp. 93–4).

16  Capp, 'The Political Dimension of Apocalyptic Thought', p. 97. The identification of the Pope with the Antichrist derived from Martin Luther's interpretation of Revelation (Bernard McGinn, 'Revelation', in Robert Alter and Frank Kermode (eds), *The Literary Guide to the Bible* (London: Collins, 1987), pp. 523–44 (p. 537)). See McGinn for a more general history of interpretations of Revelation (pp. 528ff), and Capp for an overview of Protestant interpretation of Revelation in the Tudor and Stuart periods.

17  See MacDonald, *The Jacobean Kirk*, esp. pp. 24–6, 40–1.

it clear that these meditations are meant as evidence – a 'testimonie' or 'witnes' – of James's allegiances, indicating their important public role.

What these texts represent, however, is not merely James's support of the Kirk but a complex negotiation between royal and Church authority. While the presence of a minister in the text helps to create an impression of allegiance between King and Kirk, it also suggests that James was still dependent on the Kirk's favour and approval. At the same time, by writing these texts James was stamping his authority on a crucial area of discourse, asserting royal control over texts that were the very basis of the authority of the Kirk. Galloway's first preface describes the King's meditation as 'ane worke . . . quhilk [which] Goddis Spirit did vtter be [by] our Souerane, as ane witnes of his graces knawledge in the hie [high] misteries of God' (*Ane Fruitfull Meditatioun*, sig. A2r). This is an appropriation of claims made within the Kirk: as Lee notes, 'Knox and his fellows believed that . . . in the pulpit God's spirit worked through them'.[18] Galloway is thus attributing to James the spiritual authority associated with the Kirk. The Minister's second preface goes further, beginning by stating that the Bible 'informes the christiane kirk that God sall raise vp Kinges to be nuresing [nourishing] fatheris vnto hir' (*Ane Meditatioun*, sig. A2r). Though Galloway represents the Kirk, here he seems to be supporting James's desire for authority over the Kirk.[19] He manipulates his readers into accepting this position by emphasising that it comes from the Bible and is specific to the 'christiane' church as opposed to the false church. The phrase 'nuresing fatheris' succinctly blurs the notion of James as merely nurturing and supporting the Church with the notion of him as having authority and precedence over it. These texts thus not only represent the King attempting to assume authority over the Bible but also represent him trying to assume a degree of authority over the Kirk.

### Scriptural exegesis on an international stage

The fact that James's two meditations were not anglicised in the way that *His Maiesties Poeticall Exercises* (1591) was, or even in the more partial way that *Essayes of a Prentise* (1584) was (see Chapter 1, above), may seem to suggest that in this case he was concerned only with a Scottish readership. Yet, as James was well aware, these meditations were also politically significant in an international context.[20] By publishing his own scriptural

18   Lee, *Maitland*, p. 17.
19   Galloway is described by MacDonald as one of a number of ministers previously 'involved at the forefront of opposition [who] became agents of the crown within the Kirk' (*The Jacobean Kirk*, p. 177).
20   We might speculate that the meditations were not anglicised because James was here less concerned than in the poetic works to promote an image of Scottish cultural sophistication to the general English reader; because his primary aim was to conciliate the Kirk; or because he wished the relevance of these works to an international audience to appear incidental rather than calculated. Whatever the explanation, it is clear, as we shall see, that James wanted some of their import to be recognised by at least some readers beyond the borders of Scotland.

interpretations, especially by choosing to comment on Revelation, a particularly contested area of interpretation, he was engaging in long-standing international debates. Catholic writers, such as Cardinal Bellarmine, sought to counter Protestant identification of the Pope with the Antichrist, Bellarmine publishing his three-volume *Controversies* attacking Protestant theology and exegesis from 1581 to 1593.[21] Bellarmine was the most influential advocate of the claim that popes had the right to depose rulers, and his *Controversies* therefore had troubling political implications. By offering alternative scriptural readings, which continued the established Protestant interpretation of Scripture, James was trying to undermine the authority of such Catholic interpretations, and, by extension, the political authority of the papacy and the threat it posed.[22]

The most important foreign readership for James's exegeses was, however, in England. James's strategy in domestic affairs was to play opposing groups against each other, giving himself a means to pressurise each side as required while trying to maintain favour with both.[23] He used the same strategy in foreign affairs. Having a continual eye on the English throne to which he hoped to accede, he ostensibly remained the Protestant ally of England, even after the execution of his mother in 1587.[24] Yet during the 1580s James was also trying not to alienate the Catholic powers of Spain and France and even sought aid from them. In the period 1584–5 Philip II, King of Spain, who was already considering an attack on England, believed that James was ready to convert to Catholicism.[25] Meanwhile, in May 1585 Elizabeth opened up negotiations for a Protestant league between England and Scotland, and in July of that year James accepted money from Elizabeth for a defensive alliance, which in 1586 became a formal league bringing with it a subsidy from Elizabeth.[26] Yet, as noted in the previous chapter, as the Spanish Armada headed for England in 1588, James was still trying to exploit the interest of both England and Spain in having his support. As D. H. Willson suggests, James's negotiations with foreign Catholic powers, along with his leniency towards his

21  McGinn, 'Revelation', p. 537.
22  This marked the beginning of the debate between James and Catholic interpreters, Bellarmine in particular, that would culminate in the Oath of Allegiance controversy during his English reign (see Chapter 3, below).
23  Wormald, 'Two Kings or One?', pp. 196–8. See also Goodare, 'Scottish Politics in the Reign of James VI'.
24  James's insistence on his claim to the English throne even as early as the 1580s is evident, for example, in a declaration he made in 1589 regarding his journey to Denmark, in which he refers to himself as 'air appeirand of England' (in J. T. Gibson Craig (ed.), *Papers Relative to the Marriage of King James the VI of Scotland with the Princess Anna of Denmark* (Edinburgh: Bannatyne Club, 1828), p. 12).
25  Willson, *King James*, p. 51. For the suggestion that Philip was considering an attack against England from 1583 onwards see John Guy, *Tudor England* (Oxford: Oxford University Press, 1988), p. 338.
26  Guy, *Tudor England*, p. 334; Goodare, 'Scottish Politics in the Reign of James VI', p. 38; and Goodare, 'James VI's English Subsidy'.

domestic Catholic lords, increased 'his bargaining power with Elizabeth, formed a counterpoise to the Kirk, and offered hope of survival in case of Spanish victory'.[27] James was thus trying to profit from the situation and leave himself in an advantageous position whatever the outcome.

As soon as it appeared that Elizabeth would meet James's demands, and that his interests were therefore best served by asserting his firm Protestantism and support for England, he was quick to make such assertions. He wrote the following to Elizabeth on 1 August, by which time the battle had begun and the English had succeeded in depleting the Spanish fleet:

> this tyme must move me to utter my zele to the religioun, and how neir a kinsman and neighbour I finde myself to yow and your countrey. For this effect then have I sent yow this present, hereby to offer unto yow my forces, my personn, and all that I may command, to be imployd agains yone strangearis.[28]

As we saw in the last chapter, James's wedding masque for the Earl of Huntly of only a few weeks earlier had demonstrated that he had the potential to support Catholics, and his epic poem the *Lepanto* had initially been left open to readings amenable to both Protestants and Catholics. In the same way his scriptural exegeses serve a diplomatic function, reinforcing and echoing this letter by making a public statement of his complete support for Elizabeth only when it suited him to do so.

*Ane Fruitfull Meditatioun* was printed in 1588 itself, and its preface is dated to within two months of the defeat of the Armada. Its assertion that the Pope is the Antichrist not only renders emphatic James's rejection of Catholicism but also, more subtly, implies his support for Elizabeth despite the execution of his mother a year earlier. For, particularly since that event, Catholic commentators had associated Elizabeth with the Whore of Babylon.[29] James's opposing interpretation of Revelation implicitly rescues Elizabeth from the consequences of her treatment of Mary. *Ane Fruitfull Meditatioun* further proposes that the whole island should join together in the face of external threat: 'we may . . . concur ane with another as warriouris in ane camp and citizenis of ane belouit citie, for mantenance of ye guid caus God hes cled vs with, and defence of our liberties, natiue countrie, and lyfes' (sig. B4r). This closely allies Scotland and England and emphasises their support of the same cause. It also suggests that James had supported England and perceived the Spanish attack as a threat to the whole island all along. Galloway's preface describes James 'oppinlie declaring be [by] pen, and avowing in deid the defence thairof in that maist perillous tyme quhen [when]

---

27  Willson, *King James*, p. 81.

28  John Bruce (ed.), *Letters of Queen Elizabeth and King James VI of Scotland*, Camden Society (London: J. B. Nichols and Son, 1849), pp. 51–2. On July 31 the English Ambassador had agreed to all of James's demands, but once the battle was decisively won Elizabeth outmanoeuvred James by disavowing her ambassador and refusing to grant what he had offered (Lee, *Maitland*, pp. 170–2).

29  Sandler, '*The Faerie Queene*: An Elizabethan Apocalypse', p. 162.

the foirsaid enemeis ioyned togidder did rage and bend thair force against [true religion]' (sig. A2r). Within the text James refers to 'the actioun we haue in hand presentlie' (sig. A3v) as though he were writing during the attack from a position of support for England. Yet, as we have seen, James did not make a clear statement of support for England until after the battle was well under way, and this meditation was not published until at least two months after that. The meditation is thus able retrospectively to rewrite the King's conduct during the summer of 1588; it elides the political games he played until it was clear which side it was most in his interests to support. This text is thus an important, and ultimately duplicitous, tool in James's complex international diplomacy.[30]

At the beginning of his next meditation James reflects more explicitly, and perhaps more anxiously, on the public role of his meditations, stating that they 'may efter my deith remane to the posteritie as ane certane testimonie of my vpricht and anefauld [honest or simple] meaning in this so greit and weichtie ane caus' (*Ane Meditatioun*, sig. A3v).[31] Again we have the idea of writing as testimony, and a proliferation of adjectives ('certane', 'vpricht', and 'anefauld'), that suggest the King's anxiety that he will be perceived to be duplicitous. Indeed, his allegiances were still not entirely clear in 1589.[32] Despite this hint of anxiety, he claims that his first meditation achieved its end of 'exhort[ing] yow to remane constant' and continues to assume a pedagogic and authoritative role: 'my speaches hauing taking [taken] ane euident effect, I could do no les of

---

30  James's diplomatic tactics make the Book of Revelation an appropriate choice for this meditation. As Sharpe notes, Revelation seems 'to announce both its openness and impenetrability. The first chapter promises that "blessed is he that readeth and they that heareth the words of this prophecy"; in chapter 5, by contrast, the reader confronts the sealed book that none could open' ('Reading Revelations: Prophecy, Hermeneutics and Politics in Early Modern Britain', in Sharpe and Zwicker (eds), *Reading, Society and Politics*, pp. 122–63 (p. 127)). In this way Revelation provides a model for the combination of apparent transparency with misrepresentation and omission in James's meditation, and, more broadly, for the claims that the King's 'inward intention' is open to view *and* should not be pried into that we will consider in the next chapter.

31  The word 'anefauld' is rendered as 'simple' in the 1603 English edition (*A Meditation vpon the First Booke of the Chronicles of the Kinges* (London: J. Windet for Felix Norton, 1603)), and as 'honest' in the version that appears in James's *Workes*; given the duplicitousness of James's foreign policy, it seems fitting that the meaning of this word was not entirely clear in an English context.

32  In this year James had strengthened his political connections with Protestant Europe through his marriage to Anne of Denmark. Nevertheless, he continued to refuse to repress completely the Catholic lords within Scotland or to sever unequivocally his ties with Spain, as this continued to give him bargaining power with Elizabeth and with the Kirk (Herman, '"Best of Poets, Best of Kings"', p. 81). Anne herself may later have converted to Catholicism. For discussion of the implications of her 'supposed Catholicism' see Leeds Barroll, *Anna of Denmark, Queen of England: A Cultural Biography* (Philadelphia: University of Pennsylvania Press, 2001), pp. 162–72 (quotation from p. 172).

my cairfull dewtie then out of this place cited, teache yow quhat [what] restis on your part to be done' (sig. A3v). Having thus justified writing his meditations, James goes on to stress his Protestant allegiances and to make some politically useful suggestions. He draws an analogy between the Philistines attacking Israel and the Catholic attack, maintaining that the people of England and Scotland, like the Israelites, are ruled by the pure word of God. The significance of this comparison becomes clear when he asks rhetorically 'is thair not now ane sinceir professioun of ye treuth amangest vs in this Ile oppugnit by ye natiounis about . . . hes nocht our victorie bene far mair notabill then that of Israell?' (sig. B3v). He is careful to combine England and Scotland as 'this Ile', to stress the shared religion of the two nations, to imply that the two nations must stand together in the face of external threat, to claim the victory for the whole island, and to assume the position of speaking on behalf of the English as well as the Scottish. These emphases are supported by his choice of a text about King David, as one of the legacies of this biblical figure is that he united two kingdoms (Israel and Judah).[33] James is thus not only asserting his kinship with England and distancing himself from its Catholic enemies, but also pointing towards his hoped-for future role as head of both.

James's other scriptural work of the 1580s, *A Paraphrase vpon the Reuelation*, continues in the same vein as the other two, its 'Epistle to the Church Militant' referring to Revelation as *'a speciall cannon against the Hereticall wall of our common aduersaries the Papists'*.[34] The 'Argument' also echoes the claim in *Ane Fruitfull Meditatioun* that 'of all the Scriptures, the buik of the Reuelatioun is maist meit for this our last age' (sig. A3r) by emphasising *'how profitable this Booke is for this aage'* (*Workes*, p. 5). It is, however, a much longer work: it does not merely meditate upon a few verses of one chapter but paraphrases all twenty-two chapters of Revelation. The evidence suggests that it was written around 1585, the period in which James accepted money from England for a defensive alliance. In a letter to James of circa January 1586 Elizabeth makes an apparent reference to this work: 'For your Church matters, I do both admire and rejoice to see your wise paraphrase, which far exceedeth their text.'[35] This reference is, as Daniel Fischlin notes, important evidence for the dating of this paraphrase.[36] Yet what has not been fully explored is that this reference is also highly significant in terms of the dissemination and intended function of James's writing. That he seems to have sent Elizabeth a manuscript copy of a major unpublished work suggests the important role his writing played in his diplomacy. In

---

33  King, 'James I and King David', p. 422.
34  James VI, *A Paraphrase vpon the Reuelation of the Apostle S. Iohn* in *Workes* (1616), p. 2. All subsequent references to this paraphrase refer to this edition.
35  Marcus, Mueller, and Rose (eds), *Elizabeth I*, p. 268.
36  Fischlin, ' "To Eate the Flesh of Kings" ', pp. 410–11, n. 5. Fischlin discusses the confusion surrounding the dating of this paraphrase, noting that Jenny Wormald has dated it to 1588, but that various pieces of evidence, including Elizabeth's letter and James Montague's statement in his preface to James's *Workes* that it is the earliest work in the collection and written before the King was twenty, suggest it must have been written around 1585, when James was nineteen.

this case, his paraphrase seems to have been an agent in his negotiations with Elizabeth of 1585–6, a reinforcement of the claims he was also making through letters and ambassadors as they negotiated the terms of the league and the financial support James would receive. The Queen's letter continues by referring to 'all other matters which this gentleman [the diplomat Sir Thomas Randolph] hath told me' and professing her hope in 'your faithful profession of constancy in my behalf', then asserts that 'till I see you fail me . . . I will trust your word'.[37] The letter may suggest, then, that Randolph had presented a manuscript of the paraphrase to the Queen alongside other assurances of James's constancy to her, and that the 'word' in which Elizabeth was placing her trust consisted of all of these materials. That James did not print this paraphrase after it met Elizabeth's approval reflects the complexity of his diplomacy and use of scriptural exegesis; in the mid-1580s he was giving stronger assurances to the Queen of England of his staunch Protestantism than he was willing to make in public.

Once James's other meditations were in print, however, it might have seemed appropriate to print his *Paraphrase vpon the Reuelation*. He does seem to have anticipated it would be circulated, commenting in the epistle that '*this one thing I must craue of our Aduersaries, that they will not refute any part of my Interpretation, till they finde out a more probable themselues*' (*Workes*, p. 2). The pronoun 'our' addresses the work to a readership that shares his allegiances – perhaps Elizabeth specifically – but the request he makes of these 'aduersaries' indicates he expects they too will read it, as well as acknowledging that his interpretation might not be authoritative. The extant manuscript copy of this work in the King's hand reveals the care he took with writing and revising it.[38] This care may be explicable in terms of his decision to send a copy to Elizabeth, but it may also suggest he was preparing it with publication in mind. Two apparent references in other printed works by James suggest he did indeed plan to print his paraphrase too. In the preface to *Ane Fruitfull Meditatioun* Galloway explains what he will do if the reader accept this meditation 'in gude part':

> I assure thee befoir it be lang be Goddis grace thow sall see to thy contentment and comfort a lairger pruife of his Maiesties meaning expressed be his royall pen in yat samin argument. For gif God sall grant his Maiestie may weill allow of this my doing, as I think it will be of all gude Christianes, then sall I with greater boldnes put to my hand, and communicat vnto the the greater worke. (sig. A2r)

There are two pieces of evidence here that Galloway is referring to *A Paraphrase vpon the Reuelation*, not to the second *Meditatioun* that was to be published in the following year.

37  Marcus, Mueller, and Rose (eds), *Elizabeth I*, pp. 268–9.
38  This manuscript copy (British Library, Royal MS 18 B.14) contains a number of crossings out and additions, some of which seem to be part of the initial writing process, and others of which seem to be part of subsequent revision, such as insertions between lines or in the margins. This version is largely the same as the version that appears in the *Workes*, though here it is in Scots and there it is anglicised. Notably, there are four short additions in a different hand (see fols 37v, 55r, 67r, 73r), which may indicate that James received some assistance.

Firstly, the reference to 'yat samin argument' — both *Ane Fruitfull Meditatioun* and *A Paraphrase vpon the Reuelation* are readings of the Book of Revelation, whereas the second *Meditatioun* is on the chronicle of Kings. Secondly, Galloway emphasises that this other work is 'lairger' and 'greater' — the second *Meditatioun* would hardly meet this description, being approximately the same length as the first, whereas *A Paraphrase vpon the Reuelation* is considerably longer.[39] The other reference comes three years later in James's preface to *His Maiesties Poeticall Exercises*: he proposes that his poems '*beeing well accepted, will moue mee to hast the presenting vnto thee, of my* APOCALYPS' (sig. 2v). It thus seems that at this time James was willing for the paraphrase to go into print.

This work was not, however, printed in any form until it appeared in his *Workes* in 1616. The two references cited here suggest that one possible explanation for this was that the first meditation and the second collection of poems were *not* well enough received to warrant going ahead with the proposed additional publication. But why, then, would James include it in the *Workes*, and give it pride of place as the first work in the collection? Perhaps it seemed too incendiary in the 1580s and 1590s, but James judged that circumstances had changed enough by 1616. Perhaps he felt that within the context of his *Workes* it could be presented as juvenilia. Or perhaps he decided it was a work that needed to be contextualised — introduced with suitable prefatory materials and placed alongside his other works.[40] Either way, the publication history of this work emphasises that James was cautious and thoughtful about the dissemination of his writings, and thus offers another corrective to the view of James as vain and foolish maintained in his early historiography.[41]

### The divine word and the royal author

While James thus employed his scriptural exegeses to serve specific political purposes, their significance for him went beyond the immediate context in which he wrote them. This is evident in the reprinting in anglicised versions of the two meditations in London in the year of his accession to the English throne, and his inclusion of all three early exegeses in his *Workes*. The more general function of these exegeses is to enable James to make the claims about his authority and authorship that underlie all of his writings. In particular they enable him to emphasise the divinely ordained hierarchy by which he is king by divine right, with a unique position of proximity to God, and therefore a unique ability to interpret God's word for his subjects. The subtitle of *Ane Fruitfull Meditatioun*, which James wrote when he was only twenty-two years old, states that it is 'in forme of ane sermon', placing the King in the position of a

---

39   In James's *Workes* of 1616, where all three texts are published in the same format, the two meditations run to seven folio pages, whereas the paraphrase runs to seventy-two.

40   For a discussion of the paraphrase in the context of the *Workes*, see Chapter 4, below.

41   For a brief discussion of James's early historiography and recent revisionist accounts see the Introduction, above.

preacher to his people. Galloway's claim in the preface to this work that God is speaking through James, and that James has particular access to God's mysteries, lends the King's word both political and spiritual authority, as though he were not only a ruler but also akin to a prophet. In the text itself James explains that he will first 'expone or paraphrase the hardnes of the wordis, nixt interpreit ye meaning of them, and thridlie note quhat [what] we sould learne of all' (*Ane Fruitfull Meditatioun*, sig. A3v). He is thus asserting his special ability to penetrate the difficulty of the text to reveal its single and true meaning, which he will then deliver to his readers as a lesson. This provides a model of the King as a source of knowledge and authority for his readers to follow, a model that was particularly valuable for James as he sought to establish his political authority amongst his Scottish subjects.[42] This function of the two meditations is emphasised by the fact that both were printed in gothic type: this associated them with texts of political authority, such as proclamations and ordinances, which, as Kevin Sharpe has pointed out, were also printed in gothic type at this time.[43]

James's second meditation, even more than his first, emphasises both his prophetic and his authorial claims. King David is the focus of the verses that James here seeks to illuminate, and, given David's role as a transmitter of God's word and poet-king, there is an implicit parallel between the royal subject and royal author of this meditation. This parallel is heightened by the fact that James was also, as we have seen, engaged in translating the psalms. Indeed, *Ane Meditatioun* defends one of its claims by asserting that 'we haue plane declaratioun out of Dauids awin mouth expressed weill in ye haill [whole] 101 Psalme' (sig. B1r), and this is one of the psalms James translated.[44] This means that what comes 'out of Dauid's awin mouth' is simultaneously what comes out of James's mouth, or at least pen. Given this subtle blurring of the role of King David with that of King James, it seems appropriate that the meditation should end with 'His Maiesties awin Sonnet'. This sonnet attributes the defeat of the Spanish Armada to God, but also makes a firm statement of royal authorship. Its title contrasts with 'A Sonnet of the Authour' with which James had concluded his *Essayes of a Prentise* five years earlier, further reflecting his growing concern, noted at the end of Chapter 1, with emphasising his royal identity in his writing. 'His Maiesties awin Sonnet' highlights the fact that the whole meditation is a re-presentation of God's word through the medium of royal authorship.

James's self-representation as a vehicle for God's Word is taken a step further still in his paraphrase on Revelation. The Book of Revelation begins by introducing John in

---

42 Sharpe suggests that these texts also contain a number of specific prescriptions as to how James's subjects should behave, proposing that 'exegesis of Scripture . . . becomes royal command'. See 'The King's Writ', pp. 125–6.

43 Sharpe, *Reading Revolutions*, p. 51.

44 Craigie (ed.), *Poems*, II, 163. This psalm appears in James's hand in Bodleian Library, MS 165, fols 58v–59r.

the third person: Jesus sent the Revelation 'by his angel unto his servant John' (1: 1).[45]
James's paraphrase departs from this convention to begin by speaking on behalf of John
in the first person: Jesus sent 'an Angel or Minister, to me *Iohn* his seruant, and by him
to reueale vnto mee certaine things' (*Workes*, p. 7). This establishes a more direct relationship between the King and his readers and blurs his voice with the voice of John.
Thus when James inserts comments such as 'as I did shew before', or 'this vision which
I am next to declare vnto you' (*Workes*, p. 36), the two voices become indistinguishable.
God instructs John 'What thou seest, write in a book' (1: 11) and James is reproducing
this: in writing this paraphrase he is revealing to others what the scriptural text has
revealed to him, echoing John's position as one to whom God has chosen to give a
special understanding. In these ways James is trying to strengthen his claims to having
direct access to God's truth and the capacity to reproduce it for others.

James's attempt to reinforce his authority through his authorship of scriptural works
draws upon the Bible's equation of language and authority, which is encapsulated in
John 1: 1: 'In the beginning was the Word, and the Word was with God, and the Word
was God.' The Book of Revelation extends this equation: not only does it emphasise
the power of God's word but the visions the prophet experiences include texts, and the
prophet is enjoined to write down what he sees. This may explain the appeal this Book
evidently had for James. In paraphrasing it he emphasises its equation of language and
authority, expanding on references to both the destructive and creative power of God's
word. For example, while at 1: 16 the biblical text refers to the two-edged sword coming
out of God's mouth, James emphasises that it is the 'Sword of the word' (*Workes*, p. 8);
at 3: 14 the biblical text simply refers to 'the beginning of the creation of God', but
James, echoing more closely John 1: 1, specifies that God 'is that Word which did create
all' (*Workes*, p. 12). Most tellingly, at 2: 16 the biblical text threatens that God will fight
his enemies 'with the sword of my mouth', and James explains 'the sword of my mouth,
*to wit*, by the force of my word' (*Workes*, p. 10). As Fischlin notes, the possessive case in
the phrase 'the force of my word' becomes 'a complicated metonym for James's, John's,
and Jesus' "word" *as mediated by James*'.[46] In his own writing of his paraphrase, then, the
King is reproducing the Bible's equation of language and authority, implying the power
of the royal word and using it to demonstrate and reinforce his royal authority.

The blurring of James's voice with John's voice enables the King to use the biblical
text as a vehicle for reflecting on his own concerns and instructing his own readers. This
is particularly the case in his rendering of the Book of Revelation's emphasis on the
importance of interpreting the divine word correctly. For example, the Book of
Revelation's concluding injunction that 'if any man shall add unto these things, God
shall add unto him the plagues that are written in this book: And if any man shall take

45  All quotations from the Bible are from Robert Carroll and Stephen Prickett (eds), *The Bible:
    Authorised King James Version, with Apocrypha* (Oxford: Oxford University Press, 1997) unless oth-
    erwise specified.
46  Fischlin, ' "To Eate the Flesh of Kings" ', p. 391.

away from the words of the book of this prophecy, God shall take away his part out of the book of life, and out of the holy city, and *from* the things which are written in this book' (22: 18–19) in itself reflects how James wants to be read. He expands significantly on these lines, turning them into a meditation on the art of translation and interpretation itself:

> whosoeuer in coping [*sic*] or translating this Booke, adulterateth any waies the Originall, or in interpreting of it, wittingly strayes from the trew meaning of it, and from the analogie of Faith, to follow the fantasticall inuention of man, or his owne preoccupied opinions . . . shalbe accursed as a peruerter of the trewth of God and his Scriptures. (*Workes*, p. 72)

These lines are curiously self-reflexive. James is describing the process of interpretation even as he is enacting it. Because James has blurred his voice with the voice of John, these lines also become an injunction to James's readers not to misread his book, and the paraphrase's discussion of the power of God's word becomes also a discussion of the power of the King's word. Yet as he appropriates these lines to serve his own ends, James is doing exactly what his paraphrase reiterates readers should not do, in the very moment of offering that instruction.

The paraphrase's preoccupation with interpretation extends into an explicit concern with authority and authorship. In the biblical text John says simply 'And I John saw these things, and heard *them*' (22: 8), but James adds the explanation that 'I declare you my name the oftener, lest the authority of the Booke should be called in doubt, through the vncertaintie of the Writer' (*Workes*, p. 71). This addition shifts the emphasis from experience to the recording in writing of experience – from being a prophet to being a writer – and reveals James's self-conscious concern with the biblical text *as a text*. It also has particular resonance for James, reflecting his desire for authority to lie with the writer not the reader and, more specifically, his sense that *his* royal identity should give *his* word authority, as he claims explicitly in, for example, the preface added to the *Lepanto*. Within the paraphrase this addition implies the authority of the King's book; that is, the paraphrase itself. These implications are strengthened by the fact that when printed this paraphrase opened and formed part of the King's *Workes*, an extended demonstration of royal writing.

Yet while the Bible equates divine language and divine authority, it is, as a written book, at one remove from language as authority – it is a *representation* of language as authority. This is to some extent a false distinction: in so far as biblical language is *perceived* to be performative, the difference between language as authority and language as representation of authority collapses. This is indeed precisely the kind of force that James wants his own language to have. Nevertheless, such a perception of the Bible – and likewise of James's writings – has to reconcile the fact that language is open to a range of translations and interpretations. Revelation is a particularly malleable text; Jaroslav Pelikan describes it as 'a book that was polemical in its original intent and that throughout Christian history has been a kaleidoscope in which successive generations have recognised the heresies and schisms of their own time'.[47] Interpreters such as James nevertheless maintain that this 'kaleidoscope' is, *as they interpret it*, a direct expression of God's will.

James's anxious awareness of Revelation's susceptibility to different interpretations is suggested by his emphasis on the resistance of the divine word to corruption: for example, while Revelation 6: 6 does not mention God's word, James's paraphrase adds the comment 'the word and trueth of God . . . shall neuer be destroyed, nor any wayes corrupted' (*Workes*, p. 19). This implies that his own interpretations merely reproduce God's truth, thereby supporting his explicit defences of his paraphrase in the 'Epistle to the Church Militant' that precedes the text. In this epistle he claims that in his paraphrase he has '*vsed nothing of my owne coniecture, or of the authoritie of others*' (*Workes*, p. 2), and has worked to '*square and conforme my opinions to the trew and sincere meaning*' of the biblical text (*Workes*, p. 1). He goes on, as we have seen, to write his paraphrase of Revelation as though he were the prophet. James thus remains a presence in the text, insisting that his meaning *is* God's meaning, and that his word should therefore be treated as though it has the authority of God's word.

James is here opposing his approach to those who have sought '*to wrest and conforme the meaning thereof to their particular and priuate passions*' (*Workes*, p. 1). To attack the misinterpretations of others, however, is to contradict his attempt to defend his own interpretations on the grounds that God's truth is incorruptible. While he implies that he is able to determine the 'trew and sincere' meaning of the scriptural text, he cannot escape from the fact that this is a subjective determination. His attempts to differentiate his approach from that of other interpreters betray his anxiety that he will be seen to be doing what he is actually doing – manipulating Scripture to serve his own purposes. For, as we have seen, James's exegeses reproduce established and politicised Protestant readings, thereby doing the opposite of what he claimed: using the authority of others and squaring and conforming the text to his opinions. He is, then, skilfully misleading the reader: his 'rhetorical technique disallows the notion of the interpreter as capable of manipulating Scripture even as such a manipulation occurs, almost by sleight of hand, before the reader's very eyes'.[48] James's exegeses thus attempt to construct a model of interpretation whereby authority lies with the text rather than with the reader, yet, ironically, his exegesis itself contradicts this model, shifting authority from the biblical text to James himself. In this way the King tries to claim authority both as writer and as reader, while disallowing *his* readers any such authority.

James's anxieties are further revealed when he justifies his identification of the Pope as the Antichrist. In *Ane Fruitfull Meditatioun* he states 'quhither [whether] the Pape beiris thir [bears these] markis or not, let ony indifferent man iudge: I thinke surelie it exponis the self [expounds itself]', then for half a page lists, in a rhetorically persuasive form,

---

47 Jaroslav Pelikan, 'Some Uses of Apocalypse in the Magisterial Reformers', in Patrides and
    Wittreich (eds), *The Apocalypse in English Renaissance Thought and Literature*, pp. 74–92 (pp. 81–2).
48 Fischlin, ' "To Eate the Flesh of Kings" ', p. 397.

signs that the Pope is the Antichrist (sig. B2r). If the text did expound itself James would not need to provide what he presents as evidence. The insertion of 'I thinke surelie' before 'it exponis the self' betrays the anxiety that prompts him to justify his reading. But by justifying his reading he admits that it is not a mere reproduction of God's truth but a contestable interpretation, and thereby invites debate. James could not control reading of God's word, nor could he control reading of the royal word. The irony is that his attempts to interpret the Bible expose the limitations of authorial control. For the more he manipulates the scriptural text to serve his own purposes, the more he inadvertently implies the possibility that his word too can be manipulated to serve the purposes of others; the more, in other words, he demonstrates that texts are open to the multiple interpretations of their readers.

### Writing to a monarch: the correspondence between James and Elizabeth of the late 1580s

The relationship between James and his readers is further complicated when his reader is another monarch. The scriptural paraphrase he sent to Elizabeth was only one com-ponent in the fascinating exchange between the two monarchs of the second half of the 1580s that dealt with a series of difficult, delicate, and urgent matters: the league between Scotland and England, James's claim to the English throne, the execution of Mary Queen of Scots, and the Spanish attack. The larger issues at stake were, of course, the relative power of the two monarchs and their countries, and the extent to which they were ready to support each other. As James and Elizabeth never met, their nego-tiations relied to a large extent on the written word. These letters have tended to be treated only as historical evidence, as indicated by the suggestion Grant G. Simpson makes in a discussion of the King's personal letters that '*historians* should be grateful that this extensive body of material is available for investigation' (italics mine). This view relies upon a questionable assumption. Simpson continues: 'It is tempting to say that they enable us to penetrate into James's mind. To some degree, that must be so: virtu-ally all of them are certainly composed by him.'[49] In the case of a sophisticated polit-ician, diplomat, and writer like James, personal composition is no guarantee that the letters straightforwardly represent his thoughts and intentions. Rather his letters, like many of his other writings, are carefully constructed to convey an impression of a private self, without necessarily being 'sincere'.[50] These letters therefore require a more sophisticated approach, and help to illuminate James's aims and concerns as a writer, as well as a politician.

49  Grant G. Simpson, 'The Personal Letters of James VI: A Short Commentary', in Goodare and Lynch (eds), *Reign of James VI and I*, pp. 141–53 (p. 142).
50  The potentially public nature of royal letters is indicated in the fact that a number of them were published. See, for example, *Englands Welcome to Iames* (London, 1603) which includes James's letter to the Lord Mayor of London, and *The Copie of His Maiesties Letter to the Commons* (London, 1604).

For James writing letters seems to have been continuous with writing in other forms and genres. This is reflected in his decision to send Elizabeth other kinds of writing, such as his paraphrase, alongside his letters. It is also reflected in the care he evidently took with composing his letters.[51] But this continuity was disrupted by the fact that Elizabeth was significantly different from the readers James's other writings envisage. He cannot draw on his royal authority as a means of controlling interpretation, as he does elsewhere, when he is addressing a reader over whom he does not have authority. In their writings to each other, the relationship between writer and reader becomes part of a larger conflict between the competing authority of two monarchs; James's desired authorial control is here threatened by a reader who has greater political power than he does.

Although Elizabeth seemingly approved of James's paraphrase, the terms in which its epistle addresses the reader (assuming this epistle was included in the copy she received) may not have seemed entirely appropriate to her. In particular, the 'Argument' asserts that '*this doubt onely rests now in men, that this Booke is so obscure and allegorique, that it is in a maner vnprofitable to be taught or interpreted*' (*Workes*, p. 4), then goes on to claim that James will show how profitable it is. This implies that James is teaching his reader about something difficult – hardly a stance he could maintain in relation to the older, more experienced, and more powerful English Queen. The relationship of James as writer and Elizabeth as reader was still more difficult to negotiate when James tried accompanying his letters with poems. In a letter that G. P. V. Akrigg proposes dates from 1586 (the same year as Elizabeth commented on James's paraphrase) James refers to a previous poem that he claims he sent Elizabeth without receiving a response (a communication now lost), and encloses a poem, which may be another copy of the original or a new poem.[52] This poem illuminates the complexities of addressing this particular reader.

The letter proposes that either Elizabeth, contrary to report, did not receive the first poem, or else 'ye judge it not to be of me, because it is *incerto authore* [of uncertain authorship]; for quhilk [which] cause I haue insert my name to the end of this sonnet heir inclosit'.[53] Again we see James's emphasis on his royal identity in his writing. In particular this letter echoes his assertion in his paraphrase on Revelation, noted above, that 'I declare you my name the oftener, lest the authority of the Booke should be called in doubt, through the vncertaintie of the Writer', furthering the sense of continuity between his concerns and the concerns of the biblical figures with whom he associates himself.

51  Despite the questionable assumptions underlying Simpson's analysis, he does go on to note that 'the variety of style which James is capable of employing reveals a writer who is highly conscious of the person whom he is addressing, and of the effect he wants to achieve' ('The Personal Letters of James VI', p. 145).

52  G. P. V. Akrigg (ed.), *Letters of King James VI and I* (Berkeley, Los Angeles and London: University of California Press, 1984), p. 71.

53  Bruce (ed.), *Letters of Queen Elizabeth and King James*, pp. 170–1.

The enclosed poem, 'Full many ane tyme the archier slakkis his bow', is a Petrarchan sonnet that suggests that the recent discord between the two monarchs may only kindle them to greater love.[54] As Petrarchan discourse was current in Elizabeth's court, this provides another example of James trying to exploit specific literary traditions and associations as a means of achieving particular political ends.[55] As Peter C. Herman suggests, however, James's poem was inappropriate and unsuccessful because of the disjunction between his royal status and the status of the Petrarchan lover, and the way in which the poem 'compares his relationship with Elizabeth to a series of *un*equal relationships, with *himself* as the dominant partner'.[56] Most strikingly, James compares his relationship with Elizabeth to that of a married couple: 'Full oft contentions great arise we see / Betwixt the husband and his loving wife / That sine [thereafter] they may the fermlyer agree' (lines 5–7). Where Petrarchan discourse typically represents the female beloved as unobtainable – a convention that accorded with the self-representation of the Virgin Queen – James here compares himself to a husband and Elizabeth to his wife, thereby implying that Elizabeth is to some extent bound to him and possessed by him. Moreover, in what we might see as an act of wish-fulfilment, he attaches the adjective 'loving' to the wife not the husband, implying that it is Elizabeth who is devoted to him. James was trying to exploit a particular form of address in a way that he may have seen as playful and knowing. He was also writing in a form that enabled him to play with the question of sincerity, and therefore to maintain a degree of flexibility and ambiguity entirely in keeping with his foreign policy at this point. But he was also over-stepping a mark, which other poetry circulating in Elizabeth's court was careful not to cross, in terms of the claims he implies he has over Elizabeth. Perhaps for this reason Elizabeth does not seem even to have acknowledged the poem, let alone to have responded with any indication that she had read it in a way that James might have desired.

The potential gap between expression or interpretation and experience that this poem allows is a gap that the letters of both James and Elizabeth also exploit as they engage in complex diplomatic manoeuvres. Firstly, this gap allows them to blame any dissatisfaction the other expresses on misinterpretation of their language. Thus, for example, in a letter of May 1586 Elizabeth responds to an angry reply from James to an earlier letter in a tone of wonderment: 'I muse muche, right deare brother, how

54  Craigie (ed.), *Poems*, II, 171 (based on Hatfield MSS). This poem was not included in 'All the Kings short poesis', which may indicate that James thought it suitable only for its addressee.

55  This poem thus provides further evidence of James's engagement with English literary culture as early as the 1580s (for discussion of other aspects of this engagement in this period see Chapter 1, above). It also raises the question of whether James was aware of Elizabeth's own interest in writing poetry; as noted in the Introduction, above, Elizabeth's poetry was not widely circulated, but it is not impossible that one of James's contacts in the English court informed him that writing poetry was an interest he shared with the English Queen.

56  Herman, ' "Best of Poets, Best of Kings" ', p. 71.

possiblie my wel-ment lettar, prociding from so fauteles a hart, could be ether misliked or misconstred.'[57] This carefully elides 'misliking' with 'misconstruing', allowing the Queen further room for manoeuvre. Similarly, in a letter of January 1587 expressing opposition to the death sentence placed on Mary, James claims he does not know how to write 'for ye have allreaddie takin sa evill with my playnness as I feare if I shall persist in that course ye shall rather be exasperattit to passions in reading the vordis [words] then by the plainness thairof be persuadit to consider richtlie the simpill treuth'.[58] Both monarchs thus assert the integrity and transparency of their own writing and intentions while implicitly criticising each other as readers.

Secondly, both monarchs emphasise the gap between what can be expressed and what is felt as a way of stressing the depth of their feelings. In his letter of January 1587 James tells Elizabeth that if 'ye kneu quhat dyveris thochtis [what diverse thoughts] I have bene in and quhat just greif . . . ye wold so farr pittie my cace'. This is echoed in Elizabeth's official letter after the execution, which claims she had not intended Mary to die, but, again, was misunderstood. She begins 'I wold yow knew, though not felt, the extreme dolour that owerwhelmeth my mynd for that miserable accident which farre contrary to my meening hath bene befallen'.[59] Thus both emphasise *through language* the idea of emotion that cannot be expressed in language as a strategy for manipulating the other towards pity, understanding, and agreement. At the same time both carefully word their letters to continue to assert their integrity (James's grief is 'just' and the execution of Mary was a 'miserable accident'), emphasising that they are not as overwhelmed by emotion as they claim.

This particular communication from Elizabeth further complicates the relationship between the oral and the written. Her letter claims that oral delivery by an ambassador will be better than a letter, so she has sent Robert Carey 'to instruct yow treuly of that which is to irksome for my penne to tell yow'. But what Carey presented to the King was a written account. Carey explains: 'I thought yt my best to delyver yt thus in wryting that by such meanes no words may be mistaken', prioritising writing over speaking in contradiction of Elizabeth's accompanying suggestion. Carey's account ends: 'This was the some and effect of my message, which if I could declare unto your Majestie so well, and set yt downe so lyvely as I herd her speake yt with so heavy a harte, and so discontented a countenance, I thinke verely yow would rather pitie her . . . then blame her'.[60] This account, echoing James's earlier request that Elizabeth pity him, thus constructs an absent scene. It proposes that this scene would be more affecting in reality, but this very claim is a way of affecting James, while the scene itself may have

57  Bruce (ed.), *Letters of Queen Elizabeth and King James*, p. 33. For the immediate circumstances of this letter see Herman, ' "Best of Poets, Best of Kings" ', pp. 62–3.

58  Robert S. Rait and Annie I. Cameron (eds), *King James's Secret: Negotiations between Elizabeth and James VI Relating to the Execution of Mary Queen of Scots, from the Warrenden Papers* (London: Nisbet, 1927), pp. 179–80.

59  Rait and Cameron (eds), *King James's Secret*, pp. 179, 194.

60  Rait and Cameron (eds), *King James's Secret*, pp. 194–7.

no existence beyond this text. This correspondence thus explores the possibility that written reports might be more effective than the reality of personal exchange.

Thirdly, for both monarchs the potential gap between the intention and interpretation of their letters facilitates the exploitation of ambiguity as a means of maintaining the delicate balance of their diplomacy. This was particularly valuable when it came to dealing with Mary's execution, which put both in an extremely difficult position. James had expressed his opposition to the execution but never affirmed he would avenge it, and could not have affirmed that without contradicting his arguments for opposing it. This tension is highlighted by the letter he sent Elizabeth just before the execution:

> Quhat lau [what law] of Godd can permitt that justice shall strikke upon thaime quhom [whom] he hes appointid supreame dispensatouris of the same, under Him, quhom He hath callid Goddis, and thairfore subjectid to the censoure of none in earth, quhose [whose] anointing by Godd can not be defylid be [by] man unrevenged by the authore thairof, quho [who] being supreme and immediatt lieutenant of Godd in heaven cannot thairfore be judgit by thair equallis in earth?[61]

If Elizabeth should not execute justice on Mary, then James cannot execute justice on Elizabeth; if Mary should not be subject to Elizabeth's censure, then Elizabeth should not be subject to James's; if Mary should not be judged on earth then nor should Elizabeth. James may be deliberately using terms that equate all monarchs as a way of opposing the execution while implying that he will not avenge it. The relative authority of Elizabeth and James may have caused difficulties in terms of the writer–reader relationship, but here the King is effectively exploiting the fact that all parties concerned share the same kind of authority. There is, however, a further ambiguity in the phrase 'unrevenged by the authore thairof'; while this appears to refer to God it could also refer to James, the author of this letter. This is subtle enough to be discounted, but also leaves open the possibility that James could go on to take a more hostile stance.

Elizabeth's response after the execution also paves the way for James to avoid having to act. Robert S. Rait suggests that 'Elizabeth could scarcely expect to deceive James [that the execution was an accident and not her intention]. But she hoped that James would be glad to avail himself of the pretext which she herself found so useful'.[62] This pretext was indeed a way for James to balance maintaining favour with Elizabeth, so as not to jeopardise his chance of succeeding her, with placating those of his subjects who wanted Mary's death to be avenged. In this case, their letters may be seen as a semi-public performance that forms a convenient façade for their shared political interests. It is clear, then, that, despite their protestations about the inadequacy of language and the difficulties of interpretation, negotiating through letters rather than personal contact suited the purposes of both monarchs well.

Through his correspondence with Elizabeth, James thus experienced not only the limitations of authorial control but also the value of the written word as a substitute

---

61   Rait and Cameron (eds), *King James's Secret*, p. 180.
62   Rait and Cameron (eds), *King James's Secret*, pp. 198–9.

for personal contact, and the ways in which the ambiguities and limitations of language could be exploited to political effect. These perceptions would all feed into his later writings. For example, in a letter of November 1586 he states that he wishes Elizabeth would 'see the inward partes of my harte where she should see a greate jewell of honestye toward her'.[63] This is echoed in the printed versions of his speeches to the English parliament, such as a speech of 1605 in which he states that he wishes 'that there were a Christall window in my breast, wherein al my people might see the secretest thoughts of my heart'.[64] Moreover, the terms in which James's January 1587 letter presents kings as beyond human justice clearly prefigure his later printed works on kingship. Indeed in the summer of 1598 James wrote to Elizabeth that 'I wolde wishe that all the direct or indirect dealings that euer I hadde, that micht concerne your persone or state, waire in a booke laid oppen before you, and then you woulde see, that no subject of Englande hath kept himself cleerer of any guilty [thought] against you then I haue done'.[65] The year of *The True Lawe of Free Monarchies*, the year before the first edition of *Basilikon Doron*, James suggests that letters are inadequate and books the best way of appearing to lay himself open, and, therefore, of convincing his readers of his integrity. We may see the early correspondence with Elizabeth as helping to construct the writer–king.

### Beyond the 1580s: the future role of James's scriptural exegeses

The identity as an interpreter of God's word that James created for himself through his scriptural works underlies his other writings; as his royal status lends authority to these exegeses, so scriptural interpretation in turn lends authority to the explicitly political works he would go on to write. He exploited this relationship between scriptural interpretation and political assertion by having *Ane Fruitfull Meditatioun* and *Ane Meditatioun* reprinted along with his political treatises in 1603, and by including them, with his paraphrase, in his *Workes*. He further exploited it by incorporating scriptural interpretation into his other works. For example, in his first work to offer an explicit and controversial defence of divine right kingship, *True Lawe*, James begins his argument as to the obedience the people owe to their king by explaining that he 'will set downe the true groundes, whereupon I am to builde, out of the Scriptures' (sig. B2v). He goes on to quote and discuss at length the whole of 1 Samuel 8: 9–20 (sigs B5v–C4r). Throughout *True Lawe* all of James's direct references and almost all his quotations are biblical and around one-third of the text is given over to scriptural exegesis. Yet this text exemplifies the extent to which James's manipulations of Scripture at times amount to misrepresentations. Craigie has pointed out several discrepancies between James's

63  Rait and Cameron (eds), *King James's Secret*, p. 61.
64  James I, *His Maiesties Speach in Parliament* (London: Robert Barker, 1605), sig. C3r. The relationship between the spoken and printed versions of James's speeches is considered in the next chapter.
65  Bruce (ed.), *Letters of Queen Elizabeth and King James*, p. 126.

exegesis and the scriptural text on which it is apparently based. Most notably, James writes that 'Kings are called *Gods* by the propheticall King DAVID, because they sit vpon GOD his Throne in the earth, and haue the count of their administration to giue vnto him' (sig. B3r). While the first clause paraphrases Psalm 82: 6, the 'because' clause which follows 'is not to be found either in the passage referred to or at any other place in Scripture'.[66] Nevertheless, this explicitly politicised exegesis is reinforced by the identity James had established for himself as an interpreter of Scripture, with special access to God's mysteries and the ability to expound the true meaning of the Bible.

James's paraphrases of God's word thus at times amount to rewritings as he blurs the royal word with the divine word and implies their equivalence. That he should be seen to be comparing or equating his writings with the Bible was evidently uncomfortable for him, however, and this would emerge in the preface he added to *Basilikon Doron* in 1603. The preface alleges that some people who have created a copy of his original work based only on selected notes are guilty of

> putting in the one halfe of the purpose, and leauing out the other: not vnlike the man that alleadged that part of the Psalme, non est Deus; but left out the preceding words, Dixit insipiens in corde suo. And of these notes, making a little pamphlet . . . entituled it, forsooth, the Kings Testament: as if I had eiked [added] a third Testament of my owne, to the two that are in the holy Scriptures.[67]

Even as he rejects the accusation that he has tried to give his writing comparable status to the Bible, he makes an indirect comparison between his writing and a psalm, implying that both deserve to be interpreted in their entirety, not piecemeal.[68] It seems that, while James does not want to be seen as denying the Bible's unique and superior status, the Bible nevertheless forms a frame of reference for his conceptualisation and presentation of his writing. Indeed, *Basilikon Doron*'s preface begins by emphasising Christ's revelation of divine truth: '*Charitable Reader, it is one of the golden sentences which Christ our Sauiour vttred to his Apostles, that there* is nothing so couered, that shal not be reuealed . . .' (sig. A1r). Given that this preface is part of and describes the revelation of James's book, in circumstances that we shall consider further in the next chapter, this is a rather ambiguous opening. It implies that James is both subject to God's power to bring truth to light and, like God, an agent of such revelation. In recalling these words years later, the King would even blur the distinction between God's word and his iteration of them:

66  James Craigie (ed.), *Minor Prose Works of King James VI and I* (Edinburgh: Scottish Text Society, 1982), p. 128.

67  James I, *Basilikon Doron* (London: Felix Kyngston for John Norton, 1603), sig. B2r. All subsequent references to this work in the present chapter are to this edition and given in parentheses in the text.

68  The verse James quotes in Latin is Psalm 14: 1, 'The fool hath said in his heart, "There is no God"' (Fischlin and Fortier (eds), *True Law and Basilikon Doron*, p. 100n). This verse is particularly well suited to James's purposes as it not only suggests the importance of reading words in context but also implies that as only a fool would doubt God so only a fool would doubt the King.

he refers to '*mine owne words, but taken out of the Scripture . . . in my* Basilikon Doron, that nothing is so hid which shall not bee opened, &c'.[69] The King does not merely repeat God's word – God's word becomes his word.

James was not, however, responsible for what is perhaps the fullest realisation of his desire that he be viewed as occupying a unique position of proximity to the divine that enables him to mediate the divine word for the ordinary subject. *The Psalmes of King David*, authorised and attributed to James by King Charles in 1631, has a title page that makes a bolder assertion of James's relationship to the Bible than any of the title pages of his works produced in his lifetime (see figure 2).[70] In the upper centre is a book with 'The Psalmes of King David' on its cover; on the left is a picture of King David, reaching up and holding the book with his left hand; on the right is a picture of King James, reaching up and holding the book with his right hand; and above is a hand reaching down from heaven and also holding the book. In the central column, between the two kings, are the words 'Translated by King Iames' and this is in same font type and size as 'The Psalmes of King David'. James and King David are thus rendered equivalent, and the implication is that this book is the work of God, King David, and King James collectively. Only James, however, looks towards the onlooker, indicating that it is he who is communicating the book to its readers. The irony, however, is that the authorship of this work is disputed.[71] If it was indeed written by another poet, it represents James borrowing from divine authority *and* from a subject, blurring the royal word with God's word, *and* royal authoring with royal authorising. On two different levels it emphasises that James's scriptural writings are an exercise in appropriation. *The Psalmes of King David* epitomises, then, both the ambition underlying James's translations and interpretations of Scripture, and the appropriations and deceptions that, in turn, might underlie that ambition.

While James's early scriptural exegeses thus anticipate and feed into his later political writings, and prepare for the bold claims made on his behalf on the title page of *The Psalmes of King David*, their explicit anti-Catholicism would cause problems for James later in his reign, and the initial responses they met give an early indication of this. As Capp suggests, 'it was a major step for a reigning monarch to give public endorsement to Protestant apocalyptic teaching. James's works were naturally cited and praised by numerous later commentators, who felt a new sense of authority in finding a king in their ranks.'[72] Some of these commentators, however, exploited James's works as a way

---

69  James I, *A Premonition to All Most Mightie Monarches*, in *An Apologie for the Oath of Allegiance* (London: Robert Barker, 1609), pp. 3–4.

70  James I, *The Psalmes of King David* (Oxford: William Turner, 1631). For further discussion of 'the envisioned public role of James's Psalter, and the actual reception that followed his death' see Doelman, 'The Reception of King James's Psalter' (quotation from p. 455).

71  William Alexander, one of the poets in James's Scottish coterie, was certainly involved in preparing the collection, and may indeed have written all of it. See Craigie (ed.), *Poems*, II, 269–70.

72  Capp, 'The Political Dimension of Apocalyptic Thought', p. 103.

2 Title page of *The Psalmes of King David* (Oxford: William Turner, 1631)

of pressurising him to adopt a more active anti-Catholic stance. The most prominent example of this is John Napier's *A Plaine Discouery of the whole Reuelation of Saint Iohn* (1593). The dedication to James assumes a tone of advice and even criticism, praising his writing but implying that this is not enough:

> *I say therefore, as God hath mercifully begunne the first degree of that great worke in your inward minde, by purging the same from all apparent spot of Antichristianisme, as that fruitfull meditation vpon the 7. 8. 9. and 10. verses of the 20. Chapter of the Reuelation, which your highnes hath both godly & learnedly set forth, doth beare plaine testimony, to your M. high praise and honour: So also wee beseeche your M. (hauing consideration of the treasonable practises in these present daies, attempted both against Gods trueth, your authoritie, and the commonwealth of this countrie,) to proceede to the other degrees of that reformation, euen orderly from your M. owne persone till your highnes familie, and from your family to your court. Till at last, your M. wholcountry stand reformed.*[73]

In a number of ways this passage accepts and reflects the claims made in James's meditations. It presents '*Gods trueth, your authoritie*' side by side, echoing James's equation of the two. It flatters his learning. In suggesting that *Ane Fruitfull Meditatioun* offers a '*plaine testimony*' of the godliness in James's '*inward minde*', it echoes the claim in Galloway's preface to this work that it is 'ane testimonie of his hienes maist vnfeinzeit [unfeigned] loue toward trew religioun'. Napier also proposes, however, the further consequences of this claim. The meditation is represented as only a first step towards wholesale reformation of the King, his family, and his court, and as a commitment to undertaking that larger mission. It also provides Napier with a pretext for implicitly criticising a lack of reformation to date.

These sentiments are echoed in the one significant addition to the 1603 London version of *Ane Fruitfull Meditatioun*, a poem entitled 'The Expounding of a Prophesie' by a poet identified only as 'I. St.'. This poem goes even further than Napier's dedication in urging James on to further steps against Catholicism. It claims that prophecies have long told that Rome 'To wrack and ruine should be brought, / by force of thine, O King'. It then suggests that the Pope has

> with spirituall armour thine
> receiud his deadly wound.
> Goe to likewise by dint of sword, this monster fierce and fell:
> With all his banded complices,
> bring downe and send to hell.[74]

This proposes that the pen is not enough; James must also use the sword. The King himself, as we will see, would maintain a pacifistic foreign policy throughout his English reign and attempt to challenge this kind of pen–sword dichotomy. Yet his early

73 John Napier, *A Plaine Discouery of the whole Reuelation of Saint Iohn* (Edinburgh: Robert Waldegrave, 1593), sig. A4r.

74 I. St., 'The Expounding of a Prophesie', in James I, *A Fruitefull Meditation* (London: J. Harrison, 1603), sigs A4v–5r.

scriptural exegeses were clearly appropriated as evidence to the contrary, and this would continue until the last years of his English reign.

James's scriptural exegeses form, then, a central part of his attempt to construct his authority through his authorship. They also reveal, however, the difficulties of reconciling different sources of authority: James is simultaneously deferring to divine authority, asserting royal authority, and wrestling with the question of where authority lies in the relationship between author, text, and reader. In these texts, as in the preface to the *Lepanto*, he is concerned to tell his readers what his texts mean and to prevent them from imposing their own interpretations. But readers such as Napier and 'I. St.' did impose their own interpretations on the King's exegeses, which reveal how susceptible these texts were to being used to criticise or manipulate the King, and which might in turn shape the way others read them. Throughout his English reign James would show a continuing desire to represent himself through interpretation and translation of the Bible. This is evident not only in the republication of his early scriptural works but also in his authorisation of a new translation of the Bible, a project which began after the Hampton Court Conference of 1604 and was completed in 1611; and his writing of *A Meditation vpon the Lords Prayer* (1619) and *A Meditation vpon St. Matthew. Or a Paterne for a Kings Inauguration* (1620). But having experienced the difficulties of controlling interpretation in relation to all aspects of his early writings – poetry and scriptural exegeses – his writings would increasingly attempt to deny or conceal the control of the reader over interpretation, and to dictate how he should be read as both writer and king.

# 3

## Print, authority, interpretation: the major prose works

In 1599 James circulated his political treatise and handbook for kings, *Basilikon Doron*, in only seven beautifully presented copies, amongst his intimate associates. Manuscript was the usual format of presentation copies and the most obvious and appropriate choice for a text written by a king, dedicated to his heir, and ostensibly intended for circulation only within the court. But the King chose to have these seven copies *printed*, and lavishly so (this edition is a quarto printed in large italic letter with generous margins on high-quality paper, an ornate title page, and a number of printer's ornaments throughout).[1] This choice may be evidence of his ultimate intention to publish the work for public consumption, but it may also reveal something of his attitude towards – even fascination with – print. In previous chapters we have seen several instances of James trying to appropriate and redefine various formats and genres. Here again he is not just using print but attempting to redefine print culture, to dignify it, to forge a place for it in the worlds of the court and coterie. He is trying to make the printed text a prestigious item, suitable for a work written by a king and dedicated to his heir, and to further the link between the power of print and the authority of the monarch.

Yet in the uncertainty surrounding the circumstances of the publication and republication of this work, we can also see James's awareness of the problems print could create. This chapter will explore both his exploitation of print in an effort to construct and disseminate the idea of the King as author and authority, and the limitations and difficulties involved in this self-publicisation. The discussion straddles the last decade of his Scottish reign and the first decade of his English, a period in which he wrote a number of major political, theological, and social works. These works, particularly *True Lawe* and *Basilikon Doron*, have attracted more critical attention than his earlier and later works because they have been seen as providing evidence of his views, and insights into the political, theological, and social debates in which he was engaging.[2] This book

---

1  James VI, *Basilikon Doron* (Edinburgh: Robert Waldegrave, 1599).
2  See, for example, Wormald, 'James VI and I, *Basilikon Doron* and *The Trew Law*'; Johann P. Sommerville, 'James I and the Divine Right of Kings: English Politics and Continental Theory', in Peck (ed.), *Mental World*, pp. 55–70, and 'King James VI and I and John Selden:

argues that James's works were written to present his views as persuasively as possible to a particular audience at a particular time, and to demonstrate his skill, knowledge, and authority as a writer. This is not to suggest that the King was entirely chameleonic, nor that his political views are entirely unknowable, but rather that we should be wary of reading individual texts as providing straightforward and stable 'evidence' of his political beliefs. This chapter is thus concerned not with analysing in detail the views represented in each of these works but with tracing James's aims, concerns, and development as an author.

The chapter begins with an extended close reading of James's self-construction as author and authority in his first secular prose work, published towards the end of his Scottish reign: *Daemonologie* (1597). This section emphasises both the care James took with his writing and the inherent instability of that writing by examining the different stages of *Daemonologie*'s composition and the contradictions in and between this text and royal authority. Shifting the focus to James's arrival in England in 1603, the second section examines the ambivalent attitude towards public exposure that *Basilikon Doron* highlights. As it traces James's attitude towards, and attempts to shape, the encounter of his text with his readers, this section argues against widely held critical assumptions that he was indifferent to public opinion and determined to keep his own affairs secret.

The chapter next turns to a series of royal publications of the years 1604–10 that illuminate some of the dilemmas and difficulties James faced in deciding how to write and what to print, and suggests that some of his anxieties about his readership increased after his accession to the English throne. His decision to print some works anonymously, such as *An Apologie for the Oath of Allegiance* (1607), reveals a degree of ambivalence about the relationship between his authorship and his authority. His speeches to parliament further expose his anxieties about how his word will be interpreted and reproduced by his immediate and wider audiences. These speeches were distorted as they were discussed and reproduced by his subjects, and his decision to print a number of them may suggest his belief in print as a means of arresting this process. Yet the publication history of *An Apologie for the Oath of Allegiance* highlights the instability of print itself. Ironically, then, as much as James tries to determine the interpretation of his texts and to exploit print as a way of fixing and disseminating his meaning, not even he can control what happens to his words after they leave his lips or pen but before they reach their readers in official form, let alone the response of those readers. In conclusion, the chapter examines the ways in which these various concerns are extended and commented upon in a work of this period that James did not author but authorised – the King James Bible.

Two Voices on History and the Constitution', in Fischlin and Fortier (eds), *Royal Subjects*, pp. 290–322; and Fischlin and Fortier (eds), 'Introduction', *The True Law of Free Monarchies and Basilikon Doron*, pp. 13–33. For a discussion which locates the views represented in these two texts in the context of a wide range of contemporary writings on royal authority see Burns, *The True Law of Kingship*, esp. pp. 185–255.

### Royal self-construction as author and authority: *Daemonologie*

While in the 1580s and early 1590s James tried to shape traditions of poetry and scriptural interpretation, from 1597 onwards his writings engage much more explicitly in political and social debate. Now in a more secure position politically, he was also concerned to assume an autonomous authorial persona, no longer drawing on his contemporaries for commendatory contributions as he had in all of his earlier publications.[3] His primary relationship to his literary and cultural context had been one of engaging with his supporters and associates, but in his treatises of the late 1590s it becomes one of reacting against, and attempting to discredit, those who oppose or disagree with him, such as sceptics about the existence of witches and proponents of resistance theory. Thus *The True Lawe of Free Monarchies: or The Reciprock and Mutuall Duetie Betwixt a Free King, and His Naturall Subiectes* (1598) offers a controversial defence of divine right kingship in reaction against the resistance theory advocated even by James's own tutor, George Buchanan.[4] Even the subtitle's emphasis on 'Duetie' being 'Mutuall' seems to be a specific reaction to Buchanan's comment in his dedication to James of *De Iure Regni apud Scotos* (1579) that this work 'may remind you of your duties towards your people'.[5] Where Buchanan's work had asserted that anyone is entitled to kill a tyrant, the King labours to demonstrate that a tyrannous king is sent by God 'for a cursse to his people, and a plague for their sinnes', and that wicked kings will receive their due punishment from God, 'the sorest and sharpest Schoole-maister that can be deuised for them' (*True Lawe*, sigs C7r, E3v). We might note that terming the God that will punish wicked kings as a 'Schoole-maister' is suggestive of James's fear of his old tutor. *True Lawe* nevertheless begins to suggest that James as King and author is now confident and powerful enough to take on his detractors and attack the theoretic bases to the challenges he had faced from the beginning of his reign.[6]

---

3  For a brief overview of the Scottish political context see the Introduction, above.

4  For discussion of the political views held by Buchanan and opposed by James see Burns, *The True Law of Kingship*, esp. pp. 196–205. For the view that 'the debate over the issue of sovereignty [was] both institutionalized in the conflict between the crown and the kirk and personalized in the relationship between the king and his tutor' see Roger A. Mason, 'George Buchanan, James VI and the Presbyterians', in Mason (ed.), *Scots and Britons*, pp. 112–37 (p. 114). For a discussion that questions the critical tendency to read *True Lawe* in an exclusively Scottish context and sets it instead in an international context see Peter Lake, 'The King (the Queen) and the Jesuit: James Stuart's *True Law of Free Monarchies* in Context/s', *Transactions of the Royal Historical Society*, 14 (2004), 243–60.

5  George Buchanan, *The Powers of the Crown in Scotland*, trans. Charles Flinn Arrowood (Austin: University of Texas Press, 1949), p. 37.

6  This confidence did not extend as far as publishing *True Lawe* under the King's name. At the end of the preface, however, appears the Greek name 'C. Philopatris', meaning 'a lover of his country'. This is the title of a dialogue attributed to Lucian, a Greek satirist, but subsequently realised to be spurious; this name thus makes a joke about the ambiguity surrounding the authorship of this text, and may have helped some to identify its author.

Despite this development, there are many continuities with his earlier writings, including his desire to innovate, to extend the boundaries of royal writing and publication, and to engage with continental ideas: *Daemonologie*, for example, is, as Stuart Clark points out, 'one of the first defences of Continental beliefs about witchcraft in English . . . the only book of its kind written by a monarch'.[7] *Daemonologie* has attracted less extended analysis than the two treatises it immediately precedes, *True Lawe* and *Basilikon Doron*, but it illuminates his other works and highlights the fact that James's writings – even his explicitly political writings – warrant more sophisticated literary analysis than they have so far received.

While *Daemonologie* is not even given extended consideration in Jonathan Goldberg's *James I and the Politics of Literature* (1983) or Daniel Fischlin and Mark Fortier's *Royal Subjects: Essays on the Writings of James VI and I* (2002), it has been commonly regarded as providing straightforward 'evidence' of the King's beliefs on witchcraft, and therefore as a stable text against which to read complex literary texts such as *Macbeth*. For example, a 1997 guide to *Macbeth* offers, in a chapter on 'Contexts and Sources', a series of quotations from *Daemonologie* which are introduced and related to Shakespeare's play as follows:

> Shakespeare probably read James's *Daemonologie* (1597). If so, James would have reinforced the devilish motives of the Weird Sisters . . . James would also have contributed to the play's notorious misogyny . . . James also attributes elements to the devil and to witches that do appear in *Macbeth* . . . In his preface to *Daemonologie*, James precisely expresses the conceptual basis from which the play emerges.

These quotations are not contextualised nor subjected to any analysis.[8] The title of a 1975 article, '*The Tempest* and King James's *Daemonologie*', seems to promise that both texts will be discussed, but in fact the discussion centres on the nature of Caliban and admits that the King's treatise merely 'provides a helpful gloss'.[9] More recently, Hilaire Kallendorf has noted that 'the critics who do mention *Daemonologie* . . . usually do so in a cursory manner', and suggests that it deserves to be read in its own right. Even this article, however, is concerned only to establish this treatise as an intertext for *Hamlet* and the direction of the argument runs only one way: *Daemonologie*, along with Reginald Scot's *Discouerie of Witchcraft* (1584), is used to 'illuminate certain aspects of the play' – it is not itself illuminated. Thus quotations from James's work are, again, subjected to little interrogation and introduced as straightforwardly representing his beliefs: 'King James I believed that . . .' and 'King James agrees . . .'.[10] As these examples show, the

---

7   Stuart Clark, 'King James's *Daemonologie*: Witchcraft and Kingship', in Sydney Anglo (ed.), *The Damned Art: Essays in the Literature of Witchcraft* (London: Routledge & Kegan Paul, 1977), pp. 156–81 (p. 156).

8   H. R. Coursen, *Macbeth: A Guide to the Play* (Westport, Connecticut, and London: Greenwood Press, 1997), pp. 22–3.

9   Jacqueline E. Latham, '*The Tempest* and King James's *Daemonologie*', *Shakespeare Survey*, 28 (1975), 117–23 (p. 118).

10  Hilaire Kallendorf, 'Intertextual Madness in *Hamlet*: The Ghost's Fragmented Performativity', *Renaissance and Reformation*, 22 (1998), 69–87 (pp. 72–3, 75, 76).

royal text is relegated to a secondary position and exploited as a means of elucidating other texts.

Yet close analysis of *Daemonologie* itself reveals that it does not provide a stable framework or fixed point of reference, but is – like the texts it is used to illuminate – complex and unstable. This treatise reveals the care James took in crafting his writing, his exploitation of writing and publication to reinforce his position in plural and complexly interconnecting ways, and the anxieties and contradictions that his position as a writer–king involves. The instability of the text not only lies in the interplay between these intentions, anxieties, and contradictions but also derives from its relationship to other texts and the various stages of its composition and publication.

Though not printed until 1597, *Daemonologie* may have been written as early as 1590–1, the period of the North Berwick witch trials.[11] These trials, along with various published works on witchcraft, seem to have provided much of the impetus and material for James's treatise.[12] Fragments of the text appear in MS Bodley 165, and a scribal copy of the work with James's hand-written corrections that seems to have provided the basis for the printed version (Folger MS V.a. 185) reveals something of its development. This text, then, is a reproduction of and response to various accounts of witchcraft – themselves constructed to meet certain needs in certain contexts – which was revised over an unknown period of time by the King. Finally, James's writing was anglicised for publication, presumably because he wished it to reach an English audience.[13]

James evidently took great care in revising the draft version in the Folger manuscript, and his corrections highlight some of his ambitions for his treatise. One of the most

11  The so-called North Berwick witches allegedly confessed that they had caused the storms that prevented Anne's first attempt to sail to Scotland and hindered James's attempt to reach her in Oslo, as well as making other attempts upon the King's life, at the instigation of the rebellious Protestant, the Earl of Bothwell. James was closely involved in the interrogations and trials, which were of great public interest. For further detail see Craigie (ed.), *Minor Prose Works*, pp. 147–53; Willson, *King James VI and I*, pp. 103–6; and Lawrence Normand and Gareth Roberts (eds), *Witchcraft in Early Modern Scotland: James VI's Demonology and the North Berwick Witches* (Exeter: University of Exeter Press, 2000).

12  For a brief discussion of the conventionality of James's treatise and its possible sources see Clark, 'King James's *Daemonologie*', pp. 169–73. See also Normand and Roberts (eds), *Witchcraft in Early Modern Scotland*, pp. 327–49 (esp. pp. 328–30), whose discussion of James's sources includes the pre-trial and trial materials of the North Berwick witches.

13  Even in the 1580s, as we have seen in the previous two chapters, James was in large part concerned with reaching an English readership, but from the 1590s onwards his works were more thoroughly and consistently anglicised. The publication history of *Daemonologie* reminds us, however, that 'anglicisation' in this context does not necessarily mean an absolute transition from Scots to English but a gradual and irregular process: in 1597 Waldegrave 'retained the grammar and the vocabulary of his copy-text but systematically anglicised its spelling though a few Scottish forms managed to survive this treatment', and then each successive edition removed more of the residual Scottish spellings (Craigie (ed.), *Minor Prose Works*, pp. 167–8).

striking aspects of revision is the evolution of the text's dialogue form. In the preface James explains that '*for to make this treatise the more pleasaunt and facill, I haue put it in forme of a Dialogue*', indicating a concern with both aesthetics and ease of communication.[14] In the fragments in MS Bodley 165 there are no characters, but the text is divided into 'Q' and 'A'. The copy in the Folger manuscript leaves gaps for speech prefixes, and one of James's additions to the manuscript is a note at the top of the text that 'Philomathes and Epistemon raison the matter'. For the first page their initials are inserted into the gaps that had been left.[15] Finally in the printed version, this note heads the text, abbreviations of these Greek names, meaning 'lover of knowledge' and 'knowledgeable' respectively, are used consistently as speech prefixes, and the text is set out as a dialogue with each speech beginning on a new and indented line. The use of suggestively named characters was, then, a considered addition to the work, rather than inherent to its original composition. This addition suggests that two people are jointly reasoning and discussing the issue, obfuscating the simple underlying question-and-answer structure. As we shall see, it serves James's purposes to overlay a text rich in political significance with a literary gloss that makes some of its workings more subtle; but this also makes its meanings more complex and harder to control.

Most of the more than one hundred additions and corrections on the Folger manuscript, all but seven of which are in James's hand, are minor enough to demonstrate the King's concern with form and expression, over and beyond content.[16] In some cases single words are replaced: for example, 'to cause thame' becomes 'to make thame', and 'formis' becomes 'sortis' (Folger MS, pp. 22, 24). In others phrasing is made more concise and pithy, as in a description of the Devil in which 'terrible forme that euer he appeare' becomes 'his fearefull apparition' (Folger MS, p. 22). Other more substantial changes suggest that James had acquired additional knowledge since drafting this version, both from his reading ('this worde Magie in Greke' is corrected to 'this worde Magie in the Persian tongue'), and from his experience (discussing present confessors of witchcraft, he adds an extended note, beginning '& farther experience daylie proues hou laith thay are to confesse without tortoure' (Folger MS, pp. 9, 39)). Another kind of change suggests that the situation has changed since this draft was produced: a reference to 'thair confessions that haue bene at this tyme apprehendit', is followed by a crossed-out line, 'quhilkis [which] all are to be set furthe in print' (Folger MS, verso of third sheet, unpaginated). This may be a reference to *Newes from Scotland*, a semi-official and propagandistic account of the North Berwick witch trials published in England in 1591 or 1592. All of this suggests that while the version of the text copied out in the

---

14 James VI, *Daemonologie* (Edinburgh: Robert Waldegrave, 1597), sig. A2v. Subsequent references are to this edition unless otherwise specified and given in parentheses in the text.

15 Folger Shakespeare Library, V.a. 185, p. 1. Subsequent references are given in parentheses in the text with the title 'Folger MS'.

16 See Craigie, *Minor Prose Works*, pp. 161–5, for a full list of revisions, a few of which do represent extensive additions.

Folger manuscript may have been written in 1590–1, James's revisions must have been completed later.[17]

A final, and significant, kind of change is that which makes the text less of the moment and less addressed towards an audience with first-hand knowledge of the Scottish witch trials. Thus a reference to 'thir witchis now in handis, ye knaw, confessis not' becomes 'witchis ofttymes confessis not' (Folger MS, p. 49), changing a comment on current events to a generalised statement, and losing the conversational 'ye knaw' that implies shared knowledge with the reader. Similarly, a section beginning 'And this we haue in pruif euen now be that young ane who being troubled . . .' is changed so that the point under discussion 'was lykewayes prouen by the confession of a younge lasse troubled . . .' (Folger MS, p. 107), turning an emphatic present tense ('euen now') to the past tense, and 'that young ane', with its implication that the reader will recognise the person in question, to 'a younge lass' (see figure 3). Despite what some commentators have referred to as the 'pressing topicality' indicated by the work,[18] evident in the preface's opening reference to '*the fearefull aboundinge at this time in this countrie, of these detestable slaues of the Deuill*' (*Daemonologie*, p. 2), we can thus see that James made some attempt to make his work into a more generalised, universal statement. The revisions to the Folger manuscript suggest a movement from the King simply recording and intervening in current affairs to representing himself as an author of important and broadly relevant truths to a wide and lasting readership. These revisions accord, then, with the decision to anglicise the text for publication.

*Daemonologie*'s preface situates the King within an international debate by presenting him as writing '*against the damnable opinions of two principally in our age, wherof the one called* SCOT *an Englishman, is not ashamed in publike print to deny, that ther can be such a thing as Witch-craft . . . The other called* WIERVS, *a German Phisition, sets out a publick apologie for al these craftes-folkes*' (*Daemonologie*, sig. A2v).[19] This gives those whose views he opposes more acknowledgement than he shortly would in the preface to the reader in *True Lawe*, in which he asserts he will simply '*teach you the right way, without wasting time vpon refuting the aduersaries*' (*True Lawe*, sig. A3v). Yet even in the preface to *Daemonologie* he is reconfiguring the debate in terms of his work correcting the errors that others have made. He firmly states the intention and meaning of his text: '*My intention in this labour, is only to proue*

17  Normand and Roberts favour an early date of composition (*Witchcraft in Early Modern Scotland*, p. 328), as does Dunlap, 'King James and Some Witches', p. 44, but these critics do not allow for a gap of time between composition and revision.

18  Normand and Roberts (eds), *Witchcraft in Early Modern Scotland*, p. 328.

19  James is referring to Reginald Scot, *The Discouerie of Witchcraft* (London, 1584) and Johannes Weyer, *De Praestigiis Daemonum* (Basel, 1563; reprinted Geneva, 1579). For a discussion of these works see Christopher Baxter, 'Johann Weyer's *De Praestigiis Daemonum*: Unsystematic Psychopathology', in Anglo (ed.), *The Damned Art*, pp. 53–75, and Anglo, 'Reginald Scot's *Discoverie of Witchcraft*: Scepticism and Sadduceeism', in the same volume, pp. 106–39. For a brief discussion of James's main points of opposition to Scot and Weyer see Clark, 'King James's *Daemonologie*', pp. 169–73.

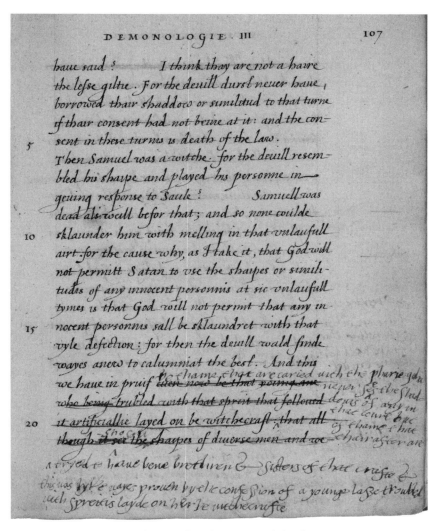

3 Manuscript copy of *Daemonologie*, showing James's hand-written corrections
(Folger Shakespeare Library, V.a. 185, p. 107)

*two things . . . the one, that such diuelish artes haue bene and are. The other, what exact trial and seuere punishment they merite'* (*Daemonologie*, sig. A3r). He thus implies that, unlike Scot and Weyer, he is writing fact not opinion, that his intention is simple and transparent, and that he has no personal investment in the subject beyond offering enlightenment.

As other critics have recognised, however, James also seems to have intended that *Daemonologie* should reinforce his image in the eyes of his subjects in various subtle and indirect ways, extending the claims already made for him in earlier accounts of the witch trials. Firstly, James's direct involvement in the trials had been represented as indicating his special ability to discover truth: for example, Robert Bowes told Lord Burghley in a letter of December 1590 that 'the King "by his own especiall travell" has drawn [Agnes] Sampson, the great witch, to confess her wicked doings'.[20] James had earlier shown in his scriptural exegeses his ability to interpret texts; now he was interpreting his subjects. This involved not only drawing out confessions but also, particularly in later years, exposing impostors.[21] In *Daemonologie* he was similarly revealing the 'truth' about witchcraft, and the treatise itself suggests the importance for his subjects of such enlightenment by claiming that the Devil has most success where he 'findes greatest ignorance and barbaritie' (*Daemonologie*, p. 69). Moreover, the treatise supports its arguments with reference to Scripture (including Revelation, which James had already meditated upon in print), exploiting and extending the King's association with scriptural interpretation.[22]

Secondly, the very notion that James was the target of the witches' practices and had survived them was presented as evidence of his godliness. *Newes from Scotland* asserts that the Devil had told the witches that 'the king is the greatest enemy he hath in the world'. It also reports that Sampson confessed that 'his Majesty had never come safely from the sea, if his faith had not prevailed above their intentions'.[23] This emphasis on James's godliness, combined with the notion that a witch lost her powers if made to face the godly magistrate, created a powerful legitimisation of the King; as Clark puts it, these notions transformed 'the very impotence of the North Berwick witches into an affirmation of [James's rule]'.[24] The King's own treatise emphasises these ideas. It is careful to explain that a witch loses her power only if apprehended by 'the lawfull Magistrate' because 'where God beginnes iustlie to strike by his lawfull Lieutennentes, it is not in the Deuilles power to defraude or bereaue him of the office, or effect of his powerfull and reuenging Scepter' (*Daemonologie*, p. 51). Thus James has justice, law, and the power of God on his side. This insistence on the special role of the monarch in the exposure and defeat of witches in turn assisted James in the ongoing debate between Crown and Church as to which had more authority. Lawrence

20  Letter quoted in Craigie (ed.), *Minor Prose Works*, p. 150.
21  The received opinion is that James grew more sceptical about witchcraft in his English reign, but Clark convincingly argues that he had always – even in 1590–1 – been sceptical and cautious about the veracity of individual cases, and cites examples of James exposing impostors in both Scotland and England ('King James's *Daemonologie*', pp. 161–3).
22  We might note that all but three of the scriptural references in the 1597 edition have been added in James's hand in the margins of the Folger manuscript (Craigie (ed.), *Minor Prose Works*, p. 166), suggesting that for James marginal references were a way of advertising scriptural authority to his readers, not intrinsic to initial composition.
23  *Newes from Scotland* (?1591), in Normand and Roberts (eds), *Witchcraft in Early Modern Scotland*, pp. 315, 317.
24  Clark, 'King James's *Daemonologie*', p. 166.

Normand and Gareth Roberts go so far as to suggest that the resolution of this debate 'in favour of the king was achieved partly through the North Berwick witch hunt'.[25]

*Daemonologie* thus implies the extent to which James's subjects need him, to discover and teach them the truth about witchcraft and to protect them from the threat it poses. What has not been explored, however, is the detailed way in which *Daemonologie*'s form extends these aims. The dialogue form places James at more of a remove, and the dialogue indeed refers to Kings in the third person. For example, it suggests that the Devil 'will make his schollers to creepe in credite with Princes' (*Daemonologie*, p. 22), implying the self-awareness that would protect James from being thus deceived. Nevertheless, Epistemon or 'knowledgeable', who takes the place of 'A[nswer]' in the early draft, seems to be a figure for the King. Epistemon's argument is the argument of the whole work; he is the one drawing authority from Scripture; and he even echoes the aim James states in the preface '*to proue . . . that such diuelish artes haue bene and are*' when he states that 'witch-craft, and Witches haue bene, and are' (*Daemonologie*, sig. A3r, p. 2). At the same time, Philomathes or 'lover of knowledge', and 'Q[uestion]' in the early draft, seems to represent James's ideal listener or reader. We might recall that in 1584 James had addressed his *Reulis and Cautelis* to '*the docile bairns of knawledge*' (*Essayes*, sig. K1v). This is an apt description of this 'lover of knowledge', whose questions are pertinent, and who is a keen, receptive and grateful listener: for example, one chapter begins with him saying 'I would gladlie first heare, what thing is it that ye call *Magie* or *Necromancie*', then he later comments 'yee haue satisfied me nowe so fullie' (*Daemonologie*, pp. 8, 27). By the end of the dialogue his doubts about the existence of witchcraft are fully assuaged and he concludes 'I pray God to purge this Cuntrie of these diuellishe practises' (*Daemonologie*, p. 81).

We might see this treatise, then, as not only teaching James's subjects about witch-craft but teaching them how to regard their King and read his writing. The lesson it offers is that the King is a source of knowledge to be appreciated and revered, and from which his readers should be ready to learn. Most striking in this regard is a moment when Epistemon rebukes Philomathes: 'I see if you had taken good tent [paid attention] . . . ye would not haue bene in this doubt, nor mistaken me, so farre as ye haue done' (*Daemonologie*, p. 15). Elsewhere in James's writings and speeches he attrib-utes disagreement or criticism to misinterpretation, and misinterpretation to a lack of due care in the reader or listener rather than to faults in him or his work. In the same way, Philomathes's continuing doubt and error are the result of his lack of atten-tion, not of any deficiency on Epistemon's behalf, nor of the possibility that there is more than one way of reading the evidence. Philomathes thus serves not only as a model for James's readers but also as a warning or counter-example. Epistemon's rebuke functions in the same way as Prospero's punctuation of his long exposition speech by telling Miranda, and by extension the audience, to pay attention – James is

25  Normand and Roberts (eds), *Witchcraft in Early Modern Scotland*, p. 74.

also reminding the reader to be attentive, in reading *Daemonologie*, and towards the King more generally.[26]

That Epistemon has become aware of how Philomathes is responding at this moment gives him the opportunity to correct Philomathes's error. Having the opportunity to offer correction was perhaps the ideal scenario for James in the face of mis-interpretation, and one which he tried to create by adding prefaces that correct alleged misinterpretations to both his epic poem the *Lepanto* (1591), as we saw in Chapter 1, and to *Basilikon Doron* in 1603, as we will consider below. That process of writing a text, allow-ing it to circulate, finding out how it has been read, then reissuing a clarified and extended version is condensed into this exchange between Epistemon and Philomathes. This argument might seem to suggest that James's ideal scenario would have been speaking to an interlocutor in person rather than writing to an absent reader, but it is evident throughout this book that the King found writing the most effective forum for his self-representation. What we see in this dialogue is James effectively exploiting some of the advantages of personal exchange *in written and printed form*, with its atten-dant advantages of greater permanence and greater scope for authorial deliberation and revision.

*Daemonologie* thus seems to acknowledge that the relationship between a monarch and his subjects/readers is not simply a one-way imposition but a dialogue, yet a particu-lar kind of hierarchised dialogue, which is between the learned and the pliant, the authoritative and the deferential. A king was indeed dependent on the perceptions of his subjects. We have seen a number of ways in which belief in the existence of witches reinforced James's position, and Fischlin has argued that his position in fact depended upon such beliefs: 'if witches did not exist they would be created in order to affirm God's presence and, by extension, the divine right of the monarch'.[27] But we can go further than Fischlin and suggest that the reality of the symbiotic relationship between a monarch and his subjects is coded into the text. For while the treatise tries to suggest that James's subjects need him to enlighten and protect them, its representation of Philomathes as a figure for the reader also inadvertently reveals that the King needs them to provide the opportunity and legitimisation for him to play his role. To admit this is to risk undermining the notion that the monarch is dependent only upon God for his authority. The substitution of named characters for the 'Q' and 'A' found in the early draft may have been in part an attempt to distract from the interdependence of the two components of the dialogue – to present Epistemon, and by extension James, as self-sufficient rather than reactive. Yet this change does not fully conceal the fact that the King can provide no answers if there are no questions.

*Daemonologie*'s strategy of voicing doubts through Philomathes in order to assuage them might seem to reflect Stephen Greenblatt's familiar argument that power produces

26  Shakespeare, *The Tempest*, I.1.78, 87, 88, 106, in Stephen Greenblatt *et al.* (eds), *The Norton Shakespeare* (New York: Norton, 1997).
27  Fischlin, ' "Counterfeiting God" ', p. 9.

and contains its own subversion to further itself.[28] But this strategy in fact risks under-mining what James is trying to achieve, creating the possibility that a reader might leave the work more convinced by the doubts raised than the responses given. The treatise's acknowledgement of alternative perspectives even extends into showing how the Bible can be interpreted in different ways: Philomathes gives his reading of 1 Samuel 28, a key text for demonologists, and Epistemon responds 'Yet if ye will marke the wordes of the text, ye will finde clearely, that . . .' and goes on to give his reading (*Daemonologie*, pp. 3–5). While the implication is that only Epistemon's reading is truly responsive to the bibli-cal text itself, and therefore 'correct', this exchange amounts to an acknowledgement of the susceptibility of texts – even the Bible, even *Daemonologie* itself – to multiple and opposing readings. This issue is further complicated by the fact that James seems to have drawn for information on Scot's *Discouerie of Witchcraft*, one of the works to which he explicitly situates himself in opposition.[29] The King was thus reappropriating Scot's materials for an opposing purpose, and this again involves not only incorporating doubt and dissent in order to challenge it, but also risks validating that doubt and dissent. Moreover, his use of Scot's work raises the possibility that aspects of his own treatise could likewise be reappropriated by people seeking to oppose him. The relationship between these different participants in the debate over witchcraft thus appears circulatory – Scot advertises the views he is refuting, providing information for James and other demonologists, and likewise James reproduces the doubts he is refuting, which could be used by other sceptics. This highlights the malleable and exploitable nature of the 'evidence' for and against the existence of witches, and the impossibility of definitively containing subversion. While James may have believed that his careful revisions and directions to the reader would prevent subversive or contesta-tory readings, we can see that he was writing about a subject the meaning of which he could not fix.

The most significant way in which the meanings of *Daemonologie* are beyond James's control concerns the issue of deception. The text repeatedly emphasises the Devil's ability to deceive, to counterfeit, and generally to make people 'beleeue that they saw and harde such thinges as were nothing so indeed' (*Daemonologie*, p. 74). As Daniel Fischlin argues, the notion that witches, like the Devil whom they served, could possess not only the body but also the imagination, was precisely what was most threatening to political and social order, not least because it formed a corollary to what he calls the 'consensual hallucination of sovereignty' which required that the monarch shape the imagination of the subject. Witchcraft thus becomes 'the site of a complex struggle over the mind and body of the political subject'. This battle between kings and witches reproduces the larger battle between God and the Devil for control over humankind. God, kings, Satan, and witches may be seen as all linked by their need to possess the imagination, and *Daemonologie* thus struggles to maintain clear binary oppositions

28  See Greenblatt, 'Invisible Bullets', esp. pp. 30, 37.
29  Normand and Roberts (eds), *Witchcraft in Early Modern Scotland*, p. 330.

between them. For example, in a passage 'addressing Satan's counterfeit of God, James is inevitably led . . . to consider the many parallels between the two', and when he derides the Devil as 'Gods Ape' it reveals his sublimated anxiety about the fact that royal power too depends upon counterfeiting God.[30]

Yet we might go even further than Fischlin by looking more specifically at how James's representation of the Devil's deceptiveness relates to his concerns not just as King but as an author. Tellingly, James proposes that the Devil is 'the author of al deceit' (*Daemonologie*, p. 20): by terming the Devil an 'author' he not only evokes the power of writing but also attributes to the Devil the originary, creative force that was more usually associated with God. James seems to have wanted to attach to himself such originary force, as is epitomised by the assertion in the epistle to the King James Bible, which we will consider further below, that the King is 'the principall moouer [mover] and Author of the Worke'.[31] James further suggests that the Devil's power lies beyond words and rituals: people are convinced of devilish practices 'by the power of the Devill for deceauing men, and not by anie inherent vertue in these vaine wordes and freites [super-stitious acts or observances]' (*Daemonologie*, p. 12). Again this is suggestive of the rela-tionship James tries to maintain between himself and language; words may be used by anyone, but when the King uses them he infuses them with his unique authority, and his words therefore should be read in accordance with that authority. In the preface added to *Basilikon Doron*, for example, he asks that his reader '*interpret fauourably this birth of mine, according to the integritie of the author, and not looking for perfection in the worke it selfe*'.[32] As in his comments on the Devil, what matters is not the words themselves but their author. Though James cannot admit it and may not even have recognised it, *Daemonologie* thus locates in the Devil the very power he wants for himself.

This treatise thus sits uncomfortably alongside the King's own imaginative writings, especially his poetry which, as we saw in Chapter 1, expresses a desire to be able to deceive its readers. Specifically, each of the twelve sonnets of invocation in *Essayes of a Prentise* emphasises a desire for readers to be convinced that they are really experiencing that which is being described. For example, the first sonnet asks Jove that he inspire the King's poetry so 'As they may suirlie think, all that it reid, / When I descryue thy might and thundring fyre, / That they do see thy selfe in verie deid' (*Essayes*, sig. A3v, lines 6–8); the sixth asks that when he describes winter 'let them think, they heare the birds that die' (*Essayes*, sig. B2r, line 11). Most strikingly, the fourth sonnet asks that all his readers' senses be 'so bereaued, / As eyes and earis, and all may be deceaued' (*Essayes*,

---

30  Fischlin, ' "Counterfeiting God" ', pp. 4–5, 15, 13.

31  *The Holy Bible, Conteyning the Old Testament and the New* (London: Robert Barker, 1611), sig. A2v. All subsequent references to the King James Bible are to this edition and given in parenthe-ses in the text.

32  James I, *Basilikon Doron* (London: Felix Kyngston for John Norton, 1603), sig. B3v. All subse-quent references to this work in the present chapter are to this edition unless otherwise specified and given in parentheses in the text.

sig. Brr, lines 13–14). This is precisely the kind of deceptive power attributed to the Devil in *Daemonologie*. These examples resonate particularly closely with the treatise's comment that 'the deuil illuded [deceived with false hopes] the senses of sundry simple creatures, in making them beleeue that they saw and harde such thinges as were nothing so indeed' (*Daemonologie*, p. 74). What the Devil has achieved is what James's poetry suggests he wants to achieve: he has affected people's senses, particularly sight and hearing, in order to make them believe they are experiencing something that does not actually exist. And the significance of this parallel goes beyond the King's desire to write powerful poetry: he wants to use writing to make his subjects believe in the reality of a royal authority that lies beyond the text. We might argue, however, that authority exists *only* in its representation.

From this perspective, then, we may see James's poetry as expressing his desire not only for poetic greatness but for a form of control over his readers/subjects that extends into their very perception and is analogous to a kind of possession. He is thus exploiting literature's capacity to affect the imagination as a means of enacting metaphorically his desired control over the minds of his subjects. This indicates the pre-eminence of literature as a means of establishing political authority. It also ties James's writings to larger debates about the metaphorical nature of all power and the relationship between literature and ideology; the King is – to paraphrase Paul de Man – trying to confuse linguistic with natural reality in order to further his own power.[33] Examining *Daemonologie* and these sonnets in this light would suggest that James is less politicising literature than exploiting something that is always-already political, and that any distinction between literary and political writing is therefore difficult to maintain. It also reveals that literature's capacity extends beyond James's ability to control it: if a piece of writing is powerful and complex enough to affect its reader's perceptions, then it is also susceptible to being interpreted in multiple ways, precisely because its power is only realised by the reader.

With all of this in mind, the tensions and contradictions in *Daemonologie* emerge still more clearly. Not only is there a parallel between the Devil and the King in terms of the desire or power to deceive, but James's very treatment of the Devil's deceptiveness is an act of deception. For even as he is warning his readers about the potential persuasiveness and deceptiveness of language, he is using language to persuade, and, indeed, to deceive, in that *Daemonologie* states one set of intentions but then also tries to reinforce the royal image in the eyes of his subjects in various subtle and indirect ways. The emphasis on the Devil's deceptiveness is to some extent a sleight of hand, a distraction from the ways in which James is trying to affect our perceptions. The dialogue seems almost to acknowledge the parallel between the royal and the diabolic when one

---

33  Paul de Man, *The Resistance to Theory* (Minneapolis: University of Minnesota Press, 1986), p. 11. The most influential post-Marx study of ideology is Louis Althusser's 'Ideology and the Ideological State Apparatuses', in *Lenin and Philosophy and Other Essays*, trans. Ben Brewster, second edition (London: New Left Books, 1977).

of Epistemon's descriptions of the Devil's ability to deceive is followed by Philomathes affirming 'Surelie ye haue made this arte to appeare verie monstruous & detestable' (*Daemonologie*, p. 24). What matters is the ability – that the Devil has and James wants – to make things 'appeare' a particular way. But 'to appear' might mean not only to bring into view (*OED*, 1), but also 'to seem, as distinguished from *to be*' (*OED*, 11): Philomathes's comment might be read as hinting that James's account of the Devil is merely a compelling representation, of which the Devil himself might have been proud.

James's first treatise thus highlights the interplay between his awareness of the power of language and his anxiety about some of the ways in which that power might be exploited. He is trying to capitalise upon the very aspect of language – its capacity to affect and deceive – that he is warning against. Put in different terms, the literary form of the work to some extent reinforces its political aims, but it also collides with those aims, risking exposing some of the deceptions and illusions that underlie kingship. It is therefore both unsurprising that James was so concerned to revise his text before publication and to guide the interpretation of his readers, and inevitable that the text should escape the fixed meanings he tried – and many later critics have tried – to impose upon it. Many of James's subsequent works, such as *True Lawe*, have a less literary form, yet the image of the King as a writer that emerges from *Daemonologie* also informs these other works. For while the mechanics of persuasion and the possibility of deception may elsewhere be more difficult to discern, *Daemonologie* alerts us to the fact that a work such as *True Lawe* is not merely a statement of belief but a carefully constructed attempt to reinforce the royal image and make something else – in the case of *True Lawe* resistance theory – '*appeare* verie monstruous & detestable'.

## To England: performing kingship in 1603

Even before 1603, James's writings had, as we have seen in earlier chapters, enjoyed some circulation amongst English readers and helped to prepare for the accession to the English throne for which he had long hoped. But when, in March 1603, Elizabeth died and the Scottish King travelled south to assume rule over the realm she left behind, there was an unprecedented wave of London printings of his works. *Ane Fruitfull Meditatioun*, *Ane Meditatioun*, the *Lepanto*, *Daemonologie*, *True Lawe*, and *Basilikon Doron* were all reprinted, in an operation that involved numerous London printers.[34] Throughout his English reign James would, as we shall see, continue to write and publish prolifically.

---

34  *A Fruitefull Meditation* was printed by J. Harrison; *A Meditation* by J. Windet for Felix Norton; the *Lepanto* by Simon Stafford and Henry Hooke; *Daemonologie* by William Aspley and W. Cotton, and by Arnold Hatfield; *True Lawe* by Thomas Creede; and *Basilikon Doron* by Felix Kyngston for John Norton, by Richard Field for John Norton, and by E. Allde. for E. White and others of the company of the Stationers. Wormald, citing the findings of Peter W. M. Blayney, suggests there may have been as many as eight editions of *Basilikon Doron* in 1603 ('James VI and I, *Basilikon Doron* and *The Trew Law*', p. 51).

This royal enthusiasm for self-representation in print is difficult to square with two related perceptions of James's English reign that have had a long currency. The first, propagated by Arthur Wilson and subsequent historians, is that he was entirely unwilling to engage in public performance, and indeed cared little for the perceptions of his subjects. For example, Wilson asserts that he 'did not love to be looked on; and those Formalities of State, which set a lustre upon Princes in the Peoples Eyes, were but so many Burthens to him'.[35] The second is that he insisted upon keeping his affairs secret. Jonathan Goldberg, for example, refers to James's 'mysteries' as 'an inner sanctum from which all subjects were excluded – or almost all'.[36] Yet the King's attitude to public exposure is far more complicated than such perceptions allow, as is emphasised not only by accounts of his early public appearances in England but also by *Basilikon Doron*, his most important exercise in public relations of 1603.

Contemporary accounts of James's public appearances in 1603–4 suggest that he in fact was willing 'to be looked on'. *The True Narration of the Entertainment of his Royall Maiestie, from the time of his Departure from Edenbrough; Till His Receiuing at London* (1603), for example, describes James refusing an opportunity for concealing himself during his progress through York: he was offered a coach 'But he graciously answered, *I will haue no Coach, for the people are desirous to see a King, and so they shall, for they shall aswell see his body as his face.* So to the great comfort of the people, he went on foote to Church'.[37] John Savile's 1603 account of James's entertainment at Theobalds gives a similar example: after having been welcomed into Theobalds by Sir Robert Cecil, James 'had not staied aboue an houre in his chamber, but hearing the multitude throng so fast into the vppermost court to see his highnesse, as his grace was informed, hee shewed himselfe openly, out of his chamber window, by the space of halfe an houre together'.[38] These accounts give no indication, however, of James interacting with his audience. Contemporary accounts of his 1604 Royal Entry into London similarly lack, as David Bergeron highlights, 'references to any impromptu speeches which he might have given along the way', thereby suggesting 'he did not exploit the dramatic possibilities'. Elizabeth's contrasting approach to public performance is illuminated by her Royal Entry of 1559, during which she engaged in what Bergeron has called 'a type of continuous dialogue with actors and audience'.[39] The authorised description reports that 'by holding vp her handes, and merie countenaunce to such as stode farre of, and most tender and gentle language to those that stode nigh to her Grace, [she] did declare her

35 Wilson, *The History of Great Britain*, pp. 12–13. For further discussion of James's historiography see the Introduction, above.

36 Goldberg, *James I*, p. 56.

37 *The True Narration of the Entertainment of His Royall Maiestie, from the Time of his Departure from Edenbrough; Till His Receiuing at London* (London: Thomas Creede for Thomas Millington, 1603), sig. D3r.

38 John Savile, *King Iames His Entertainment at Theobalds* (London: Thomas Snodham, 1603), sig. B1v.

39 David Bergeron, *English Civic Pageantry, 1558–1642* (London: Edward Arnold, 1971), pp. 74–5.

selfe no lesse thankefullye to receiue her peoples good wyll, than they louingly offred it vnto her'. It is, then, less in a complete disdain for public appearance than in an unwillingness to interact with a crowd of spectators that James differed markedly from Elizabeth.[40]

James's attitude to public appearance was thus analogous to his self-representation in print. This is aptly figured by the image of him sitting in his chamber window at Theobalds, distanced from the 'multitude' beneath but available to their gaze; being behind a window or in a book makes him visible to his subjects but at a remove from them. Framed in the window, he was making even his own person into a silent, static, and fixed representation, in the same way that he repeatedly translates his views and claims into writing, and attempts to fix the meaning of that writing. He seems to have believed that if he was the agent of his own exposure – putting himself in the window or putting himself in a book – he could take more control over the meanings he generated; and that if his audience were kept at a distance they would be less able to assume any agency in questioning, challenging or disagreeing with him.

The question of agency also informs his attitude towards state secrets, in ways that complicate the traditional view of James influentially maintained by Goldberg. Goldberg describes James's attitude thus:

> His theme, as it was in his first appearance before the Star Chamber in 1616, was, repeatedly, 'the mysterie of the Kings power' . . . The meaning of that phrase was remarkably straightforward: 'Incroach not upon the Prerogative of the Crown:' James said, 'If there fall out a question that concernes my Prerogative or mystery of State, deale not with it' . . . The mysteries, or as James called them in the *Basilikon Doron*, his 'secretest drifts' . . . were the center of the royal sphere of power, an inner sanctum from which all subjects were excluded – or almost all.

Having made these assertions, Goldberg turns to discussing at length other writers' engagement with this royal attitude.[41] Yet his whole argument depends upon the two quotations included in this extract, both of which are taken out of context. The first part of Goldberg's quotation from James's speech to the Star Chamber continues as follows: 'the mysterie of the Kings power, is not lawfull to be disputed'.[42] His quotation from *Basilikon Doron* comes in the context of James's reflecting on the fact that

---

40  *The Passage of Our Most Drad Soueraigne Lady Quene Elyzabeth through the Citie of London to Westminster the Daye before her Coronacion* (London: Richard Tottill, 1558 [1559]), sig. A2r. This is not to deny that there was a decline in the number of public entries and progresses in the Jacobean period, in comparison to the Elizabethan. See, for example, Peck, 'Introduction', *Mental World*, pp. 1–17 (p. 7).

41  Goldberg, *James I*, pp. 56–112 (quotation from p. 56). Goldberg's argument has been influential: Fischlin and Fortier, for example, quote part of the passage quoted above without commenting upon or interrogating it, or returning to the primary texts Goldberg cites ('Introduction', *Royal Subjects*, pp. 37–58 (p. 42)).

42  James I, *His Maiesties Speach in the Starre-Chamber, 1616* (London: Robert Barker, 1616) sig. D2r.

Kings are '*publike persons . . . all the beholders eyes are attentiuelie bent, to looke and pry in the least circumstance of their secretest driftes. Which should make Kings the more carefull, not to harbour the secretest thought in their minde, but such as in the* [their] *owne time they shall not be ashamed openlie to avouche*' (sig. A1v). Looking at these quotations in full reveals that James did not maintain that there was 'an inner sanctum from which all subjects were excluded'. Rather the key for James is the question of control over exposure: subjects must not presume to encroach upon, discuss, or dispute royal mysteries, but the King has no secrets that he would be unwilling to reveal *in his own time*. This is not to deny that James may have resented and feared the public scrutiny to which he was subject, or that he was capable of harbouring secrets, but to make the important distinction that he was concerned less with maintaining his right to secrecy than with denying his subjects any agency in exposing his secrets.

The question of how far James actually had agency in revealing himself to his subjects and how far he was forced into self-revelation – and of the relationship between 'public' and 'private' – is complicated by the opaque nature of the circumstances surrounding the publication of *Basilikon Doron*. This treatise was dedicated to, and presented as a guide for, his heir, Prince Henry, its title meaning 'the kingly gift', and the extant draft of the treatise in James's handwriting (British Library, Royal MS 18. B. 15) was probably written in 1598 when the Prince was four years old. What we know of its publication history is as follows. In 1599 Waldegrave printed a limited edition of only seven copies in Edinburgh, and this edition, like all subsequent editions, is anglicised. Rumours about the work were in circulation as early as May 1599, and quickly spread to England.[43] In late March 1603 a revised version was printed in Edinburgh, also by Waldegrave. A copy of this was sent to London, and then on 28 March, the very day on which James received the news that Elizabeth was dead and he was King of England, *Basilikon Doron* was entered on the Stationers' Register to a syndicate of booksellers. Two days later copies were available in London, giving James's new subjects a means of access to the King, and his apparent ideals of rule, before they had the opportunity to see him in person.[44] The opportunity to gain such an insight was fully exploited: Jenny Wormald characterises the printings of *Basilikon Doron* in the first two and a half weeks

43 At this time Sir Robert Bowes wrote to Cecil from Edinburgh about the book, commenting that 'though it be secret, whereof a few coppies onely printed, yet as it is spreading, it is likely to grieve many'. By October 1602 John Chamberlain could write from London in terms that echo what James, as we shall see, states in the preface added to the 1603 edition: because the King's work 'hath gon abrode subject to many constructions and much depraved by many copies, he will now set yt out under his owne hand' (letters quoted in James Craigie (ed.), *The Basilikon Doron of King James VI*, 2 vols (Edinburgh and London: William Blackwood & Sons, 1950), II, 7, 19).

44 Craigie (ed.), *Basilikon Doron*, II, 4, 6, 19–20. Though he acceded to the English throne in March 1603, James did not arrive in London until the middle of May, and soon after the plague forced him to retreat from the city. He would not make his Royal Entry into London until March 1604.

of the reign as 'frenzied' and gives the estimate that there were between 13,000 and 16,000 copies printed.[45]

Despite the anglicisation, the failure to keep information about the book secret, and the timely nature of the March 1603 reprint, the preface added to the 1603 edition maintains that James had not intended that the work should ever be publicly circulated. This preface claims that Waldegrave was *'sworn for secrecie'* and the seven copies of the original edition dispersed amongst the King's *'trustiest seruants, to be keeped closelie by them: least in case . . . any of them might haue bene loste, yet some of them might haue remained after me, as witnesses to my Sonne'* (sig. A2v). It is only because, James goes on to explain, *'contrarie to my intention and expectation, . . . this booke is now vented, and set foorth to the publike view of the world'* that he is *'now forced . . . to publish and spred the true copies thereof, for defacing of the false copies that are alreadie spred'* (sigs A2v–3r). This echoes the preface he added to the *Lepanto* in which he also claims he is printing in order to replace the false copies in circulation. In both cases we have no evidence that the circulation of pirated editions ever took place; this may be simply a strategy to legitimise changing and printing the works.[46] Given these circumstances, commentators have disagreed as to James's original intentions for his treatise.[47]

The extent and nature of the changes in the text between 1599 and 1603 suggest, I would argue, that we may believe James's claim that he had not intended the original edition to reach a general readership. While the most substantial changes are the removal of the dedicatory sonnet and the addition of the preface 'To the Reader', there are numerous minor changes in presentation and content, indicating that, as with *Daemonologie*, James undertook a detailed process of revision in order to prepare the text for public consumption.[48] For example, the representation of kingship becomes more

45  Wormald, 'James VI and I, *Basilikon Doron* and *The Trew Law*', p. 51, again citing Blayney's findings. Wormald further suggests that *Basilikon Doron* aroused unprecedented interest abroad (p. 52). See also Craigie (ed.), *Basilikon Doron*, II, 1–2.

46  The false copy of *Basilikon Doron* to which James refers may, however, have been a version based on notes taken by Andrew Melville who had somehow gained access to it. Offended by what he had seen, Melville produced a list of eighteen conclusions derived from James's work which were presented to the disapproving Synod of Fife. James intervened and the matter was dropped. See Craigie (ed.), *Basilikon Doron*, II, 21, 10–14.

47  For example Craigie accepts unquestioningly a contemporary account that proposes that James was motivated to provide his son with written advice through fear of his own early death (*Basilikon Doron*, II, 4–5). Wormald claims that James wrote primarily for himself, and that this work was not 'written with an English readership particularly in mind' ('James VI and I, *Basilikon Doron* and *The Trew Law*', pp. 49–50). Sommerville raises the possibility that James 'hoped from the first that the work would be widely read' and proposes that his claims in the added preface may simply represent his exploitation of a common strategy for excusing publication (*King James VI and I: Political Writings*, p. xix).

48  See Craigie (ed.), *Basilikon Doron*, I, which prints these two versions, and the manuscript version, as parallel texts. For ease of reference I am citing this edition in considering differences between the two printed versions.

idealised, as in the removal of the rather Machiavellian suggestion that in certain circumstances a king should engage in 'fair generall speeches, (keeping you as far as ye can
from direct promises)'. An English readership is more obviously courted, as in an added
passage that praises Elizabeth and emphasises the 'fruitful effects of the vnion' between
the two kingdoms. James even addresses his own son more warmly: the 1603 title page
adds a subtitle, 'His Maiesties Instructions to His Dearest Sonne, Henry the Prince',
and where the epistle to the Prince had concluded simply 'Finis', in 1603 it concludes
'Your louing Father I. R.'.[49] These addresses to Henry are thus part of presenting the
relationship between King and heir to the public, rather than integral to the original
work.

This revision does not mean, however, that we may likewise believe James's claims
that copies of the original edition were distributed only for safekeeping. The remarkable degree of care that Waldegrave's printing house took with producing each copy of
the first edition, presumably on his instruction, suggests that it represented something
more than simply a record of advice to be preserved for his son.[50] A letter written to
Cecil in June 1599 by an anonymous Scotsman lists the people to whom James distributed his work as follows: 'ane to the queynis Majestie, another to the princis schole-
maister, ane to ather of the Catholique erlis, and ane to the Marquiss of Hamiltoun'.[51]
Craigie identifies the schoolmaster as Adam Newton, the Catholic earls as Angus,
Huntly, and Errol, and the Marquis of Hamilton as Lord John Hamilton (leaving one
copy unaccounted for, which, he suggests, is that intended for Prince Henry himself).[52]
These earls were now nominally Protestant but had a past record of armed opposition
to the Crown, whereas Hamilton, who had only recently had his marquisate conferred
on him, had loyally served James and his mother before him.[53] These four choices of
*'trustiest seruants'* would seem, then, to be strategic: James was honouring key individuals
with a beautifully prepared copy of *Basilikon Doron* as a way of extending favour and reconciliation, and rewarding loyalty.[54]

---

49 Craigie (ed.), *Basilikon Doron*, I, 182, 201, 10–11.

50 In both extant copies (National Library of Scotland, shelfmark Ry.II.e.11 and British
Library, shelfmark G.4993) printing errors have been meticulously corrected by hand. These
corrections range from adding scriptural references to the margins (see, for example, p. 68
in both copies) to perfecting the form of individual letters (see, for example, the British
Library copy, p. 29, where the first 'l' in the word 'well' has been printed slightly shorter than
the second and extended to the same length by hand).

51 Quoted in Craigie (ed.), *Basilikon Doron*, II, 7.

52 Craigie (ed.), *Basilikon Doron*, II, 7. The *Dictionary of National Biography* notes that Newton continued in the service of the royal family in England (XL, 689). The translation into Latin
of James's *Declaration Touchant le Faict de Conradus Vorstius* in 1612 has been attributed to him.

53 Craigie (ed.), *Basilikon Doron*, II, 7–8.

54 The limited circulation of James's unpublished poetry in the 1580s and 1590s may similarly
have served to identify an exclusive circle and to strengthen its sense of intimacy with the
King (see Chapter 1, above).

Similarly, we might question James's claim that he was ultimately forced into producing a second edition that he had never intended to produce. It may be the case that
he was in part using this selection of readers to test how his book might be received
more widely; this would be consistent with the concern to judge his audience in advance
that we shall consider more below. Notably, where the 1599 edition advises Henry that
he should return to drafts of his writings and revise them 'ouer again', the 1603 edition
adds 'before they be published'.[55] It may be that *Basilikon Doron* was always intended
ultimately for public consumption but that the 1599 version was not yet ready, and that
this comment reflects James having learned the danger of letting his writings circulate
at all before final revision.

Maintaining that this work was not originally intended for public consumption was,
of course, of considerable benefit to James. He exploits this notion in order to emphasise his claim that it really does represent his true and private thoughts and beliefs, not
a version of those cynically represented simply to impress. Thus he asserts in the
preface's final paragraph that since his book '*was first written in secret, and is now published,
not of ambition, but of a kinde of necessitie; it must be taken of al men, for the true image of my very
minde, and forme of the rule, which I haue prescribed to my selfe and mine*' (sig. B3v). This proposes
an absolute identification between representation and reality, and presumes the value of
such insight into the royal mind. He also claims that '*the greatest part of the people of this whole
Ile, haue been very curious for a sight*' of his treatise (sig. A8r), indicating his concern to
exploit the situation as a way of reaching both his current and his shortly-to-be subjects, as well as his awareness of their desire 'for a sight' of a representation of the King.
Curiosity was indeed a likely response, particularly since the work ostensibly represents
a private communication between the King and his heir, and James may have allowed
information about his book to leak before 1603 precisely in order to increase this curiosity. As Fischlin and Fortier suggest, James 'understood the need for personal myth-
making' and the secrecy surrounding *Basilikon Doron* gave it the added allure 'of
representing, however fictively, the immensely attractive spectacle of the king's private
self'.[56] Yet the 'myth' that *Basilikon Doron* constructs is, paradoxically, that the King has
been demystified – that his private self is the same as the self now on public view, so
his subjects need look no further than the 'true image' with which he is providing them
in his book.

*Basilikon Doron* thus indicates that publication was for James not merely an alternative to public display but rather a textual version of public display. The preface not only
describes but enacts his willingness to put himself on display before his subjects in his
own time. He is reversing a situation in which, he implies, others assumed agency in
circulating his writing. This had left his book '*subiect to euery mans censure, as the current of
his affection leades him*' (sig. A2v) – a phrase that suggests James's awareness that how a book
is interpreted may be dictated by the preconceived notions of its reader. Now he has

55  Craigie (ed.), *Basilikon Doron*, I, 184–5.
56  Fischlin and Fortier (eds), *Basilikon Doron and The True Law*, p. 28.

regained the initiative by bringing his book into circulation himself, offering a model of royal representation as ideally under royal control.

At the same time, however, *Basilikon Doron* maintains a sense of the limitations of that control, and self-consciously uses a theatrical metaphor to convey the idea that kingship is so public in nature that not even a royal book may be kept secret. The preface proposes that '*Kings . . . are as it were set (as it was sayd of olde) vpon a publique stage, in the sight of all the people; where all the beholders eyes are attentiuelie bent, to looke and pry*' (sig. A1v). This echoes the following comment within the treatise:

> It is a true old saying, That a King is as one set on a stage, whose smallest actions and gestures, all the people gazinglie doe behold: and therefore although a King be neuer so precise in the discharging of his office, the people, who seeth but the outward part, will euer judge of the substance, by the circumstances: and according to the outward appearance, if his behauiour bee light or dissolute, will conceiue preoccupied conceits of the Kings inward intention. (pp. 103–4).

These comments emphasise the public exposure and performative nature of kingship, but do so in textual form. It is notable that the 1599 edition and the original manuscript version of this passage had used the word 'skaffold', which is here replaced with 'stage'.[57] Given the subtly different connotations of the two words, this substitution emphasises public performance and submerges the more anxious sense that such performance might entail facing public retribution.[58] Even with this revision, however, the passage retains a sense that James is vulnerable and not entirely in control of his self-exposure; he is 'as one set on a stage', not as one who chooses to put himself on a stage. The passage reveals the anxiety that underlies James's desire to produce texts that show his subjects — or at least convince them he is showing them — '*the true image of my very minde*': being seen in person is not in itself enough because people will then reach their own conclusions about 'the Kings inward intention', which might be inaccurate or hostile.

James thus seems to have had a strong sense that certain kinds of exposure were variously unavoidable and necessary, coupled with a determination to control the interpretation of his texts and, by extension, of his actions and intentions. The preface he

---

57  See Craigie (ed.), *Basilikon Doron*, I, 162–3.

58  At this time 'skaffold' could mean not only a platform for a theatrical performance (*OED*, 4) but also an elevated platform on which a criminal is executed (*OED*, 6). 'Stage' could also have both meanings, but the second usage seems to have been less common than the first (*OED*, 5a, 4b). The *Dictionary of the Older Scottish Tongue* lists 'skaffold' as having both meanings but does not list 'stage' as meaning a platform for executions specifically (see 'stage', 5). This passage resonates eerily with the execution of James's son, Charles I, half a century later, and with Andrew Marvell's account of this event: 'thence the royal actor borne, / The tragic scaffold might adorn' ('An Horatian Ode upon Cromwell's Return from Ireland', in Elizabeth Story Donno (ed.), *Andrew Marvell: The Complete Poems* (Harmondsworth: Penguin, 1972), pp. 55–8, lines 53–4).

added to *Basilikon Doron* is one of a series of prefaces in which he attempts precisely this. This preface, like the preface to the *Lepanto*, uses the notion that the text has been unofficially circulated and misinterpreted to justify explaining how it should be interpreted. James suggests that criticisms have been made on the basis of this false copy, concerning '*doubt of my sinceritie in that Religion, which I haue euer constantly professed*' and suspicion that he is harbouring '*a vindictiue resolution against England*'.[59] But he emphasises that these criticisms derive solely from misreadings, made as the result of malice or simple error: '*the malitious sort of men haue detracted therein; and some of the honest sort haue seemed a little to mistake*'.[60] He refutes these accusations and explains his text, concluding firmly '*that this is the onely meaning of my booke*' (sigs A3r–6v). This is James's clearest statement of his desire that his writing be interpreted as having only a single, fixed, and royally sanctioned meaning. It also reveals his desire to maintain ownership of his texts even after they have entered the public sphere; while the book's title claims it is a 'kingly gift', the King continues to consider it '*my booke*'. The preface thus reveals his ambivalence towards being publicly exposed in print: he is not only keen to create an impression of honesty and integrity but also anxious about being scrutinised in ways beyond his control, misinterpreted, criticised, or challenged.

James's determination to explain his meaning puts him into a contradictory position, however. Even as he explains his meaning, he defends his original writing by suggesting that meaning is already self-evident. He maintains, for example, that '*if there were no more to be looked into, but the very methode and order of the booke, it will sufficientlie cleare me of that first and grieuousest imputation, in the point of Religion: since in the first part, where Religion is onely treated of, I speake so plainly*' (*Basilikon Doron*, sig. A4r–v).[61] Here he sounds a little like Epistemon chiding Philomathes for not listening properly (*Daemonologie*, p. 15): James's meaning is already clear, so if it has been misunderstood it is because his readers have

59  Craigie suggests that James is here responding to criticisms that do seem to have been circulating in England at this time (*Basilikon Doron*, II, 14–17). Yet in 1603 *Basilikon Doron* seems to have been well received (see Doelman, ' "A King of Thine Own Heart" ', pp. 1–2). This might suggest that the preface and revisions were remarkably successful in dispelling such concerns, but it more likely reflects a shift in perception of James once he became King of England, and a diminished willingness to criticise him publicly.

60  James's response to these alleged criticisms may, however, be disingenuous. As the preface he added to the *Lepanto* emphasises his Protestantism while the poem itself balances Catholic and Protestant interests, so, as James Doelman suggests, the preface James added to *Basilikon Doron* brought about inconsistencies with the existing text, especially over the issue of the Puritans (' "A King of Thine Own Heart" ', p. 5). Again it may be that rather than James having been misinterpreted, reception or changed circumstances made it desirable for him to encourage his readers to read his text differently.

61  This recalls the preface he added to the *Lepanto*, which also both explains his meaning and claims that meaning is self-evident, stating, for example, that he was moved to write the poem in response to the persecution of Protestants, '*as the exhortation to the persecuted in the hinmost eight lines therof doth plainely testifie*' (*Poeticall Exercises*, sig. G4v).

not attended to his words carefully enough. At the same time he seems aware that the *'onely meaning'* of his texts – like the validity of his actions and the basis of his authority – is not as self-evident and beyond question as he would wish. This leaves him unwilling to risk letting others interpret for themselves the meaning that he claims is self-evident. Thus, in such documents as the preface to *Basilikon Doron*, we find the King paraphrasing his own word as elsewhere he paraphrases God's word.

James's desire to control the ways in which he is scrutinised by his subjects is, then, analogous to his desire to control interpretation of the divine word from which his authority derives. Indeed, *Basilikon Doron's* instructions to Prince Henry as to how to read the Scriptures reflect how James too wants to be read:

> admire reuerentlie such obscure places as ye vnderstand not . . . the Scripture is euer the best interpreter of it selfe. But preasse not curiously to seek out farther then is contained therein; for that were ouer vnmannerly a presumption, to striue to be further vpon Gods secrets, then he hath will ye be: for what he thought needfull for vs to know, that hath he reuealed there. (p. 10)

This echoes passages from other parts of this book, and other works by James, in which he is discussing not God but kings. The notion that God has revealed as much of his secrets as we need to know, and therefore we should not seek to know more, is reproduced in royal terms in the preface when James implies that subjects need not pry into kings' secrets because kings will reveal their secrets *'in the* [their] *owne time'* (sig. A1v). That God's mysteries, rather than being pried into, should be treated with reverence is likewise translated into royal terms in James's speech to the Star Chamber of 1616, when he suggests that what 'concernes the mysterie of the Kings power, is not lawfull to be disputed; for that is to wade into the weakenesse of Princes, and to take away the mysticall reuerence, that belongs vnto them that sit in the Throne of God'.[62] Such parallels suggest James's sense of the vulnerability of both divine and royal mysteries to demystifying interrogation. Indeed we might see his whole writing career – particularly given his proclivity for including explanatory prefaces – as evidence that he believed that he, like Scripture, was his own 'best interpreter'. Of course his own politically motivated interpretations of Scripture rather undermine the claim that Scripture is the best interpreter of itself, as we saw in Chapter 2, and his interpretations of his own texts are at times disingenuous. Nevertheless his handbook for kings remains one of his most extended attempts to interpret himself to his subjects.

James seems to have been relatively successful in presenting *Basilikon Doron* as *'the true image of* [his] *very minde'*: James Doelman suggests in his study of its reception that, at a time 'when rumours about the King were rife', it 'was perceived as a hard core of indisputable evidence about the personality and policy of the new King'.[63] Yet even this perception of *Basilikon Doron* would ultimately be problematic for James, as one insightful

---

62  James, *His Maiesties Speach in the Starre-Chamber*, sig. D2r.
63  Doelman, ' "A King of Thine Own Heart" ', pp. 1–2.

contemporary appears to have realised. Samuel Daniel's *Panegyrike Congratulatorie* of 1603 expresses the hope that James's actions will confirm what he has written in this treatise:

> We haue an earnest that doth euen tie
> Thy Scepter to thy word, and binds thy Crowne
> (That else no band can binde) to ratifie
> What thy religious hand hath there set downe,
> Wherein thy all-commanding Sov'raintie
> Stands subiect to thy Pen and thy Renowne,
> There we behold thee King of thine own hart,
> And see what we must be, and what thou art.[64]

There is a note of warning in these lines: what James had written in this treatise may have been well-received, but he would now be expected to live up to it; he might be 'all commanding', but he was 'subiect to [his] Pen'. In thus subjecting himself, he had empowered his subjects, giving them an 'earnest' that could and would be used to hold up against the reality of Jacobean rule. James may not have performed in public to the extent that his predecessor in England had. But the 'common touch' Elizabeth displayed during her public appearances was, as Wormald suggests, 'in fact a dazzling display of the majesty and mystique of monarchy, and in that sense evidence of the remoteness of the late-sixteenth-century English monarchy'.[65] Even where James did attempt to maintain the mystique of kingship, he still tried to communicate that mystique to his subjects – an act of communication that is itself demystifying. By putting himself into print as he did, he – ironically enough – exposed himself far more than Elizabeth ever had.

### The dilemmas of royal publication and the vagaries of print

The first new work James printed in England, only a year after his accession, was a social treatise, *A Counterblaste to Tobacco*.[66] In the years following the Gunpowder plot of 1605, however, his attention turned towards defending his religious policy and engaging in theological debates with leading religious figures in continental Europe. He responded to the Catholic threat that the Gunpowder plot seemed to announce by introducing the Oath of Allegiance, requiring all of his subjects to affirm that their first allegiance was

---

64  Samuel Daniel, *Panegyrike Congratulatorie* (London: Edward Blount, 1603), sig. A6v.

65  Jenny Wormald, 'Two Kings or One?', p. 204.

66  The debate over whether tobacco was beneficial or harmful was already well under way in 1604, and James was seeking to make a decisive intervention, as he earlier had with regard to resistance theory versus divine right and the question of the existence of witches. For a suggestive discussion of the ways in which *A Counterblaste to Tobacco* participates in the rhetorical and political strategies characteristic of James's early English reign see Sandra J. Bell, ' "Precious Stinke": James I's *A Counterblaste to Tobacco*', in Fischlin and Fortier (eds), *Royal Subjects*, pp. 323–43.

to the King, and that the Pope had no authority to depose him or release his subjects from that allegiance. After this act had been attacked by the Pope and his followers, James printed *Triplici Nodo, Triplex Cuneus. Or An Apologie for the Oath of Allegiance, against the Two Breues of Pope Paulus Quintus and the Late Letter of Cardinal Bellarmine* (1607), defending the act and disputing the arguments that had been mounted against it on the Catholic side. The *Apologie* was reprinted in Latin in 1607, 1608, and 1609, and reissued in 1609, along with an extended preface (*A Premonition to All Most Mightie Monarches*), in English, Latin, and French. As the titles and use of Latin and French indicate, these works were largely aimed at powerful European individuals, yet the fact that each also appeared in English suggests that James intended his own subjects should likewise read them. Similarly, he printed many of his speeches to his English parliament for the perusal of his subjects more generally.

While this list of publications might suggest the confident continuation and development of James's writing career in his new realm, the reality is more complicated. *A Counterblaste to Tobacco* (1604) and the first edition of *An Apologie for the Oath of Allegiance* (1607) were published anonymously. James only printed a revised edition of the latter work, with a title page that states *An Apologie for the Oath of Allegiance. First Set Foorth Without a Name: And Now Acknowledged by the Authour, the Right High and Mightie Prince, Iames*, after it had been attacked by Catholic writers and the identity of its author had become clear. This 1609 edition, particularly because *A Premonition* returns to the concerns of his earlier scriptural writings and identifies the Pope with the Antichrist, elicited a still more vehement wave of counter-attacks.[67] Where his speeches are concerned, the King seems to have printed in part for the negative reason that he could not prevent the circulation of unauthorised versions, and he did not print all of them. And the publication history of the *Apologie* highlights the extent to which even a king was subject to the vagaries of the printing process. In this section we shall see, then, the considerable dilemmas and difficulties attendant upon royal publication, and the ways in which some of these seem to have been intensified in the years after 1603.

*A Counterblaste to Tobacco* and *An Apologie for the Oath of Allegiance* were not James's first anonymous publications: *Essayes of a Prentise* and *True Lawe* were printed anonymously in 1584 and 1598 respectively. Comparing these four works reveals a pattern. The King prints anonymously when he is trying out something new – these represent his first ever publication, his first treatise on kingship, his first work produced in England, and his first intervention in the Oath of Allegiance controversy. In each case, once there has been some opportunity to gauge the response, he follows these up with further publications under his name: the *Essayes of a Prentise* was followed by another collection of poetry, *His Maiesties Poeticall Exercises*; *True Lawe* was followed by that other treatise on kingship, *Basilikon Doron*; *A Counterblaste to Tobacco* was followed by various publications in

---

67 For a detailed discussion of this 'bitter European-wide theological controversy', which involved various writers on both sides over a number of years, see Patterson, *King James VI and I*, pp. 75–123 (quotation from pp. 76–7).

England; and *An Apologie for the Oath of Allegiance* was not only reissued in 1609 but followed by further interventions in the same debate. This pattern recalls the model of
assertion, response, and correction played out between Epistemon and Philomathes in
*Daemonologie*, and emphasises how concerned James was to judge the audience that would
judge him.

James's anxieties about how readers might respond to a royal author seem to have
been greater after 1603: where *A Counterblaste to Tobacco* and the *Apologie* differ from
the two earlier anonymous publications is in their adoption of the persona of one of
the King's subjects, who represents him in the third person. James's reasons for at times
publishing anonymously were, then, more complex than he himself suggests in *A
Premonition to All Most Mightie Monarches* in 1609. Here he claims that he originally printed
the *Apologie* anonymously out of a concern for what is appropriate in a king: '*I thought it
not comely for one of my place, to put my name to bookes concerning Scholasticke* Disputations.'[68] This
amounts to an acknowledgement of the public concerns about his writing activities
that, as we shall see in the next chapter, would be voiced in Bishop Montague's preface
to James's *Workes*. Yet making this remark within a further publication seems only a
slight concession to such sensibilities, and the anonymity of the original version
appears less a necessity forced on the King by public expectation than a strategy that
he is choosing to exploit.

As the persona of a loyal subject he writes, for example, that 'as well for the discharge
of my particular duetie, as for the loue of Veritie; I must next performe my duetie to
his Maiestie present, in testifying likewise the truth of his Actions in this matter'.[69] The
King's security and legitimacy having been threatened by the Gunpowder plot and the
debates that ensued, he puts his usual claims of truthfulness into the mouth of his own
construction of the ideal subject, as though this might lend those claims greater credibility while emphasising that he already has the support of his subjects. But even before
these events, the preface to *A Counterblaste to Tobacco* had similarly ventriloquised James's
subjects: '*wee are of all Nations the people most louing and most reuerently obedient to our Prince.*'[70]
These acts of ventriloquy may reflect not only a degree of wish-fulfilment on James's
behalf but a belief in representation as a means of shaping reality; if his subjects read
enough times that they are loving and obedient to the King, then perhaps this will

---

68  James I, *A Premonition to All Most Mightie Monarches* in *An Apologie for the Oath of Allegiance. First Set
    Foorth Without a Name: And Now Acknowledged by the Authour, the Right High and Mightie Prince, Iames.
    Together with a Premonition of his Maiesties, to All Most Mightie Monarches* (London: Robert Barker,
    1609), p. 4. As we shall see below, two editions of this work were printed in 1609; unless oth-
    erwise specified, references are to the second of these (STC 14402). Note that though *A
    Premonition* is printed as part of the *Apologie*, the two pieces are not continuously paginated.
    Where a page number refers to *A Premonition* this is specified; otherwise page numbers refer
    to the *Apologie* itself.
69  James I, *Triplici Nodo, Triplici Cuneus. Or An Apologie for the Oath of Allegiance* (London: Robert
    Barker, 1607), p. 18.
70  James I, *A Counterblaste to Tobacco* (London: R. B. [Robert Barker], 1604), sig. A3r.

encourage them to enact it. This is, then, an extension of James's strategy in *Daemonologie*; there Philomathes functions as a figure for the reader/subject, but here the subject is directly represented.

In the 1609 edition of the *Apologie* the persona is altered so that all references to the King in the third person are changed to the first person. The comment quoted above, for example, becomes 'I may next with S. *Paul* iustly vindicate my owne fame, from those innumerable calumnies spred against me, in testifying the trueth of my behauiour toward the Papists'.[71] This defence in the first person is more specific and defensive, perhaps in part because of a perception on James's behalf that *self*-defence might be greeted with more suspicion than an expression of support from a subject. Such changes also reveal, however, the extent to which James's representation of his subjects was merely a fiction readily exchangeable for another, which might make us more suspicious of all of his claims about his subjects. Likewise the fact that he was able to move between writing as a subject and writing as a king emphasises that the personas we find in his works, even when the persona appears to be the King, are not necessarily fully identifiable with James himself.

That James experimented with publishing anonymously, creating fictional personas, and writing about himself in the third person suggests a notable ability to separate himself from his role, and to see that role from a range of perspectives. He seems to have realised that in some cases his readers – perhaps, in particular, his readers in his new realm – might hold expectations and associations regarding the King that would prejudice their reading, and that they might therefore be more likely to believe the protestations of a fellow (English) subject. If so then this aspect of James's writing career suggests his awareness that royal authority might have its limitations in the sphere – or certain spheres – of writing and publication. The King was thus aware of the complexity of the interrelationship between writing and ruling, and willing to configure that interrelationship in different ways according to his sense of audience or occasion. He could not, however, entirely control the form in which his word circulated, either orally or in print, as we shall see in considering his speeches to parliament and then returning to the *Apologie*.

Parliament formed a particularly important occasion for royal self-representation and here, as he was acutely conscious, James was facing an often resistant audience, and engaging in a public act that would be reported and discussed beyond its immediate context.[72] In his speech to parliament of March 1609 he claims he is offering the 'great

71  James, *An Apologie for the Oath of Allegiance* (1609), p. 18.
72  The King was financially dependent on parliament, but it was not obliged to grant him as much in subsidies as he wanted, and this was one of several grounds for conflict between the King and the English parliament (see the Introduction, above). Wormald has suggested that the set speech was all the more important to James because the English parliamentary system cut him off from the centres of debate, denying him the political asset of his skill in personal debate, which he had been able to use effectively in Scotland ('Two Kings or One?', p. 205).

and rare Present' of a mirror in his chest, but 'not such a Mirror wherein you may see
your owne faces, or shadowes; but such a Mirror, or Christall, as through the
transparantnesse thereof, you may see the heart of your King'.[73] He seems aware of the
ambiguity that glass is not only transparent but also reflective; even as he tries to emphasise his transparency, his audience may see in him only the reflection of their own preconceptions, and report his speech accordingly. He goes on to add, apparently
spontaneously, 'I wish you here now to vnderstand me rightly. And because I see many
writing and noting, I will craue your pardons, to holde you a little longer by speaking
the more distinctly, for feare of mistaking' (sig. D4v). This begins to suggest James's
discomfort with the kind of scrutiny to which he was here subject, his awareness of the
potential difference between the spoken word and its written record, and his anxious
desire to control the transition from the one to the other.

These comments are, of course, quoted from the printed version of the speech,
and so enact an official attempt to control the transition between his word as spoken
and his word as reported. James's sense of the relationship between the two is illuminated by this speech's reference to *Basilikon Doron*: 'As I haue already said, Kings
Actions (euen in the secretest places) are as the actions of those that are set vpon the
Stages, or on the tops of houses: and I hope neuer to speake that in priuate, which I
shall not auow in publique, and print if it need bee, (as I sayd in my *Basilikon Doron*.)'
(sig. C1r). The very fact that the speech recalls a printed text suggests James's sense of
the continuity between speech and print, a continuity that he would later emphasise
by including speeches in his *Workes*. More specifically, while he here represents print
as the ultimate public statement – indicating his willingness to print his speeches –
he twice uses the verb *said* to denote what he has *written*. By referring to his writings
in his speeches, printing those speeches, and even presenting writing as itself a form
of speech, James collapses the difference between the two. This works to question the
primacy of speech and to lend its written form a sense of immediacy and royal textual
presence.

By printing his speeches, James was attempting to replace the inaccurate reports that
circulated outside parliament. That such reports did circulate is reflected by the preface
to the printed version of his 1607 speech, in which the printer refers to '*the publishing
of so many false copies that begin already to be spread thereof*'.[74] John Chamberlain would
observe of James's speech to the Star Chamber of 1616 that 'beeing long and of many

---

73  James I, *The Kings Maiesties Speach to Parliament, 1609* (London: Robert Barker, 1609), sig. A2v.
    Subsequent references are to this edition and given in parentheses in the text. According to
    our dating system, parliament took place in 1610, but I refer to James's printed speech of
    March as given in 1609 in accordance with its title page. This was the Jacobean parliament
    that involved the most extended debates over royal expenditure and the level of parliamen-
    tary subsidy. See Kishlansky, *A Monarchy Transformed*, pp. 86–8.

74  James I, *His Maiesties Speech to Both the Houses of Parliament, 1607* (London: Robert Barker, 1607),
    sig. A3v.

matters is so mangled in the rehersall of them that heard yt, that I can make no coherence, nor wherto yt principally tended'.[75] Chamberlain here suggests that these
rehearsals of the speech have destroyed it to the point that not even its principal focus
is clear, but that this is the fault of the speech itself being so long and wide-ranging.
His reference is all the more ironic because for James this speech had a clear message
that he instructed his audience to spread: 'informe my people trewly of me, how zealous
I am for Religion, how I desire Law may be maintained and flourish; that euery Court
should haue his owne Iurisdiction; that euery Subiect should submit himselfe to Law'.[76]
These lines are, however, quoted from the printed version of the speech, and may reflect
not what those who tried to rehearse it heard but subsequent addition or revision, in
which case this instruction is rather disingenuous. It creates the impression that James
is instructing his immediate audience to inform others of his honourable intentions,
when in fact he is doing this informing himself by printing the speech. That providing
printed versions might indeed prevent interested subjects from concerning themselves
with 'mangled' reports is suggested by Chamberlain's further comment on this particular speech: he is 'the lesse curious to inquire after yt because I presume we shall shortly
have yt in print'.[77]

This meant, however, that James was in a difficult position if a speech was controversial or badly received: if he published, the speech itself would be subjected to wider
scrutiny; if he did not publish, rumours about the speech might circulate that were even
more damaging. Nevertheless, he was selective about which speeches he printed, as is
emphasised by the fact that his speech of March 1609, which was printed, was followed
two months later by a speech that he did not print. This second speech seems to have
been more antagonistic: James told parliament 'I will not have you to call my prerogative in question' and made the controversial assertion that 'Kings elective as well as successive have ever had power to lay impositions'.[78] The decision to print the first speech
but not the second suggests that he believed this would help him to maintain a public
image that was more benign and conciliatory than his behaviour might actually be in
parliament.

This strategy does not seem to have been particularly effective. Firstly, news of the
May speech spread beyond parliament even though the speech itself had not been
printed, Chamberlain commenting that 'yt bred generally much discomfort; to see our
monarchicall powre and regall prerogative strained so high and made so transcendent
every way'.[79] Secondly, even the March speech, which James thought fit for publication,
attracted some negative comment. Within this speech James made in explicit terms the

75  McClure (ed.), *Letters of John Chamberlain*, II, 11.
76  James, *His Maiesties Speach in the Starre-Chamber*, sig. H3v.
77  McClure (ed.), *Letters of John Chamberlain*, II, 11.
78  As reported in records of House of Lords, in Elizabeth Read Foster (ed.), *Proceedings in
    Parliament, 1610*, 2 vols (New Haven and London: Yale University Press, 1966), I, 88.
79  McClure (ed.), *Letters of John Chamberlain*, I, 301.

parallel between the royal and divine that is so often implicit in his writings: 'if you will consider the Attributes to God, you shall see how they agree in the person of a king' (sig. B1r); 'as to dispute what God may doe, is Blasphemie . . . so is it sedition in Subiects, to dispute what a King may do in the height of his power' (sig. B4v). A letter of the same month from John More to Sir Ralph Winwood reports that 'the most strictly religious could have wished *that his Highness would have been more spareing in using the Name of God, and comparing the Deity with Princes Soveraignty*'.[80] These comments reveal the limitations of James's attempt to judge and control his audience.

Any comparison between these two speeches is, of course, complicated by the impossibility of discerning how accurately either a printed text or parliamentary records represent what James said at the time. In the case of the March 1609 speech, where we have both, we can see the discrepancies between printed text and parliamentary record. These discrepancies are particularly ironic where they concern the issue of interpretation itself; in the printed version James ends by asking parliament not to wrong the mirror he has offered them:

> First, I pray you, looke not vpon my Mirrour with a false light: which ye doe, if ye mistake, or mis-vnderstand my Speach, and so alter the sence thereof. But secondly, I pray you beware to soile it with a foule breath, and vncleane hands: I meane, that ye peruert not my words by any corrupt affections, turning them to an ill meaning, like one, who when hee heares the tolling of a Bell, fancies to himselfe, that it speakes those words which are most in his minde. And lastly (which is worst of all) beware to let it fall or breake; (for glasse is brittle) which ye doe, if ye lightly esteeme it, and by contemning it, conforme not your selues to my perswasions. (sig. I1v)

In the House of Lords these instructions were paraphrased as:

> A mirror may be abused in three kinds: first with the carriage; secondly, with foul hands or stinking breath; thirdly with a fall and with the beholding it in a false light, which will darken it, therefore must be held with a true light.[81]

This rather garbled and condensed version lacks the logic that informs the metaphor in the printed version, failing to convey the parallel James constructs between a mirror and a king's words. It is difficult to imagine anyone attending only to this paraphrase gleaning more than a general sense that the King's word should be treated carefully, whereas the printed version makes the specific point that interpretation should conform with what James says he means, and not with the preconceptions of the listener. The paraphrase does, however, contain a version of the striking reference in the printed text to 'foule breath, and vncleane hands'; though the terms are confused in the paraphrase – 'foul hands or stinking breath' – it appears that the recorder of the

---

80  Extract in Ashton (ed.), *James I*, pp. 67–8.
81  Foster (ed.), *Proceedings in Parliament*, I, 52; for the paraphrase of these instructions in the records of the House of Commons, see II, 62–3; for full parliamentary records of the speech, see I, 45–52 and II, 59–63.

speech found this a noteworthy reference. In both versions this phrase is suggestive of the royal desire noted earlier to be visible without being in physical proximity to his audience.

There are a number of possible explanations for the discrepancies between the printed version and the parliamentary records. Firstly, these discrepancies may reflect the degree to which James revised the speech before publication, in order to make it more lucid and impressive.[82] While this would suggest the importance he attached to his image in textual form, other possibilities would reveal the distortions involved in the recording of speeches. One such possibility is that the printed version of the 1609 speech *is* an accurate representation of what James said, but the parliamentary records were, despite his best efforts, inaccurate.[83] Or other people involved in the printing process may have altered the speech in reproducing it: although there is no indication of this within the edition, comments made in other printed royal speeches alert us to it as a possibility. For example, the version of James's 1607 speech printed by Robert Barker includes a preface explaining that it is a collaborative reconstruction of James's speech, based on '*diuers and different Copies*' and prepared '*with the helpe of some gentlemen that were auditors thereof*'. It is not '*a true and full relation of all his Maiestie spake . . . a thing desired by so many, though not rightly related by any*'.[84] This preface makes it clear that even the printed version does not directly represent the speech of 1607 as the King delivered it, and the same may also be true of the speech Barker published in 1609. However these different possibilities played out, for us as for James's contemporaries, the speech as delivered recedes out of view to be replaced by the textual version.

While re-presenting speech in print was part of James's attempt to fix meaning and control interpretation, print was itself unable to provide textual stability. This is epitomised in the different stages of the composition and circulation of his *Apologie for the Oath of Allegiance* in the years 1607–9, which is particularly ironic given that the debate in which this work participates was itself largely about the interpretation of textual authorities. *A Premonition* plays down the extent to which the *Apologie* has been changed since it appeared in 1607, James claiming that he has '*in a maner corrected nothing but the Copiers or Printers faults therein*'.[85] This claim is, however, disingenuous. He is here trying to exploit public awareness that the printing process might introduce errors in order to give himself the opportunity not only to change the text from a third person to a first person account but to make more substantial changes. Some of these were, as Johann Sommerville notes, intended to meet the criticisms of those who had written against

82 This is the view of Foster who suggests that parliamentary records reflect 'the speech actually given, and actually heard, not as later revised' (*Proceedings in Parliament*, I, 451n).
83 For a brief discussion of the inaccuracy of parliamentary sources and the difficulties even
   members found in reconstructing speeches see David Colclough, *Freedom of Speech in Early Stuart
   England* (Cambridge: Cambridge University Press, 2005), pp. 127–30.
84 James, *His Maiesties Speech, 1607*, sig. A3r-v.
85 James, *A Premonition* in *An Apologie for the Oath of Allegiance* (1609), p. 113.

the original work.[86] What emerges, then, is a writer well aware of some of the potentials and the problems of print, and trying hard to exploit both to his own advantage.

Ironically, however, James's revised edition of 1609 was itself, he claimed, subjected to 'Copiers or Printers faults'. On 7 April he issued a proclamation explaining these faults and recalling the first 1609 edition, which had been printed around a week earlier:

> which Booke, by the rashnesse of the Printer, and errour of the Examiner, is come forth vncorrected of some faults varying from the Originall Copie, and which doe not a little peruert the sense: Like as we disclaime from all the Copies published before the date hereof, as adulterate, and set out contrary to our express Commandement to the Printer giuen: So . . . we doe hereby straitly charge and command all . . . that they doe presently, and without delay, bring in all such Bookes as they haue, to our Printer: from whome they shall haue other Copies for the same, corrected to the trueth.[87]

Robert Barker, who printed this proclamation, also printed another edition of the *Apologie* with the following day's date (8 April) on its title page and the following warning on the verso of the title page:

> Whereas the rashness of the Printer and error of the Examiner hath made a number of his Maiesties books to be put forth and sold, being still full of the Copiers faults, and before his Maiestie had fully reuised and compared the Copie with the Originall: These are to forewarne all Readers, that they shall no way trust to any Copie, but such as hath this present admonition imprinted and that they holde all other imprinted Copies in English to be erroneous, and surreptitiously solde by the vnder Officers in the Printing House, without either his Maiesties approbation of his owne worke, or the allowance of any, who had the charge and ouersight of the imprinting thereof. And therefore that they are all to be held as vtterly disclaimed by his Maiestie.[88]

Even as the proclamation and printer's warning jointly attempt to impose order, they form a striking public acknowledgement of the limitations of royal control over the behaviour of a printing house. Neither document clarifies whether the 'faults' in the text were introduced by a scribe producing a fair copy from James's original manuscript or by a compositor setting the text for the press, but even Barker is forced to admit that members of his printing house have behaved rashly and surreptitiously. These documents expose an act of disobedience to the King, his inability to prevent the circulation of an unauthorised edition of his work, and his resulting concern and personal

---

86  Sommerville, *King James VI and I: Political Writings*, p. 283n. Sommerville lists some of these changes, pp. 283–92.

87  James I, *Proclamation* (London: Robert Barker, 1609) (STC 8431).

88  This edition is STC 14402. Barker himself evidently managed not to lose the King's favour over these events, continuing to print for him over the next decade. For further discussion of Barker's position as one of the King's printers in the later Jacobean period see Maria Wakeley and Graham Rees, 'Folios Fit for a King: James I, John Bill, and the King's Printers, 1616–1620', *Huntington Library Quarterly*, 68 (2005), 467–95.

involvement. As in the *Lepanto* and *Basilikon Doron*, we see him trying to make a clear distinction between true and false copies of his work, but this time he is accusing not a reader but those involved in the production process of 'peruert[ing] the sense'. Yet the claim made in both proclamation and printer's warning that the only problem with the first edition is that there are copier's errors seems at odds with the extremity of the reaction. These documents reveal the remarkable extent of James's desire to maintain control over the final format of his work, and his surprising willingness to be publicly represented as doing the manual work of comparing 'the Copie', whether this means a scribal copy or proofs, with 'the Originall' himself.[89]

One might imagine that James would have gone so far as to recall the first edition only if it contained politically dangerous material that required significant revision. Yet the differences between these two 1609 editions are slight. These differences may be attributable to the scribe or compositor failing accurately to reproduce what James had originally submitted. Given the nature of the differences, however, it seems more likely that he fictionalised, or at least exaggerated, what had happened in order to give himself the opportunity to complete a relatively cosmetic round of revisions. In either case his behaviour reflects his concern with minor textual detail.[90] That he recalled the first 1609 edition of the *Apologie* thus suggests again the extent of his concern with how he

89  In this regard James had not changed his approach since 1591 when, as we saw in Chapter 1, he complained in print about not having the time '*to re-mark the wrong orthography committed by the copiars of my vnlegible and ragged hand*' (*Poeticall Exercises*, sig. 2v).

90  Comparing copies of the first 1609 edition, STC 14401 (British Library, shelfmark 714.c.9; Henry E. Huntington Library, shelfmark RB 61867; and Bodleian Library, shelfmark Marl.N.31), and of the second 1609 edition, STC 14402 (British Library, shelfmark 1009.c.7. [2]; Huntington Library, shelfmark RB 433495; National Library of Scotland, shelfmarks H.32.d.37 and Abbot.104 [20]; and Bodleian Library, shelfmarks Pamph.C7 [8] and Tanner 821), reveals that there are numerous differences between the two editions, particularly within *A Premonition*, but none that significantly change the arguments. There are some additions to *A Premonition* that further support the arguments being made: for example, an argument about the Apocrypha is lent greater weight by '*Concluding this point with* Ruffinus', a five-line addition (STC 14402, p. 37). There is some nuancing of phrasing in *A Premonition*: '*the Pope now will haue no lesse then the third part of euery Kings* Subiects *and* Dominions' (STC 14401, p. 21) is changed to the more cautious '*the Pope now will haue little lesse then* . . .' (STC 14402, p. 21). Marginal references are corrected: for example, in the *Apologie* itself 'I. Chron. 4. 18' (STC 14401, p. 106) is changed to 'I. Sam. 24. 11' (STC 14402, p. 106), and this is the correct reference. While these changes are likely authorial, there are a number of other minor differences between the two editions that appear consistently in all copies consulted and appear, therefore, to be changes made before the start of the second print-run, but which may be attributable to either James or the compositor. These include in *A Premonition* long paragraphs (STC 14401, pp. 21, 32) being split into two (STC 14402, pp. 21, 32) and the addition of two sets of parentheses (STC 14402, p. 36). If James were indeed responsible for such minor adjustments, this would be entirely in keeping with what we have already seen of his careful and deliberative style of authorship.

appeared not only as king, theologian, and debater but as author. A further issue that may be at stake here is the principle of royal texts being issued without authorisation. This again recalls the preface to *Basilikon Doron*; however close to being ready for the press his work was, James may simply have been unwilling in principle for the text to be issued in anything other than his '*owne time*'.

Although the claim of the proclamation and printer's warning that James wanted only to correct 'Copiers faults' may be disingenuous, these documents suggest his underlying desire that the printed copies should correspond exactly to the authorised copy-text. This desire was in conflict with the realities of the printing process. As David McKitterick puts it, 'So long as proof-reading and consequent correction continued throughout a press-run' and imperfect sheets 'were put into circulation as an ordinary part of everyday production . . . variant copies were the norm'.[91] The second, 'corrected', 1609 edition of the *Apologie* exhibits such variation.[92] McKitterick suggests that 'most authors and readers' accepted that this was necessarily an aspect of the printing process, but perhaps James provides us with an example of an author who did believe 'Copiers faults' might be eliminated.[93]

It transpires, however, that he could not even ensure that his readers knew which edition to 'trust'. The Huntington Library holds a variant copy of the first 1609 edition in which the warning appears on an extra leaf at the back.[94] In this case, then, the warning lends an appearance of authenticity to a copy of the very edition James was trying to disclaim. Perhaps this copy too was 'surreptitiously solde by the vnder Officers in the Printing House' – keen to make money on a copy of the otherwise redundant first edition – in direct violation of what the warning itself is trying to achieve. A reader buying this copy would presumably have been reassured upon reading the warning

---

91  McKitterick, *Print, Manuscript and the Search for Order*, p. 123.

92  For example, the Huntington copy of the second 1609 edition, shelfmark RB 433495, retains the reading from the 1607 edition and the first 1609 edition of 'and of all Kings in generall, thus he speaketh' (*An Apologie for the Oath of Allegiance*, p. 100), which is corrected in other copies of the second 1609 edition to 'and of all things in generall, thus he speaketh'.

93  McKitterick, *Print, Manuscript and the Search for Order*, p. 111. We might remember here that 'Copiers faults' *were* in effect eliminated from the 1599 edition of *Basilikon Doron*, as noted above; perhaps for James this set a standard, but it was one that could not be maintained for larger print-runs.

94  Shelfmark RB 61867. This copy of the warning was printed separately from those that appear on the verso of the title page in STC 14402, and the wording is slightly different: it has a more vituperative tone, beginning 'Whereas the ignorance and greedie gaine of the vnder-Printers . . .'; 'at the ende thereof' is added after 'such as hath this present admonition imprinted' in order to accommodate it to the position in which it appears in this copy; and the date of 8 April is not printed but added by hand. Perhaps this version of the warning – which, since it was printed on an extra leaf, could be added to sets of sheets which were already assembled – represents yet another abortive stage in James's attempts to assume control over the publication of his work.

that he or she had successfully acquired the authorised edition. Particularly ironic is the possibility that the person who unknowingly bought this false copy was Sir Thomas Egerton, a member of James's own government.[95]

There is still another version that bears the same date on its title page as the revised edition (8 April), but lacks the printer's warning altogether.[96] Where this version is concerned, then, the proclamation and the printer's warning contradict each other: the proclamation disclaims only 'all the copies published before the date hereof [7 April]', which would *authorise* this version on the basis of the date on the title page; the printer's warning orders that the reader 'shall no way trust to any Copie, but such as hath this present admonition imprinted', which would *disclaim* this version on the basis of its lack of the admonition. This contradiction leaves the reader unable to ascertain whether they may 'trust' this particular version or not. While it is difficult to recover exactly what happened in the printing house, the textual history of the *Apologie* highlights just how far the vagaries of printing house processes exceeded even a king's attempts to control the publication of his works. We have a warning appended to and therefore legitimising a copy of the unrevised edition, which is exactly what it is supposed to be warning against, and a version that escapes being clearly identified as either revised or unrevised. These mistakes have still not been fully disentangled and are further compounded by cataloguing errors.[97] The case of the *Apologie* utterly ironises, then, the royal desire for authorial control that we have seen throughout this chapter.

Moreover, the amount of time James seems to have devoted to this text was a cause

95  Egerton was the founder of his family's library, the Bridgewater library from which the copy in question comes. For discussion of the history of the Bridgewater library see Stephen Tabor, 'The Bridgewater Library' in *Dictionary of Literary Biography*, 213 (1999), 40–50. Of course, even if, as seems likely, it were Egerton who obtained this copy, it is possible that he did so in full knowledge of the circumstances of its publication, or indeed acquired the warning separately and chose to have it bound with this copy.

96  This version is STC 14401.5. As the *ESTC* notes under STC 14402, sheets are found mixed between 14401.5 and 14402. 14401.5 may have been a 'stopgap' edition, produced after the King had both made his displeasure known and provided a corrected text, but before the printer's warning was decided upon. Some of the sheets produced for this edition may then have been re-used for 14402. This possibility is supported by the fact that there are far fewer copies of 14401.5 in existence than there are of the other two editions (the *ESTC* lists only 6 copies of 14401.5, as against 18 of 14401 and 42 of 14402, though, as indicated below, these figures may not be accurate). I am grateful to Steve Tabor, curator at the Huntington Library, for helpful discussion of these issues.

97  At the time of writing the *ESTC* and the National Library of Scotland's catalogue list this library as having a copy of STC 14401 (shelfmark H.32.d.37), but this is actually a copy of STC 14402; the Folger Shakespeare Library's copy of STC 14401.5 (shelfmark ac142019) is listed in its own catalogue as STC 14401; the *ESTC* does not include the Bodleian Library's copy of 14401.5 (quarto A 41 TH); in *ESTC*'s note under STC 14401.5, 'Sheets are often found mixed with 14401', '14401' is a typing error for '14402'; and Early English Books Online's entry for STC 14402 gives images from the Latin edition of the *Apologie* of 1607.

for concern for some. The process of researching and writing the text must itself have taken up a considerable amount of time, particularly since it is so dense with references (one sentence draws on no fewer than ten biblical references to the status of kings).[98] Then revising the text and dealing with the printing house was evidently also a time-consuming process. Chamberlain's 1608 comment on the *Apologie* thus seems plausible: he hears the king is 'so wholy possest and over-carefull about his booke, that till that be finished to his liking, he can brooke no other sport or busines'.[99] The pejorative tone here – '*wholy* possest and *over*-carefull' suggests the critical nature of the comments Chamberlain has heard and adds to the implication that James's priorities are askew, while indeed seeming quite apt to describe the degree of care we have seen he took. According to Malcolm Smuts, similar questioning of James's priorities took place in this period amongst several of his continental allies, who were growing impatient with him for dealing with religious controversy by writing books instead of by taking decisive action.[100] This was perhaps, then, a decisive moment in terms of the perception that writing books took the King away from other important responsibilities.

James's interventions in this debate may also have served to demystify him before his subjects. John Donne suggests in his dedicatory epistle to *Pseudo-Martyr* (1610), a text commissioned by James as part of the Oath of Allegiance controversy, that James 'had vouchsafed to descend to a conuersation with your Subiects, by way of your Bookes'.[101] The word 'vouchsafe', which could mean 'to give, grant or bestow in a gracious or condescending manner' (*OED*, 2) might suggest royal generosity, but it also emphasises that in his books James is addressing himself to those beneath him, and this means he has to 'descend' to their level. By writing, James was lowering himself to a position in which not only the likes of the Pope and Bellarmine but even his own subjects could respond to him. And such response did not necessarily consist of admiration and reverence for the King: one seventeenth-century reader of the 'corrected' 1609 edition of the *Apologie* responded to some of James's arguments by repeatedly writing a resounding 'no' in the margin.[102] As we will see even more clearly in Chapter 5, James's writings involved him in a 'conversation' with his subjects that he could not control.

98  James, *An Apologie for the Oath of Alliegiance* (1609), pp. 106–7. Even if, as Willson proposes, James was aided by eminent churchmen ('James I and His Literary Assistants'), his evident concern with this work suggests he would at the very least have closely supervised their contributions.

99  McClure (ed.), *Letters of John Chamberlain*, II, 291.

100  Smuts, 'The Making of *Rex Pacificus*', p. 382. Patterson suggests that James's conduct in the controversy did, however, win him much support in the Protestant community (*King James VI and I*, pp. 124–5).

101  John Donne, *Pseudo-Martyr* (London: W. Stansby, 1610), sig. A3r.

102  National Library of Scotland, shelfmark H.32.d.37. This copy exhibits a range of annotations, including the word 'no', alongside part of the text that has been underlined, in *A Premonition*, pp. 2, 25, 44, 49, 69, 108, 110, 123. There are far fewer annotations in the second part of the book, the *Apologie* itself.

## James as principal mover and author: the King James Bible

James's sponsorship of a new translation of the Bible in the first decade of his English reign does not only represent the culmination of much of what he tried to achieve through his writings. This Bible's dedication and preface also bear traces of some of the anxieties, contradictions, and problems involved in royal self-representation. While we do not know what direct influence James may have had on the writing of these prefatory materials, they thus offer a further perspective on the issues with which this chapter has been concerned, and suggest the extent to which his engagement with writing and print blurred the distinction between authoring, authorising, and authority.

Each of the royal texts considered in this chapter is to some extent an attempt to intervene decisively in a debate and quash opposition. The King James Bible of 1611 is likewise in part an attempt to intervene in debates about how the Bible should be interpreted and presented, and, in particular, to replace the Geneva Bible. The major change was the removal of the Geneva Bible's copious marginal notes, which formed an acknowledgement of the interpretative openness of the text, even as they sought to guide interpretation, and which, where they dealt with doctrinal and moral points, could be read as anti-monarchist. At the Hampton Court conference James, according to William Barlow's account, explicitly stated that no marginal notes should be added to the authorised version, having found in the Geneva Bible 'some notes very partiall, vntrue, seditious, and sauouring too much, of daungerous, and trayterous conceipts'.[103] The 1611 Bible firmly countered any association between the Bible and anti-monarchism and aimed to present a single, authoritative text. The fact that this Bible, unlike the Geneva Bible, was published in gothic type associated it with texts of political authority, such as proclamations and ordinances, which were also printed in gothic type at this time.[104] Thus the ways in which the King James Bible differed from the Geneva Bible were attempts to present the later Bible as more authoritative and to prevent its readers being guided towards anti-monarchism; to accommodate it to, and to reinforce, the monarch–subject relationship. The King James Bible was even printed by '*Robert Barker, printer to the Kings most Excellent Maiestie*', who would also, with John Bill, print James's *Workes*. The King James Bible thus attempts to assert royal authority over the most important text of authority.

103  James went on to give the following examples: '*Exod* I. 19. where the marginall note alloweth *disobedience to Kings*. And 2. *Chron* 15. 16. the note taxeth *Asa* for disposing his mother, *onely*, and *not killing* her' (William Barlow, *The Summe and Substance of the Conference at Hampton Court* (London: John Windet for Mathew Law, 1604), pp. 46–7). The Geneva Bible was the first English bible printed in Scotland, financed by a vote of the Scottish Church (W. H. Stevenson (ed.), *King James Bible: A Selection* (London and New York: Longman, 1994), p. 28). This may have fuelled James's enthusiasm for the production of the King James Bible early in his English reign.

104  Sharpe, *Reading Revolutions*, p. 51. The Geneva Bible was printed in Roman type (Stevenson (ed.), *King James Bible*, p. 28).

The ambivalence of James's attitude towards public exposure that *Basilikon Doron* highlights is also reflected upon here. As James made himself available to his subjects through his publications, so, by sponsoring the King James Bible, he was participating in the reformist drive to make God's word directly accessible to his people. But the translators' preface suggest the risks of this exercise in terms that recall James's claim that kings are set '*vpon a publicke stage, in the sight of all the people*'. The translators state that, as the King 'knew full well',

> whosoeuer attempteth any thing for the publike, (specially if it pertaine to Religion, and to the opening and clearing of the word of God) the same setteth himselfe vpon a stage to be glouted vpon by euery euil eye, yea, he casteth himselfe headlong vpon pikes, to be gored by euery sharpe tongue . . . Notwithstanding his Royall heart was not daunted . . . but stood resolute, *as a statue immoueable.* (*Holy Bible*, sig. A4r)

These lines combine images from theatre, war, and the visual arts, and praise James's courage for an action that has nothing to do with visual performance or war. This supports his attempt to redefine kingship in terms that are not primarily performative or martial. The comparison of James to a '*statue immoueable*' even recalls what seems to have been his attitude to public performance – displaying himself but not interacting with the crowds. If these lines suggest that James has to some extent shifted the terms of royal self-representation, however, they also suggest that books are simply another kind of self-exposing performance. They might also be read as implying that he was insufficiently sensitive or responsive to his audience. And while James only imagined himself being *seen* onstage, the translators imply what Donne also implied, and what several examples we have considered demonstrate; royal self-exposure might elicit response and even criticism, for spectators, far from being merely passive onlookers, also have tongues.

James's ambivalence about public exposure was tied to his anxiety about controlling interpretation, and in some cases this led him explicitly to impose his royal authority on his writings. Similarly, the King James Bible presents God's word to be interpreted through the framework of royal authority. Readers are greeted with a title page that proclaims this version of the Bible is '*Newly Translated out of the Originall tongues: & with the former Translations diligently compared and reuised by his Maiesties Speciall Comandement*'. The text then begins with an 'Epistle Dedicatorie' to the King. Known as the *authorised* version, or later as the *King James* Bible, the 1611 translation clearly associates James, the Bible, and authority. Unsurprisingly, James involved himself very closely in the translation, seemingly adopting the same degree of care we have see him adopt in his own writings.[105] We might say, then, that these framing devices are to the King James Bible as

---

105  'Bishop Bancroft's Rules for the Revisers' reflect James's involvement: 'as any one Company hath dispatched any one book in this manner, they shall send it to the rest, to be considered of seriously and judiciously, for his Majesty is very careful in this point' (quoted in Stevenson (ed.), *King James Bible*, p. 497).

James's various prefaces are to his own writings: he is willing to make both the Bible and his image available to his subjects but at the same time keen to control the ways in which both are interpreted.

James's attempts to imply parallels between royal and divine authorship and authority are supported by the translators. The prefatory material projects on to the King the different meanings of 'author' intrinsic to the Bible's representation of language and authority. 'The Epistle Dedicatorie' states that James's subjects bless him as 'that sanctified person, who vnder GOD, is the immediate authour of their true happinesse', presenting James as 'author' in the sense of 'creator'. It renders explicit the fact that James is himself making a statement through this Bible: 'there are infinite arguments of this right Christian and Religious affection in your MAIESTIE: but none is more forcible to declare it to others, then the vehement and perpetuated desire of accomplishing and publishing of this Worke'. The previous paragraph identifies one of those 'infinite arguments' as James's own anti-Catholic works, representing him as 'author' in the sense of 'writer' by referring to him 'writing in defence of the Trueth, (which hath giuen such a blow vnto that man of Sinne, as will not be healed,)' (*Holy Bible*, sig. A2v). The suggestion that James is making the same statement through the King James Bible as he is through his own writings implicitly aligns the two. Indeed, in the preface 'To the Reader' that follows the dedication the translators even explicitly identify the word of God with the word of the King:

> the very meanest translation of the Bible in English, set foorth by men of our profession . . . containeth the word of God, nay, is the word of God. As the Kings Speech which hee vttered in Parliament, being translated into *French, Dutch, Italian* and *Latine*, is still the Kings Speech, though it be not interpreted by euery Translator with the like grace. (*Holy Bible*, sig. A6v)

This suggests that James's language, like God's language, has a fixed and reproducable 'true' meaning that exists unchanged through the processes of translation and interpretation. This reflects the King's desire that his exegeses should be seen as reproducing the 'trew and sincere' meaning of Scripture, and that his own works be interpreted only as he intends.

Yet even the translators' preface seems to raise the doubts about the nature of textual authority that trouble James's writings (not least because it takes the example of the King's speech as uttered, which, as we have seen, was not necessarily the same as its textual versions). It confidently asserts that a translation 'is the word of God', and dismisses both the doubt that it only 'containeth the word of God', and the possibility that poor translation might fundamentally change that which it translates. But it thereby acknowledges the distinction between text as authority and text as mere representation of authority, raising the possibility that even a translation of the Bible may be no more than the latter. James's writings try to maintain that the Bible, and by extension his own writing, *is* the authority it represents, while struggling against the possibility that a text can only *represent* authority, and is open to multiple interpretations. But even the King James Bible was not an entirely authoritative text: as James could not determine how his own writings would be read, so too would it be impossible to control how people responded to the new Bible, or indeed to dictate that this Bible should be favoured over others.[106] Moreover, ironically enough, even the King James Bible was printed with numerous printer's errors.[107]

As these various parallels between James's writings and the King James Bible blur the distinction between royal authoring and authorising, so they complicate the relationship between royal and divine authority. The King elsewhere uses divine authority to reinforce his works, but here royal authority authorises the Bible. This reciprocity is particularly striking in the relationship between this Bible and the collection of his *Workes* that James, as we shall see in the next chapter, would publish five years later. For, despite the problems and limitations of royal writing and printing that we have seen throughout this chapter, he would in the coming years collect and reprint all of his prose works. His decision to do this reflects the rather paradoxical tendency that we have begun to see, and will see increasingly in the remaining chapters: James tries to resolve the problems his publications reveal or create by writing and publishing more. He seems to have hoped that by revising, reprinting, extending, or recontextualising his writings, he would eventually achieve his goal of a text that no one could criticise or misinterpret.

Perhaps what this chapter has above all suggested, however, is the various kinds of deception involved in royal representation. *Daemonologie* reveals the relationship of James's desire to control the imagination of his subjects through writing to the deceptive power he attributes to the Devil. The 1603 version of *Basilikon Doron* obfuscates the circumstances of its publication, and conceals the fact that it was revised as it was prepared for a wider public, while maintaining that it presents a 'true image' of the King's mind. The printed versions of James's speeches to parliament create the impression that the general reader is being given direct access into parliamentary proceedings, but only some of these speeches were printed, and, before publication, they may have been revised by the King or reconstructed by listeners and printers. The various editions of *An Apologie for the Oath of Allegiance* construct a fictional persona, try to present politically motivated alteration as mere correction of printer's error, and inadvertently call into question how far a reader may 'trust to any Copie'. And even the epistle to the King James Bible subtly confuses the distinction between the royal authoriser of this translation and its divine author by terming James 'the principall moouer and Author of the Worke' (*Holy Bible*, sig. A2v). James was the author of texts that were designed to reflect

106  The King James Bible did not entirely replace the Geneva Bible, which continued to be published until 1644 (Stevenson (ed.), *King James Bible*, p. 28). Tribble suggests that the Geneva Bible remained the most popular bible until about ten years after the King James Bible was published (*Margins and Marginality*, p. 32).

107  See Adam Nicolson, *Power and Glory: Jacobean England and the Making of the King James Bible* (London: Harper Collins, 2003), pp. 225–6.

his authority, respond to opposition, and control their own interpretation and reproduction, but that also attempt to efface some of the processes of revision, the mecha-
nisms of persuasion, and the realities of his position. He could not, then, avoid also
becoming an 'author of . . . deceit'.

# 4

# Monumentalising the royal author:
## *The Workes* (1616)

The largest, grandest, and in many ways the most significant, of James's publications was the folio edition of his *Workes*, published in 1616, republished in Latin translation in 1619 and in another English edition in 1620. No monarch before James had ever published their writings in a collected edition, while folio collections of the work of authors of any kind were still rare. James's *Workes* was a major intervention in the political and literary climate of the period. It was no doubt in part an attempt to bolster the royal image in the face of increasingly difficult and controversial political matters, but its significance clearly extends beyond this even for James himself. It is a highly prestigious and carefully presented publication that reflects the King's desire to consolidate, elevate, and monumentalise his writing – the culmination of his ambitions as an author. It also represents an established King reflecting upon, and even celebrating, his long reign, and it may be no coincidence that it was printed in the year he reached the notable age of fifty. At the same time, however, the *Workes* extends the tensions we have seen in preceding chapters between James's literary and political aims, and exists in an ambivalent relationship to the political and literary contexts in which it was produced.

The *Workes* is a large and imposing folio which includes engravings on the frontispiece, the title page, and at the start of the preface, and is lavish in its use of paper (an expensive item), with wide margins on all four sides of the text, all of which emphasises that it is a luxury commodity.[1] It runs to over five hundred pages and includes all of James's major prose writings to date, all of which had already been published as separate quarto and octavo editions, with the exception of the opening scriptural paraphrase. After this paraphrase and two further scriptural exegeses, the collection continues with treatises on social and political matters, interventions in theological debates, and finally political speeches. The *Workes* continues to attract surprisingly little critical consideration as a text in itself.[2] Yet it is not merely a collection of individual

---

1 James I, *The Workes of the Most High and Mighty Prince, Iames* (London: Robert Barker and John Bill, 1616). All subsequent references to James's *Workes*, and to his individual prose works, in the present chapter are to this edition unless otherwise specified and given in parentheses in the text.

2 While some recent studies have acknowledged the importance of this collection, it has still not been the focus of sustained enquiry. Goldberg briefly juxtaposes it with that of Jonson

writings but a book that is carefully introduced and organised, and that attempts to function as a single and coherent entity. The title page states that the collection was published by James Montague, Bishop of Winchester, and Montague contributes a dedication to Prince Charles and a preface to the reader in which he takes responsibility for gathering the King's works. Yet Montague's apparent assumption of responsibility may simply represent James attempting to deflect away from himself some of the criticisms that his production of a collected works seems, as we shall see, to have attracted. For it seems highly unlikely that the King – who, as we have seen repeatedly, was anxious to control interpretation of his texts, careful with their final format, and willing to be personally involved in the printing process – would not have played a major role in the preparation of his most prestigious publication. I am working on the assumption that he made or at least approved all of the major decisions regarding the contents, order, and presentation of the collection.[3]

This chapter first locates the *Workes* in its literary and political contexts, and suggests that the associations developing around collected editions of literary works accorded with, and may have helped to shape, James's authorial ambition. It then examines what texts he chose to include and how these texts were altered from earlier editions. This reveals that the collection attempts not only to strengthen his image as author and authority in the book's present but retrospectively to reshape his political and literary career to date, through various suppressions and elisions. This leads into considering the careful presentation of the collection, focusing in particular on its prefatory materials and opening text. The presentation of the volume cannot, however, entirely suppress its internal contradictions, and while the preface attempts to defend the King's book, this involves the representation of other dissenting voices. What emerges is that multiple claims are being debated in the King's *Workes* – it functions not only as a symbol of royal authority but as an anxious defence of royal writing that registers the concerns and resistance of its readership, and is itself susceptible to reappropriation. As the *Workes* relates in complex ways to its readership, so too it relates in complex ways to other contemporary publications. The final section of the chapter briefly compares the

but subjects it to no analysis (*James I*, p. 56). Masten explores its representation of authority and authorship as intimately related, but his purpose is to use it as an example of a 'patriarchal absolutist' model of authorship against which he sets the collaborative model of authorship which is the focus of his study (*Textual Intercourse*, pp. 64–73). I would suggest this is anyway too sharp a distinction, particularly given the collaborations that, as we will see, were involved in James's *Workes*. An article of 2005 by Maria Wakeley and Graham Rees considers James's *Workes* alongside other special folios produced by the King's Printing House in the years 1616–20 ('Folios Fit for a King'). Fischlin's essay, ' "To Eate the Flesh of Kings" ', is one of the few studies of James as an author to consider the *Workes* in its own right, but is mainly concerned with the apocalyptic writings with which the collection begins.

3   In this regard I concur with Fischlin and Fortier, who also suggest that 'we can assume, given James's reputation for pedantry, that he had a hand in the choice, order, and shape of the texts that were printed' (*The True Law of Free Monarchies and Basilikon Doron*, p. 29).

King's *Workes* with the folio collection of *Workes* Ben Jonson published in the same year. The parallels between the two collections emphasise that James's aspirations for his writings were similar to those of some of his contemporaries, indicate a complex picture of influence and appropriation, and highlight the constructedness and contingency of both political and literary authority.

### Why publish a collected edition?

The reasons for which James published a major work in 1616 may have been primarily political, yet the particular choice of a collected edition with the title 'Workes' (a translation of the Latin 'opera') suggests that literary motivations were also at play. To some extent the *Workes* seems to have been an attempt to respond to growing disenchantment with the King and his court. The Crown was suffering from severe financial problems, while the court was seen by many as corrupt, wasteful, and immoral.[4] This was brought into sharp focus in the period 1613–16 when the Essex affair, the Overbury murder, and James's handling of these events caused public scandal.[5] As we shall see in the next chapter, from 1616 onwards the financial and political influence held by Buckingham was widely criticised, and from 1618 the King also faced increasing opposition to his pacifist foreign policy. James thus needed to reinforce his public image, but he did not respond by making more public appearances. Indeed, he made few civic appearances after the first two years of his reign, and the other major public occasions of his reign – the visit of Christian IV in 1606, the ceremonies for the creation of Henry as Prince of Wales in 1610, the wedding of Princess Elizabeth in 1613 – all came in its first half. Instead, he published and republished a book that asserted his piety and authority, and that, by including texts that spanned his reign, provided a timely reminder of happier days. In particular the collection's inclusion of James's first speech to his English parliament offers a reminder of the widespread joy his accession had occasioned (or that he at least could plausibly claim it had occasioned): in this speech he thanks his people for 'your so ioyfull and generall applause to the declaring and receiuing of mee in this Seate (which GOD by my Birthright and lineall descent had in the fulnesse of time prouided for me)' (*Workes*, p. 485). This serves as a rebuke to those who in 1616 were daring to challenge his authority.

Even as the *Workes* attempts to intervene in contemporary politics, however, it also locates James's writings as transcending immediate political circumstance, as we will see below. This is of course a false distinction: representing the King's transcendent

---

4  See the Introduction, above.
5  The controversial divorce of the Earl of Essex and Lady Frances Howard was followed by the remarriage of Lady Frances to the royal favourite Robert Carr in 1613, and the discovery in 1616 of the involvement of Lady Frances and Carr in the murder of Sir Thomas Overbury. For a detailed study of representations of Overbury's murder, the circulation of those representations, and the political significance of this court scandal see Bellany, *The Politics of Court Scandal.*

authority is a way of encouraging obedience and reverence amongst his contemporaries. Yet James's choice of a prestigious collected folio edition suggests that the extent of his authorial ambition extended beyond the immediate moment and into posterity, beyond the political and into the literary. This is reflected in Montague's preface: the Bishop notes that through time other monuments fade but writings *'gaine strength and get authori-tie'* (sig. Dιr). The notion of writing as a lasting monument is a literary commonplace, echoing claims by numerous contemporary writers including Jonson and Shakespeare, but it accords with what we have seen in James's writings themselves: he was seeking to derive authority not only from God, not only from his political status, but from literature and the values attached to it by his contemporaries. The particular nature of his aspirations for his collection are illuminated by considering the associations of the folio format and the development of the collected edition as a genre in the years leading up to 1616.

The folio format lent a work weight and authority: as Stephen B. Dobranski notes, 'because folios required both greater workmanship and more paper than was needed for books printed in smaller formats, they had traditionally been reserved for the period's most serious and important publications', many of them historical and philosophical.[6] Moreover, the folio format was conducive to the preserving and individualising of an author's work: while most early modern books were sold unbound, and then often bound together with other books, folios were usually bound separately and before being sold.[7] The collected edition also had significant associations: ever since the sixteenth century, it has played a central role in the construction of authorial identity, literary reputation, and the canon of individual authors, as well as the literary canon as a whole. While authors can never have complete control over their own reputations, producing a collected edition is a way of attempting to shape how posterity will view an author and their work. A collected edition creates 'an air of finality and completeness; a sense of personal and artistic investment and embodiment'.[8] We might also add to this list a sense of personal and artistic *achievement*.

The late Elizabethan and Jacobean periods produced several folio collections of literary works, but these were mainly posthumous editions of the revered poets of the past. These include the works of ancient writers, such as the *Workes* of Seneca, translated by Thomas Lodge (1614), and *The Whole Works of Homer in his Iliads and Odysses*, translated by George Chapman (1616?), both of which are presented by the translator as

6 Dobranski, *Readers and Authorship in Early Modern England*, p. 104.

7 Sharpe and Zwicker, *Reading, Society and Politics*, pp. 5, 29n.

8 Andrew Nash, 'Introduction: The Culture of Collected Editions: Authorship, Reputation and the Canon', in Nash (ed.), *The Culture of Collected Editions* (Basingstoke: Palgrave Macmillan, 2003), pp. 1–18 (p. 2). While any collected edition may have these associations, Nash speculates that Jonson may have been the first major author consciously to attempt to use his collected edition in this way. See this study for a range of perspectives on collected editions from Jonson to the present.

having a didactic dimension.[9] They also include works from the relatively recent past, such as *The Workes of Our Ancient and Learned Poet, Geffrey Chaucer* (1598 and 1602) and Sir Philip Sidney's *The Countesse of Pembroke's Arcadia*, which is supplemented by his other works (1598). Kevin Pask suggests that the Chaucer edition 'marked a watershed in the authorization of Chaucer as well as of the English poet altogether', and that the Sidney edition was a 'best seller' in elite circles.[10] In 1609 the first folio edition of *The Faerie Queene* was published, and this was followed two years later by another folio, *The Faerie Queen: The Shepheards Calendar, Together with the Other Works of England's Arch-poet, Edm. Spenser*, which would be reprinted three times within the decade. The proliferation of editions such as these both emphasises the role of the collected edition in preserving a writer's work for future generations, and suggests that the production of such an edition is the result of − and therefore the mark of − a writer's greatness.

This period also saw writers beginning to publish collected editions of their *own* work, reflecting the growing authority of the author, but these tended to be confined to poetry and in quarto rather than folio size. These include *The Workes of John Heywood* (1562; reprinted 1566, 1576, 1587 and 1598) and *The Whole Workes of George Gascoigne* (1587). Samuel Daniel was the first to publish his *Works* in folio, though still he included only poetry (1601; reprinted in 1602, and in 1623 as *The Whole Workes of S. Daniel in Poetrie*). This was an age in which a considerable amount of writing was collaborative and many publications were anonymous, or at least did not emphasise the identity of their authors, but each of these publications gives the individual author's name prominence in the very title of the book, suggesting that the name is its greatest selling point.[11]

These collections tend to emphasise the patronage connections of their writers or translators, and several locate the monarch in the familiar position of dedicatee and patron. Daniel's *Works*, for example, was originally dedicated to Elizabeth, and this dedication emphasises the favour he has already won with her, claiming he has received 'That comfort which my Muse and me hath blest'.[12] Similarly, the term 'Arch-poet', used in the title of the 1611 folio edition of Spenser's poetry, emphasises the poet's association with monarchy: the *OED*, defining it as 'Chief or first poet' (a) and 'A poet-laureate' (b), cites its first usage as 1610, in reference to Henrie of Aurenches as 'Archpoet to King

9   The date of Chapman's edition of Homer is conjectural, but if this collection was indeed published in the same year as Jonson's *Workes* it intensifies the contrast between Jonson's aspirations and those of his contemporaries and rivals: while Chapman was translating a classical writer into English, Jonson was trying, as we will consider further below, to translate his work into a classical format.

10  Kevin Pask, *The Emergence of the English Author: Scripting the Life of the Poet in Early Modern England* (Cambridge: Cambridge University Press, 1996), pp. 6, 73.

11  The last years of the sixteenth century and beginning of the seventeenth also saw authors' names beginning to appear on the title pages of playbooks. For a recent consideration of this related development see Lukas Erne, *Shakespeare as Literary Dramatist* (Cambridge: Cambridge University Press, 2003), esp. pp. 34–41.

12  Daniel, *Works* (1601), sig. A2.

Henrie the Third'. This was a new term, then, and in using it the printer, Matthew Lownes, was emphasising not only Spenser's connections but the exceptional nature of his poetry. These examples thus emphasise the traditional pattern whereby the monarch enables and authorises the author's work and the author serves the monarch – but these were roles that James would seek to conflate.

By the 1610s, then, the collected edition had emerged as a genre that resonated with James's aspirations. Collected editions were associated with the notion of a singular author, posterity, literary greatness, the educative function of literature, and monarchical authority. Such editions were also, the frequency of republication would suggest, popular with their market. The collected edition's creation of an 'air of finality' made it an appropriate venture for James's mature years, while its sense of 'embodiment' accorded well with his attempts in many of his writings to create the impression his texts represented his *self*. Moreover, some of the writers involved in this burgeoning production of collected editions were writers in which James had a particular interest. In Chapter 1, we saw that he was familiar with some of Spenser's work, and may even have considered him a poetic rival. The construction of Spenser as 'England's Archpoet' may thus have fed into James's literary aspirations. We also saw the King's explicit admiration for, and emulation of, Du Bartas, and Du Bartas's works too were collected by Joshua Sylvester, and dedicated to the King (*Du Bartas His Deuine Weekes and Workes Translated and Dedicated to the Kings Most Excellent Maiestie* (1605; reprinted 1606, 1608, 1613, and 1621). Again this collection may have helped to persuade James of the merits of collected editions. The King thus had various opportunities to see the role such editions were increasingly playing in constructing the author and preserving writing for posterity, and seems to have felt this was a model that he wanted to exploit.

The most striking aspect of the relationship of James's *Workes* to contemporary literary culture is, however, the fact that it was published in the same year as that of Ben Jonson. Jonson's *Workes* has received a considerable amount of critical attention, often being described as an unprecedented publication which marked an important step in the 'emergence of the author' and the acceptance of drama as literature.[13] John Velz goes so far as to claim of Jonson that 'one man can be said to have . . . changed literary history abruptly'.[14] Lukas Erne has recently attempted to qualify such views by

13  See, among others, Richard Helgerson, 'The Elizabethan Laureate: Self-Presentation and the Literary System', *English Literary History*, 46 (1979), 193–220; Richard C. Newton, 'Jonson and the (Re-)invention of the Book', in Claude J. Summers and Ted-Larry Pebworth (eds), *Classic and Cavalier: Essays on Jonson and the Sons of Ben* (Pittsburgh: University of Pittsburgh Press, 1982), pp. 31–55; David Riggs, *Ben Jonson: A Life* (Cambridge, Mass., and London: Harvard University Press, 1989); Jennifer Brady and W. H. Herendeen (eds), *Ben Jonson's 1616 Folio* (Newark: University of Delaware Press, 1991); Richard Dutton, *Ben Jonson: Authority: Criticism* (London: Macmillan Press, 1996); Butler (ed.), *Re-Presenting Ben Jonson*; and Joseph Loewenstein, *Ben Jonson and Possessive Authorship* (Cambridge: Cambridge University Press, 2002).

14  John Velz, 'From Authorisation to Authorship, Orality to Literature: The Case of Medieval and Renaissance Drama', *Text: An Interdisciplinary Annual of Textual Studies*, 6 (1994), 197–211 (p. 204).

suggesting that Shakespeare and other writers of the period were also concerned with authorship.[15] But critics and historians have not considered the ways in which James's contemporaneous publication might make Jonson's less unique, and little attempt has been made to compare the two.[16]

While it is difficult to establish at what point between 25 March 1616 and what we would term 24 March 1617 the collections of James and Jonson were published, and therefore to establish which came first, what evidence we have would suggest Jonson's did: by November 1616 a York stationer had a copy,[17] whereas the first mention of James's *Workes* of which we have record is a letter by John Chamberlain of February 1617 (according to our dating system).[18] What is certain is that work on these two collections was under way at the same time. Were James and Jonson simply participants in the same cultural moment? Did their shared concerns as writers take their writing careers along independent but parallel lines? Or was there a more complex exchange between them? As King, James could hardly be seen to be influenced by a commoner, and yet Jonson had the kind of literary authority James seems to have wanted himself. Jonson was one of the most prominent and successful writers of the Jacobean period, and one of the writers to whose work, in the form of masques and plays, James was most frequently exposed. That 1616 was also the year in which Jonson received a royal pension, by which time 'he was in all but name Poet Laureate',[19] suggests that the period leading up to the publication of both folios was one in which Jonson was increasingly winning royal favour. Considered from the perspective of James's earlier interest in other contemporary writers, it seems feasible that Jonson may have formed an unacknowledged model for James's literary aspirations, and, as I shall suggest below, James's collection is illuminated through comparison with that of his more studied subject.[20]

15  See Erne, *Shakespeare as Literary Dramatist*.
16  Study of the relationship between James and Jonson has largely been confined to examining the ways in which Jonson's writing for the Jacobean court negotiated patronage relationships and the demands of panegyric and decorum. See Jennifer Brady, 'Jonson's "To King James": Plain Speaking in the *Epigrammes* and the Conversations', *Studies in Philology*, 82 (1995), 380–99, and Jean le Drew, 'Subjecting the King: Ben Jonson's Praise of James I', *English Studies in Canada*, 17 (1991), 135–49, as well as extensive recent work on Jonson's court masques, including David Bevington and Peter Holbrook (eds), *The Politics of the Stuart Court Masque* (Cambridge, Cambridge University Press, 1998), and Martin Butler, 'Ben Jonson and the Limits of Courtly Panegyric', in Sharpe and Lake (eds), *Culture and Politics*, pp. 91–116. Recently, Perry's *The Making of Jacobean Culture* has explored some of Jonson's work in terms of it responding to and negotiating with James's style of self-representation. James and Jonson have not, however, been compared as writers.
17  Gants, 'The Printing of Jonson's Folio *Workes*', p. 39.
18  Letter to Sir Dudley Carleton, McClure (ed.), *Letters of John Chamberlain*, II, 51.
19  Richard Dutton, 'Jonson: Epistle to Volpone', in *Licensing, Censorship and Authorship in Early Modern England: Buggeswords* (Basingstoke: Palgrave Macmillan, 2000), pp. 114–31 (p. 127).
20  A full consideration of the two-way relationship between the *Workes* of James and Jonson is beyond the scope of the present study, but will be undertaken in my next book, *Writing the*

## Which 'workes'? Constructing a canon

When James embarked upon the project of producing a collected edition of his works, he decided to include all of his prose works to date. These texts incorporate two poems: one of the scriptural exegeses concludes with a sonnet, and the political treatise *Basilikon Doron* begins with a sonnet. But James decided not to include poetry in its own right, even though he had two volumes' worth of printed poetry, and a considerable number of poems that had never been printed. Contemporary comments suggest that the King was still thought of as a poet and that this omission was therefore noticed: John Chamberlain, for example, wrote that 'the Kings workes (all save his Poetrie) are abrode in one volume'.[21] Edmund Bolton suggests the significance of this omission, writing in *Hypercritica* (1618?) 'I dare not speak of [James's poems] because I see them all left out in that Edition which *Montague . . .* hath given us of his royal Writings'.[22] James was still writing poetry and circulating it in manuscript in this period, and people such as Bolton were evidently familiar with his poetry, but by excluding it from his prestigious *Workes* he rendered its status – its availability for public comment – ambiguous.

James himself perhaps considered his poetry inappropriate for inclusion in this collection. It may have seemed to him less serious and weighty than his prose works. Or perhaps he felt that most of his poetry was more specifically 'Scots' and less translatable into the English context than his other works. Certainly, *Scots* poetry is, as we saw in Chapter 1, the specific concern of his poetic treatise, *Reulis and Cautelis*, and his two collections of poetry are the only Scottish works that were not reprinted in England in 1603. It may also be the case that excluding poetry was part of an attempt to redefine the format of the collected works, which usually consisted primarily of poetry; James may have wanted to exploit the associations of this format while ensuring that his collection was distinct from the collections of others.

The picture is complicated, however, by the existence of a manuscript collection of short poems by James entitled 'All the Kings short poesis that ar not printed' (BL Add. MS 24195), which was probably prepared between the start of 1616 and the later part of 1618. This collection consists of three sections: 'Amatoria', a sequence of love lyrics; 'Miscellanea', most of which are to or about other literary figures; and 'Fragmenta'. Most of these poems were written in the 1580s and 1590s, some appearing in James's hand in a manuscript of this period (Bodleian Library, MS 165), and are here anglicised.[23] A few were written later, the latest probably being 'A Sonet against the could that was in January 1616'. Like the *Workes*, then, this collection is a retrospective

*Monarch in Jacobean England.* See also my 'The "First" Folio in Context: The Folio Collections of King James, Ben Jonson, and Shakespeare', in Richard Wilson, Richard Meek, and Jane Rickard (eds), *Shakespeare's Book: Essays on Writing, Reading and Reception* (Manchester: Manchester University Press, forthcoming).

21  McClure (ed.), *Letters of John Chamberlain*, II, 51.
22  Quoted in Craigie (ed.), *Poems*, I, 278.
23  For a discussion of some of the material this collection includes see Chapter 1, above.

reflection upon James's career, from the 1580s to the collection's present. The manuscript also includes at the end some miscellaneous prose items, such as letters from the King to Du Bartas, which further suggests that it is attempting to emphasise James's literary connections. Significantly, some of the corrections in James's hand reveal a desire to extend the relevance of the early material; in particular, a reference to 'the treatise of Scottish poesie' (*Reulis and Cautelis*) is corrected to 'the treatise of the arte of poesie' ('All the Kings short poesis', fol. 41r). This suggests that the collection was being prepared not merely as a monument to the past but as a potential intervention in the present.

This collection may, as Craigie suggests, have been intended for publication in connection with the 1616 *Workes*.[24] Herman has responded to this suggestion by arguing that 'given that the manuscript was revised by Prince Charles and Thomas Carey, James's Groom of the Chamber, and corrected by the King himself, it is equally plausible that they wanted this collection to remain private'.[25] It seems to me unlikely that such trouble would have been taken with the collection if no circulation were intended. We can only speculate, however, as to whether it was intended for a limited degree of manuscript circulation that did take place, or for a publication that did not, and whether intentions or circumstances changed. James's priorities seem to shift in his post-1618 poetry, as we will see in the next chapter, and this may have led to the abandonment of this project. Yet if this collection were indeed intended for publication, this might explain the absence of poems in the *Workes* and provide further evidence of James's literary ambitions.

Either way, the prose edition was evidently the greater priority. The *Workes* was to include even James's early scriptural exegeses, written in the same period as his poetry. His *Paraphrase vpon the Reuelation* was, as far as we know, the only major prose work he had written and not printed, but it would play a key role in the *Workes*, as will be considered further below. All of the other works had already been printed, though *The True Lawe of Free Monarchies*, *A Counterblaste to Tobacco* and *A Discourse of the Powder-Treason* had never been printed under the King's name before. Many of these works were responses to specific circumstances, events, or debates; many were explicitly addressed to particular audiences; some may not even have been written by the King in any straightforward sense. But they would all be made to play their part in this broad and prestigious reconstruction of James's authorship. He not only published these writings as a collection but removed some of their original extra-textual material. He was thereby asserting that the individual texts transcended their contexts of production, were relevant to more general audiences, and deserved reading and rereading for their own sake. Yet even this attempt to separate texts and contexts served, as we shall see, political purposes.

The two meditations on Scripture originally printed in Scotland in the late 1580s are significantly changed. Both originally included a preface written by Patrick Galloway, a minister of the Scottish Church, in which, as we saw in Chapter 2, Galloway both

24  Craigie, *Poems* (ed), II, xxii–xxiii.
25  Herman, ' "Best of Poets, Best of Kings" ', p. 99.

defends James to the Church and constructs him in the image the Church wanted, which is to say James as staunch Protestant opposing the papacy. As a young King of Scotland, James needed this kind of support. When these texts were reprinted in London in 1603 this additional prefatory material remained, though it was anglicised and even added to, perhaps because James still felt the need for this support, or perhaps because there was no opportunity for royal intervention. For the *Workes*, however, all of this material is removed; the texts do not even give their original dates of publication. They are no longer presented as what indeed they were – texts written in a specific political and religious context. What is being elided in particular, of course, is James's troubled Scottish reign; these are the *Workes* of a mature English King.[26]

In other cases the removal of prefatory material helps to conceal the provenance of texts not solely written by the King. This is particularly clear in the case of his 1607 speech to parliament. As we saw in Chapter 3, when this speech was first published the printer added a preface 'To the Reader' in which he explains that the ensuing text is a collaborative reconstruction of the speech, based upon various copies and guided by '*some gentlemen that were auditors thereof*'. He therefore dares not maintain that this text is '*a true and full relation of all his Maiestie spake*'.[27] The same text is reproduced in the *Workes* but this preface is removed, leaving the reader to think that it is a direct representation of the speech as delivered. Here, then, we see royal representation as a collaborative construction, and the removal of the traces of that collaboration; a process that is by definition rarely available to our gaze but which, Curtis Perry has suggested, we should suspect more often than we do.[28] The fact that James accepted this text for inclusion in a celebration of his authorship despite its provenance, provides further evidence that his own definition of himself as author was a generous one.

The very inclusion of speeches in the *Workes* is significant in terms of James's aspirations as an author. In the period between 1603 and 1616 five of his speeches were printed, but always in the year that they were delivered. The interest of political speeches, then as now, was primarily topical, and the title pages and prefatory material of the original editions of James's speeches market them on these grounds. The title

26  We might note, however, the parallel between the role Galloway played in the earlier texts and the role Montague plays in the *Workes*; James might be eliding his Scottish reign, but he remains concerned to emphasise that he has the support of the Church, and, perhaps, to have these churchmen deflect criticism for his publications away from himself.

27  James, *His Maiesties Speech* (1607), sig. A3r.

28  Perry, 'Royal Authorship and Problems of Manuscript Attribution'. James's concern to remove the traces of collaboration may not seem to extend to *A Discourse of the Powder-Treason*. Willson suggests that others substantially wrote this text, and that this is indicated in its opening pages, and notes that these pages are not removed for the *Workes* ('Literary Assistants', p. 53). As noted in the Introduction, above, Willson's view of textual production is, however, anachronistic. The fact that the opening pages are written from the perspective of a subject does not in itself prove that James was not heavily involved in writing this work; as we saw in Chapter 3, James wrote from such a perspective on a number of occasions.

pages of the 1603 and 1609 speeches, for example, indicate that they were given in a session of parliament still under way at the time of printing ('*this present Parliament*'). The printer of the 1605 speech explains in a preface that, as it concerns '*that fearefull accident*' (the Gunpowder plot), he is printing it with *A Discourse of the Maner of the Discouery of this Late Intended Treason*, which '*is presently comen to my handes*'.[29] There is a sense that these printed royal speeches were an important source of up-to-date information about current affairs, at a time when there was limited publication of 'news'.[30] These examples indicate that there was a market for printed royal speeches, and this was perhaps one market that James satisfied more than Elizabeth had.[31] In the *Workes*, however, such prefatory material is removed and 'this present parliament' becomes simply 'the parliament'. By reprinting these speeches, thirteen years after originally delivered in the case of the first speech, and by thus altering their presentation, James makes a claim, unprecedented among his predecessors, that their interest extends beyond the topical, into the historic, and even perhaps the literary.

James wrote two texts after 1616, *A Meditation vpon the Lords Prayer* (1619) and *A Meditation vpon St. Matthew. Or a Paterne for a Kings Inauguration* (1620), which were included at the end of the 1620 edition of his *Workes* (which is otherwise the same as the first edition).[32] While both of these meditations were also printed as separate books, they extend James's concern at this time, evident in his production of a collected edition of prose and a manuscript collection of poetry, with reflecting on his writing career, and may even have been written with a view to being added to the *Workes* as a kind of coda. In the preface to *A Meditation vpon the Lords Prayer*, James recalls the scriptural exegeses with

29  James, *His Maiesties Speach* (1605), sig. A3r-v.

30  The first news-sheets printed in London did not appear until 1621, and even then were able only to represent 'news' from abroad (Adam Fox, *Oral and Literate Culture in England, 1500–1700* (Oxford: Oxford University Press, 2000), p. 394). For discussion of the growth of 'news' culture in the last years of the Jacobean period see Chapter 5, below.

31  Copies of many of Elizabeth's speeches circulated widely in manuscript within and beyond her lifetime, reflecting the public interest they aroused. But *The Copie of a Letter to the Right Honourable the Earle of Leycester* (1586), containing two speeches concerning the proceedings against Mary Queen of Scots, and a 1601 edition of Elizabeth's 'Golden Speech' were the only official editions of her speeches printed in her reign. See May (ed.), *Queen Elizabeth I: Selected Works*, pp. xxiii–xxv, 69. Elizabeth thus provided no precedent for James's practice of regularly printing his speeches as self-contained works.

32  James I, *The Workes of the Most High and Mighty Prince, Iames* (London: Robert Barker and John Bill, 1620). *A Meditation vpon the Lords Prayer* also appears in all editions of the Latin translation of James's *Workes, Opera Regia* (London: Robert Barker and John Bill, 1619). Two editions of the Latin version were issued in quick succession and *A Meditation vpon St. Matthew* is included only in the second, where its omission from the contents page and positioning after the final iteration of the printers' date and names suggests it was a late addition. The *ESTC* notes that the second Latin edition of the *Workes* was probably published early in 1620, though its title page gives the date as 1619. All subsequent references to the Latin edition refer to this second edition.

which his *Workes* begins: he has come from '*wading in these high and profound Mysteries in the Reuelation, wherein an Elephant may swimme; to meditate vpon the plaine, smoothe and easie* Lord's Prayer . . . *the reason is, I grow in yeeres*'.[33] Despite the self-deprecation, he is indicating the length, range, and smooth progression of his writing career, which the collection as a whole also attempts to reflect. *A Meditation vpon St. Matthew*, the last piece in the 1620 edition, also glances towards the past: its discussion of the inauguration of kings implicitly recalls the beginning of James's reign. In addition it not only refers to *Basilikon Doron*[34] but, in being dedicated to his heir and offering advice on kingship, it recalls this earlier handbook for princes, one of the first pieces in the *Workes*. This again lends this edition a further sense of completeness and coherence.

These self-conscious reflections and parallels may also form a politically motivated attempt to distract from the very different contexts in which these early and late texts were written. As we saw in the second chapter, the early scriptural exegeses assume an anti-papal stance for specific political and diplomatic purposes, while in *Basilikon Doron* James advises Prince Henry 'I would rathest haue you to Marie one that were fully of your owne Religion' (*Workes*, p. 172). By the time he republished his *Workes*, James was seeking a Catholic marriage for Prince Charles. It was, then, politically useful for him to veil these changes in his stance with an emphasis on the literary coherence of the texts in which those changes are represented.

In constructing a canon of works James thus seems to have wanted to present his texts as separate from their contexts, and establish himself as author, broadly defined, and authority for posterity as well as for his subjects. Yet his collection would be printed as *The Workes of the Most High and Mighty Prince, Iames*, and there is a fundamental contradiction between authorising the text by attaching it to the King's name and trying to present it as transcending specific contexts. The attempt to separate texts from contexts itself has a political motivation, making such a separation still less achievable. This again highlights one of the central questions of this book: how could James reconcile being a writer and a king? The prefatory materials that others contributed to the King's *Workes*, and that help to combine these disparate works as an impressive and coherent whole, seek to find in divine precedence a way of achieving this reconciliation.

### '*Knowledge makes the KING most like his maker*': representing the King in the prefatory materials of his *Workes*

As this quotation from the frontispiece of James's *Workes* highlights, the extensive prefatory materials produced on the King's behalf are primarily concerned with reinforcing the claims the King had long been making about his relationship to the divine. Throughout his writings, as we have seen, James not only draws on the divine as an external source of authority, in much the same way that other contemporary writers

33  James, *Workes* (1620), pp. 571–2.
34  James, *Workes* (1620), pp. 611, 621.

draw on other external sources of authority, but also implies the proximity, and even comparability, of the royal and the divine. The prefatory materials to his *Workes* both extend and prepare for these claims. These introductory pages draw in particular on the Book of Revelation, James's paraphrase of which is the first of his works in the collection, to establish, through analogy, association, implication, and assertion a series of related identifications: divine authority and the divine word; the divine and the royal; royal authority and the royal word. The boundaries between these are blurred so that the royal word is increasingly presented as an earthly version of the divine word. This provides a framework within which each text is to be viewed, predisposing the reader not only to approach each successive text in terms of these claims but to view each as further evidence to support these claims. For the reader who starts at the first page and continues reading, the effect of the collection is thus a cumulative one, as we will see by examining the opening pages in sequence.

The frontispiece depicts James with a book showing the title *Verbum Dei*, but this image is complicated so that divine authority is not represented as something external to the King (see figure 4). Rather, the frontispiece implies a parallel: God is here represented through the book, as James is representing himself through this book. This paralleling of royal and divine is intensified by the relationship of this image of James on a throne with the Bible at his right to the Book of Revelation: as Fischlin points out, the image recalls Revelation 5:1, 'And I saw in the right hand of him that sat on the throne a book written within and on the backside, sealed with seven seals'.[35] This prepares for the implicit claim in James's paraphrase of this text that he has privileged access to divine truth. The relationship between this visual image and the later paraphrase also serves to emphasise that James represents the Bible in two ways: in his person he is a realisation of the kingly power described in the Bible and in his writing he reproduces biblical truths. The short verse at the bottom of the page that concludes '*knowledge makes the KING most like his maker*' reinforces the parallels depicted in the image of King and Bible, though we might also note that 'King' is in block capitals but 'maker' is not, ensuring it is not God but James who dominates this opening page. The claim of likeness between God and King reverberates throughout the collection.

What is also notable about the frontispiece is the way it configures the relationship between the visual and the verbal. While it pictures James sitting on a throne with royal regalia, language is used to interpret the visual images: the Bible has words on it to explain what it is, as does the sword of justice that lies across it, and James wears a medallion which bears a motto. Language is also used in preference to visual images: rather than a symbol of peace we get James's motto, the divine words *Beati Pacifici*, written on the cloth of state in front of which he sits. Above all, the verses at the bottom not only interpret the visual in verbal terms but suggest the transience of the visual sign, beginning '*Crounes haue their compasse*'. What the verses attach most value to is 'knowledge', something not easily represented in anything other than verbal terms. Thus, although

35  Fischlin, ' "To Eate the Flesh of Kings" ', p. 412.

BEATI PACIFICI

*Crounes haue their compasse, length of dayes their date,*
*Triumphes their tombes, felicitie ee fate :*
*Of more then earth, can earth make, none partakers,*
*But knowledge makes the KING most like his maker.*

Simon Passeus sculp:Lond.                    Ioh: Bill excudit.

**4** Frontispiece of *The Workes of the Most High and Mighty Prince, Iames*
(London: Robert Barker and John Bill, 1616)

the frontispiece is a visual representation, the impression it creates is one that confirms the prioritisation of the verbal that the book as a whole enacts. In particular its depiction of the sword of justice, lying across the book of God, resonates in the emphasis in James's *Paraphrase vpon the Reuelation* on the sword of God's mouth as the force of his word.[36] This resonance contributes to the collection's insistence that both divine and royal authority be exercised and comprehended in verbal terms. From the very opening page then, the book functions as a defence of itself; it justifies James's prioritisation of the word and implies that even this is a way in which the royal and the divine are related.

The title page following the frontispiece has been described in a study of early modern title pages as 'one of the most ornate of English examples'.[37] This not only helps to lend the book dignity; it is also a rich interweaving of royal and religious imagery (see figure 5). At the top of what is an architectural design it pictures the four crowns of England, Scotland, Ireland, and Wales, topped by a divine crown, 'the crown of glory which awaits the righteous in heaven'.[38] John N. King suggests that, 'shaped like the imperial crown of England', this is 'a distinctly regal variation of the celestial crown'.[39] Moreover, the sun directly above the tier of crowns is a symbol for God, and a common symbol for royalty. Thus, as the frontispiece implies parallels between the royal and the divine, so too the iconography of the title page blurs the distinction between them. There are two figures in the side niches between the columns: on the left is Religion and on the right is Peace, picking up on the themes of the frontispiece and emphasising these as the pillars of James's reign. Religion is holding an open book towards the onlooker, as though inviting us to enter it. But the book we are entering as we view this image is of course James's – and the figure of Religion indeed holds the open book next to the words at the centre of the title page, 'THE WORKES OF THE MOST HIGH AND MIGHTY PRINCE, IAMES'. Again the boundary between religious and royal text is thus blurred, while the implication is made that religion itself dictates we read the King's book. That his book has won religious support is further emphasised by the statement made on the title page that it has been published by the Bishop of Winchester, Montague. The title page also appropriates God's words to Solomon '*Loe I haue giuen thee a wise and an vnderstanding heart*' (1 Kings 3: 12). This again celebrates the knowledge and understanding that James derives from God, drawing on the Bible to support the text that we are about to read.

This title page further emphasises James's relationship with religion by having the kind of architectural design common in bibles of the period,[40] and by recalling the

36  John N. King points out that the sword, traditionally signifying justice, and the book had also been defining symbols of Tudor majesty, which first appear in Henry VIII's hands in the Coverdale Bible title page ('James I and King David', p. 432).

37  Margery Corbett and Ronald Lightbown, *The Comely Frontispiece: The Emblematic Title Page in England 1550–1660* (London: Routledge and Kegan Paul, 1979), p. 139.

38  Corbett and Lightbown, *The Comely Frontispiece*, p. 139.

39  King, 'James I and King David', p. 435.

40  See Corbett and Lightbown, *The Comely Frontispiece*, p. 110.

King James Bible in particular.[41] Both James's *Workes* and the King James Bible involved the same printer, Robert Barker, who is presented in both cases as '*Printer to the Kings most excellent Maiestie*' (see figures 5 and 6). The title pages of both have central panels giving the title in bold print, a depiction of the light of heaven at the top middle, and key figures standing in the left and right niches, and, as the figure on the left of James's title page holds an open book towards the onlooker, so the figure on the left of the Bible's title page holds an open tablet.[42] Other details of form and presentation throughout both books are also similar.[43] While some of these similarities may be attributed to the fact that both involved Barker, the extent of the similarities – and the very fact that the same printer was employed for both – indicates an attempt not only to impose royal authority on the Bible but also to associate the two books. These associations enrich the earlier book's ambiguous representation of James as 'the principall moouer and Author of the Worke', by further blurring the distinction between authorising and authoring, between Bible (which is also a 'work') and *Workes*, and between the King as vehicle for divine truth and source of divine truth.

Both the King James Bible and James's *Workes* are, then, monumental publications that emphasise the relationship between royal and divine authority, but while royal authority provides, as we saw in the last chapter, a frame through which to read the King James Bible, divine authority provides a frame through which to read the *Workes*. In the *Workes*, the primarily visual representations of the opening pages are followed by a dedication of the book to Prince Charles and a lengthy preface to the reader, both by Montague. The Bishop's presence in the volume continues the sense that James's book is authorised not only by God but also by the Church. It is of course a reversal of James authorising the King James Bible – we might observe that in these two books there is a mutually reinforcing relation between the Church and the Crown. Yet the fact that James can authorise the Bible, but draws on the Church to authorise his book, raises the question of where earthly authority actually resides and reflects its constructed and contingent nature. Authority is here constructed through a process of exchange between

41  Sharpe, Foreword, Fischlin and Fortier (eds), *Royal Subjects*, pp. 15–36 (p. 19).

42  The title pages were not, however, produced by the same engraver: that in James's *Workes* bears the name 'Renold Elstrack', and that in the Bible 'Iaspar Isac'.

43  Both the King James Bible and James's *Workes* are folios, though the Bible is much bigger. Both begin with an 'Epistle Dedicatory' and in both cases this serves as a running heading with the first word on the verso and the second on the recto. Then in the King James Bible comes 'The Translators to the Reader', in the *Workes*, 'The Preface to the Reader', and in both cases the running heading is split so that the recto pages read 'to the Reader'. Both employ the same printers' decoration of a crown above a rose, surrounded by a garland and held by two cherubs (*Holy Bible*, sigs A3r, D4r; *Workes*, pp. 136, 286). In the King James Bible, after the tables, calendars, and contents page, is a full-page image of the royal coat of arms, with supports and the motto 'Dieu et mon Droit' (*Holy Bible*, sig. 2A1r), which is identical to the page following the title page in the *Workes*. This might have been a frequently used image, but its reproduction as a full folio page forms a further association between these two books.

5 Title page of *The Workes of the Most High and Mighty Prince, Iames*
(London: Robert Barker and John Bill, 1616)

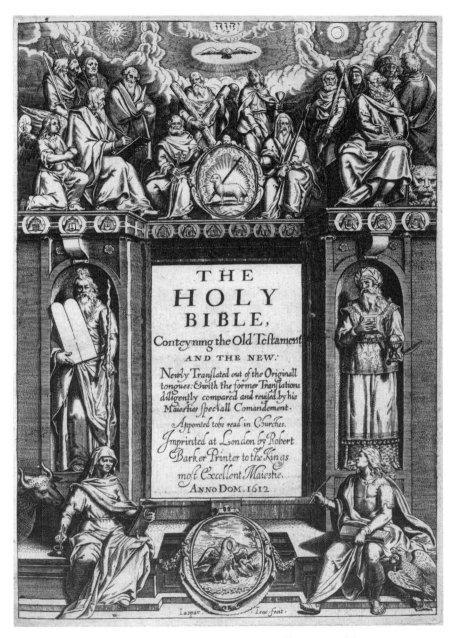

6 Title page of *The Holy Bible, Conteyning the Old Testament and the New* (London: Robert Barker, 1612). This exceptionally well-preserved copy of the title page is identical to that in the original edition of 1611, in all except the date.

Crown and Church, and this is analogous to the exchange we have elsewhere seen between James and other writers.

Montague's contributions echo many of the claims James made on his own behalf, and develop the preoccupation of the opening pages with the relationship between the royal and the divine, the word and the deed. His dedicatory epistle tells Prince Charles to 'Let these *Workes* . . . lie before you as a Patterne' (sig. A4r). His preface then justifies collecting James's works, and James writing these texts in the first place, by explicitly citing God as a precedent (sig. B1r–v).[44] Thus God provides a pattern for James, and James in turn provides a pattern for his son. This structure would be echoed in James's *A Meditation vpon St. Matthew*. Justifying his dedication of this text to Prince Charles, James asks '*whom can a paterne for a Kings Inauguration so well fit as a Kings sonne and heire, beeing written by the King his Father, and the paterne taken from the King of all Kings?*'.[45] This play on the ambivalence of the terms 'Father' and 'King' emphasises the proximity of God and God's Elect. Montague's preface reinforces such royal claims of proximity to, and comparability to, the divine.

Montague not only represents James's word as a vehicle for the divine, asserting that all of James's writings '*carry in them so much diuine trewth and light*' (sig. D4v), but establishes associations between '*the Workes* of GOD' (sig. B1v) and James's *Workes*, in ways that play on the ambiguity of the word 'works' (as meaning both 'acts' and 'texts'). In the phrase '*the Workes* of GOD' the primary meaning is 'acts', but the notion that God's creative and destructive power is verbal is fundamental to Genesis and to Revelation. The generic title of the King's book primarily suggests 'texts', but Montague is implicitly emphasising that in the particular case of the King's *Workes*, the word again carries both meanings; in effect he is re-presenting the title as not only a translation of the Latin 'opera' but as reflective of the power of the royal word. He goes on to represent that power in terms that recall the Bible's representation of the power of God's word: James's adversaries '*are not safe from being blasted by the breath of his* Maiesties *Bookes*' (sig. C4v). This emphasises that the royal word, like the divine word, does not merely describe or represent but *acts*, that it contains its speaker, and that it dictates its own meaning to its readers. This association of the divine and the royal, and emphasis on the notion of the royal word as performative, underlies Montague's defence of the King's book against the perception (that the preface acknowledges exists) that the King wrote *instead* of acting. The Bishop again uses an implicit comparison with God to defend the King's use of his own writing when he stresses that '*the Workes* of GOD' began with God's direct and unmediated production of his word: '*hee beginnes with the word out of his owne mouth, proceeds with the*

---

44 Montague goes on to give a range of biblical and historical precedents, up to Queen Elizabeth (sigs B3r–C4r), citing the presence of kings as writers in the Bible as a particular divine justification for James's identity as a writer: '*if* GOD *had thought it a matter derogatory to the Maiestie of a King to bee a Writer, he would not haue made choice of those, as his chiefe* Instruments *in this kinde, who were principalls in that other Order*' (sig. B4r).

45 James, *Workes* (1620), p. 603 (misprinted as 593).

Tables *written by his owne fingers'* (sig. Bɪv). This hints at some of the other contemporary criticisms against which the preface is defending the King; namely, that it was inappropriate for a king to write for himself, and that writing and publishing were akin to the work of artisans or tradesmen. Montague goes on to discuss these objections in detail in terms that, as we shall see later, suggest some ambivalence on his behalf about royal publication and risk undermining the very texts he is introducing.

### *'This* Paraphrase . . . *leades the way to all the rest of his* Maiesties Workes'

When, after all of these detailed prefatory materials, we finally reach James's writings, we find that they have been carefully ordered. We first encounter his 'Epistle To The Whole Church Militant, in whatsoeuer part of the Earth' and 'Argument of this Whole Epistle', which introduce and further shape our response to his *Paraphrase vpon the Reuelation*, and then the paraphrase itself (see figure 7). As this was James's earliest prose work, its positioning at the beginning of the collection accords with the organisation of the collection as a whole, which is largely chronological and reflective of his progression as a writer. Yet several departures from chronology reveal that the texts have been ordered so as to maximise the impact of each and of the collection as a whole. For example, the popular *Basilikon Doron*, which offers an idealised view of kingship, is placed before the more confrontational and controversial *True Lawe*, after which it was printed, presumably in order to make *True Lawe* seem more palatable.[46] The speeches are all grouped in the final section rather than being chronologically interspersed with other texts, which further separates them from the contexts in which they were originally produced. *A Discourse of the Powder-Treason* is separated from the 1605 speech with which it was originally printed, and placed in chronological sequence with other social and religious treatises. In the 1620 edition the opening and closing texts are scriptural exegeses and this framing subtly suggests that the King's authority is contained within the bounds of the divine. Such examples suggest that James's *Paraphrase vpon the Reuelation* is positioned as the first text in the collection not merely because of when it was written but also because its concerns with authorship and interpretation make it appropriate to this position.[47]

James had written this paraphrase in the 1580s but it had not been printed before, making it an effective selling point for the collection. More importantly, it continues the preoccupations of the prefatory materials which, as we have seen, seem to have been prepared with this text in mind. Revelation is of course the last text of the Bible; perhaps

---

46  For further discussion of these works see Chapter 3, above.

47  Fischlin also points out that 'the choices made in deploying a particular sequence of texts in the *Workes* are far from random and unconsidered', and that it is 'not surprising' that James's *Workes* should begin with his 'apocalyptic texts, which testify to his faith while highlighting the importance of the book . . . in relation to his sovereign position as *fidei defensor*' (' "To Eate the Flesh of Kings" ', pp. 390–1).

CHAP. I.　　　　　　　　　　　　　　　　　7

# A PARAPHRASE VPON
## THE REVELATION OF
### THE APOSTLE S. IOHN.

## CHAP. I.

### ARGVMENT.

*The Booke, the Writer, and the Inditer ; the end and vse thereof : The dedication of this Epistle to the Churches and Pastors, vnder the vision of the seuen Candlesticks and seuen Starres.*

OD THE FATHER hath directed his Sonne and Word, IESVS CHRIST, to send downe an Angel or Minister, to me *Iohn* his seruant, and by him to reueale vnto mee certaine things which are shortly to come to passe, to the effect in time the chosen may be forewarned by me; ² Who haue borne witnes that the word of God is true, and that IESVS CHRIST is, and was a faithfull witnesse, and haue made true report of all I saw. ³ Happy are they that read and vnderstand this Prophesie, and conforme themselues thereunto in time, for in very short space it will be fulfilled : ⁴ I am directed to declare the same, specially to you the *seuen Churches of Asia*, with whom be grace and peace from the Eternall, the Father, and from the Holy Spirit : ⁵ And IESVS CHRIST, that faithfull witnesse, the first borne of the dead, the Mightie King of the world, and head of his Church; Who for the loue he bare vs, hath made vs innocent by his blood in the worke of Redemption; ⁶ To him then we, whom hee hath made Spiritual Kings and Priests, in Honour and Holinesse, and ordained to serue and praise his Father, giue all glory and power for euer : so be it. ⁷ Assure your selues of his comming againe *from Heauen* in all glory, and all eyes shall see him ; Yea the wicked shalbe compelled to acknowledge that it is euen very he, whom

so

7　The first page of *A Paraphrase vpon the Reuelation* in *The Workes of the Most High and Mighty Prince, Iames* (London: Robert Barker and John Bill, 1616), p. 7

it is not attributing too much to James's desire to associate the royal word with the divine to suggest that the positioning of his paraphrase deliberately implies that his book is on some level a continuation of the Bible, particularly given his association with the King James Bible of only five years earlier. His paraphrase forms the basis of his book, and by implication, of his writing career, as Montague's preface indicates: 'GOD *hath giuen him an vnderstanding Heart in the Interpretation of that* Booke, *beyond the measure of other men . . . this* Paraphrase *. . . leades the way to all the rest of his* Maiesties Workes' (sig. D3v). This echoes the title page's key claim of divinely inspired royal wisdom, thereby positioning the paraphrase as evidence for the truth of this claim. The paraphrase thus forms a transition between the claims made in the prefatory materials and the more explicitly political texts to come, and exemplifies the ways in which individual texts reinforce the rest of the collection, and are in turn reinforced by being part of the collection.

The opening paraphrase, like the prefatory materials, is concerned with the relationship between royal and divine authorship and authority. We saw in the second chapter that the paraphrase blurs John's voice with James's voice and makes implicit claims about royal authorship; revisiting these aspects of the text reveals that these implications are more effective still in the context of the *Workes*. The paraphrase's explanation of John's comment, 'And I John saw these things, and heard *them*' (22: 8), which is that 'I declare you my name the oftener, lest the authority of the Booke should be called in doubt, through the vncertaintie of the Writer' (*Workes*, p. 71), has greater resonance here. It implies that the identity of the writer of the *Workes*, which is clearly stated and often reiterated (several of the texts included have separate title pages) gives the whole book authority.

Similarly, the paraphrase's comments upon translation and interpretation, which are suggestive of James's attitude towards his own readers, are here lent additional significance. James expands upon the biblical text to emphasise that anyone who strays from 'the trew meaning' of 'this Booke' by following 'his owne preoccupied opinions . . . shalbe accursed as a peruerter of the trewth of God and his Scriptures' (*Workes*, p. 72). As the paraphrase serves as an introduction to the rest of the volume, 'this Booke' is connected to the *Workes* itself. Moreover, the instructions on interpretation given here are echoed later in the volume in moments when James is explicitly talking about himself. For example, in a speech to Parliament given in March 1609 he tells his audience, as we saw in the last chapter, 'peruert not my words by any corrupt affections, turning them to an ill meaning, like one, who when hee heares the tolling of a Bell, fancies to himselfe, that it speakes those words which are most in his minde' (*Workes*, pp. 547–8). In both cases we have the notion of readers deliberately 'perverting' truth in accordance with their own preconceptions. Such echoing between different texts by James, emphasised by collecting them together in one volume, reinforces the implication that James's word should be treated as God's word should be treated, and forms an attempt to control interpretation of the King's *Workes* itself.

James's paraphrase also emphasises the destructive and creative power of God's word. For example, at 2: 16 the biblical text threatens that God will fight his enemies 'with the

sword of my mouth', and James explains 'the sword of my mouth, *to wit*, by the force
of my word' (*Workes*, p. 10). This echoes the implication in Montague's preface that
words and actions are not opposed, or even necessarily separable. The paraphrase
implicitly makes claims for the power not only of the divine word but of the royal word,
and these claims are strengthened by the fact that here it opens and forms part of an
extended demonstration of royal writing. Similar claims recur more explicitly later in
the volume in James's boast to the parliament of 1607 that 'This I must say for Scotland,
and I may trewly vaunt it; Here I sit and gouerne it with my Pen, I write and it is done,
and by a Clearke of the Councell I gouerne Scotland now, which others could not doe
by the sword' (*Workes*, pp. 520–1). This not only elevates the pen over the sword but blurs
the distinction; James here suggests that his language is performative, and writing therefore *is* the act of governing. In conjunction then, the preface, the paraphrase, and this
speech imply that the performative power of James's word is comparable to that of
God's word.

James's *Paraphrase vpon the Reuelation* thus develops the prefatory materials and forms
the basis for the texts to come. It reflects his literary as well as his political concerns,
and provides a model for the relationship between authorship and authority that works
to reinforce his *Workes* as a whole. After this paraphrase, and two further scriptural
exegeses, the collection continues with his writings on political and social matters,
implicitly suggesting that God's word is the foundation for the whole book and that all
of the King's writings are on some level a revelation of divine truth. But just as there
are some discrepancies between the opening paraphrase and the biblical text on which
it is based, so too, as we have seen, the collection as a whole does not merely translate
James's career to date into a text, but, through its choice, arrangement and alteration of
individual works, effectively rewrites certain aspects of that career.

As James's *Workes* begins with a paraphrase in which God tells John how to inform
God's people truly of him, so, in its 1616 edition, it ends with a speech in which James
gives his audience a comparable instruction. This speech, given in the Star Chamber in
1616, brings us to the collection's present and concludes, as we saw in Chapter 3, with
James telling his audience to 'procure reuerence to the King and the Law, enforme my
people trewly of mee, how zealous I am for Religion, how I desire Law may bee maintained and flourish' (*Workes*, p. 569). This synopsis in fact elides some of the more controversial aspects of the foregoing speech. Procuring reverence and obedience, while
maintaining that James is 'trewly' pious and supportive of the law, is precisely the effect
that the whole collection in which this speech appears has been seeking to achieve,
but the collection has been likewise selective in what it includes. This instruction to a
specific audience becomes also a closing instruction to the reader of the *Workes* and
takes us back to the opening paraphrase's concern with 'true' representation. Yet it
also exposes the fact that royally sanctioned 'truth' is in fact a matter of subjectively
selecting certain representations and not others, on the basis of political efficacy.
And the ironic failure of this royal attempt to control representation becomes more
and more apparent in considering the readers of the King's works that contribute to

the collection (Montague and the translators of the 1619 Latin edition), and the readers whose views Montague represents.

## Readers in the *Workes*

James attempts, as we have seen repeatedly, to dictate to his readers the singular meaning of his writings, the clearest example of this being his assertion in the preface to *Basilikon Doron* that the explication of the text he has given '*is the onely meaning of my Booke*' (*Workes*, p. 144). Accordingly, he seems to have wanted to fix the meaning of his *Workes* and to make it into a monumental symbol. This desire, the importance of the *Workes* to the royal image, and the ambitiousness of the claims made for it, are suggested by an official and publicly sold engraving of the royal family by Willem van de Passe, first published in 1622 (see figure 8). This engraving depicts James and his royal progeny, with the family of the King of Bohemia, and his *Workes*, with its Latin title, *Opera Regia* (perhaps we are invited to see his book also as one of his offspring). In the picture Charles stands with his hand placed on the open Bible (the book of his divine father), and beside the Bible is placed, in a remarkably bold gesture, the book of his father. This furthers James's attempt to equate God's word and the King's word, not only by suggesting that they play a parallel role in the education of the heir to the throne but also, more subtly, by locating James's book in the position that the Bible occupies in his book's frontispiece. The later engraving further recalls the King's *Workes* in that his depiction here – his dress, posture, and expression – is similar to that in the engraving in the frontispiece of his *Workes*, and, indeed, the engraver of that frontispiece was Simon van de Passe, the brother of Willem van de Passe.[48] More significantly, this engraving enacts Montague's advice to Prince Charles that he should 'let these *Workes* . . . lie before you as a Patterne'. This establishes alongside the blood lineage a textual lineage: the Bible informs James's *Workes*, which in turn can instruct his heir and, if not replace the Bible, certainly supplement it. The engraving thus represents the *Workes* as a symbol of royal authority and offers to public view a model of reading – the heir to the throne reading the *Workes* alongside the Bible – that operates within the terms of that authority. By locating the book between its royal author, its royal dedicatee, and the Bible, the engraving attempts to fix its meaning.[49]

48  In addition the engraving of James and his family was printed by John Bill, who was also involved in printing the *Workes* (Griffiths, *The Print in Stuart Britain*, p. 65).

49  See also Goldberg, *James I*, pp. 90–1, who discusses this portrait alongside others primarily in terms of its representation of the relation between father and son. Ironically, even this portrait was to be re-presented in ways far beyond James's control. An engraving from Passe's original forms the centrefold, and first of a series of pictures of James, in an 1817 edition of Weldon's *The Court and Character of King James* (London: G. Smeeton, 1817). Given that Weldon's book was designed to expose James as weak and corrupt (the series of images ends with a copy of a emotional letter hand-written by James to Buckingham), this picture was presumably chosen for the centrefold to emphasise the pretensions and hypocrisies of James and his successor. This

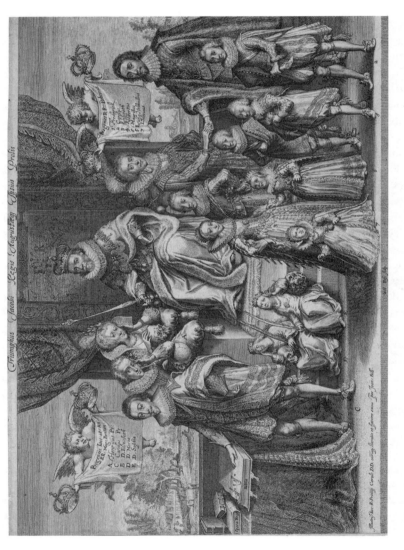

8 Engraving of the 'Triumphus Iacobi Regis Augustaeque Ipsius Prolis' ('Triumph of King James and of his August Progeny), by Willem van de Passe, 1622 (this state 1623)

Yet several acknowledgements of the impossibility of fixing the meaning of a text, and of other models of reading that exist outside the terms James attempts to dictate, find their way into the pages of the *Workes* itself. While such acknowledgements are implicit in moments when James uses his writings to defend himself against criticism or to attack writings by others, as we have seen in considering these writings individually in earlier chapters, the preface to the *Workes* by Bishop Montague renders them explicit. Firstly, the preface acknowledges that works of art are '*accepted or reiected, as it pleaseth the seuerall apprehensions of men to conceiue of them*', and are therefore '*subiect to so many Interpretations*' (sig. B1v). This places agency on the side of the reader; in a reversal of the king–subject power dynamic it is the King's writings that are subjected. Secondly, having acknowledged the rather democratic nature of interpretation, Montague engages with negative responses to James's writings, returning them to a context of popular judgement and resistance to his literary aspirations:

> But while I am collecting workes one way, I heare others scattering wordes as fast an other way, affirming, it had beene better his Maiestie had neuer written any Bookes at all; and being written, better they had perished with the present, like Proclamations, then haue remayned to Posterity. (sig. B2v)

This strong sense that royal utterances should not be preserved, and that proclamations are the appropriate forum for them, emphasises the difficulty for James of separating his texts not only from the present moment but from specific public expectations of royalty. Though the preface appears to justify James's use of print, it thus acknowledges that 'Whether it may sorte with the Maiestie of a King, to be a writer of Bookes, or no' is a debatable issue, ensuring that the words others have 'scatter[ed]' against royal writings are, ironically enough, preserved for posterity alongside those writings (sigs B2v–3r). This preface is, then, a significant and complex document that provides us with an insight into contemporary perceptions of royal publication, and attitudes towards book-writing more generally, and that suggests that James's prolific writing career to this point had not succeeded in changing some of these perceptions. While we cannot be sure exactly how accurately the preface represents other readers, it does – however opaquely – represent the Bishop himself as a reader of the King.[50]

Footnote no. 49 (*cont.*)

sequence also includes an undated reproduction of the picture of James in the *Workes* frontispiece, which alters the image to make it a less positive representation of the King. The image has been trimmed to remove the Bible at James's right, and the verse below the picture has been rewritten as follows: 'Kings have their Periods by Dame Natures date, / The poore man dies, so doth the Potentate; / And though to the Worlds eye Kings seeme compleater, / Their standing high makes but their fall the greater.' An engraving of Passe's portrait and this altered reproduction of the *Workes* frontispiece also appear in an illustrated version of Arthur Wilson's *Life and Reign of James I* (Folger, Art vol. b16; no date). These official images were, then, as susceptible to reappropriation as the royal books they attempt to promote.

50  Omitted from the facsimile reprint of James's *Workes* (Hildesheim and New York: Georg Olms, 1971), Montague's preface has received virtually no critical attention. Where it has

The objections to royal writing that Montague reproduces fall into three main categories. Firstly, there are objections that concern the nature of the medium: as noted
in the Introduction, above, Montague reflects the contemporary perception that the
commercialisation of the book has demeaned book-writing to the level of a profession,
the implication being that it does not require a particular talent or status but might be
practised by anyone (sig. B2v). It is therefore doubly dishonourable for the King: it
involves him in a sphere that is commercial and that does not reflect his privileged position. The list of contents at the end of Montague's preface notes which texts were originally published anonymously, reminding the reader that even the King himself was
earlier ambivalent towards publication (sig. E3r–v). Concern about the commercialisation of the book is of course prominent in the work of various writers of the period,
most notably Jonson. But such writers had an alternative to demeaning their work by
selling it: writing to patrons. James had no such alternative, and Montague labours to
emphasise this point in his dedication to Prince Charles: 'these *Workes* come not to you,
as vsually Bookes doe to men of great *Dignitie*, for *Patronage* and *Protection*; for Protection
is properly from iniurie; and that the Royall *Author* of them is best able to right' (sig.
A3v). This concern to differentiate James from court writers betrays the anxiety that
what he is doing by writing books rather aligns him with them. It also leaves it difficult
to justify why he writes at all – it is beneath him to write either for money or for patronage, but these were the existing systems within which he was located. Montague's dedication hints that royalty should only receive not produce writings, that as the King is
the source of patronage – and it is nonsensical for him to write to himself – James's
writings have a certain redundancy.

Secondly, there is the issue of the nature and content of James's writings. Montague
is particularly equivocal about those that engage in religious controversies.[51] While
the grouping of these texts in the *Workes*, in isolation from all of the responses and

Footnote 50 *(contd)*
> been considered, its ambivalence and the effect it has on the volume as a whole has not been
> sufficiently acknowledged. One of the few commentators even to mention the preface,
> Patterson, reads Montague's assertion that James's writings are a political weapon that his
> theological opponents look upon with amazement and fear (sig. C4v) as evidence that they
> caused apprehension in the Catholic world, without considering that the exercise required
> Montague to engage in this kind of rhetoric (*King James VI and I and the Reunion of Christendom*,
> p. 97). Fischlin and Fortier cite Patterson in their introduction to *Royal Subjects* without exam-
> ining the primary text (pp. 45–6). None of the contributors to *Royal Subjects* engages with
> Montague's preface. Masten briefly considers the preface's representation of the royal
> 'author', but only in terms of the notion of patriarchal authorship (*Textual Intercourse*,
> pp. 67–73).

51  Montague had in fact assisted James in the Oath of Allegiance controversy (Kenneth
    Fincham, *Prelate as Pastor: The Episcopate of James I* (Oxford: Oxford University Press, 1990),
    p. 37). His particular ambivalence towards his King's engagement in religious controversies
    thus derives at least in part from personal experience.

challenges they met, creates the impression of a one-sided debate that James won, Montague's preface returns these texts to a context of controversy. Montague recalls that, when James wrote against the Pope and Cardinal Bellarmine, there was such a commotion that there is scarce a nation '*out of which his* Maiestie *hath not receiued some answere or other; either by way of refuting, or at least by rayling*' (sig. D2r). His most suggestive reflection on this matter is that in religious controversies '*the person of a* King *is more exposed and lyes more open, then the person of a poore Scholler can doe; for as he is a farre greater marke, so he may farre more easily be hit*' (sig. D1v). Montague here implies that engaging in religious controversy is more appropriate for a scholar than for a king and that James is confusing what should be two distinct roles. While the King repeatedly tries to draw on his royal status to authorise his writings, Montague claims it is that very status that makes him open to attack. The Bishop reflects James's own awareness that writing was a form of, not an alternative to, public exposure, but adds a greater sense of the dangers of such exposure. His assertion that it is the 'person of a King' that is exposed in written debates is a reiteration of the claim of royal textual presence he had made in stating that his enemies are '*blasted by the breath of his Maiesties Bookes*', but shows the negative corollary of this authorising presence; not only the text but the King it contains may be 'hit'. He implies that by engaging with issues which produce '*diuersity of Opinions*' (sig. D1v), with people who are not subject to his authority, James is writing in a context in which his writing will not be perceived as authoritative, exposing not only his texts but his person to disagreement and vilification on a large scale. While Montague does not go so far, we might add that such engagement reveals the limits of royal authority.

Thirdly, Montague addresses the issue of the relationship between writing and acting. As noted above, in the period of the publication and republication of the *Workes*, James's pacifist stance was increasingly coming under strain, and Montague's preface responds to this in its attempt to present writing as a forceful political weapon, not an alternative to political engagement. Nevertheless, he engages with the view that '*Little it befitts the Maiesty of a* King *to turne Clerke, and to make a warre with the penne, that were fitter to be fought with the Pike*' (sig. B2v). This conveys a view of writing and acting as opposing endeavours and, again, a sense that James's writings involve him in assuming roles that are beneath him. While Montague is ostensibly reproducing such a view in order to reject it, the issue is complicated by a related comment made by James in one of the texts in the collection. In the preface to *Basilikon Doron* James claims that '*I haue euer thought it the dewtie of a worthie Prince, rather with a pike, then a penne, to write his iust reuenge*' (*Workes*, p. 145). He wrote this in the context of defending himself against accusations allegedly made against the first edition of *Basilikon Doron* (namely, that it urged his son to seek revenge for the death of Mary Queen of Scots). James's apparent elevation of the pike over the pen is itself, however, compromised by his use of writing as a metaphor to describe exacting revenge with a pike ('*to write his iust reuenge*'), and by the fact that this claim is itself made in print. This creates the impression that even when he tries to engage with the notion of military action, he cannot think outside of textual terms. Montague's reproduction of the view that war should be fought with the pike not the pen echoes – perhaps deliberately – these words of the King, inviting the reader of the *Workes* to connect them. And what the connection suggests is that James's statement in the preface to *Basilikon Doron* confirms the objection to his prioritisation of writing that Montague's preface is apparently trying to dismiss, both by on the surface suggesting the superiority of the pike to the pen, and by implicitly representing the King as unable to escape the textual. This in turn ironises and undermines the *Workes* which, as an elaborate book that brings together his extensive writings, epitomises the King writing rather than acting.

What we have seen, then, is that the *Workes* functions as a defence of itself and of the King's pacifist stance – celebrating James's writings, blurring the distinction between word and deed, and countering criticism – but at the same time it stands as a monument to the King's failure to act instead of writing. In other words, the terms of its defence could also be seen as further evidence of the tendency that it is attempting to defend. At least one contemporary publication picks up on this central instability of meaning. Thomas Scott's *Vox Regis*, a pamphlet of the early 1620s advocating war against Spain, refers to the book in order punningly to suggest that the King should turn his words into actions: Scott asserts that James's writings are '*called his* Works, *because they should be turned into workes*'.[52] The ambiguity of the word 'works', which James's collection itself attempts to exploit, could also be used to undermine it.[53]

While it is difficult to determine precisely what Montague's attitude towards his King's proclivity for writing was, he presents the following advice forcefully enough to suggest he condones it: '*If a* King *will needs write; Let him write like a* King, *euery Lyne a* Law, *euery Word a* Precept, *euery Letter a* Mandate' (sig. B2v). This is the view of word as action that had been central to the representation of the royal word since before the Jacobean period; that James tries to emphasise by associating his word with the divine word; and that Montague, at least ostensibly, tries to maintain throughout his preface. Yet the desire expressed here for James to write in a uniquely kingly way seems to arise from the anxiety, which underlies each of the objections to royal publication discussed above, that through his writings the King is slipping out of his role and assuming other roles that were not unique to his position. By presenting an ideal of kingly writing in the imperative, the preface acknowledges that a King's writing does not automatically have this unique force. Montague is admitting the possibility of – and perhaps even reflecting upon experience of – James not writing 'like a King'.

The Bishop's ideal of kingly writing is not what we might call 'literary'. Again we see one of the problems at the heart of James's writing: to a large extent he was drawing on the styles, genres, and aspirations of other contemporary writers, but, as far as at least some contemporary commentators were concerned, a king's writing should be

---

52  Thomas Scott, *Vox Regis* ([Utrecht, 1624]), preface, sig. 2v.

53  This is an example of the kind of reappropriation of James's words that Goldberg fails to acknowledge when he confidently asserts 'royal power expresses itself by giving others words' (*James I*, p. 19).

absolutely distinct from that of anyone else. James had tried in the course of his long writing career to redefine what it meant to 'write like a King', but Montague here suggests that there were still external standards of kingliness by which he could be judged. Such judgement is also discernible in the contributions made to the book in its Latin edition by two more readers of the King, the translators, Thomas Reid and Patrick Young.[54] The translators create new contexts for the texts, shifting their emphases to present them in a different light. They omit from the preface to *True Lawe* the signature in Greek 'C. Philopatris', a playful pseudonym for James that appears in all previous editions of this treatise. To the title page of *A Counterblaste to Tobacco* they add the phrase 'Lusus regius' ('royal sport').[55] This addition not only describes, or even excuses, the text to come, but shapes the reader's perception of it; the text is re-presented not as an important social and political treatise but as something not to be taken too seriously. This tendency to remove that which may seem playful, or to redefine and excuse it, suggests that the translators were trying to re-present James as 'writing like a King' according to a particular set of standards that were not his.

The translators also alter the presentation of the King's writings to shift the focus away from the general reader. In the 1616 version Montague's preface has as its running heading 'THE PREFACE / TO THE READER', but in 1619 this becomes simply '*Praefatio*'. Similarly, in the 1616 version, as in the earlier editions of each of these texts, the prefaces of *Daemonologie* and *Basilikon Doron* have 'To the Reader' as their running headings, while *True Lawe* has 'AN ADVERTISEMENT / TO THE READER', but in 1619 their running headings become 'PRAEFATIO', 'Prooemium' and 'PRAEFATIO' respectively. This is in accordance with other changes in presentation that make the Latin edition more austere, but this change seems also to have an ideological basis. The translators appear to be curtailing the attempt of James's writings to engage with the reader, making this edition feel more remote. This is analogous to – perhaps even indicative of a desire for – a style of kingship that remains aloof and mystified, as opposed to James's tendency to explain, justify, and persuade. The 'King's' *Workes*, and to an even greater extent his *Opera*, are, then, collaborative constructions that, like the court masque as described in the work of Martin Butler, incorporate and reflect numerous 'competing voices' – here, the King, Montague, the readers whose resistance is figured in the text, and the translators.[56]

The separation of the King's writings from the general reader represented within the *Opera* was extended in the giving of presentation copies to both the universities. In 1620 a copy bound in red velvet, with the royal arms stamped in gold on the side, and a Latin inscription, headed by the King's autograph signature and subscribed by Secretary

---

54  Patrick Young was the son of Peter Young, who had been tutor to James in his youth, and royal librarian from 1609 to 1647 (Warner (ed.), *The Library of James VI*, p. xv).

55  James, *Opera*, pp. 179, 198.

56  See Butler, 'Courtly Negotiations' in Bevington and Holbrook (eds), *The Politics of the Stuart Court Masque*, pp. 20–40; and 'Ben Jonson and the Limits of Courtly Panegyric'.

Calvert, was given to the Bodleian Library. This was carried to Oxford by a special dep-
utation including Patrick Young, and was received by Oxford University with great ceremony. The library keeper's speech for the occasion describes wondering 'what place
can be found good enough for so incomparable a treasure?' and placing it in the
Bodleian's archives, noting 'nothing vulgar here, nothing common to the mass'.[57] Here,
then, we see James's *Opera* being treated with the kind of reverence and admiration he
desired for his writings, and we see it being – unlike many of his writings – purpose-
fully kept separate from the masses. But, as we have seen, this required, or at least followed, James's original writings being altered by others. The case of this Latin edition
thus reflects the tension inherent in James's desire to represent the mystique of kingship; the translators and the officials of the Bodleian Library seem to have realised that
for this book to have mystique it must be kept separate from the majority of readers.
James presumably approved of their treatment of his book, but his continuing desire
to communicate with his subjects more widely is apparent in his decision to reprint his
*Workes* in English in 1620, an act that to some extent undoes the attempt of the translators and library officials to elevate those works beyond his subjects.

### James, Ben Jonson, and the authorisation of the author

By publishing and republishing his *Workes*, the King was, then, participating in a literary marketplace in ways that might diminish the distance between the King and his subjects. This is further illuminated by comparing his collection to that of a writer who
frequently wrote for him and to whom much credit for shaping that marketplace has
been given: Ben Jonson. For those people who, according to Montague's preface to
James's *Workes*, were critical of the King's book-writing, the fact that King and court
writer both produced comparably ambitious and ostentatious folio collections of their
own works in the same year may have provided further evidence that, far from writing
'like a King', James was writing like a writer. Further, the relationship between these two
collections suggests the co-dependence of political and literary authority.

As noted above, many contemporary literary collections were of great writers from
the past, and what collections of contemporary literary works did precede 1616
tended to contain predominantly poetry. No monarch had ever published their writings as a collection, and no playwright had ever published plays written for the public

---

57   The library keeper further stated that 'Henry VIII wrote certain sheets against Luther, which
     were so valued at Rome, that to this day they hold no mean place in the caskets of the
     Vatican. But what are they, compared to the writings of James? Like tradesmen's tokens in
     comparison with good coins of the realm.' Cambridge University had also been sent James's
     collection but had received it with less ceremony, although the Public Orator, George
     Herbert, returned thanks in a Latin letter of acknowledgement, representing the book as a
     weapon against Jesuits (William Dunn Macray, *Annals of the Bodleian Library* (Oxford: Oxford
     University Press, 1890), pp. 58–62; speeches translated by Macray from the original Latin).

stage – an often denigrated form – as a collection. James and Jonson not only employed the format of a collected works in equally unprecedented ways but attempted to redefine that format. Both were seeking to elevate and monumentalise their *own* writing, and to construct their collection to reflect the range and chronology of their careers, which in both cases stretch back into the Elizabethan period (the first text in James's collection, *A Paraphrase vpon the Reuelation*, was written in the 1580s, the first in that of Jonson, *Every Man in His Humour*, was written in 1598). This meant including material previously considered unsuitable for such collections, particularly texts that were performed – speeches to parliament, and plays, masques and, entertainments respectively.

In this attempt simultaneously to redefine the format of collected works and reshape their long literary careers, both writers faced perceptions of inappropriateness – inappropriateness in terms of the status of the author in the case of James, and inappropriateness in terms of the status of dramatic texts in the case of Jonson.[58] Both responded to such perceptions by taking great care to dignify, justify, and authorise their collections within the collections themselves, and making the presentation of the collections impressive and lavish.[59] Jonson, like other early modern authors, needed to draw on external sources of authority to authorise his work, but, as many critics have noted, was exceptionally concerned with attempting to assert his own authority.[60] The main external authority Jonson drew on was the work of classical writers, but he does so in such a way as to make bold claims for his own work. As Richard C. Newton suggests, Jonson 'labors throughout his writing, through allusion and imitation, to appropriate to himself the epithet "classical"', and 'in the 1616 *Workes*, his translation of the Latin *opera* specifically makes the claim that Jonson as a writer is a classic'.[61] What has not been considered is that this is analogous to James's use of the Bible as a source of authorisation. While the different authorities on which the two draw – classical and divine respectively – reflect their very different position in society, the particular ways in which they draw on them are closely related, as is highlighted by comparing the presentation of the two 1616 folios.

58 Jonson's collection would indeed attract satiric comment. For example Suckling wrote of Jonson in verses published in 1646, 'he told them plainly he deserv'd the Bayes, / For his were calld Works, where others were but Plaies' (C. H. Herford and Percy and Evelyn Simpson (eds), *Ben Jonson*, 11 vols (Oxford: Oxford University Press, 1925–52, IX, 13).

59 See Gants, 'The Printing of Jonson's Folio *Workes*', for a detailed analysis of Jonson's involvement in the printing of the folio, and Douglas A. Brooks, *From Playhouse to Printing House: Drama and Authorship in Early Modern England* (Cambridge: Cambridge University Press, 2000), pp. 104–39, for a discussion of the inconsistent nature of this involvement.

60 Tribble, for example, suggests that in his earlier work Jonson uses plural external authorities, including royal authority, but that he moves towards abandoning such authorities in 'an early anticipation of the eighteenth-century construction of the literary subject, of the authored – and owned – text' (*Margins and Marginality*, p. 10).

61 Newton, 'Jonson and the (Re-)invention of the Book', pp. 39, 37.

We have seen that the frontispiece of James's *Workes* implies that the King's book is informed by God's book and that the King is like God in the power of his word. This is paralleled by the engraved portrait of Jonson produced in the mid-1620s and subsequently bound in to some copies of his 1616 *Workes*.[62] While this frontispiece is thus not part of Jonson's collection as originally constructed, it does seem, like James's frontispiece, to reflect some of the claims the collection implicitly makes. The portrait depicts Jonson as a classical poet, complete with laurel wreath, with books at either side. As James's frontispiece implies that his word is like God's word and should be treated as such, so that added to Jonson's collection implies that his writings are worthy of the status of classical texts, comparable to the works of Seneca and Homer that his contemporaries and rivals were translating and publishing in folio in the same period. As the image of James supports his claim to be God's representative on earth, so that of Jonson supports his claim to be the representative of a poetic tradition. Moreover, on the frontispiece added to Jonson's *Workes* is an inscription in Latin that presents the picture of Jonson as the 'true image of the greatest teacher of English poetry', and this echoes the pedagogic stance that James adopts towards his readers in, for example, his scriptural exegeses. Both James and Jonson are represented as being capable, like the authorities on which they draw, of teaching others; as they refer to various texts, so others are invited to refer to theirs.

If the title page of James's *Workes* is one of the most elaborate of English examples, then the title page of Jonson's *Workes* is not far behind, and the two are strikingly similar (see figures 5 and 9). They have similar architectural designs, with key figures in the niches between the pillars at either side of the central panel. Such architectural designs for title pages were not only common in bibles of the period but also feature in Thomas Lodge's translation of the *Workes* of Seneca (1614) and George Chapman's translation of *The Whole Works of Homer* (1616?). Thus the design reinforces the association between James's book and the Bible, and between Jonson's book and the works of his classical precursors. The figures at the sides of Jonson's title page are the muses of 'Tragoedia' and 'Comoedia'. This implies that his career and book are supported by the precepts of classical theatre, as the figure of 'religio' on James's title page implies that religion is the support of his reign and book. At both top corners of Jonson's title page we see laurel, implying that this is what his career and book lead towards, as the celestial crown at the top of James's title page implies that the divine is what his reign and book point towards. Jonson's title page presents a quotation from Horace as that of James presents a quotation from the Bible. On both title pages the words 'The Workes' and the author's name are given similar prominence by being placed in the central panel. In both cases then, the author is at the centre, supported by and aspiring towards the classical and the divine respectively.

62  Mark Bland, 'William Stansby and the Production of *The Workes of Beniamin Jonson, 1615–16*', *The Library: The Transactions of the Bibliographical Society*, 20 (1998), 1–33 (p. 24n). For the engraved portrait see the first leaf of some copies of Ben Jonson, *The Workes of Beniamin Jonson* (London: William Stansby, 1616).

9 Title page of *The Workes of Beniamin Jonson* (London: William Stansby, 1616)

After the title pages, the reader of the King's *Workes* encounters, as we have seen, a dedication and preface by the Bishop, Montague, while the reader of Jonson's *Workes* encounters a series of contemporary poems. As Montague is a representative of the church, his support of James's book reinforces the King's claims of proximity to God. Likewise, the contributions to Jonson's *Workes* by a number of contemporary poets emphasise Jonson's important place in a continuing poetic tradition. James's *Workes* then includes his interpretations of Scripture and his secular writings which also draw on the Bible, often adopting the practice of placing the biblical reference in the margins. Jonson's *Workes* includes his interpretations of classical forms, such as the epigram, and his use of new forms such as the court masque, which also incorporate classical ideas and references. Again, his classical references are often placed in the margins of his texts. Thus throughout both *Workes* divine and classical authorities respectively are appropriated in an attempt to present the collections themselves as comparable to those authorities. The implied status of the collections is reflected in their employment of the folio format, which, as noted above, was usually reserved for serious and important works. This association supports the lofty claims James and Jonson are making for the authority of their writings.

Unlike the King, Jonson was also drawing on patrons as external sources of authority, and one of the sources of patronage and authority he advertised in his *Workes* was of course that of James himself. Again, however, Jonson is not only drawing on James as an external source of authority but also appropriating that authority to serve his own ends. In particular James had validated poetry through his own practice, and had presented the roles of poet and king as complementary; Jonson appropriates this aspect of James's self-representation in order to present himself as poet as though on a level with the King. For example, Jonson's *Panegyre, on the Happy Entrance of Iames, Our Soueraigne, to His First High Session of Parliament in this His Kingdome, the 19 of March, 1603*, which appears in his *Workes*, ends 'Solus Rex, aut Poeta non quotannis nascitur' (only the King and the Poet are not born every day).[63] Jonson is thus suggesting a kind of equivalence between himself and the King, and, to the extent that James's own writing makes it easier for Jonson to make this suggestion, this reflects the King's failure to write in a uniquely kingly manner. Whether the external authority is classical or royal then, Jonson not only refers to it but uses it as a basis for self-authorisation, to a degree that sets him aside from many of his contemporary writers but is comparable to James's engagement with biblical authority.

The attempts of both James and Jonson to authorise their own texts through other texts are, however, inherently self-defeating. Jonson explicitly advocated moving beyond classical writings: 'I know nothing can conduce more to letters than to examine the writings of the ancients, and not to rest in their sole authority . . . It is true they opened the gates and made the way, that went before us; but as guides not commanders.'[64] Yet the more James and Jonson attempt to reinforce their authority as authors through their manipulations and appropriations of the texts they have read, the more – paradoxically – they implicitly

63  Jonson, *Workes*, p. 868.
64  Jonson, *Timber: or Discoveries*, in Donaldson (ed.), *Ben Jonson*, p. 525.

acknowledge that their texts might also be susceptible to such treatment in the hands of readers not content to 'rest in their sole authority'. This paradox is exemplified even on the title pages of their collections: the biblical and classical quotations help to authorise their texts and exemplify the kind of authority James and Jonson want their own texts to have, but the quotations also compete with, and function independently of, that authority, and demonstrate how words may be reappropriated.

Neither writer, then, is a fixed source of authority, but rather both are participants in a process of authority being created through exchange as they variously borrow authority from, and lend authority to, kingship, other writers, and the divine. The relationship between the writings of James and Jonson is, then, analogous to what we found in considering both the poetry of James and his early poetic circle in Chapter 1, and the relationship between his *Workes* and the King James Bible above. As an author Jonson draws on royal authority to authorise his work, but the King himself is trying to reinforce his authority through authorship. James, as King and patron, has the political and social authority on which Jonson needs to draw, but at the same time Jonson, as a successful writer, has the literary authority which James wants for himself. It is through his ability as a writer that Jonson gains himself willing publishers and a readership. As King, James automatically has these two things, but he does not necessarily have the writing ability to win admiration and support that Jonson has. This relationship complicates any attempt to judge which of the *Workes* published in 1616 has more 'authority', and suggests that both writers – despite their differences in status and role – recognised that textual authority needed to draw on both the literary and the political.

James's *Workes* thus exists in an uncomfortable relation to its literary context. For just as the collection both engages with and seeks to transcend its political moment, so it exploits the literary associations of its format while trying to present the King's writings as unique. The collection succeeded in preserving his works for future readers, but not in preventing the King from meeting further criticism and opposition, nor in being widely recognised as a major literary work. Nevertheless, he was participating in a literary marketplace and his concerns and aspirations were analogous to those of other contemporary writers. This marketplace was not, as far as his detractors were concerned, an accepted arena for royal authority, but at least his *Workes* was an impressive and dignified publication that could function as a symbol of that authority. As either cause or effect of his decision to publish his *Workes*, the collection does seem to have had an 'air of finality and completeness' for James in so far as he published no further major works after the 1620 edition. In the final years of his reign he would return to writing poetry that circulated only in manuscript. This poetry, some of which engages with manuscript verse libel, exists at the opposite end of the spectrum from the *Workes* in terms of its material authority and symbolic capital. As we will see in the following chapter, this poetry in various ways registers the fissures that were more and more evident in James's political position, and that had always been inherent in his attempt to be both King and author.

# 5

# The late poetry and the deconstruction of authority

If euer in the Aprill of my dayes
I satt vpon Parnassus forked hill:
And there inflam'd with sacred fury still
By pen proclaim'd our great Apollo's praise.[1]

In these lines of 1621 James reflects upon the poetic endeavours of his youth, implies the extent of his writing career, and even recalls, as we shall consider in more detail below, specific works of that period in his language and grammatical structure. In this regard this poem – like his decision to collect all of his prose writings in his *Workes* of 1616 and his preparation of the manuscript collection 'All the Kings short poesis that ar not printed' around 1616–18 – suggests that in the final years of his reign James was concerned to consolidate his image as a mature author.[2] Yet, at the same time, his writings after 1616 also mark a return to his beginnings as a writer in terms of the genres he prioritised. After publishing his *Workes*, James's attention turned away from secular prose – this climactic publication symbolically as well as literally marked the effective end of his career as a secular prose writer.[3] He turned back towards the genres that he had employed

---

1 James, 'A Vow or Wish for the felicity & fertility of the owners of this house', Craigie (ed.), *Poems*, II, 177 (based on MS Rawlinson Poet. 26).
2 For discussion of James's *Workes* and 'All the Kings short poesis that ar not printed', which may have been intended for publication alongside the *Workes*, though this did not take place, see Chapter 4, above.
3 The only new secular prose works issued in the King's name between 1616 and 1620 were *A Declaration of Sports* (1617) and *The Peace-Maker: or, Great Brittaines Blessing* (1618), but James's decision not to include either in the 1620 reissue of his *Workes* suggests they did not come within his conception of his authorship. *A Declaration of Sports* was written by Thomas Norton, though James may have made some revisions (see Craigie (ed.), *Minor Prose Works*, pp. 217–37). *The Peace-Maker* has been attributed to Thomas Middleton in Gary Taylor and John Lavagnino (gen. eds), *The Collected Works of Thomas Middleton* (Oxford: Oxford University Press, forthcoming). After 1620 James printed only *His Maiesties Speach in the Vpper House of Parliament 1621* (1621); *His Maiesties Declaration, Touching His Proceedings in the Late Assemblie and Conuention of Parliament* (1622); and *The Kings Maiesties Letter Touching Preaching, and Preachers* (1622), containing his directions for preachers.

in the troubled years of his early Scottish reign – poetry and scriptural exegeses.[4] Like that earlier period, the final years of James's reign were marked by widespread opposition and political difficulty. This was the result, in particular, of the power and influence of his favourite George Villiers, created Earl of Buckingham (and later Duke); his unwillingness to adopt a militaristic foreign policy; and his related policy of pursuing a Spanish marriage for Prince Charles.[5] Perhaps James still believed that in such hostile climates poetry and scriptural exegeses were a better means of reinforcing his image than the more explicitly political works of the middle years of his reign.

In James's early Scottish reign, opposition to royal authority had circulated in various forms, including satirical poetry, and his policy had been simultaneously to quash such representations while writing, and encouraging others to write, the kind of poetry that might bolster his image. Similarly, the criticism of king and court in the last years of his reign often took the form of manuscript verse as this provided a way of avoiding censorship.[6] James responded, as he had in Scotland, with a dual strategy of trying to censor all opposition while at the same time providing alternative poetic representations of his authority. There are, however, some significant shifts in the King's use of poetry from the early years of his Scottish reign to the last years of his English.

Firstly, he no longer engaged explicitly with other poets as fellow poet, patron, or translator to the extent that he had in the earlier period. This meant that James's claimed poetic authority now lacked reinforcement from other quarters; in keeping with the overall progression of his career, his late poetry presents him as an autonomous, independent author. Thus while the collections of poetry he published in 1584 and 1591 each contain a series of commendatory verses contributed by other writers, the royal manuscript collection 'All the Kings short poesis that ar not printed' contains no commendatory material. Equally, James did not engage in the practice of contributing commendatory sonnets to the works of other writers to the extent that, as we saw in the first chapter, he did in Scotland. This suggests that he had not established the same intimate and reciprocal relationship with the writers he encountered in England as he had with other writers in Scotland.[7]

---

4  While the last years of James's reign involve neither a sudden return to poetry (he seems to have written poetry from time to time throughout his reign) nor poetry writing on the scale of the 1580s and early 1590s, he wrote poetry more regularly in the years 1618–23 than he had in the intervening years (seven poems attributed to James survive from this period). As we shall see, in this period poetry again assumes a central role in royal public relations. He wrote two scriptural exegeses after 1616, *A Meditation vpon the Lords Prayer* (1619) and *A Meditation vpon St. Matthew* (1620), both of which he included in the reissue of his *Workes* (1620).

5  For a brief overview of the main events and developments of this period see the Introduction.

6  Marotti, *Manuscript*, p. 76.

7  Perry offers an interesting discussion of the difficulties poets in England experienced in responding to James's self-styling as a poet in *The Making of Jacobean Culture*, but more work needs to be done on the differences between the literary cultures of James's Scottish and English courts.

Secondly, his late poems deal much more directly and explicitly with political matters than his earlier poems had done. In the early years of his Scottish reign James had used poetry to reinforce and promote his image, and to reflect his authority, in general, indirect ways; his poems never risked being politically inflammatory. Some of his late poems, conversely, unflinchingly rehearse the arguments of divine right kingship, address complaints and fears about the crown, and offer specific instructions to their readers. In other words James is no longer using this literary form as a discreet means of prosecuting his political aims, but rather he is using it as a vehicle for explicitly political material. This makes these poems the fullest realisation of his attempt to forge a direct link between literature and politics.

Thirdly, there is a major shift in terms of the nature of the dissemination of James's poems. The vast majority of James's earlier poetry had been printed, or was included in 'All the Kings short poesis that ar not printed'. The poems he wrote from 1618 onwards, however, were not printed, or even collected.[8] Moreover, while the poems that were not printed in the earlier period reached, as noted in Chapter 1, only a small number of readers, these late poems have survived in numerous copies in private poetical miscellanies and other manuscript collections of the time, indicating relatively wide circulation. Given how careful James had earlier been to control manuscript circulation of his poetry, its sudden increase seems likely a reflection of his intentions: he is no longer using manuscript circulation for the poems he wanted to keep semi-private, but for poems he wanted to make public to a specific readership.[9] And this was not necessarily a small readership. One of James's most widely circulated manuscript poems, 'On the death of Queene Anne' of 1619, exists in more than thirty contemporary manuscript collections.[10] We might compare this to the fifteen or so extant copies of his *Opera Regia* – the prestigious Latin edition of his works, copies of which were

8   This makes it difficult to be certain that James was sole author of any of this group of poems, but this book has argued for adopting his broad definition of 'authorship' (see, in particular, the Introduction). Rather than lessening the relevance or significance of this group of poems, the questions of attribution and the authority of any version are, as we shall see, integral to – and illuminating of – the participation of verse associated with the King in manuscript culture.

9   For a list of the manuscripts containing James's unprinted poems which clearly shows this shift see May, 'Circulation in Manuscript'. One exception to which May draws attention is his poem to Buckingham of 1621, which was not circulated in manuscript. As we shall see below, this poem is distinct from the others of this period in that it does not explicitly address political affairs and seems addressed to an exclusively courtly audience. This would seem to be, then, the exception that proves the rule: James was still capable of limiting manuscript circulation, but chose to allow it for most of his poems of this period.

10  May lists 32 in 'Circulation in Manuscript', and, since completing this article, has discovered that there are at least six more texts of the poem with a variant in the first line ("'Twas thee to Invite' for 'Thee to Invite'). I am grateful to Steve May for sharing this work with me.

presented to the universities – of the same year.[11] Given the uncertainty of the relationship between the number of copies that survive and the number of copies that
were in circulation at the time, it is difficult to draw precise conclusions from these
figures. However, they do suggest that for James the choice between print and manuscript circulation was not a choice between wide and limited circulation. Rather, it was
a choice between different, though no doubt in some cases overlapping, readerships,
and between the different associations of the two media.

James's circulation of his late poems in manuscript relates, as we shall see, to a rise
in the exchange of news, comment, and libel in the form of manuscript verse. He seems
to have realised that this was a sphere of representation that was difficult to censor and
that could be penetrated only in kind – with short manuscript poems that could be
easily passed around, transcribed, and even memorised, not with expensive printed
books.[12] As Curtis Perry argues, by injecting his voice into the decentralised form of
discourse represented by manuscript verse, James was trying to extend his 'powers of
"discursive imposition" beyond the immediate reach of the law' and to reassert his centrality.[13] At the opposite end of the cultural spectrum from his prestigious *Workes*,
James's late poetry thus further demonstrates his consciousness of the need to address
different audiences in different ways; his belief that his word should have authority
whatever medium he writes in; and his desire to control through direct participation
all the spheres of discourse in which he might be represented or invoked. This meant,
however, descending to the level of his detractors; worse still, these poems were circulating at a time when his subjects were also appropriating various of his earlier writings
as a means of opposing his current policies.

This chapter explores the specific political uses to which James tried to put his poetry
of 1618–23, and argues that this body of poetry illuminates and extends the problems
of being a writer–king that have emerged throughout this book. It also outlines the
specific political uses to which some of his earlier writings were put by his subjects in
this period, suggesting the extent to which James's self-representation through writing
had empowered his readers. In other words this chapter looks more closely at James's
inadvertent engagement in what Donne termed a 'conversation' with his subjects – a
mode of communication that did not enable the King simply to dictate, but rather that

11  According to the *ESTC*, fourteen libraries, including a number of cathedral and Oxford
    college libraries, have copies. Each has only one copy, except the British Library which has
    two.

12  It may also be the case that, as Kevin Sharpe argues, James regarded personal interventions
    as more authoritative than printed proclamations and statutes (Foreword, Fischlin and
    Fortier (eds), *Royal Subjects*, pp. 15–36 (p. 20)). Moreover, as Andrew McRae points out, most
    major writers of the period valorised manuscript circulation, with the result, he suggests,
    that even topical or libellous verse might acquire a degree of literary status by virtue of cir-
    culating in this form (*Literature, Satire and the Early Stuart State* (Cambridge: Cambridge
    University Press, 2004), p. 41).

13  Perry, ' "If Proclamations Will Not Serve" ', p. 210.

enabled the reader/subject to respond. The chapter begins by looking at a series of texts that have the very specific agenda of defending the King's unpopular favourite, Buckingham, from the criticism he was increasingly facing, and thus illuminate James's belief in the political potential of his poetry. It then addresses several poems that, in attempting to counter public discussion more generally, further reveal the ways in which the King's poems of this period were not only reactive but also exist in a complex inter-relationship with the discussion they attempt to subdue. The third section is devoted to what is perhaps the most remarkable of James's poems, 'King Iames his verses made vpon a Libell lett fall in Court and entituled "The wiper of the Peoples teares / The dryer vpp of doubts & feares" ' (1622/3). This poem exemplifies the anxieties and con-tradictions that royal writing involves, and represents the culmination of a process of James yielding authority to his subjects through his writing. The final section examines the ways in which certain of James's earlier writings were being used as fuel for the very opposition that he was seeking to contain with further writing, emphasising the fun-damental irreconcilability of his project for his writing with actual processes of reading and interpretation. In this final chapter, then, we see that the King's attempt to main-tain a mutually reinforcing relationship between his political and textual authority ulti-mately exposed the limitations of both forms of authority.

## 'Now let us reioice sing Peans all / For Buckingham is now made Admirall': defending the royal favourite

George Villiers rapidly rose to a position of wealth and power from 1616 onwards; bestowed with royal favours, created Earl of Buckingham in 1617 and Duke in 1623, he was by 1620 among the wealthier members of early Stuart society, and, according to one biographer, 'the major single political influence at court'.[14] He was not, however, of noble blood and his elevation offended many people, especially amongst the ancient peerage.[15] In 1628, three years after James's death, Buckingham would be assassinated by a soldier who maintained he believed that his act would do 'his country great service', and was lauded in popular verse.[16] Unsurprisingly, then, the rise of Buckingham, and his alleged corruption and influence over the King, was a favourite topic amongst

14  Roger Lockyer, *Buckingham* (London and New York: Longman, 1981), pp. 61, 65.

15  Lawrence Stone, *The Crisis of the Aristocracy* (Oxford: Oxford University Press, 1965), p. 123. In 1622 Girolamo Lando wrote of the favourite that people 'cannot endure that one born a simple gentlemen [*sic*], a rank slightly esteemed there, should be the sole access to the Court, the sole means of favour' (*Calendar of State Papers, Venetian*, ed. Rawdon Brown *et al.* (vols XIII to XVIII for 1613–25 ed. Allen B. Hinds), 38 vols (London, 1864–1947), XVII (1621–3), 439). Buckingham's 1623 promotion was still more controversial: he 'was the first duke for nearly a century to have no royal blood in his veins' (Lockyer, *Buckingham*, p. 155).

16  For this claim see Bodleian MS Rawl. B 183, 191. For contemporary verse on Buckingham's assassination see Frederick W. Fairholt, *Poems and Songs Relating to George Villiers, Duke of Buckingham; and His Assassination by John Felton* (London: Percy Society, 1850).

satirists and libellers, whose criticisms of the favourite could imply indirect criticism of the monarch who favoured him.[17] One of the poems circulated upon Buckingham's death exemplifies the perception of the favourite as hated and dangerous:

If heaven admitt of treason, pride & lust
Expect a damned soule among ye just
The Countreys bayne the Courtiers hate
An agent for the Spanish state
The Romish friend the gospells foe
The Church and kingdome overthrow.

In one contemporary manuscript miscellany, this energetic denunciation of Buckingham follows the King's own poem on the death of his Queen. This juxtaposition emphasises that such satirical verses had the potential to compete with any writings the King produced.[18]

As Buckingham attracted more and more criticism, James was evidently keen to defend him, and, by extension, his own integrity in having chosen to elevate him. He made some attempt to bolster Buckingham's image through his own printed works. He dedicated *A Meditation vpon the Lords Prayer* (1619) to his favourite and justified doing so in the preface by stating that Buckingham gives '*so good example to the rest of the Court, in frequent hearing the word of God*' and '*in so often receiuing the Sacrament, which is a notable demonstration of your charitie in pardoning them that offend you*'.[19] This emphasis on Buckingham's piety seems carefully designed to counter the perception, expressed in the verse quoted above, that he is 'the gospells foe', while claiming he sets a pious example to the rest of the court challenges the perception that he leads the court in immorality and extravagance. The King was evidently aware that Buckingham was meeting opposition,

---

17  See Marotti, *Manuscript*, p. 83. Marotti later notes that 'By far the largest number of topical political poems about a person other than a reigning monarch was associated with George Villiers' (p. 107). Another topic much represented in manuscript libel was the Essex affair and the Overbury murder (see Bellany, *Court Scandal*). The other issue to attract most attention was the Spanish match negotiations, as we shall consider more below. For further discussion of manuscript verse libel in the Jacobean period see McRae, *Literature, Satire and the Early Stuart State*, esp. pp. 23–82; Thomas Cogswell, 'Underground Verse and the Transformation of Early Stuart Political Culture', in Susan D. Amussen and Mark A. Kishlansky (eds), *Political Culture and Cultural Politics in Early Modern England* (Manchester: Manchester University Press, 1995), pp. 277–300; Alastair Bellany, ' "Rayling Rymes and Vaunting Verse": Libellous Politics in Early Stuart England, 1603–1628', in Sharpe and Lake (eds), *Culture and Politics*, pp. 285–310; and Adam Fox, 'Popular Verses and Their Readership in the Early Seventeenth Century', in James Raven, Helen Small, and Naomi Tadmor (eds), *The Practice and Representation of Reading in England* (Cambridge: Cambridge University Press, 1996), pp. 125–37.

18  British Library, Egerton 923, 'Vpon the duke of Buckingham' appears on fol. 45v, and 'King James on Queene Annes death', which we will consider more below, on fol. 45r.

19  James, *Workes* (1620), p. 573.

acknowledging as much in referring to '*them that offend you*', and of the nature of that opposition. Indeed, the publication of this work amounts to an acknowledgement that the royal favourite needs to be publicly defended; James was failing to transcend the debates Buckingham was causing. A year later he employed Buckingham as his amanuensis for *A Meditation vpon St. Matthew* (1620), a fact that he reveals in the dedication, which is to Prince Charles.[20] The King was thereby partly transferring to his favourite the role of acting as the mediator of God's word for others, using the same strategy for enhancing his favourite's status that he had long been using for himself. By going to such lengths to defend his favourite, however, the King risked adding to the perception that he was dominated by him.

In manuscript poems, which were, perhaps, aimed more specifically at Buckingham's detractors, James seems still more anxious to generate support for his favourite. In 1619 he appointed Buckingham as Admiral of the Fleet, and wrote a poem encouraging universal celebration of this appointment that begins, as quoted above, 'Now let us reioice sing Peans all / For Buckingham is now made Admirall'.[21] Yet the opening 'now', which might be read as acknowledging that such celebration would be a change from what has gone before; the shift from 'let us reioice' to the imperative 'sing', and the emphasis placed on 'all', betray an anxiety that the promotion of an unpopular favourite was in reality unlikely to be celebrated by many. Such anxiety appears more prominently in the final lines of the poem:

> Why then should any grudge that favour graces
> The meritt of one person with two places
> Since it is soe amongst the states of heaven
> Where none dare doubt but things are carried even.                (15–18)

Although the question is here rhetorical, it reveals James's awareness that there were in fact many people who begrudged the favour he bestowed on Buckingham. His strategy in this poem is to propose that the order on earth is the same as the divine order, and none dare question the divine order so nor should they question that order as reproduced on earth. Yet the implication remains that whereas 'none dare doubt' in heaven, the King has not quite managed to reproduce that situation on earth. He thus seems aware that his poem is swimming against the current of opinion, but hopeful that it may help to reverse the trend.

James's most intriguing use of his own writing to defend and promote Buckingham came two years later. In August 1621 Buckingham, who was newly married, entertained the King at his new home, Burley-on-the-Hill. Buckingham provided entertainment that on 3 August included Ben Jonson's masque, *The Gypsies Metamorphosed*, in which Buckingham

---

20  James, *Workes* (1620), p. 602.
21  James, 'To the Duke of Buckingham' (Craigie (ed.), *Poems*, II, 176 (based on MS Egerton 2725)). In some manuscripts this is accompanied by a verse in Latin that is attributed to James, but this is elsewhere attributed to Sir Robert Ayton who is its more likely author (see Craigie, p. 259n).

played the leading gypsy and was given lines in which he praised the King.[22] James responded by not only writing the poem with which this chapter began but reading it aloud to Buckingham and his wife at a banquet on the very next day. The King was returning the praise he had received the day before, and emphasising that he too was a poet:

> If euer in the Aprill of my dayes
> I satt vpon Parnassus forked hill:
> And there inflam'd with sacred fury still
> By pen proclaim'd our great Apollo's praise:
> Grant glistringe Phoebus with thy golden rayes
> My earnest wish which I present thee heere:
> Beholdinge of this blessed couple deere,
> Whose vertues pure no pen can duly blaze.
> Thow by whose heat the trees in fruit abound
> Blesse them with fruit delicious sweet & fayre,
> That may succeed them in theyr vertues rare.
> ffirme plant them in theyr natiue soyle & ground.
>     Thow Jove, that art the onely God indeed,
>     My prayer heare: sweet Jesu interceed.[23]

The sonnet not only makes explicit reference to his earlier poetry but also implies the length of his poetic career, and enacts its continuation. The poem thus presents the King as a poet, through both reference and demonstration, and not as a king.

The ways in which this poem recalls James's earlier poetic career exceed what it acknowledges. Firstly, it is strikingly similar to the opening lines of the wedding masque that, as we saw in Chapter 1, James had written in 1588, a full thirty-three years earlier. The masque begins: 'If euer I ô mightie Gods haue done yow seruice true / In setting furth by painefull pen your glorious praises due'.[24] Both pieces follow the structure 'If ever I . . . then grant me this', as both ask God to grant the King's wish for the married couple in return for the service he has rendered through his poetry. This may suggest that James used the masque as a model for writing the sonnet. What is surprising, however, is that both begin with the same questioning note ('If ever'); despite the passage of time, James is still maintaining a stance of poetic humility. Secondly, the opening line of the sonnet echoes earlier poems by other poets. Du Bartas's dedication of *L'Vranie* begins 'Je n'estoy point encor en l'Auril de mon aage', which James rendered in his translation of 1584 as 'Scarce was I yet in springtyme of my years'.[25] The French

22  Buckingham had moved into Burley-on-the-Hill, a great estate in Rutland, during the early summer of 1621 (Lockyer *Buckingham*, p. 63). For a discussion of the masque see Martin Butler, '"We are one mans all": Jonson's *The Gypsies Metamorphosed*', *Yearbook of English Studies*, 21 (1991), 253–73.

23  Craigie (ed.), *Poems*, II, 177.

24  BL Add. MS 24195, fol. 52r.

25  Both versions are given in James, *Essayes of a Prentise*, sigs C4v–D1r.

version, in particular, is recalled in James's sonnet, which also employs 'April' as a term that suggests the beginnings of maturity. This sonnet also faintly echoes the thirty-first sonnet of Daniel's *Delia* (1592), which uses 'April' in a similar way, beginning 'The starre of my mishap impos'd this payning, / To spend the Aprill of my yeeres in wayling'.[26] Thirdly, James's 1621 poem recalls the past in its sonnet form. In the 1580s the King himself had written a number of sonnets, and in the 1590s a vogue for sonnets had swept England. By 1621, however, that vogue had long faded. His employment of the sonnet form at this time thus creates a sense of nostalgia. This echoing of earlier texts and choice of the sonnet form may reveal a desire, whether conscious or not, to return to earlier days of poetic and political promise.

Moreover, in his 1621 sonnet James seems to be trying to re-emphasise his literary credentials. According to the Venetian ambassador, Girolamo Lando, after reading out his verses James even 'ordered that they should be written on the walls, and carved in the marble of the doors, for a perpetual memorial'.[27] This grand gesture suggests the King's desire to memorialise his poetry and preserve his image as poet for posterity, albeit within a highly elite context. Ironically, however, the poem itself functions as a memorial to his earlier poetry in ways that suggest his failure to progress as a poet or to keep up with changing poetic fashions, and this literary aspiration towards memorialisation was, as we shall see below, increasingly problematic for the King. Given the self-consciously literary nature of his poem, the fact that the reading took place the very day after the performance of Jonson's masque is significant. James had had the opportunity to see the extent of Jonson's literary success, culminating in his publication of his *Workes* in 1616, and was evidently impressed by his latest masque.[28] By responding with a poem of his own James seems, though this could never have been acknowledged, to be trying to match Jonson, and, again, to be trying to draw to himself the kind of literary fame Jonson was achieving.

At the same time, the 1621 sonnet is politically significant, even though, unlike other royal poems of these years, it does not explicitly portray James as a king or engage directly with current political affairs. This is illuminated by the parallels between the circumstances surrounding this performance and those surrounding his 1588 masque. The masque celebrated the marriage of a Catholic favourite at a time when the Spanish Armada was on its way northwards and James was still bargaining with Elizabeth. He may have hoped that this court occasion would encourage England to meet his demands by serving as a warning that he had the potential to support Catholics, but in a manner subtle enough that he could continue to keep his options open. The masque's

26  Samuel Daniel, *Delia. Containing Certaine Sonnets: With the Complaynt of Rosamond* (London: J. C. for S. Watersonne, 1592), sig. E4r.

27  Girolamo Lando, despatch to the Doge and Senate (27 August 1621), *C.S.P., Ven.*, XVII, 117.

28  *The Gypsies Metamorphosed* was so well received that, unusually for a masque, it was performed two further times, at Belvoir on 5 August and at Windsor, probably early in September, in a revised version (Herford and Simpson (eds), *Ben Jonson*, VII, 541).

emphasis on his poetic rather than his royal identity was thus politically useful; it allowed him to make a statement but also to disassociate any such statement from his actual policies if circumstances should change. The masque thus served a particular political purpose while, or even by, appearing to be apolitical. In 1621 James was again showing support for a favourite in a context that made this particularly controversial. Not only was Buckingham highly unpopular, but in the 1621 parliament he was indirectly attacked over the matter of monopolies.[29] The royal visit to Burley-on-the-Hill took place in the summer recess of this parliament. In his verses, then, James was defending his favourite while trying not to appear involved in political controversy. Again, he was attempting to defuse the potentially insensitive implications of his writing by distancing his poetry from his kingship.

The apparently apolitical nature of the 1621 sonnet has further political significance. In the parliament of 1621 the King was seeking backing for his unpopular foreign policy of seeking a Spanish match for Prince Charles, and there was, as already noted, a broader context of controversy surrounding this foreign policy. James issued two proclamations against public discussion of political affairs, one at the end of 1620, and one in July 1621, only a month before his performance of his poem to Buckingham.[30] The timing of this proclamation points to the possibility that James's disengagement from political concerns in his poem was in part a further attempt to shift attention away from the matters he did not want others to discuss. Not to refer to such immediate, pressing concerns is a statement in itself. Though he would contradict this claim in other poems, as we shall see, he implies in this sonnet that poetry is not an appropriate forum for political discussion.

These attempts to appear to separate poetry and politics are furthered by several details shared by masque and sonnet. Both present James's claimed poetic achievement in mythological terms, the masque asking 'If one [*sic*] the forked hill I tredd' (3), and the sonnet 'If euer . . . I satt vpon Parnassus forked hill' (1–2). Both present poetry as sacred, James claiming in the first to have written 'from that sacred hill' (5) and in the second while 'inflam'd with sacred fury' (3). This implies that poetry transcends the world of political debate, while his claim in the sonnet that he has previously written while 'inflam'd with sacred fury' subtly implies that he does not have full responsibility for his poetry. Both pieces were performed to a court audience, but were neither printed nor widely circulated in manuscript, suggesting James's desire to keep them apart from the larger political context. In this late sonnet, then, the King was trying to manage the relationship between literature and politics in the same way as he had in his early Scottish reign.

29 For a general account of the 1621 parliament see Russell, *Parliaments and English Politics*. See also Butler, ' "We are one mans all" ', which places the occasion of James's visit to Burley-on-the-Hill in the context of the 1621 parliament.

30 James F. Larkin and Paul L. Hughes (eds), *Stuart Royal Proclamations*, 2 vols (Oxford: Oxford University Press, 1973), I, 495–6, 520.

While the masque may have been well enough received in Scotland, however, the reading of 1621 was commented upon with some ambivalence. Differences in reaction may be partly attributable to James's greater maturity and Buckingham's unpopularity, but comments from 1621 suggest that the King's behaviour was perceived as inappropriate in a way it may not have been formerly in Scotland, indicating the limitations of his attempt to judge his audience. Girolamo Lando reported on the reading on two occasions. His despatch to the Doge and Senate, sent on the 27 August 1621, *begins* with an account of the reading:

> The king showed the favourite as much honour at Burli as he received from his Excellency, as at a state banquet . . . his Majesty rose from the table where he was sitting apart with the prince [Charles], and went to the head of another at which were the leading lords and ladies, and drank standing and uncovered to the health of the Lord High Admiral [Buckingham], spoke in the highest terms of his merits and qualities . . . , and finally read some verses which he had composed in honour of this splendid host.

Over a year later, on 21 September 1622, in an extended 'relation of England', Girolamo Lando describes Buckingham's unpopularity and dominance of the King's affections and in this context recalls James reading out his verses. Lando observes that James's reading 'caused more comment than if he had done some great wrong to his kingdom'.[31] A letter of 18 August 1621 by John Chamberlain confirms that, despite James's apparent intentions, news of the incident quickly spread beyond its immediate audience; within only two weeks of the occasion Chamberlain is able to include in a letter a paraphrase of the verses. He offers the opinion that James 'was so pleased and taken' with the entertainment provided for him during his stay 'that he could not forbeare to express his contentment in certain verses'.[32] These contemporary accounts reflect the public nature of the occasion, attended by 'the leading lords and ladies'; the perception of such acts of royal self-representation as significant enough to re-present them, at home and abroad; and the fact that James was thus figuratively, as well as literally, 'uncovered' before an audience whose response he could not control. They also indicate several possible bases for objections to the reading.

Firstly, there is the question of appropriateness and decorum, in terms of both the nature of the performance and the content of the poem. Lando describes James adopting an inappropriate stance for the reading – he was 'standing and uncovered', as though affecting courtly servility – and thereby implies that the reading itself was also inappropriate. Chamberlain suggests that James showed a lack of self-restraint – 'he could not forbeare' – which might also seem inappropriate in a ruler. These details reflect the inappropriateness of the stance James adopts within the poem, which is the relatively lowly stance of the panegyrist. James himself had earlier acknowledged '*it becomes not the honour of my estate, like an hireling, to pen the praise of any man*'.[33] Yet not only does he appear to defer to Buckingham in the manner of his performance, but the verses consist of

31  *C.S.P., Ven.*, XVII, 117, 439.
32  McClure (ed.), *Letters of John Chamberlain*, II, 397.
33  James, the *Lepanto*, in *His Maiesties Poeticall Exercises*, sig. H1r.

conventional praise of the royal favourite and his wife, even using the poetic trope that 'no pen can duly blaze' their virtues (line 8). This implies the inadequacy of even royal poetry. By returning the praise Buckingham had offered the previous day in *The Gypsies Metamorphosed* in verses of his own, before what was presumably the same audience, James risked being perceived as lowering himself to the level of those, such as the noble Buckingham, and worse still the court poet Jonson, who needed to engage in panegyric in order to win favour. Moreover, the object of this poetic praise from the King was a favourite of relatively lowly origins, and an unpopular figure at that. The comparison made in the first line of Lando's 1621 despatch – 'the king showed the favourite as much honour at Burli as he received from his Excellency' – emphasises the inappropriateness of a king showing a mere favourite so much honour. James's attempt to construct an apparent separation between poetry and politics in fact meant that he was playing the role of poet at the expense of the role of king, and his promotion of his poetry seems to have been badly judged in this context.

Secondly, the sonnet's apparent disengagement from a context of European political instability and domestic political controversy, criticism and censorship, risked exacerbating the problem James faced of his writing being viewed as a distraction from state affairs. Lando, having described the reading at the beginning of his 1621 despatch, goes on to discuss the latest news and notes that 'in the variety and uncertainty of the news one fears the ill rather than expects the good'.[34] This implies the impropriety of James praying to God about the fertility of Buckingham and his wife at a time of major international political difficulty. It may well have seemed not only inappropriate but also irresponsible for the King to be writing and reading out this poem at such a time. For even if James emphasised that he was writing as a poet, he would still be read as a king.

Buckingham and the responses he was generating appear, then, to have played a major role in determining the agenda of the King's writing. This subtle shift in agency is aptly figured by the favourite acting as amanuensis for *A Meditation vpon St. Matthew*; on a literal level, the King is dictating to his subject, but it is the subject – Buckingham – who is not only literally but also metaphorically moving the royal pen. If the 1621 sonnet, in particular, was a spectacular failure as an attempt to rescue Buckingham and bolster the royal image, however, the problems generated and exacerbated by James's poetry would increase the more that he allowed his writing agenda to be dictated not just by criticism of his favourite but by public discussion of his affairs more generally.

### 'I wish the Curious man to keep / His rash Imaginations till he sleepe': public discussion and royal poetry

The late Jacobean period saw not only widespread opposition to royal policies and the court but also a marked rise in the discussion and representation of current affairs.[35]

---

34 *C.S.P., Ven.*, XVII, 117–18.
35 Fox, *Oral and Literate Culture*, p. 350.

St Paul's Cathedral became renowned as a location for the exchange of news, either orally or via materials pinned up in the church or churchyard, and newsmongers quickly relayed information gained here to others elsewhere. Manuscript verse increasingly responded to, and provided an impetus for, this growing demand for news and political commentary, and was one of the main ways in which 'Pauls walkers' heard or read 'news'.[36] The continuing negotiations for the Spanish match, and James's related refusal to enter into war against Spain, was a matter of particular concern, as is exemplified in the anti-Spanish pamphlets of Thomas Scott. Scott, a minister at Utrecht, was unusual only in that he criticised royal policy openly and managed to get his criticisms into print; according to Peter Lake, he was dealing in 'the common currency of contemporary political debate'.[37] Scott's pamphlets not only argue against the Spanish match and for going into war against Spain, but also – perhaps more worryingly for the Crown – defend a subject's right to engage in such discussion and valorise popular opinion. His first pamphlet, printed in 1620, is even entitled *Vox Populi*. In another pamphlet of the early 1620s, *Vox Regis*, he argues explicitly that 'Truth comes sometimes amongst the vulgar . . . so Kings from these may gather the best and most certaine intelligence of their Domestick affaires'.[38] These pamphlets thus not only represent the failure of royal attempts to censor popular voices but also call the legitimacy of such censorship into question.

Richard Corbett's 'Dr Corbet to the Duke of Buckingham being in Spayne', a satirical poem presumably written during the trip to Spain of Buckingham and Prince Charles in 1623, reflects explicitly on this proliferation of discussion and representation. The poem suggests wryly that if only Buckingham could be at 'Paules next Sunday' he could hear all about what he and Charles are allegedly getting up to in Spain. It then proposes what would happen 'If for a good euent the Heauens doe please' (the implication is 'if the Spanish match were to go ahead'):

Mens tongues should become rougher than the seas,
And that th'expense of paper should be such

36  Cogswell, 'Underground Verse', p. 281. Further evidence of growing public interest in news is provided by the appearance in 1621 of the first news-sheets printed in London (Fox, *Oral and Literate Culture*, p. 394). These corantos, which represented only 'news' from abroad, appeared at roughly weekly intervals and from 1622 began to construct narratives around the events they recorded (Joad Raymond, *The Invention of the Newspaper: English Newsbooks, 1641–1649* (Oxford: Oxford University Press, 1996), p. 8). For further discussion of the various ways in which news was circulated, and of its impact on politics and public perception of politics, in the 1620s specifically, see Richard Cust, 'News and Politics in Early Seventeenth-Century England', *Past and Present*, 112 (1986), 60–90.

37  Once his identity as the writer of *Vox Populi. Or Newes from Spayne* (1620) became known, Scott fled to the Low Countries. From there he wrote further pamphlets, while *Vox Populi* itself was reprinted a number of times in the following five years (P. G. Lake, 'Thomas Scott and the Spanish Match', *Historical Journal*, 25 (1982), 805–25 (pp. 806, 805)).

38  Scott, *Vox Regis*, p. 18. For further discussion of the strategies Scott's pamphlets employ to justify free speaking see Colclough, *Freedom of Speech*, pp. 102–19.

First written, then translated out of Dutch,
Corrantoes, dietts, packets, newes, more newes.[39]

These lines imply that, whatever the dangers faced by Prince and favourite during their journey over the seas to Spain, the hostile response to the match at home would be worse. Crucially, they make a direct correlation between the occurrence of controversial events and the rate at which news is produced, implying that the discussion and representation about which James was so worried was a symptom and consequence of his unpopular policies.[40] This suggests the difficulties of the King's position: the more he pursued the policies he wanted to pursue, the more he encouraged the responses he wanted to avoid.

Despite these contemporary suggestions that public opinion might be valid and that royal policies only encouraged public discussion, James continued to pursue his unpopular policies while trying to tighten censorship. He issued, as noted above, a proclamation at the end of 1620 (reissued in July 1621), against 'excesse of Lavish and Licentious Speech of matters of State', asserting that his subjects should not 'intermeddle by Penne, or Speech' with matters 'above their reach and calling'.[41] He seems to have been particularly anxious about discussion of the Spanish match, and responded to such discussion in parliament in December 1621 by sending a letter commanding that none 'shall presume henceforth to meddle with anything concerning our government or deep matters of State, and namely not to deal with our dearest son's match with the daughter of Spain'.[42] This exchange formed part of the most extended of the parliamentary debates on freedom of speech, which ended in James dissolving parliament in January 1622.[43] In 1622 he responded to discussion of the Spanish match in the pulpits by having 'a procession of clergymen' reprimanded,[44] and by issuing directions

---

39 The poem is quoted from a manuscript miscellany of around 1650 (Folger, V.a. 262, pp. 62, 64).

40 Although this poem has worrying implications for James, Corbett had close ties with Buckingham and his satire is directed more against public discussion than the royal court or policies. For further discussion of Corbett see McRae, *Literature, Satire and the Early Stuart State*, pp. 155–87.

41 Larkin and Hughes (eds), *Stuart Royal Proclamations*, I, 495–6.

42 J. R. Tanner (ed.), *Constitutional Documents of the Reign of James I* (Cambridge: Cambridge University Press, 1930), pp. 278–9.

43 For James's account of this conflict with parliament see *His Maiesties Declaration, Touching his Proceedings in the Late Assemblie and Conuention of Parliament* (London: Bonham Norton and John Bill, 1621 [1622]). For discussion of James's disagreements with parliament over the issue of freedom of speech throughout his English reign see Colclough, *Freedom of Speech*, pp. 138–86. It was not, of course, unusual for a monarch to try to control the subjects discussed in parliament. For example, in 1585 Elizabeth, using similar language to James, threatened those members of parliament who 'meddle with matters above their capacity' (Haigh, *Elizabeth I*, p. 124).

44 Cogswell, *The Blessed Revolution*, p. 27.

for preachers in August that year. These directions state that henceforth no preacher 'shall presume . . . to declare, limit, or bound . . . in any Lecture or Sermon, the Power, Prerogatiue, Iurisdiction, Authoritie, or Duty of Soueraigne Princes; or otherwise meddle with these matters of State'.[45] In November 1622 he issued a proclamation instructing people to leave London, a move that may in part have been intended to reduce opportunities for discussion of his policies.[46] None of these measures seems to have met with a great deal of success.[47]

Even before he began to take such drastic measures, however, James tried to use poetry to redirect public discussion. In the years 1618–19 he produced two poems that engage with popular concerns and allowed, or even encouraged, their wide circulation in manuscript. An event that seems to have captured the popular imagination in this period was the appearance of a comet, visible in Britain from 18 November to 16 December 1618. Negotiations for the Spanish match had become very active in the earlier part of 1618 and many saw the comet as a portent of evil to come, perhaps as a consequence of royal policy. According to Sir Simonds D'Ewes, the comet 'gave all men a sad occasion of several dismal conjectures from the view of it, for divers weeks after'.[48] Scott would later reflect on how 'That Comet which appeared to vs . . . gaue occasion of much discourse to all sorts of men'.[49] One interpretation of the comet concerned

---

45  *The Kings Maiesties Letter Touching Preaching, and Preachers* (London, 1622), sigs A2v–A3r.

46  Larkin and Hughes (eds), *Stuart Royal Proclamations*, I, 561–2.

47  Cogswell suggests that the unofficial market for news could not be controlled (*Blessed Revolution*, p. 21). This is reflected in a letter of 1621 in which Chamberlain refers to the reissued proclamation against public discussion of matters of state, 'which the common people know not how to understand, nor how far matter of state may stretch or extend; for they continue to take no notice of yt, but print every weeke (at least) corantas with all manner of newes' (McClure (ed.), *Letters of John Chamberlain*, II, 396). Despite James's attempts to control parliament, the parliament that reassembled in 1624 continued to favour war with Spain (see Russell, *Parliaments and English Politics*). Peter Lake argues that despite his 'Directions for preachers', the court sermons of 1622–5 represent a coherent attempt to argue for war with Spain ('Joseph Hall, Robert Skinner and the Rhetoric of Moderation at the Early Stuart Court', in Lori Anne Ferrell and Peter McCullough (eds), *The English Sermon Revised: Religion, Literature and History 1600–1750* (Manchester: Manchester University Press, 2000), pp. 167–85 (p. 175)). The reissue of the proclamation instructing people to leave London in December 1622, March 1623, and October 1624 suggests its inefficacy (Craigie (ed.), *Poems*, II, 261). McRae proposes that James's 'attempts to control legitimate speech may actually have contributed to a proliferation of unauthorised texts' in that he redefined all commentary as illicit, with the result that there was no incentive for commentators to operate within previously acceptable bounds (*Literature, Satire and the Early Stuart State*, p. 98). For further assessment of the effectiveness of censorship in relation to foreign policy in the years 1619–24 see Cyndia Susan Clegg, *Press Censorship in Jacobean England* (Cambridge: Cambridge University Press, 2001), pp. 161–96.

48  Quoted in Craigie (ed.), *Poems*, II, 255.

49  Thomas Scott, *Vox Populi. Or Newes from Spayne* ([Holland], 1620 [1624]), sig. *2r.

the Queen, as the following extract from a letter written in November 1618 by the Venetian ambassador, Antonio Donato, to the Doge and Senate of Venice reflects:

> Yesterday at sunrise a large and long comet appeared in the air towards the east. Everyone considers this unlucky, and a certain prognostication of ill. Accordingly they fear that the Queen will not live much longer. She is in a very bad condition.[50]

Queen Anne's death in 1619 seemingly confirmed that the comet had indeed been a sign.

The King was evidently aware that such perceptions of the comet were feeding into the kind of widespread discussion of his policies about which he was so anxious. Upon the death of his Queen he wrote a short poem that accepts the popular association of the comet with Anne's death, but re-presents in benign terms the symbol that many saw in such an ominous light. The poem begins 'Thee to inuite the great God sent a starre', and goes on to represent Anne's death in positive, reassuring terms, conventionally suggesting that she left 'the Earth to be enthroned aboue'.[51] While this poem is ostensibly about the death of the Queen, James is evidently using it as an opportunity to insert a redefinition of the troubling symbol of the comet, and a positive image of royalty, into popular culture. Even as he tries to bring the meaning of the comet into his control, however, he is accepting the terms of discussion that his subjects have dictated, and participating in the kind of interpretation of divine signs he elsewhere seeks to condemn.

While 'On the death of Queene Anne' represents the comet without acknowledging the popular discussions surrounding it, James's poem of the previous year, 'King Iames on the blazeing starr', explicitly responds to contemporary news culture and directly attacks public interest in the comet. This poem begins 'You men of Britaine, wherefore gaze yee so / Vppon an Angry starr', immediately identifying itself as a topical, reactive work.[52] It then warns against the misinterpretation of heavenly signs:

> And misinterpret not with vaine Conceit
> The Caracter you see on Heauen gate.
> Which though it bring the world some news fro fate
> The *letters* such as no man can translate
> And for to guesse at God Almightys minde
> Weere such a thing might cozen all mankinde.

> (7–12)

Describing heavenly signs in verbal terms – 'Caracter', '*letters*', 'translate' – enables James to emphasise the uselessness of gazing, seeing, and guessing without understanding. But this also reflects his preoccupation with verbal representation and the interpretation of language; even heavenly signs are comprehended and represented in verbal terms. While the King is here ostensibly concerned with defending God against misinterpretation, other more personal concerns are evidently at play. James had on other occasions, as we

50   *C.S.P., Ven.*, XV (1617–19), 366.
51   Craigie (ed.), *Poems*, II, 174, 'a' text (based on MS Harley 6917, fol. 32r), lines 1, 6.
52   Craigie (ed.), *Poems*, II, 172, 'a' text (based on MS Rawlinson Poet. 84, fol. 72).

have seen, implied that his word should be treated as God's word should be treated, and revealed his sense of the parallel vulnerability of divine and royal mysteries to demystifying interrogation. That his concern in this poem is in fact primarily with how he is being interpreted by his subjects is here suggested by his use of the term 'news' (9), a later reference to Paul's walkers (20), and the acknowledgement that some people 'thinke the match with spaine hath causd this star' (16). The poem implies, then, that people should not misinterpret the King, nor guess at his mind, nor read too much significance into 'news'. Establishing this association between heavenly signs and royal affairs involves, however, reproducing the very link between the Spanish match and the comet that James was trying to undermine.

As well as trying to defend the King against speculation and interrogation, the poem seeks to reassure the reader by dismissing popular fears. In order to do so, however, it has to reiterate these fears:

> Wherfore I wish the Curious man to keep
> His rash Imaginations till he sleepe
> Then let him dreame of ffamine plague and war
> And thinke the match with spaine hath causd this star
> Or let them thinke that if their Prince my Minion
> Will shortly chang, or which is worse religion.
>
> (13–18)

This act of reiteration risks appearing to give these ideas credence and legitimising the kinds of popular discussion James is trying to condemn. The poem tries to undermine and contain such ideas by situating them within the realm of imagination and dreams, as opposed to the realm of actuality and rationality. Yet this amounts to an acknowledgement that these fears, however misguided, cannot be entirely removed from circulation and, indeed, require an outlet. James may try to suggest that dreams are so far from actuality as to pose no threat, but he is also acknowledging that dreams form a sphere beyond official regulation. And by re-presenting public speculation and discussion as belonging to that sphere, he inadvertently implies that this too is beyond his control. The fear that this poem tries to relieve but in fact reveals is that the King cannot control what his subjects are thinking.

This fear of that which lies beyond official regulation recalls James's much earlier representation of witchcraft and demonic possession in *Daemonologie* (1597), which had just been reprinted as part of his *Workes*. As we saw in Chapter 3, this treatise reveals that what makes these forces so threatening is their potential for controlling the mind of the subject; but it also suggests that this is precisely the power the King wants for himself. Even as he warns against the ability of the Devil to affect the perceptions of his victims, he echoes his own expressions of his desire to shape the perceptions of his subjects through his writing. Strikingly, in his 1618 poem James compares those who peddle news with the Devil: 'Let him [the 'Curious man'] walke Pauls, and meet *the* Devills there' (20). As in *Daemonologie* James is trying to set up a clear distinction between his official truth, as embodied in his texts, and the Devil's misleading falsities, while revealing that for him the Devil epitomises the power to persuade and mislead. His comparison of the news-peddlers that walked Paul's to the Devil thus not only works to condemn them as corrupt and dangerous; it also acknowledges the extent of their ability to affect what people think. And, as in the earlier treatise, there is a sense that the power James attributes to the Devil is the power he wants for himself – that he wants to be the persuasive figure encountered by subjects curious for news. Indeed, by writing and circulating this poem the King was offering the curious man who walks Paul's an alternative source of 'news', in the hope of shaping his thought in accordance with royal design.

Again, then, James's awareness of the power of verbal representation places him in a double bind: he cannot exploit or invoke this power in his own texts without simultaneously acknowledging the power and importance of the other representations of 'news' he is seeking to counter. To an even greater extent than when he opposed his treatise to the Devil's ability to seduce with language and tricks, he is here trying to fight fire with fire. Moreover, he is now on shakier ground: while the Devil and his witches were unlikely to elicit sympathy from James's readers, the rights of subjects to hear news and engage in discussion were being upheld by some in the late years of his reign. We might say, then, that the influence of the 'Devils' that were walking Paul's in 1618 was even harder to police and more of a threat to royal authority than the influence of the Devil that James had represented two decades earlier.

The King's attempts to counter this threat are not only self-contradictory but risk fuelling the very discussion he was trying to contain: although his 1618 poem implies that people cannot guess at his meaning, by writing about state affairs he is creating the opportunity for them to attempt to do so, and giving them something more to talk and write about. Moreover, while it warns against misinterpretation, the poem itself was altered as it entered manuscript circulation, appearing in multiple contemporary versions.[53] James was not, however, deterred, but would go on to write a further poem in which these ironies are only extended.

### 'Such were A king but in A play / If hee might beare no better sway': royal poetry and the limitations of authority

'King Iames his verses made vpon a Libell lett fall in Court and entituled "The wiper of the Peoples teares / The dryer vpp of doubts & feares"' (hereafter referred to as

---

53  Craigie publishes two different versions, and the various manuscripts in which it exists reveal further textual variants. For example the lines quoted above as 'Or let them thinke that if their Prince my Minion / Will shortly chang, or which is worse religion', appear as 'And let him thinke that I theyr Prince, and Mynion . . .' in a version in the state papers (Craigie, (ed.), *Poems*, II, 173); as 'Or let them think that I their Prince, his minion . . .' in Folger, V.a. 345, p. 143; and as 'Or lett them thinke that I their prince my mind . . .' in Folger, V.a. 162, fol. 31r. The instability of this line mirrors the very uncertainties it is trying to quash. The significance of such textual instability is considered further in the next section.

'The wiper of the Peoples teares'), written in late 1622 or early 1623, was one of the last works to be attributed to the King.[54] Where 'King Iames on the blazeing star' engages with contemporary news culture in general, this poem responds explicitly to a specific libel. The apprehension of libellers was, Cogswell argues, so difficult and counter-productive that 'the best response . . . was not to investigate but to counter-attack', a purpose for which court poets were employed.[55] But for the King to respond person-ally with verses that, unlike most libels, circulated under the author's name, was an extra-ordinary act.[56] This response is in keeping with the willingness to engage in debate rather than to remain above it that we saw in Chapter 3, but the forum and nature of this debate made effective intervention difficult if not impossible. This poem epito-mises the potential of royal writing to demystify and undermine royal authority.

James's poem appears to have been written as an answer to a libel entitled 'The Comons Teares'.[57] Its concern is to deter such 'railing rymes and vaunting verse' (23), and it begins by responding to the metaphor of crying: 'O stay your teares yow who complaine / Cry not as Babes doe all in vaine' (1–2). This is in keeping with the poem's representation of subjects as uncomprehending and dependent upon royal care and dis-cipline, but the comparison also works against James's purposes: crying is a way in which babies seek attention and the satisfaction of their needs, which is precisely what the King's subjects have achieved through their complaints. Far from being 'all in vaine', their 'teares' have led the King to defend his policies and authority in an answering poem. Indeed, the poem seems directly to respond to criticisms and requests made in the original libel: it explains royal intentions, such as 'The parliament I will appoint / When I see thyngs more out of ioynt' (60–1), and justifies royal decisions, as in the lines 'The men you nam'd seru'd in their tyme / And soe may myne as cleere of cryme' (35–6). James is thereby contradicting the aloof, inscrutable, God-like position the poem claims for him in such lines as 'Striue not to see soe high A steeple' (92) and 'Kings cannot comprehended bee / In Comon circles' (145–6). This poem is itself demystifying the King, making his intentions and decisions more comprehensible and visible. As in earlier works, James appears opposed to the presumptuous prying, doubting, and

54  Craigie (ed.), *Poems*, II, 182–90, 'a' text (based on MS Malone 23, p. 49). This poem is attributed to the King in a number of contemporary manuscript collections and there is no competing attribution. One contemporary, however, seems to suggest that the King disclaimed it, and the significance of this is considered below. In spring 1623 James wrote, or was at least involved in the writing of, one further poem, 'Off Jacke and Tom', which is less explicitly political, but attempts to transform the controversial Spanish trip of Prince Charles and Buckingham into a pleasant pastoral jaunt (see Craigie (ed.), *Poems*, II, 192–3). For a brief discussion of questions surrounding the authorship of 'Off Jacke and Tom', see the Introduction, above.

55  Cogswell, 'Underground Verse', p. 285.

56  Bellany notes that 'Libels were nearly always anonymous: they were too stigmatised a form of expression for anyone to advertise their authorship' (*Court Scandal*, p. 101).

57  British Library, Add. MS 52585, for example, gives James's poem the title 'K James his Answer vnto the libell called ye Comons Teares' (fol. 4r). The original libel has not been traced.

meddling of his subjects, rather than determined to maintain a right to secrecy. Yet whereas the preface to *Basilikon Doron* emphasises that kings will reveal their secrets '*in the* [their] *owne time*', 'The wiper of the Peoples teares' suggests that his subjects have forced him to make these revelations at this point.[58]

As the act of responding to criticism involves the King in self-disclosure, so the act of denouncing manuscript verse culture involves participating in that culture. James's poem becomes another example of 'railing rymes and vaunting verse', reflecting the original libel not only in its engagement with criticism and circulation in manuscript but also in its form: as Cogswell notes, having used complex metres and rhymes elsewhere, here James uses rhyming couplets, the preferred form of writers of verse libels.[59] The King's familiarity with popular forms of discourse had long been evident: in an unprinted speech of 1614, for example, he proposes to proceed 'as they doe in Ballades to end as I beganne'.[60] This explicit emulation of a ballad in a royal speech hints at the tendency to erode distinctions between official and unofficial forms of discourse, and, by extension, between the voice of the King and the voice of the subject, that culminates in James writing a poem in the form of a libel. He was thus compromising the ideal of affinity between royal writing and status that Montague had voiced in his preface to the King's *Workes* – '*If a King will needs write; Let him write like a King*' (*Workes*, sig. B2v). In the case of 'The wiper of the Peoples teares', James was writing not 'like a king' but like his detractors. Indeed we might say that he was here not even writing 'like a poet', for he was writing a kind of doggerel that some contemporary poets considered beneath them – this is hardly 'the diuine art of poesie'.[61] His attitude towards the culture of manuscript verse libel was, as Perry has argued, deeply contradictory. On the one hand, he tries to play down its political importance, and denounces it for its decentralisation of political discourse and its meddling in state secrets. On the other, he desires to exploit it for public relations purposes and to redirect its perceptions. By participating in manuscript libel culture, James in fact acknowledges not only its political importance but also the Crown's failure to contain it.[62]

---

58   James, *Workes* (1616), p. 141. All references to James's prose works in the present chapter are to this edition unless otherwise specified and are given in parentheses in the text.

59   Cogswell, 'Underground Verse', p. 286.

60   Henry E. Huntington Library, HM 1554, p. 33.

61   Jonson, for example, expressed disdain for such verse. In a masque written shortly after 'The wiper of the Peoples teares', he distinguishes true poetry from 'th'abortive and extemporal din / Of balladry' and from 'what tumultuous verse / Or prose could make, or steal' (*Neptune's Triumph for the Return of Albion* (1624), in David Lindley (ed.), *Court Masques: Jacobean and Caroline Entertainments 1604–1640* (Oxford: Oxford University Press, 1995), lines 115–20). McRae has recently argued persuasively, however, that 'libels were also acknowledged as literary products, and it is important to appreciate the significance of literary codes and expectations in the culture of early Stuart libelling' (*Literature, Satire and the Early Stuart State*, p. 25).

62   Perry, ' "If Proclamations Will Not Serve" ', pp. 224, 211. Unsurprisingly, James's poem did not prevent the production and circulation of further 'railing rhymes'. Indeed one of the

The poem not only risks validating the very culture it is seeking to denounce, however, but also calls into question the efficacy of other forms of discourse at the King's disposal. The poem situates its specific responses to complaint within a reiteration of the ideology of divine right kingship (for example, it asserts that 'God aboue all men Kings enspires' (14) and rhetorically demands 'Was euer king call'd to Account' (66)). This recalls assertions James had earlier made in various specifically political contexts, particularly his two treatises on kingship and speeches to parliament. The poem also recalls James's proclamations, letter to parliament, and directions to preachers of the early 1620s in instructing its readers 'The moddell of our princely match / You cannot make but marr or patch' (85–6), so 'Meddle not with your princes Cares' (97). While this recollection of other royal texts in itself suggests that poetry might be at least *as* effective a vehicle for political statement as official media, the poem goes on to imply that poetry might even be *more* effective: towards the end, James remarks 'If proclamations will not serue / I must do more' (175–6). These lines suggest that writing this poem is part of the 'doing more' that the inefficacy of proclamations necessitates, a suggestion that is even clearer in the opening of his poem of 1622 asking people to leave London; 'You women that doe London loue so well / whome scarce a proclamacon can expell'.[63] In both poems he is suggesting the inefficacy of official, specifically royal, forms of discourse while validating through his practice manuscript poetry, an unofficial form of discourse in which his subjects can also engage. It is as though he has recognised that a form of representation that could be used to oppose royal authority might, after all, be more powerful than those forms conventionally used in its service. He seems to remain unaware, however, of the contradictions inherent in a King trying to exploit popular media as a means of bolstering his own authority.

We might go further than Perry, then, and suggest that this poem represents the King not only acknowledging the political importance of the culture of manuscript libel but yielding authority to his subjects. Not only is James engaging in a two-way 'conversation' with his subjects – as is emphasised in those copies of the poem that describe it as an 'answer' to other verses – but he may not even be the dominant party in terms of controlling the nature of that conversation. It is his subjects who have dictated which issues are to be discussed, demonstrated that manuscript verse might be a better way of affecting perception and behaviour than official pronouncements, and elicited from the King a series of demystifying revelations. The question as to where authority really lies in the interaction between ruler and ruled is itself anxiously encoded in the text:

Footnote no. 62 (*cont.*)
> most subversive verse representations of the King, 'The Five Senses', which prays for his deliverance from captivating favourites and thereby implies his vulnerability to them, was likely written in late 1623, shortly after 'The wiper of the Peoples teares'. See McRae's discussion of the subversive potential of this libel (*Literature, Satire and the Early Stuart State*, pp. 75–82).

63  Craigie (ed.), *Poems*, II, 178 ('a' text based on MS Egerton 923).

O what A calling weere A King
If hee might giue, or take no thing
But such as yow should to him bring
Such were A king but in A play
If hee might beare no better sway.                              (41–5)

James is here trying hard to maintain a clear distinction between real kings, who have intrinsic power, and theatrical kings, who have no power other than that brought by others, but seems anxiously aware of their comparability. Indeed, in earlier printed works he had compared his position to that of being on stage. In the preface to *Basilikon Doron*, for example, he had written that kings are set '*vpon a publike stage, in the sight of all the people*' (*Workes*, p. 141). There the theatrical metaphor served to emphasise the exposure of his position, but this later poem suggests that in the intervening years he had realised the full implications of his comparability to an actor. As though prescient of the arguments Stephen Greenblatt and David Scott Kastan would later make about Shakespeare's history plays, James now seems anxiously aware that kings might indeed be dangerously like actors in terms of being dependent on their audiences, and that others might make that connection.[64]

This poem is not only haunted by the fear that royal power might be at least in part a fictional construction, and therefore dependent on the perceptions of its beholders, but itself participates in the realisation of that fear. While it tries to disassociate the King from the 'king in a play', there is rather a sleight of hand, for James is here making himself a king *in a poem*. His poem, like a play, substitutes literary representation for reality, offering a 'king' that is constructed by a writer and dependent upon being per-ceived and read by others. The possibility the poem thereby raises – that its represen-tation of royal power may be little more than a fictional representation – is intensified by its employment of what Perry has called 'impractical threats based on ideological fantasies of omnipotent kingship'.[65] Moreover, the threats made by this 'king in a poem' echo threats made by kings in plays of the period. For example, when James tells his readers that 'Hee doth disdaine to cast an eye / Of Anger on you least you die' (149–50), it recalls Shakespeare's Richard II self-reflexively describing kings as being given 'a little scene, / To monarchise, be feared, and kill with looks'.[66] This shows the extent to which

64  For further discussion of the ways in which James's writings complicate the work of Greenblatt and Kastan on the connections between kingcraft and statecraft see the Introduction and Chapter 1, above. James would of course have seen some of Shakespeare's history plays, including, perhaps most pertinently here, *Henry V*, which according to Alvin Kiernan was performed at Whitehall in the 1604–5 season (*Shakespeare the King's Playwright: Theater in the Stuart Court 1603–1613* (New Haven and London: Yale University Press, 1995), p. 205). Perhaps the experience of being part of the audience for these plays fed into his anx-ieties about his relationship to the audiences he faced.

65  Perry, ' "If Proclamations Will Not Serve" ', pp. 216–17.

66  Shakespeare, *Richard II*, III.2.160–1, in Greenblatt, *et al.* (eds), *The Norton Shakespeare*.

the language and illusions of royal power overlap with those of theatrical performance, in ways that even a king trying to maintain a clear distinction between the two inadvertently emphasises.

At the same time as hinting at the partially fictional nature of royal power, the poem acknowledges the agency of the subject. In protesting 'Why doe you push me downe to hell / By making me an Infidell' (133–4), the poem ascribes a surprising amount of power to the language of those subjects who wrote the original libel – the libel does not merely call the King an infidel, it *makes* him an infidel. Even as James tries to construct 'the King' in his own poem, then, he implies that a king can also be constructed by his subjects – that, as the Chorus in *Henry V* suggests, it is the 'thoughts' of the onlookers that 'deck' a king.[67] And even as he attempts to shape those thoughts through a poem that defends royal policies, he tacitly admits that he needs to win his subjects' support and approval.

The poem thus raises the possibility that the authority of the King lies partly in the hands of the subject, and this is further played out in the circumstances of its production and circulation. The uncertainty as to whether James was sole author that surrounds his unprinted poems is extended in the case of 'The wiper of the Peoples teares'. For although it is attributed to the King in a number of contemporary manuscript collections, we have a contemporary comment that calls its authorship into question. Chamberlain wrote in January 1623 that 'touching libells the report goes there be many abrode, and yt shold seeme the Kings verses I herewith send you were made in aunswer to one of them', but in the following month offers the correction that 'The King disclaimes those I sent you last that went about in his name, and sayes they are the worst libell of all'.[68] We cannot be certain whether Chamberlain is referring to 'The wiper of the Peoples teares' or to a similar poem of the same period, or whether his account of what James said, which was presumably not first-hand, is accurate. Even if James did disclaim 'The wiper of the Peoples teares' after it had entered circulation, this does not necessarily mean he did not write it; he may rather have changed his mind about being associated with it because of a negative response. What Chamberlain's comment does tell us, however, is that the King was associated with a kind of writing that creates uncertainty as to attribution, and that might itself be considered libellous. James had created a situation in which his authorial voice lacked authority, in that it was not necessarily readily identifiable.

Given the extent to which this poem echoes the claims he makes and anxieties he reveals elsewhere, I would argue that James did write it, or was at least closely involved in its writing. But even if it were written by someone else in the person of the King, that person was drawing upon the disclosures James had made in other texts, and responding to the fact of his engagement with poetry; as we saw in the first chapter, by writing poetry the King created a poetic persona that others could appropriate.

---

67  Shakespeare, *Henry V*, Prol., 28, in Greenblatt, *et al.* (eds), *The Norton Shakespeare*.
68  McClure (ed.), *Letters of John Chamberlain*, II, 473, 478.

Whether or not James personally penned this poem, then, he was responsible for it being written, and, either way, its content was dictated largely by the concerns of his subjects. This echoes the case of Buckingham acting as amanuensis for a text that he and the criticisms he was meeting had indirectly produced: whether the King is directly or indirectly responsible for the writing of the text, he is both accountable as named author and not solely in control of its creation.[69]

The question of the 'authorship' of this poem, and of other uncollected poems by the King, is further complicated by the nature of manuscript circulation.[70] While his strategy of inserting poetic defences of his policies into popular culture through manuscript poetry seems to have been successful in terms of the apparent popularity of these poems, looking more closely at the collections in which they appear reveals a more complicated picture. As these poems were copied out in multiple contemporary manuscripts, variations were introduced, to the extent that authoritative texts have not been established.[71] This forms an important way in which James is not sole author, and ironises his attempt to make a decisive intervention in contemporary debate. Some variants call into question the poem's key claims. For example, while some versions refer to 'railing rymes and vaunting verse / Which your kings brest shall neuer peirce' (23–4), in other versions 'shall neuer' reads 'should neuer'.[72] The slippage between these two possibilities encapsulates one of the tensions at the heart of the poem. For while it ostensibly maintains an ideal of royal power, inscrutability and imperviousness to threat, it also reveals that James was both hurt and exposed by the libel to which the poem is responding. He would presumably have preferred the reading 'shall', but someone transcribing the poem might well have chosen 'should' as making more sense given the context of the poem as a whole and the period in which it was written. Other variants further enact the questions the poem raises as to where authority lies. The line

69  The potential for textual meaning to exceed the control of any individual has been recognised as a quality of literary texts in particular. Frank Kermode, for example, notes in his discussion of 'classic' works that 'the text is under the absolute control of no thinking subject' (*The Classic* (London: Faber and Faber, 1975), p. 80). What is distinctive in the case of James's poem is that this lack of control derives not only from the inherent nature of the text but from the position of the author; paradoxically, his royal status means he is answerable and knowable to his readers, in ways that allow them to shape or appropriate his authorial voice.

70  For general discussions of manuscript circulation, or 'scribal publication', see Harold Love, *The Culture and Commerce of Texts: Scribal Publication in Seventeenth-Century England* (Amherst: University of Massachusetts Press, 1998 (first pub 1993)), and Peter Beal, *In Praise of Scribes: Manuscripts and Their Makers in Seventeenth-Century England* (Oxford: Oxford University Press, 1998).

71  Craigie notes this in the introduction to his edition (*Poems*, II, xxvii) and goes on to include at least two versions of each of these poems.

72  Craigie's 'a' text, based on MS Malone 23, p. 49 and his 'b' text, based on MS Harley 367, fol. 151r, provide examples of the two different versions of this line (*Poems*, II, 182–3).

'And what I say yow shall finde true' (108) becomes in at least one version 'And what you say, you shall finde true'.[73] Though only one pronoun is altered, this turns the assertion that the reader should trust the royal word into an admission that the doubts voiced in the original libel will be proved true and, more broadly, into a radical empowerment of the reader/subject as the source of truth.

The empowerment of the reader/subject that this version of the poem proposes is an apt reflection of what the process of transcription represents; whether consciously or not, the subjects who transcribed royal poems were playing a part in constructing royal 'truths'. James had thus provided another way in which Scot's subversive claim, quoted above, that 'Truth comes sometimes amongst the vulgar' might be realised. The meanings thereby created might be utterly at odds with James's intentions, but, for the reader of these manuscript collections, they appear royally authored. While any of James's writings were susceptible to being inaccurately transcribed, the fact that there was no official version of his late poems, against which a conscientious subject might compare a given copy, means that all versions become effectively 'true'.[74] By participating in manuscript culture, the King made the truths he tried to represent not only available to scrutiny and even misinterpretation, but susceptible to being quite literally rewritten by his subjects. And if writing and ruling were as closely allied as James had always maintained, to rewrite the King is to assume control over him.

A further way in which the inclusion of royal poems in manuscript collections might alter their meaning is through the range and organisation of the collections themselves. Manuscript miscellanies tend to gather a diverse range of materials, with the result that royal poems might appear alongside poems that represent the same events in different – even oppositionist or satirical – terms. These various perspectives might then work to contradict, undermine, or ironise each other. For example, one manuscript miscellany that contains 'King Iames on the blazing starr' and his 'On the death of Queene Anne', also includes 'To Bucckinghame', a satire on the King's fondness for his undeserving favourite; 'On the princes goeing to Spayne', which expresses opposition to the Spanish trip and the match it was designed to finalise; 'On a Blazing Starre', which associates the comet and the Spanish match in exactly the way James's poem on the subject tried to counter; and the irreverent and popular verse 'On a fart in ye Parliament house'.[75] 'The wiper of the Peoples teares', in which James demands 'Content yourself with such as I / Shall take neere me, and place on high' (33–4), appears in one collection that includes not only the verse condemning Buckingham as

---

73  I have found the second version of this line only in Folger, V.b. 303, p. 264.

74  The notion of an 'official version' is problematic even in the case of printed texts, as we saw in the case of James's *Apologie for the Oath of Allegiance* in Chapter 3, but the existence of an authorised version of a given text, even if it does contain some variants and errors, provides a mechanism for rejecting other versions as unauthorised, which is absent in the case of these poems.

75  Folger, V.a. 162, fols 31r, 33v, 35v, 73r, 88v, 86r.

the 'The Countreys bayne the Courtiers hate' quoted above but two verses defending Felton, the soldier who assassinated the favourite James had tried so hard to defend.[76] Manuscript miscellanies represent, then, a dialogic context – the King's voice, which, as we have seen, may itself be collaboratively constructed, becomes only one voice among many and the debate between opposing representations remains unresolved.[77] In this regard these collections reflect the culture from which they emerged: authority could not fully contain or exclude opposition, but rather was forced into existing alongside it, and being shaped by it.

### 'We haue an earnest that doth euen tie / Thy scepter to thy word': reading the King, 1618–24

While James was trying unsuccessfully to control public discussion of state affairs through further writing, his subjects were continuing to read his earlier texts, which he had returned to the public eye by publishing his *Workes*. His writing career spanned over forty years ('the first verses that euer the King made' were likely written in 1582 and he continued writing poems into the 1620s). We might see this as quite an achievement, but it was also long enough for his policies to change significantly. In particular he appeared to have changed his foreign policy: as we have seen, he had earlier written vehemently against the papacy and advised Prince Henry not to marry outside of his religion, but now he was seeking a marriage for Prince Charles with Catholic Spain. James may have been responding wisely to a changed political landscape, but he was thereby failing to uphold the ideal of constancy that Elizabeth had emphasised in her motto, '*Semper Eadem*' ('always the same').[78] While he appeared to have changed, he had monumentalised in print the views he now seemed to be contradicting, and this gave his subjects a way in which to judge and oppose his current policy.

In the last years of his reign, then, James's readers were increasingly exposing the tensions between his aims as an author and his position as King. As we saw in Chapter 4, by collecting and republishing his works, James had implied that they transcended the contexts of their production. He had even stripped his scriptural exegeses – the earliest works in the collection – of the extra-textual material that tied them to 1580s Scotland. But this only made it easier for opponents of his foreign policy to use these works against him. Thus, for example, in 1618, at the outbreak of the Thirty Years War, Archbishop George Abbot directed James himself back to his own earlier *Paraphrase vpon*

76 British Library, Egerton 923, 'The wiper of the Peoples teares' is split between fols 32r–33v and fols 37r–38r; the verses on Buckingham and Felton appear on fols 45v–46r.

77 Cf. McRae's comment that the verse miscellany 'characterizes a culture within which people were becoming increasingly fascinated by the emergent phenomena of political contestation and ideological division' (*Literature, Satire and the Early Stuart State*, p. 43).

78 Malcolm Smuts convincingly argues that despite the apparent change in James's attitude towards Protestant resistance he was not inconsistent, but rather adept at adjusting theoretical positions to meet immediate needs ('The Making of *Rex Pacificus*').

*the Reuelation*, thereby suggesting that James should carry out the role of militant Protestant king he had once assigned himself.[79] In a sermon preached in Northampton in 1621 Robert Bolton directed his audience to the full range of the King's anti-papal writings. While he was ostensibly praising James for his anti-Catholicism as demonstrated in these earlier writings, in 1621 this implied criticism of his current policy.[80] Having been written in a different set of circumstances, these works were no longer entirely politically relevant, but James's literary aspirations had denied him this line of defence; in separating his texts from their contexts of production his readers were only doing what he had invited them to do.

James, as we have seen, wanted to invest his works with his authority, and even implied that his word should be treated as God's word should be treated. To some extent he seems to have achieved this, particularly with *Basilikon Doron* which was often cited in other texts as an 'authority', and which, according to James Doelman's study of its reception, was treated by some like holy writ.[81] Yet, as Doelman argues, this authority became detached from the King and was even used against him; by reflecting back to James the ideals and principles he had articulated in *Basilikon Doron*, 'English readers attempted to govern the King by his own words'. Doelman gives the example of a sermon in which William Thorne encouraged James to 'read himselfe as it were, & rule out of his owne booke'.[82] What these instances show is that, in claiming that his authority was embodied in his texts, James had made that authority available to his subjects,

79 Richey, *The Politics of Revelation*, pp. 3–4.
80 Bolton makes his point even clearer by praising England for the military valour it has enjoyed since the beginning of Elizabeth's reign and focusing on the problems caused by the presence of papists in England (Robert Bolton, *Two Sermons Preached at Northampton* (London: George Miller, 1635), pp. 12–15, 30–1). James's anti-papal writings were also used to authorise militantly Protestant scriptural exegeses throughout the Jacobean period. For example, in a work on Revelation the Puritan preacher Richard Bernard establishes that James's *Premonition* has '*made known to the Christian world . . . that the supremacie of the Pope, is a proud vsurpation*', then goes on to assert 'Cursed be he, that doth the worke of the Lord negligently, or deceitfully: and cursed be hee that keepeth back his sword from bloud' (*A Key of Knowledge for the Opening of the Secret Mysteries of St Iohns Mysticall Reuelation* (London: Felix Kyngston, 1617), C4v, C5r). While this is less directly an attack than the other examples cited, Bernard is nevertheless appropriating James's writings to help support his call for the kind of aggressive policy the King himself was unwilling to pursue.
81 Doelman, '"A King of Thine Own Heart"', p. 2. For an example of James's writings being used as a source of authority in works published in the last years of his reign see William Pemberton, *The Charge of God and the King* (Oxford, 1619), which places references to the King's word in the margin, alongside references to biblical and classical sources of authority.
82 Doelman, '"A King of Thine Own Heart"', pp. 1, 6. See also Joseph Marshall, who similarly suggests that, in the last years of his reign, James's 'readers felt they should make the king live up to his words' ('Reading and Misreading King Iames 1622–42', in Fischlin and Fortier (eds), *Royal Subjects*, pp. 476–511 (pp. 478–9)).

inadvertently empowering them to judge, question, and manipulate him. The ironic outcome of his attempt to authorise himself through his writings was that he had inadvertently authorised his subjects.

The contemporary response that most neatly sums up both the achievement and the failure of James's writings comes from a fellow poet, George Herbert, in an oration to James of 1620:

> Sanè, gestarbaris antea in cordibus nostris; sed Tu vis etiam manibus teri, semotâque Maiestate, chartâ conspiciendum Te praebes, quò familiarùs inter nos verseris. (Truly thou wast borne before in our hearts; but thou wishest also to be thumbed in our hands; and laying aside thy majesty, thou dost offer thyself to be gazed upon on paper, that thou mayest be more intimately conversant among us.)[83]

These lines reflect James's claims of textual presence, affirming that writing is an effective way for him to reach his subjects. But the suggestion that to offer himself on paper James lays aside his majesty implies that his self-presentation in his writings is incompatible with his kingship – that authorship and authority are not after all complementary. Herbert also, in emphasising the reader's physical handling of the text, points to the agency of the reader. 'Teri' from the verb 'terō', meaning not only to rub but 'To destroy gradually by attrition, wear down, wear away' or 'To handle (an article) constantly (so as to wear away)' (here translated as 'thumbed'), is particularly suggestive.[84] It intensifies the sense that offering himself on paper leaves the King vulnerable to being manipulated and even diminished by his subjects. What Herbert captures here, then, is what we have seen increasingly throughout this book: by putting himself into his writings James inadvertently created a shift in the power dynamic, allowing some of his authority to be worn off and giving his subjects the power to interpret, manipulate, even construct their King.

In the last years of his reign James seems to have become aware that the writings of his past had left him little room to manoeuvre, and attempted, yet again, to respond to this problem in writing. In 'The wiper of the Peoples teares' he challenges the expectation that kings should remain constant, but appears uncertain as to whether or not he wants his subjects to read his previous writings:

> Tis true I am A Craddle King
> Yet doe remember euery thinge
> That I haue heeretofore putt out
> And yet beginn not for to doubt
> But oh how grosse is your deuise
> Change to impute to kings for vice

83  F. E. Hutchinson (ed.), *The Works of George Herbert* (Oxford: Oxford University Press, 1941), p. 458. The translation is from *Complete Works in Verse and Prose of George Herbert*, ed. and trans. A. B. Grosart, 3 vols (London: Robson and sons, 1874; reprinted New York, 1982), III, 449.

84  Glare (ed.), *Oxford Latin Dictionary*, 'terō' (4) and (5a).

The wise may change yet free from fault
Though change to worse is euer nought. (135–42)

This passage, like the poem as a whole, repeatedly shifts its argument (here this is clearly signalled by 'yet', 'yet', 'but', and 'though'). This reflects James's uncertainty, and implies a loss of linguistic control and, by extension, political control. On the one hand, he wants his readers to remember everything he has so far 'putt out', presumably because he believed this material emphasises his authority and integrity. This is one of the sentiments he acted upon in collecting all his prose writings in his *Workes*. On the other, he seems anxiously aware that the changes this body of works reveals might automatically be seen in negative terms, and thus seems almost to retract the request that his earlier works be remembered. It is as though James has finally begun to realise the implications of the warning that, as we saw in Chapter 3, Samuel Daniel offered in 1603 with regard to *Basilikon Doron*: his writings have formed an 'earnest' that tie his actions to his word, and the more he has written, the more subject he has become to his texts and their readers. Yet he is still trying to deal with this problem in writing. Here, then, we see the fundamental futility of James's strategy: even at a time when what he had written previously was being used against him, he continued to produce still more works which could, in turn, provide his subjects with further means of questioning, doubting, and judging him.

We have seen, then, that whether James appears to separate poetry and politics, as in the 1621 sonnet to Buckingham, or explicitly combines them, as in the other poems considered here, there is a political agenda behind his writing that requires the impossible: that the poems be read in only one way. While any of his writings were susceptible to being altered, misinterpreted, reappropriated, and criticised, the medium of poetry seems particularly ill-matched with his desire to control meaning. More so than the other genres in which he also wrote, poetry involves conventions, such as the trope of humility, that are incompatible with monarchical status. It invites unauthorised transcription and rewriting. Unlike specifically royal forms of discourse, such as proclamations, it allows others to respond in kind. Poetry might even invite the reader to participate more actively in constructing textual meaning; as we saw earlier, James himself was aware of the possibility that the Poet 'Doeth graue so viue [lifelike] in vs his passions strange, / As maks the reader, halfe in author change'.[85] By the end of his reign he had indeed created various opportunities for his readers to author – to shape, direct, and rewrite – their King.

Given the analogy that James had long sought to maintain between literary and political authority, the problems of his writings reflect, and play a part in, the problems of his rule. There is a fundamental incompatibility between his claims of unique and unassailable political authority and the representation of those claims in writing – a medium democratic in terms both of the fact that people of any status can write and of the

---

85  James, *Essayes of a Prentise*, sig. E2r.

uncontrollability of interpretation. His continual attempts to explain and justify his political authority reveal that this authority is not self-evident and indisputable, and, in the same way, his various attempts to explain and dictate the meaning of his texts reveal that textual meaning is also not self-evident and indisputable. Moreover, by implying at times that literary authority *requires* an explicit emphasis on the political authority of the writer, and, at others, that political authority *requires* literary representation, James only emphasises that neither form of authority can exist in isolation. As he struggles to bolster one with the other, he inadvertently acknowledges the very source of authority that he is trying to suppress: as the meaning of a text is largely dependent on and constructed by the reader, so the authority of a king is largely dependent on and constructed by the subject. His attempts to impress, manipulate, and coerce his subjects through writing serve only to underscore and extend this dependency, and the more he exposed and demystified himself through his writing the more his subjects were able to assume agency in interpreting and responding to him. As royal authority was constructed through a process of exchange, so, then, could its deconstruction be a collaborative endeavour.

The overall impact of James's writings on the political developments of his reign and beyond is difficult to gauge. With regard to the impact of court scandal in the first half of the seventeenth century, Bellany notes cautiously that 'the extent of delegitimation is hard to measure, and it is much easier to track the possible contours of the process than prove a direct link from scandal to delegitimation and on to revolution'.[86] We might say the same about James's writings – it is difficult to prove a direct link from their empowerment of the reader/subject to a loss of royal political power and on to Civil War. Yet a number of critics have made considerable claims for the long-term impact of other cultural developments occurring during James's lifetime. As Bellany suggests that scandal may have worked to delegitimise authority, so Cogswell claims that manuscript verse was a factor in 'the emergence of popular political awareness', McRae suggests that satire helped 'to make radicalism thinkable', and Kastan argues that the Elizabethan theatre 'nourished the cultural conditions that eventually permitted the nation to bring its King to trial'.[87] James's writings not only voice anxieties about these developments but also participate in them from a position of cultural and political centrality and high visibility. His writings, more so than the theatre or popular verse, allow subjects to assume greater authority in their interactions with the monarch himself. The great irony, then, is that King James's very attempts to wipe away the 'doubts & feares' of his subjects may have contributed to a process that extended beyond his lifetime of such doubts and fears gaining credence, finding voice, and, ultimately, shaping the fate of the monarchy.

86   Bellany, *Court Scandal*, pp. 22–3.
87   Cogswell, 'Underground Verse', pp. 294–5; McRae, *Literature, Satire and the Early Stuart State*, p. 107; Kastan, 'Proud Majesty Made a Subject', pp. 460–1.

# Afterword

Throughout this book we have seen the tensions and contradictions inherent in James's writings, and the problems these writings exacerbated and created. To acknowledge these, however, is not to reject the emphasis of revisionist historians on James's perspicacity as a ruler. It is to complicate further our sense of his relationship to the audiences of his rule, and of the ways in which that relationship was shaped by his various attempts to construct and promote himself as a wise and powerful monarch. In trying to use authorship to reinforce his authority he was, to a large extent, attempting the impossible. For the authority of Renaissance monarchs required the *perception* of authority and therefore had to be represented, but representation requires interpretation, which cannot be controlled. In the specific case of writing, it requires a reader, but becomes to some extent subject to its reader. We might say, then, that no attempt to represent the authority of a Renaissance monarch could be guaranteed to have the required effect on every recipient, but that James's style of self-representation exacerbated this unavoidable problem.

This is not to suggest that writing is necessarily more open to multiple interpretations than, for example, portraits or civic ceremonies. But, by attempting to take control of his own public relations, James left himself unable to attribute blame elsewhere when those public relations exercises failed. His various writings do not simply assert his authority but attempt to explain and justify it, to manipulate and even deceive his readers, and to exploit the value increasingly attaching to literary uses of language. In each of these ways James inadvertently multiplied the susceptibility of his writing to different, and even critical or oppositionist, readings. His writings reveal, then, some of the ways in which literature is both valuable to and not wholly compatible with a political system that maintains it is not consensual. Literature's value to such a system lies in its power to manipulate perception and to lend prestige and lustre to authority. But literature is also incompatible with any attempt to impose authority because it invites different interpretations, and its effect on the perceptions of its recipients is in part determined by those recipients.

James himself was not, however, unaware of these difficulties. By printing some works anonymously he admitted that for a king to represent *himself* was not always the most effective way for him to be defended and promoted. His employment of the trope of humility in some of his works may be not only conventional but indicative of his awareness of the limitations of language. His works repeatedly show that he was painfully aware of the difficulty of controlling reader response. One of his most suggestive reflections on this matter comes in the preface to *Basilikon Doron*: having commented upon the misreadings to which he claims various readers have already subjected his work, he adds that to this 'hydra *of diuerslie enclined spectators, I haue no targe to oppone but plainnesse, patience, and sinceritie . . . Though I cannot please all men therein, I am contented so that I onely please the vertuous sort*'.[1] It is striking that, in this consideration of the kinds of readers who pose a challenge to the King, the term 'spectator' creeps in, emphasising his awareness that writing was a form of public exposure, and that 'readers' were not a category distinct from the general mass of his subjects who would scrutinise his every move. As complex as the publication history of *Basilikon Doron* is, and as mediated as I have argued all of James's published works are, we might see this as a moment of honest reflection: the King seems to have realised that his subjects had varied and even conflicting perspectives and expectations, and that his writings could therefore never please all of them.

Of course, this raises the question of why he persisted in writing none the less. Diana Newton's recent study of the early years of James's English reign emphasises how determined he was to intervene personally in every aspect of government rather than trusting others to do things for him, and this is illuminating here.[2] James knew that his political, religious, and cultural authority needed to be repeatedly represented, and he was unwilling to trust this vital task entirely to others. He therefore took personal responsibility for it, and used the medium within which he was personally competent, and which involved less direct contact with his subjects, and less (though not, as we have seen, a complete lack of) dependence on court writers, image-makers, or government and Church officials than other forms of royal representation. He seems to have felt that he had '*no targe to oppone*' against the challenges and criticisms he faced except his writings – that he had no choice but to write.

We should also remember that he did not persist in writing exactly the same kinds of things throughout his reign but rather tried out a whole range of strategies: writing poetry and prose; writing directly and indirectly about his authority; circulating his writing in manuscript and in print; circulating his writing under his own name and anonymously; printing cheap quartos and octavos, and expensive folios; writing for specific and general audiences; publishing in different languages. None of these strategies may have solved the problems he faced, but they reveal an impressive degree of versatility and creativity. In addition to trying different kinds of writing, he also recalled and changed various of his works according to the reception they had met, revealing that he was anxious to judge and respond to his audience. His ability to judge his audience seems, perhaps unsurprisingly, to have diminished as he moved on to a wider and less

---

1  James, *Basilikon Doron* (1603), sig. A8v.
2  Newton, *The Making of the Jacobean Regime*.

familiar stage in 1603, but he continued to respond to his audience, and to larger cultural developments, by, for example, entering into the culture of manuscript libel. All of this suggests that he was not, at least with regard to his writing, the '*statue immoueable*' that he is depicted as in the preface to the King James Bible.

James was, then, constantly trying to contain subversion through his writing, but, unlike 'authority' as represented in much New Historicist work, seems only ever to have fuelled the debates he was trying to contain, and thereby to have exposed the limits of his authority. His writing exists in a complex interrelationship with other contemporary writing, within which questions of authority, authorship, influence, attribution, collaboration, and patronage are significantly complicated. This emphasises that any attempt to divide the various texts circulating in a given period into 'texts' and 'contexts' is necessarily a simplification. Rather than separating all texts from any sense of context like the New Critics, or going so far as presenting all texts as 'a mass of disembodied discourse' with some of the New Historicists, this book has argued that examining the material form, circulation, and reception of a given set of texts can reveal these texts to be both distinctive and reactive, both embedded in specific contexts and not entirely reducible to them.[3] The writings of a king are not the same as the writings of any one of his subjects. But nor do they exist in isolation from them.

This leads us to the larger question of James's role in Jacobean literary culture more broadly, and some preliminary comments may be made here.[4] To explore, as the present book has done, the ways in which James's writings exposed and extended his dependence on his subjects is not to deny that he may also have shaped their writings. *Henry V*'s representation of the paradoxical nature of kingship might help us to understand the ways in which James both did and did not have agency, and was and was not able to influence his subjects. Henry claims in the final act that monarchs are the 'makers of manners'.[5] By putting this claim in the mouth of a king whose rhetoric we know by the end of the play cannot always be trusted, Shakespeare suggests that the nature of royal authority and influence is more complex than monarchs themselves might be willing to admit. If we read Henry's claim in the context of the implication at the start of the play that kings are dependent on their subjects – ''Tis your thoughts that now must deck our kings' (Prologue, 28) – it suggests that monarchs might be able to make manners, but only with the co-operation of their subjects. That is, authority and influence run in both directions, and the 'manners' – or trends or developments – thereby created are the product of interaction not imposition.

James's interactions with his subjects through his writings may thus have helped to shape Jacobean literary culture, but not necessarily in ways entirely to his advantage. To take but one example, 'The wiper of the Peoples teares', as we saw in the final chapter, both acknowledged and tried to deny the ways in which real kings are like kings in plays.

3  The quotation is from Helgerson's review of Goldberg's *James I*, p. 182.
4  This subject will be addressed in my next monograph, *Writing the Monarch in Jacobean England*.
5  Shakespeare, *Henry V*, V.2.252, in Greenblatt *et al.* (eds), *The Norton Shakespeare*.

This anxiety may itself have been shaped by the popularity in James's lifetime of theatrical representations of kingship, while his poem further testifies to the power of such representations. Within a year of this poem the Shakespeare First Folio (1623) gave James's subjects an extended opportunity to perceive kingship through the lens of theatrical and literary representation. Moreover, this collection made a bold statement of Shakespeare's independence from real kings: nowhere does it mention that he had been a 'King's Man'.[6] Shakespeare's authority as an author was thus decisively severed from royal authority, and this severance may, ironically, have been facilitated by James himself, who had asserted the authority of authorship through his own folio collection seven years earlier. The King's attempts to borrow authority from literature may ultimately have done less to reinforce kingship than to authorise authorship. The writings of King James VI and I give us, then, a unique perspective on two of the most significant developments of the early seventeenth century: the diminished prestige of the monarchy and the increased prestige of authorship. They also suggest some of the ways in which these developments were not unrelated.

6  Leah S. Marcus, *Puzzling Shakespeare: Local Reading and Its Discontents* (Berkeley, Los Angeles, and London: University of California Press, 1988), p. 106.

# Bibliography

## Manuscript sources

Bodleian Library, MS 165

Bodleian Library, MS Rawlinson B 183

British Library, Additional MS 24195 ('All the Kings short poesis that ar not printed')

British Library, Additional MS 22601

British Library, Additional MS 52585

British Library, Egerton 923

British Library, Royal MS 18 B.14

British Library, Royal MS 18 B.15

British Library, Royal MS 18 B.16

Folger Shakespeare Library, Art vol. b16

Folger Shakespeare Library, V.a. 162

Folger Shakespeare Library, V.a. 185

Folger Shakespeare Library, V.a. 262

Folger Shakespeare Library, V.b. 303

Folger Shakespeare Library, V.a. 345

Henry E. Huntington Library, HM 1554

## Early editions of printed works by and attributed to King James VI and I

*The Essayes of a Prentise, in the Diuine Art of Poesie* (Edinburgh: Thomas Vautroullier, 1584)

*Ane Fruitfull Meditatioun* (Edinburgh: Henry Charteris, 1588)

*Ane Meditatioun vpon the First Buke of the Chronicles of the Kingis* (Edinburgh: Henry Charteris, 1589)

*His Maiesties Poeticall Exercises at Vacant Houres* (Edinburgh: Robert Waldegrave, 1591)

*Daemonologie* (Edinburgh: Robert Waldegrave, 1597)

*The True Lawe of Free Monarchies: or The Reciprock and Mutual Duetie Betwixt a Free King, and His Naturall Subiectes* (Edinburgh: Robert Waldegrave, 1598)

*Basilikon Doron* (Edinburgh: Robert Waldegrave, 1599)

*Basilikon Doron or His Maiesties Instructions to His Dearest Sonne, Henry the Prince* (Edinburgh: Robert Waldegrave, 1603)

*Basilikon Doron or His Maiesties Instructions to His Dearest Sonne, Henry the Prince* (London: Felix Kyngston for John Norton, 1603)

*Basilikon Doron or His Maiesties Instructions to His Dearest Sonne, Henry the Prince* (London: Richard Field for John Norton, 1603)

*Basilikon Doron or His Maiesties Instructions to His Dearest Sonne, Henry the Prince* (London: E. Allde. for E. White and others of the company of the Stationers, 1603)

*Daemonologie* (London: William Aspley and W. Cotton, 1603)

*Daemonologie* (London: Arnold Hatfield, 1603)

*A Fruitefull Meditation* (London: J. Harrison, 1603)

*A Meditation vpon the First Booke of the Chronicles of the Kinges* (London: J. Windet for Felix Norton, 1603)

*His Maiesties Lepanto* (London: Simon Stafford and Henry Hooke, 1603)

*The True Lawe of Free Monarchies* (London: Thomas Creede, 1603)

*The Kings Maiesties Speach, as it was deliuered by him in Parliament, 1603* (London: Robert Barker, 1604)

*The Copie of His Maiesties Letter to the Commons* (London, 1604)

*A Counterblaste to Tobacco* (London: R. B. [Robert Barker], 1604)

*His Maiesties Speach in Parliament. Together with a Discourse of the Maner of the Discouery of this Late Intended Treason* (London: Robert Barker, 1605)

*His Maiesties Speach to Both the Houses of Parliament, 1607* (London: Robert Barker, 1607)

*Triplici Nodo, Triplex Cuneus. Or An Apologie for the Oath of Allegiance, against the Two Breues of Pope Paulus Quintus, and the Late Letter of Cardinal Bellarmine* (London: Robert Barker, 1607)

*An Apologie for the Oath of Allegiance. First Set Foorth without a Name: And Now Acknowledged by the Authour, the Right High and Mightie Prince, Iames. Together with a Premonition of His Maiesties, to All Most Mightie Monarches* (London: Robert Barker, 1609)

*The Kings Maiesties Speach to Parliament, 1609* (London: Robert Barker, 1609)

*Declaration Touchant le Faict de Conradus Vorstius* (London: John Norton, 1612)

*Declaration du Roy Iacques I. Pour le Droit des Rois* (London: John Bill, 1615)

*A Remonstrance for the Right of Kings* (C. Legge, printer to the Universitie of Cambridge, 1616)

*The Workes of the Most High and Mighty Prince, Iames* (London: Robert Barker and John Bill, 1616)

*His Maiesties Speach in the Starre-Chamber, 1616* (London: Robert Barker, 1616)

*A Declaration of Sports* (London: Bonham Norton and John Bill, 1617)

*The Peace-Maker: or, Great Brittaines Blessing* (London: Thomas Purfoot 1618)

*A Meditation vpon the Lords Prayer* (London: Bonham Norton and John Bill, 1619)

*Opera Regia* (London: Robert Barker and John Bill, 1619)

*A Meditation vpon St. Matthew. Or A Paterne for a Kings Inauguration* (London: Robert Barker, 1620)

*The Workes of the Most High and Mighty Prince, Iames* (London: Robert Barker and John Bill, 1620)

*His Maiesties Speach in the Vpper House of Parliament 1621* (London: Bonham Norton and John Bill, 1621)

*His Maiesties Declaration, Touching His Proceedings in the Late Assemblie and Conuention of Parliament* (London: Bonham Norton and John Bill, 1621 [1622])

*The Kings Maiesties Letter Touching Preaching, and Preachers* (London, 1622)

*The Psalmes of King David* (Oxford: William Turner, 1631)


### Other printed primary sources

*Academiae Cantabrigiensis Lachrymae Tumulo Philippi Sidneii Sacratae* (London: Ioannis Windet, 1587)

Akrigg, G. P. V. (ed.), *Letters of King James VI and I* (Berkeley, Los Angeles and London: University of California Press, 1984)

Ashton, Robert (ed.), *James I by His Contemporaries* (London: Hutchinson, 1969)

Atkins, Ivor, and Neil R. Ker (eds), *Catalogus Librorum Manuscriptorum Bibliothecae Wigorniensis, made in 1622–3 by Patrick Young, Librarian to King James I* (Cambridge: Cambridge University Press, 1944)

*Ave Caesar. God Saue the King* (London, 1603)

B., A. D., *The Court of the Most Illustrious and Most Magnificent James* (London, 1619)

Barlow, William, *The Summe and Substance of the Conference at Hampton Court* (London: John Windet for Mathew Law, 1604)

Bernard, Richard, *A Key of Knowledge for the Opening of the Secret Mysteries of St Iohns Mysticall Reuelation* (London: Felix Kyngston, 1617)

Bodin, Jean, *On Sovereignty*, ed. Julian H. Franklin (Cambridge: Cambridge University Press, 1992)

Bolton, Robert, *Two Sermons Preached at Northampton* (London: George Miller, 1635)

Bruce, John (ed.), *Letters of Queen Elizabeth and King James VI of Scotland*, Camden Society (London: J. B. Nichols and Son, 1849)

Buchanan, George, *The Powers of the Crown in Scotland*, trans. Charles Flinn Arrowood (Austin: University of Texas Press, 1949)

Budé, Guillaume, *Tesmoignage de Temps, ou Enseignemens et Enhortemens pour l'Institution du Prince* (Paris, 1547)

Calderwood, David, *The History of the Kirk of Scotland*, ed. Thomas Thomson, 8 vols (Edinburgh: Wodrow Society, 1843)

*Calendar of State Papers, Venetian*, ed. Rawdon Brown *et al.* (vols XIII to XVIII for 1613–25 ed. Allen B. Hinds), 38 vols (London, 1864–1947)

*Calendar of State Papers, Domestic*, ed. R. Lemon, 12 vols (London, 1856–72)

*The Cambridge Geneva Bible of 1591*, facsimile reprint (Cambridge: Cambridge University Press, 1992)

Carroll, Robert, and Stephen Prickett (eds), *The Bible: Authorised King James Version with Apocrypha* (Oxford: Oxford University Press, 1997)

Craig, J. T. Gibson (ed.), *Papers Relative to the Marriage of King James the VI of Scotland with the Princess Anna of Denmark* (Edinburgh: Bannatyne Club, 1828)

Craigie, James (ed.), *Thomas Hudson's History of Judith* (Edinburgh and London: William Blackwood & Sons, 1941)

—— *The Basilikon Doron of King James VI*, 2 vols (Edinburgh and London: William Blackwood & Sons, 1950)

—— *The Poems of James VI of Scotland*, 2 vols (Edinburgh and London: William Blackwood & Sons, 1955–1958)

—— *Minor Prose Works of King James VI and I* (Edinburgh and London: William Blackwood & Sons, 1982)

Cranstoun, James (ed.), *Satirical Poems of the Time of the Reformation* (Edinburgh: Blackwood, 1891–3; reprint, New York: AMS, 1974)

Crockett, Thomas (ed.), *Poems of John Stewart of Baldynneis*, 2 vols (Edinburgh and London: Blackwood, 1913)

Daniel, Samuel, *Delia. Containing Certaine Sonnets: With the Complaynt of Rosamond* (London: J. C. for S. Watersonne, 1592)

—— *The Works of Samuel Daniel* (London: Simon Waterson, 1601)

—— *Panegyrike Congratulatorie* (London: Edward Blount, 1603)

Dekker, Thomas, *The Magnificent Entertainment* (London, 1604)

Donaldson, Ian (ed.), *Ben Jonson* (Oxford: Oxford University Press, 1985)

Donne, John, *Pseudo-Martyr* (London: W. Stansby, 1610)

Donno, Elizabeth Story (ed.), *Andrew Marvell: The Complete Poems* (Harmondsworth: Penguin, 1972)

Dutton, Richard (ed.), *Sir Philip Sidney: Selected Writings* (Manchester: Carcanet Press, 1987)

*Englands Welcome to Iames* (London, 1603)

*An Excellent New Ballad, Shewing the Pedigree of our Royall King Iames* (London, 1603)

Fairholt, Frederick W., *Poems and Songs Relating to George Villiers, Duke of Buckingham; and His Assassination by John Felton* (London: Percy Society, 1850)

Fischlin, Daniel, and Mark Fortier (eds), *The True Law of Free Monarchies and Basilikon Doron* (Toronto: Centre for Reformation and Renaissance Studies, 1996)

Foster, Elizabeth Read (ed.), *Proceedings in Parliament, 1610*, 2 vols (New Haven and London: Yale University Press, 1966)

Greenblatt, Stephen *et al.* (eds), *The Norton Shakespeare* (New York: Norton, 1997)

Greene, Thomas, *A Poets Vision, and a Princes Glorie* (London: William Leake, 1603)

Grosart, A. B. (ed.), *Complete Works in Verse and Prose of George Herbert*, 3 vols (London: Robson and sons, 1874; reprinted New York, 1982)

Grundy, Joan (ed.), *The Poems of Henry Constable* (Liverpool: Liverpool University Press, 1960)

Hayes, William, *The Lawyers Looking-Glasse* (Oxford, 1624)

Herford, C. H., and Percy and Evelyn Simpson (eds), *Ben Jonson*, 11 vols (Oxford: Oxford University Press, 1925–52)

Holland, Henry, *Baziliologia, a Booke of Kings* (London, 1618)

Holmes, Urban Tignier, John Coriden Lyons, and Robert White Linker (eds), *The Works of Guillaume De Salluste Sieur Du Bartas*, 3 vols (Chapel Hill: University of North Carolina Press, 1935–40)

*The Holy Bible, Conteyning the Old Testament and the New* (London: Robert Barker, 1611)

Hudson, Thomas, *The Historie of Judith* (Edinburgh: Thomas Vautroullier, 1584)

Hutchinson, F. E. (ed.), *The Works of George Herbert* (Oxford: Oxford University Press, 1941)

Jack, R. D. S., and P. A. T. Rozendaal (eds), *The Mercat Anthology of Early Scottish Literature 1375–1707* (Edinburgh: Mercat Press, 1997)

James VI and I, *Basilikon Doron*, ed. Charles Butler (London, 1887)

Jonson, Ben, *The Workes of Beniamin Jonson* (London: William Stansby, 1616)

Larkin, James F., and Paul L. Hughes (eds), *Stuart Royal Proclamations*, 2 vols (Oxford: Oxford University Press, 1973)

Law, Thomas Graves (ed.), 'Documents Illustrating Catholic Policy, 1596–98', *Miscellany of the Scottish History Society* (Edinburgh: Edinburgh University Press, 1893), I, 1–70

*The Laws and Actes of Parliament Maid be King James the First and His Successours* (Edinburgh: Waldegrave, 1597)

Lindley, David (ed.), *Court Masques: Jacobean and Caroline Entertainments 1604–1640* (Oxford: Oxford University Press, 1995)

McClure, Norman Egbert (ed.), *The Letters of John Chamberlain*, 2 vols (Lancaster: Lancaster Press, 1939)

McIlwain, Charles Howard (ed.), *The Political Works of James I* (Cambridge, Mass.: Harvard University Press, 1918; reprinted New York: Russell and Russell, 1965)

Marcus, Leah S., Janel Mueller, and Mary Beth Rose (eds), *Elizabeth I: Collected Works* (Chicago and London: University of Chicago Press, 2000)

May, Steven W. (ed.), *Queen Elizabeth I: Selected Works* (New York: Washington Square Press, 2004)

Meikle, Henry W. (ed.), *The Works of William Fowler*, 3 vols (Edinburgh and London: William Blackwood & Sons, 1914–40)

Napier, John, *A Plaine Discouery of the whole Reuelation of Saint Iohn* (Edinburgh: Robert Waldegrave, 1593)

Nichols, John (ed.), *The Progresses and Public Processions of Queen Elizabeth*, 3 vols (London: John Nichols, 1823)

—— *The Progresses, Processions and Magnificent Festivities of King James the First, His Royal Consort, Family and Court*, 4 vols (London: John Nichols, 1828)

Parkinson, David L. (ed.), *Alexander Montgomerie: Poems*, 2 vols (Trowbridge: Cromwell Press, 2000)

*The Passage of Our Most Drad Soueraigne Lady Quene Elyzabeth through the Citie of London to Westminster the Daye before Her Coronacion* (London: Richard Tottill, 1558 [1559])

Pemberton, William, *The Charge of God and the King* (1619)

Pitcher, John (ed.), *Francis Bacon: The Essays* (Harmondsworth: Penguin, 1985)

Rait, Robert S., and Annie I. Cameron (eds), *King James's Secret: Negotiations between Elizabeth and James VI Relating to the Execution of Mary Queen of Scots, from the Warrenden Papers* (London: Nisbet, 1927)

Rhodes, Neil, Jennifer Richards, and Joseph Marshall (eds), *King James VI and I: Selected Writings* (Aldershot: Ashgate, 2003)

Savile, John, *King Iames His Entertainment at Theobalds* (London: Thomas Snodham, 1603)

Scot, Reginald, *The Discouerie of Witchcraft* (London, 1584)

Scott, Thomas, *Vox Regis* ([Utrecht, 1624])

——— *Vox Populi. Or Newes from Spayne* ([Holland], 1620 [1624])

Sommerville, Johann P. (ed.), *King James VI and I: Political Writings* (Cambridge: Cambridge University Press, 1994)

Spenser, Edmund, *The Faerie Queene*, ed. A.C. Hamilton (Harlow: Longman, 2001)

Steuart, A. Francis (ed.), *Memoirs of Sir James Melville of Halhill, 1535–1617* (London: Routledge, 1929)

Stevenson, George (ed.), *Poems of Alexander Montgomerie: Supplementary Volume* (Edinburgh and London: William Blackwood and Sons, 1910)

Tanner, J. R. (ed.), *Constitutional Documents of the Reign of James I* (Cambridge: Cambridge University Press, 1930)

Thomson, T. (ed.), *The Acts of the Parliaments of Scotland*, 12 vols (Edinburgh, 1844)

*The True Narration of the Entertainment of His Royall Maiestie, from the Time of His Departure from Edenbrough; Till His Receiuing at London* (London: Thomas Creede for Thomas Millington, 1603)

Warner, George F. (ed.), *The Library of James VI, 1573–1583, from a manuscript in the hand of Peter Young, his tutor* (Edinburgh: Edinburgh University Press, 1893)

Westcott, Allan F. (ed.), *New Poems of James I of England* (New York: Columbia University Press, 1911)

Weyer, Johannes, *De Praestigiis Daemonum* (Basel, 1563; reprinted Geneva, 1579)

## Secondary sources

Adamson, John (ed.), *The Princely Courts of Europe, 1500–1750* (London: Weidenfeld and Nicolson, 1999)

Akrigg, G. P. V., 'The Literary Achievement of King James I', *The University of Toronto Quarterly*, 44 (1975), 116–29

Aldis, Harry, *A List of Books Printed in Scotland before 1700* (Edinburgh: Edinburgh Bibliographical Society, 1904)

Alter, Robert, and Frank Kermode (eds), *The Literary Guide to the Bible* (London: Collins, 1987)

Althusser, Louis, 'Ideology and the Ideological State Apparatuses', in *Lenin and Philosophy and Other Essays*, trans. Ben Brewster, second edition (London: New Left Books, 1977)

Amussen, Susan D., and Mark A. Kishlansky (eds), *Political Culture and Cultural Politics in Early Modern England* (Manchester: Manchester University Press, 1995)

Anglo, Sydney, *Images of Tudor Kingship* (London: Seaby, 1992)

——— (ed.), *The Damned Art: Essays in the Literature of Witchcraft* (London: Routledge & Kegan Paul, 1977)

Anglo, Sydney, 'Reginald Scot's *Discoverie of Witchcraft*: Scepticism and Sadduceeism', in Anglo (ed.), *The Damned Art*, pp. 106–39

Axton, Marie, *The Queen's Two Bodies: Drama and the Elizabethan Succession* (London: Royal Historical Society, 1977)

Baldwin, T. W., *William Shakspere's Small Latine & Lesse Greeke*, 2 vols (Urbana: University of Illinois Press, 1944–50)

Barnard, John, and D. F. McKenzie (eds), *The Cambridge History of the Book in Britain, Volume IV, 1557–1695* (Cambridge: Cambridge University Press, 2002)

Barroll, Leeds, 'A New History for Shakespeare and His Time', *Shakespeare Quarterly*, 39 (1988), 441–64

—— 'The Court of the First Stuart Queen', in Peck (ed.), *Mental World*, pp. 191–208

—— 'Assessing "Cultural Influence": James I as Patron of the Arts', *Shakespeare Studies*, 29 (2001), 132–62

—— *Anna of Denmark, Queen of England: A Cultural Biography* (Philadelphia: University of Pennsylvania Press, 2001)

Barthes, Roland, 'The Death of the Author', in *Image Music Text*, ed. and trans. Stephen Heath (London: Fontana Press, 1977), pp. 42–8

Bawcutt, Priscilla, 'James VI's Castalian Band: A Modern Myth', *Scottish Historical Review*, 80 (2001), 251–9

Baxter, Christopher, 'Johann Weyer's *De Praestigiis Daemonum*: Unsystematic Psychopathology', in Anglo (ed.), *The Damned Art*, pp. 53–75

Beal, Peter, *In Praise of Scribes: Manuscripts and Their Makers in Seventeenth-Century England* (Oxford: Oxford University Press, 1998)

Bell, Sandra J., 'Writing the Monarch: King James VI and *Lepanto*', in Mary Silcox, Helen Ostovich, and Graham Roebuck (eds), *Other Voices, Other Views: Expanding the Canon in English Renaissance Studies* (Newark: University of Delaware Press, 1999), pp. 193–208

—— ' "Precious Stinke": James I's *A Counterblaste to Tobacco*', in Fischlin and Fortier (eds), *Royal Subjects*, pp. 323–43

Bellany, Alastair, ' "Raylinge Rymes and Vaunting Verse": Libellous Politics in Early Stuart England, 1603–1628', in Sharpe and Lake (eds), *Culture and Politics*, pp. 285–310

—— *The Politics of Court Scandal in Early Modern England: News Culture and the Overbury Affair, 1603–1660* (Cambridge: Cambridge University Press, 2002)

Bennett, Andrew, *The Author* (London and New York: Routledge, 2005)

Bennett, H. S., *English Books and Readers, 1558–1603* (Cambridge: Cambridge University Press, 1965)

—— *English Books and Readers, 1603 to 1640* (Cambridge: Cambridge University Press, 1970)

Bergeron, David, *English Civic Pageantry, 1558–1642* (London: Edward Arnold, 1971)

—— *James I and Letters of Homoerotic Desire* (Iowa City: University of Iowa Press, 1999)

—— 'Writing King James's Sexuality', in Fischlin and Fortier (eds), *Royal Subjects*, pp. 344–68

Bevan, Jonquil, 'Scotland', in Barnard and McKenzie (eds), *The Cambridge History of the Book*, pp. 687–700

Bevington, David, and Peter Holbrook (eds), *The Politics of the Stuart Court Masque* (Cambridge: Cambridge University Press, 1998)

Birrell, T. A., *English Monarchs and Their Books* (London: British Library, 1987)

Bland, Mark, 'William Stansby and the Production of *The Workes of Beniamin Jonson*, 1615–16', *The Library: The Transactions of the Bibliographical Society*, 20 (1998), 1–33

Brady, Jennifer, 'Jonson's "To King James": Plain Speaking in the *Epigrammes* and the *Conversations*', *Studies in Philology*, 82 (1995), 380–99

—— ' "Noe Fault, but Life": Jonson's Folio as Monument and Barrier', in Brady and Herendeen (eds), *Ben Jonson's 1616 Folio*, pp. 192–216

—— and W. H. Herendeen (eds), *Ben Jonson's 1616 Folio* (Newark: University of Delaware Press, 1991)

Brennan, Michael G., *The Sidneys of Penshurst and the Monarchy, 1500–1700* (Aldershot: Ashgate, 2006)

Brooks, Douglas A., *From Playhouse to Printing House: Drama and Authorship in Early Modern England* (Cambridge: Cambridge University Press, 2000)

Bruster, Douglas, *Shakespeare and the Question of Culture: Early Modern Literature and the Critical Turn* (New York: Palgrave, 2003)

Burke, Sean (ed.), *Authorship from Plato to the Postmodern: A Reader* (Edinburgh: Edinburgh University Press, 1995)

Burns, Jimmy H., *The True Law of Kingship: Concepts of Monarchy in Early Modern Scotland* (Oxford: Oxford University Press, 1996)

Bushnell, Rebecca, 'George Buchanan, James VI and Neo-classicism', in Mason (ed.), *Scots and Britons*, pp. 91–111

Butler, Martin, ' "We are one mans all": Jonson's *The Gypsies Metamorphosed*', *Yearbook of English Studies*, 21 (1991), 253–73

—— 'Ben Jonson and the Limits of Courtly Panegyric', in Sharpe and Lake (eds), *Culture and Politics*, pp. 91–116

—— 'Jonson's Folio and the Politics of Patronage', *Criticism*, 35 (1993), 377–90

—— 'Courtly Negotiations', in Bevington and Holbrook (eds), *Politics of the Stuart Court Masque*, pp. 20–40

—— (ed.), *Re-Presenting Ben Jonson: Text, History, Performance* (London: Macmillan Press, 1999)

Callaghan, Dympna C., 'Recent Studies in Tudor and Stuart Drama', *Studies in English Literature, 1500–1900*, 44 (2004), 405–44

Capp, Bernard, 'The Political Dimension of Apocalyptic Thought', in Patrides and Wittreich (eds), *The Apocalypse in English Renaissance Thought and Literature*, pp. 93–124

Carpenter, Frederick Ives, *A Reference Guide to Edmund Spenser* (Chicago: University of Chicago Press, 1923)

Carpenter, Sarah, 'Early Scottish Drama', in Jack (ed.), *The History of Scottish Literature*, I, 199–212

Chambers, E. K., *The Elizabethan Stage*, 4 vols (Oxford: Oxford University Press, 1923)

Chartier, Roger, *The Order of Books: Readers, Authors, and Libraries in Europe between the Fourteenth and Eighteenth Centuries*, trans. Lydia G. Cochrane (Cambridge: Polity Press, 1994)

Christianson, Paul, 'Royal and Parliamentary Voices on the Ancient Constitution, c. 1604–1621', in Peck (ed.), *Mental World*, pp. 71–98

Clare, Janet, *'Art made tongue-tied by authority': Elizabethan and Jacobean Dramatic Censorship* (Manchester: Manchester University Press, 1990)

Clark, Stuart, 'King James's *Daemonologie*: Witchcraft and Kingship', in Anglo (ed.), *The Damned Art*, pp. 156–81

Clegg, Cyndia Susan, *Press Censorship in Jacobean England* (Cambridge: Cambridge University Press, 2001)

Clewett, Richard M., 'James VI of Scotland and His Literary Circle', *Aevum*, 47 (1973), 441–54

Cogswell, Thomas, *The Blessed Revolution: English Politics and the Coming of War, 1621–1624* (Cambridge: Cambridge University Press, 1989)

—— 'England and the Spanish Match', in Cust and Hughes (eds), *Conflict in Early Stuart England*, pp. 107–33

—— 'A Low Road to Extinction? Supply and Redress of Grievances in the Parliaments of the 1620s', *Historical Journal*, 33 (1990), 283–303

—— 'Underground Verse and the Transformation of Early Stuart Political Culture', in Amussen and Kishlansky (eds), *Political Culture and Cultural Politics*, pp. 277–300

Colclough, David, *Freedom of Speech in Early Stuart England* (Cambridge: Cambridge University Press, 2005)

Cole, Mary Hill, *The Portable Queen: Elizabeth I and the Politics of Ceremony* (Amherst: University of Massachusetts Press, 1999)

Corbett, Margery, and Ronald Lightbown, *The Comely Frontispiece: The Emblematic Title Page in England 1550–1660* (London: Routledge and Kegan Paul, 1979)

Coursen, H. R., *Macbeth: A Guide to the Play* (Westport, Connecticut, and London: Greenwood Press, 1997)

Cressy, David, *Bonfires and Bells: National Memory and the Protestant Calendar in Elizabethan and Stuart England* (Berkeley and Los Angeles: University of California Press, 1989)

Croft, Pauline, 'Robert Cecil and the Early Jacobean Court', in Peck (ed.), *Mental World*, pp. 134–47

—— *King James* (Basingstoke: Palgrave Macmillan, 2003)

Cruickshanks, Eveline (ed.), *The Stuart Courts* (Stroud: Sutton Publishing, 2000)

Cuddy, Neil, 'Reinventing a Monarchy: The Changing Structure and Political Function of the Stuart Court, 1603–88', in Cruickshanks (ed.), *The Stuart Courts*, pp. 59–85

Cust, Richard, 'News and Politics in Early Seventeenth-Century England', *Past and Present*, 112 (1986), 60–90

—— and Ann Hughes (eds), *Conflict in Early Stuart England* (London and New York: Longman, 1989)

Daly, James, 'The Idea of Absolute Monarchy in Seventeenth-Century England', *Historical Journal*, 21 (1978), 227–50

Díaz, José Simón, *Relaciones Breves de Actos Públicos Celebrados en Madrid, 1541–1650* (Madrid: Instituto de Estudios Madridleños, 1982)

Dickens, A. G., *The Courts of Europe: Politics, Patronage and Royalty, 1400–1800* (London: Thames and Hudson, 1977)

Dobranski, Stephen B., *Readers and Authorship in Early Modern England* (Cambridge: Cambridge University Press, 2005)

Doelman, James, ' "A King of Thine Own Heart": The English Reception of King James VI and I's *Basilikon Doron*', *Seventeenth Century*, 9 (1994), 1–9

—— 'The Reception of King James's Psalter', in Fischlin and Fortier (eds), *Royal Subjects*, pp. 454–75

Drew, Jean le, 'Subjecting the King: Ben Jonson's Praise of James I', *English Studies in Canada*, 17 (1991), 135–49

Dunlap, Rhodes, 'King James's Own Masque', *Philological Quarterly*, 41 (1962), 249–56

—— 'King James and Some Witches: The Date and Text of the *Daemonologie*', *Philological Quarterly*, 54 (1975), 40–6

Dunnigan, Sarah M., *Eros and Poetry at the Courts of Mary Queen of Scots and James VI* (Basingstoke: Palgrave Macmillan, 2002)

Durkan, John, 'The Library of Mary, Queen of Scots', in Lynch (ed.), *Mary Stewart*, pp. 71–104

Dutton, Richard, *Jacobean Civic Pageants* (Keele: Keele University Press, 1995)

—— *Ben Jonson: Authority: Criticism* (London: Macmillan Press, 1996)

—— *Licensing, Censorship and Authorship in Early Modern England: Buggeswords* (Basingstoke: Palgrave Macmillan, 2000)

Eagleton, Terry, *Literary Theory: An Introduction*, second edition (Oxford: Blackwell, 1996)

Eisenstein, Elizabeth L., *The Printing Press as an Agent of Change: Communications and Cultural Transformations in Early Modern Europe*, 2 vols (Cambridge: Cambridge University Press, 1979)

Erne, Lukas, *Shakespeare as Literary Dramatist* (Cambridge: Cambridge University Press, 2003)

Ferrell, Lori Anne, and Peter McCullough (eds), *The English Sermon Revised* (Manchester: Manchester University Press, 2000)

Figgis, John N., *The Divine Right of Kings* (Cambridge: Cambridge University Press, 1914)

Fincham, Kenneth, *Prelate as Pastor: The Episcopate of James I* (Oxford: Oxford University Press, 1990)

Firth, Katherine R., *The Apocalyptic Tradition in Reformation Britain* (Oxford: Oxford University Press, 1979)

Fischlin, Daniel, ' "Counterfeiting God": James VI (I) and the Politics of *Daemonologie* (1597)', *The Journal of Narrative Technique*, 26 (1996), 1–29

—— ' "To Eate the Flesh of Kings": James VI and I, Apocalyse, Nation and Sovereignty', in Fischlin and Fortier (eds), *Royal Subjects*, pp. 388–420

Fischlin, Daniel, ' "Like a Mercenary Poet": The Politics and Poetics of James VI's *Lepanto*', in Sally Mapstone (ed.), *Older Scots Literature* (Edinburgh: John Donald, 2005), pp. 540–59

—— and Mark Fortier (eds), *Royal Subjects: Essays on the Writings of James VI and I* (Detroit: Wayne State University Press, 2002)

Fleming, Morna R., 'The *Amatoria* of James VI: Loving by the *Reulis*', in Fischlin and Fortier (eds), *Royal Subjects*, pp. 124–48

Foucault, Michel, *Discipline and Punish: The Birth of the Prison*, trans. Alan Sheridan (Harmondsworth: Penguin, 1977 (first published as *Surveiller et punir*, 1975))

—— 'What Is an Author?', in *Language, Counter-Memory, Practice: Selected Essays and Interviews*, ed. Donald F. Bouchard and trans. Bouchard and Sherry Simon (Oxford: Blackwell, 1977), pp. 113–38

Fox, Adam, 'Popular Verses and Their Readership in the Early Seventeenth Century', in Raven, Small, and Tadmor (eds), *The Practice and Representation of Reading in England*, pp. 125–37

—— *Oral and Literate Culture in England, 1500–1700* (Oxford: Oxford University Press, 2000)

Frye, Susan, *Elizabeth: The Competition for Representation* (Oxford: Oxford University Press, 1993)

Gallagher, Catherine, and Stephen Greenblatt, *Practicing New Historicism* (Chicago and London: University of Chicago Press, 2000)

Gants, David L., 'The Printing of Jonson's Folio *Workes*', in Butler (ed.), *Re-Presenting Ben Jonson*, pp. 39–58

Gardiner, Samuel R., *History of England from the Accession of James I to the Outbreak of Civil War 1603–1642*, 10 vols (London: Longmans, Green, and Co., 1883)

Genette, Gérard, *Paratexts: Thresholds of Interpretation*, trans. Jane E. Lewin (Cambridge: Cambridge University Press, 1997 (originally published in French as *Seuils*, 1987))

Goldberg, Jonathan, *James I and the Politics of Literature: Jonson, Shakespeare, Donne, and Their Contemporaries* (Baltimore and London: Johns Hopkins University Press, 1983)

Goodare, Julian, 'Scottish Politics in the Reign of James VI', in Goodare and Lynch (eds), *Reign of James VI*, pp. 32–54

—— 'James VI's English Subsidy', in Goodare and Lynch (eds), *The Reign of James VI*, pp. 110–25

—— and Michael Lynch (eds), *The Reign of James VI* (East Lintin: Tuckwell Press, 2000)

Grady, Hugh, 'Shakespeare Studies, 2005: A Situated Overview', *Shakespeare*, 1 (2005), 102–20

Gray, Douglas, 'The Royal Entry in Sixteenth-Century Scotland', in Mapstone and Wood (eds), *The Rose and the Thistle*, pp. 10–37

Greenblatt, Stephen, *Renaissance Self-Fashioning from More to Shakespeare* (Chicago and London: University of Chicago Press, 1980)

—— *Shakespearean Negotiations: The Circulation of Social Energy in Renaissance England* (Oxford: Oxford University Press, 1988)

—— *Learning to Curse: Essays in Early Modern Culture* (New York and London: Routledge, 1990)

Griffiths, Antony, *The Print in Stuart Britain, 1603–1689* (London: British Museum, 1998)

Gurr, Andrew, *The Shakespearean Stage, 1574–1642* (Cambridge: Cambridge University Press, 1970)

Guy, John, *Tudor England* (Oxford: Oxford University Press, 1988)

—— (ed.), *The Reign of Elizabeth I: Court and Culture in the Last Decade* (Cambridge: Cambridge University Press, 1995)

Haigh, Christopher, *Elizabeth I*, second edition (London: Longman, 1998)

Hale, John, *The Civilisation of Europe in the Renaissance* (London: Fontana, 1994)

Helgerson, Richard, 'The Elizabethan Laureate: Self-Presentation and the Literary System', *English Literary History*, 46 (1979), 193–220

—— *Self-Crowned Laureates: Spenser, Jonson, Milton, and the Literary System* (Berkeley, Los Angeles, and London: University of California Press, 1983)

—— Review of Jonathan Goldberg, *James I and the Politics of Literature*, *Renaissance Quarterly*, 38 (1985), 180–3

—— 'Milton Reads the King's Book: Print, Performance, and the Making of a Bourgeois Idol', *Criticism*, 29 (1987), 1–26

Herman, Peter C., ' "Best of Poets, Best of Kings": King James and the Scene of Monarchic Verse', in Fischlin and Fortier (eds), *Royal Subjects*, pp. 61–103

—— (ed.), *Reading Monarchs Writing: The Poetry of Henry VIII, Mary Stuart, Elizabeth I, and James VI/I* (Tempe, Arizona: Arizona Center for Medieval and Renaissance Studies, 2002)

Holstun, James, 'Ranting at the New Historicism', *English Literary Renaissance*, 19 (1989), 189–225

Hopkins, Lisa, *Writing Renaissance Queens: Texts by and about Elizabeth I and Mary, Queen of Scots* (Newark: University of Delaware Press; London: Associated University Presses, 2002)

Howard, Jean E., 'The New Historicism in Renaissance Studies', *English Literary Renaissance*, 16 (1986), 13–46

Howarth, David, *Images of Rule: Art and Politics in the English Renaissance, 1485–1649* (Hampshire and London: Macmillan, 1997)

Ives, Carolyn, and David J. Parkinson, ' "The Fountain and Very Being of Truth": James VI, Poetic Invention, and National Identity', in Fischlin and Fortier (eds), *Royal Subjects*, pp. 104–23

Jack, R. D. S., 'James VI and Renaissance Poetic Theory', *English*, 16 (1967), 208–11

—— 'Poetry under James VI', in Jack (ed.), *History of Scottish Literature*, I, 125–40

—— (ed.), *The History of Scottish Literature*, 4 vols (Aberdeen: Aberdeen University Press, 1988)

Jardine, Lisa, *Worldly Goods* (London: Macmillan, 1996)

—— and Anthony Grafton, ' "Studied for Action": How Gabriel Harvey Read His Livy', *Past and Present*, 129 (1990), 30–78

Johns, Adrian, *The Nature of the Book: Print and Knowledge in the Making* (Chicago and London: University of Chicago Press, 1998)

Kallendorf, Hilaire, 'Intertextual Madness in *Hamlet*: The Ghost's Fragmented Performativity', *Renaissance and Reformation*, 22 (1998), 69–87

Kantorowicz, Ernst H., *The King's Two Bodies: A Study in Mediaeval Political Theology* (Princeton: Princeton University Press, 1957)

Kastan, David Scott, 'Proud Majesty Made a Subject: Shakespeare and the Spectacle of Rule', *Shakespeare Quarterly*, 37 (1986), 459–75

Kermode, Frank, *The Classic* (London: Faber and Faber, 1975)

Kiernan, Alvin, *Shakespeare the King's Playwright: Theater in the Stuart Court 1603–1613* (New Haven and London: Yale University Press, 1995)

King, John N., 'James I and King David: Jacobean Iconography and Its Legacy', in Fischlin and Fortier (eds), *Royal Subjects*, pp. 421–53

King, Stephen, ' "Your Best and Maist Faithfull Subjects": Andrew and James Melville as James VI and I's "Loyal Opposition" ', *Renaissance and Reformation*, 24 (2000), 17–30

Kishlansky, Mark A., *A Monarchy Transformed: Britain, 1603–1714* (London: Allen Lane, 1996)

Knapp, Jeffrey, 'What Is a Co-Author?', *Representations*, 89 (2005), 1–29

Lake, P. G., 'Thomas Scott and the Spanish Match', *Historical Journal*, 25 (1982), 805–25

—— 'Joseph Hall, Robert Skinner and the Rhetoric of Moderation at the Early Stuart Court', in Ferrell and McCullough (eds), *The English Sermon Revised*, pp. 167–85

—— 'The King (the Queen) and the Jesuit: James Stuart's *True Law of Free Monarchies* in Context/s', *Transactions of the Royal Historical Society*, 14 (2004), 243–60

Latham, Jacqueline E., '*The Tempest* and King James's *Daemonologie*', *Shakespeare Survey*, 28 (1975), 117–23

Lee, Maurice, *John Maitland of Thirlestane and the Foundation of the Stewart Despotism in Scotland* (Princeton: Princeton University Press, 1959)

—— *Great Britain's Solomon: James VI and I in His Three Kingdom* (Urbana and Chicago: University of Illinois Press, 1990)

Lindley, David, 'Embarrassing Ben: The Masques for Frances Howard', *English Literary Renaissance*, 16 (1986), 343–59

Lockyer, Roger, *Buckingham* (London and New York: Longman, 1981)

Loewenstein, David, and Janel Mueller (eds), *The Cambridge History of Early Modern English Literature* (Cambridge: Cambridge University Press, 2002)

Loewenstein, Joseph, 'The Script in the Marketplace', *Representations*, 12 (1985), 101–14

—— *Ben Jonson and Possessive Authorship* (Cambridge: Cambridge University Press, 2002)

Love, Harold, *The Culture and Commerce of Texts: Scribal Publication in Seventeenth-Century England* (Amherst: University of Massachusetts Press, 1998 (first published 1993))

Lyall, Roderick J., 'James VI and the Sixteenth-Century Cultural Crisis', in Goodare and Lynch (eds), *The Reign of James VI*, pp. 55–70

Lynch, Michael, (ed.), *Mary Stewart, Queen in Three Kingdoms* (Oxford: Blackwell, 1988)

—— *Scotland: A New History* (London: Pimlico, 1991)

—— 'Court Ceremony and Ritual during the Personal Reign of James VI', in Goodare and Lynch (eds), *The Reign of James VI*, pp. 71–92

McCabe, Richard A., 'The Masks of Duessa: Spenser, Mary Queen of Scots, and James VI', *English Literary Renaissance*, 17 (1987), 224–42

MacDonald, A. A., 'Early Modern Scottish Literature and the Parameters of Culture', in Mapstone and Wood (eds), *The Rose and the Thistle*, pp. 77–100

MacDonald, Alan R., *The Jacobean Kirk, 1567–1625* (Aldershot: Ashgate, 1998)

McFarlane, I. D., *Buchanan* (London: Duckworth, 1981)

McGinn, Bernard, 'Revelation', in Alter and Kermode (eds), *The Literary Guide to the Bible*, pp. 523–44

Mackechnie, Aonghus, 'James VI's Architects and Their Architecture', in Goodare and Lynch (eds), *Reign of James VI*, pp. 154–69

McKitterick, David, *Print, Manuscript and the Search for Order, 1450–1830* (Cambridge: Cambridge University Press, 2003)

McManus, Clare, 'Marriage and the Performance of the Romance Quest: Anne of Denmark and the Stirling Baptismal Celebrations for Prince Henry', in L. A. J. R. Houwen, A. A. Macdonald, and S. Mapstone (eds), *A Palace in the Wild* (Leuven: Peeters, 2000), pp. 177–98

McPherson, David, 'Ben Jonson's Library and Marginalia: An Annotated Catalogue', *Studies in Philology*, 71 (1974), 1–106

McRae, Andrew, *Literature, Satire and the Early Stuart State* (Cambridge: Cambridge University Press, 2004)

Macray, William Dunn, *Annals of the Bodleian Library* (Oxford: Oxford University Press, 1890)

Man, Paul de, *The Resistance to Theory* (Minneapolis: University of Minnesota Press, 1986)

Mann, Alastair, *The Scottish Book Trade 1500–1720: Print Commerce and Print Control in Early Modern Scotland* (East Linton: Tuckwell Press, 2000)

Mapstone, Sally, and Juliette Wood (eds), *The Rose and the Thistle: Essays on the Culture of Late Medieval and Renaissance Scotland* (East Linton: Tuckwell Press, 1998)

Marcus, Leah S., *Puzzling Shakespeare: Local Reading and Its Discontents* (Berkeley, Los Angeles, London: University of California Press, 1988)

Marotti, Arthur F., *Manuscript, Print and the English Renaissance Lyric* (Ithaca: Cornell University Press, 1995)

Marshall, Joseph, 'Reading and Misreading King James 1622–42', in Fischlin and Fortier (eds), *Royal Subjects*, pp. 476–511

Mason, Roger A. (ed.), *Scots and Britons: Scottish Political Thought and the Union of 1603* (Cambridge: Cambridge University Press, 1994)

—— 'George Buchanan, James VI and the Presbyterians', in Mason (ed.), *Scots and Britons*, pp. 112–37

Masten, Jeffrey, *Textual Intercourse: Collaboration, Authorship, and Sexualities in Renaissance Drama* (Cambridge: Cambridge University Press, 1997)

May, Steven W., 'Tudor Aristocrats and the Mythical "Stigma of Print"', in A. Leigh Deneef and M. Thomas Hester (eds), *Renaissance Papers 1980* (Durham, NC: The Southeastern Renaissance Conference, 1981), 11–18

—— *The Elizabethan Courtier Poets: The Poems and Their Contexts* (Columbia and London: University of Missouri Press, 1991)

—— 'Renaissance Manuscript Anthologies: Editing the Social Editors', *English Manuscript Studies, 1100–1700*, 11 (2002), 203–16

—— 'The Circulation in Manuscript of Poems by King James VI and I', in James Dutcher and Anne Lake Prescott (eds), *Renaissance Historicisms: Essays in Honor of Arthur F. Kinney* (Newark: University of Delaware Press, forthcoming)

Miller, Jacqueline T., *Poetic License: Authority and Authorship in Medieval and Renaissance Contexts* (Oxford: Oxford University Press, 1986)

Montrose, Louis, 'New Historicisms', in Stephen Greenblatt and Giles Gunn (eds), *Redrawing the Boundaries: The Transformation of English and American Literary Studies* (New York: Modern Language Association of America, 1992), pp. 392–418

Morrill, John, Paul Slack and Daniel Woolf (eds), *Public Duty and Private Conscience in Seventeenth-Century England* (Oxford: Oxford University Press, 1993)

Morse, Ruth, 'The Year's Contributions to Shakespeare Studies: 1. Critical Studies', *Shakespeare Survey*, 56 (2003), 300–31

Nash, Andrew (ed.), *The Culture of Collected Editions* (Basingstoke: Palgrave Macmillan, 2003)

Newman, J., 'Inigo Jones and the Politics of Architecture', in Sharpe and Lake (eds), *Culture and Politics*, pp. 229–56

Newton, Diana, *The Making of the Jacobean Regime: James VI and I and the Government of England, 1603–1605* (Woodbridge: Boydell, 2005)

Newton, Richard C., 'Jonson and the (Re-)invention of the Book', in Summers and Pebworth (eds), *Classic and Cavalier*, pp. 31–55

Nicolson, Adam, *Power and Glory: Jacobean England and the Making of the King James Bible* (London: Harper Collins, 2003)

Normand, Lawrence, and Gareth Roberts (eds), *Witchcraft in Early Modern Scotland: James VI's Demonology and the North Berwick Witches* (Exeter: University of Exeter Press, 2000)

Orgel, Stephen, *The Jonsonian Masque* (Cambridge, Mass.: Harvard University Press, 1965)

—— *The Illusion of Power: Political Theater in the English Renaissance* (Berkeley, Los Angeles, and London: University of California Press, 1975)

Osborne, Francis, *Historical Memoirs on the Reigns of Queen Elizabeth and King James* (London, 1658)

Parry, Graham, *The Golden Age Restor'd: The Culture of the Stuart Court* (Manchester: Manchester University Press, 1981)

Pask, Kevin, *The Emergence of the English Author: Scripting the Life of the Poet in Early Modern England* (Cambridge: Cambridge University Press, 1996)

Patrides, C. A., and Joseph Wittreich (eds), *The Apocalypse in English Renaissance Thought and Literature: Patterns, Antecedents, Repercussions* (Manchester: Manchester University Press, 1984)

Patterson, Annabel, *Censorship and Interpretation* (Wisconsin and London: University of Wisconsin Press, 1984)

Patterson, W. B., *King James VI and I and the Reunion of Christendom* (Cambridge: Cambridge University Press, 1997)

Peck, Linda Levy, *Northampton: Patronage and Policy at the Court of James I* (London: Allen and Unwin, 1982)

—— ' "For a King not to be bountiful were a fault": Perspectives on Court Patronage in Early Stuart England', *Journal of British Studies*, 25 (1986), 31–61

—— (ed.), *The Mental World of the Jacobean Court* (Cambridge: Cambridge University Press, 1991)

—— 'The Mentality of a Jacobean Grandee', in Peck (ed.), *Mental World*, pp. 148–68

Pelikan, Jaroslav, 'Some Uses of Apocalypse in the Magisterial Reformers', in Patrides and Wittreich (eds), *The Apocalypse in English Renaissance Thought and Literature*, pp. 74–92

Perry, Curtis, *The Making of Jacobean Culture* (Cambridge: Cambridge University Press, 1997)

—— 'Royal authorship and Problems of Manuscript Attribution in the Poems of King James VI and I', *Notes and Queries*, n.s. 46 (1999), 243–6

—— ' "If Proclamations Will Not Serve": The Late Manuscript Poetry of James I and the Culture of Libel', in Fischlin and Fortier (eds), *Royal Subjects*, pp. 205–32

Phillips, J. E., 'George Buchanan and the Sidney Circle', *Huntington Library Quarterly*, 12 (1948–9), 23–55

—— *Images of a Queen: Mary Stuart in Sixteenth-Century Literature* (Berkeley and Los Angeles: University of California Press, 1964)

Pitkin, Hanna Fenichel, *The Concept of Representation* (Berkeley, Los Angeles: University of California Press, 1967)

Platt, Colin, *The Great Rebuildings of Tudor and Stuart England* (London: UCL Press, 1994)

Pocock, J. G. A., *Politics, Language and Time: Essays on Political Thought and History* (London: Methuen, 1972)

Raven, James, Helen Small, and Naomi Tadmor (eds), *The Practice and Representation of Reading in England* (Cambridge: Cambridge University Press, 1996)

Raymond, Joad, *The Invention of the Newspaper: English Newsbooks, 1641–1649* (Oxford: Oxford University Press, 1996)

Redworth, Glyn, *The Prince and the Infanta: The Cultural Politics of the Spanish Match* (New Haven, Connecticut, and London: Yale University Press, 2003)

Relle, Eleanor, 'Some New Marginalia and Poems of Gabriel Harvey', *Review of English Studies*, 23 (1972), 401–16

Richey, Esther Gilman, *The Politics of Revelation in the English Renaissance* (Columbia: University of Missouri Press, 1998)

Riggs, David, *Ben Jonson: A Life* (Cambridge, Mass., and London: Harvard University Press, 1989)

Robertson, James, 'Stuart London and the Idea of a Royal Capital City', *Renaissance Studies*, 15 (2001), 37–58

Russell, Conrad, *Parliaments and English Politics 1621–1629* (Oxford: Oxford University Press, 1979)

—— *The Addled Parliament of 1614: The Limits of Revisionism* (Reading: University of Reading, 1992)

—— 'Divine Rights in the Early Seventeenth Century', in Morrill, Slack and Woolf (eds), *Public Duty and Private Conscience*, pp. 104–17

Said, Edward, *Beginnings: Intention and Method* (New York: Basic, 1975)

Sandler, Florence, '*The Faerie Queene*: An Elizabethan Apocalypse', in Patrides and Wittreich (eds), *The Apocalypse in English Renaissance Thought and Literature*, pp. 148–74

Saunders, J. W., 'The Stigma of Print: A Note on the Social Bases of Tudor Poetry', *Essays in Criticism*, 1 (1951), 139–64

—— 'From Manuscript to Print: A Note on the Circulation of Poetic MSS in the Sixteenth Century', *Proceedings of the Leeds Philosophical and Literary Society* (1951), 507–28

Scott, Sir Walter, *The Secret History of the Court of James I* (Edinburgh, 1811)

Sharpe, Kevin (ed.), *Faction and Parliament: Essays in Early Stuart History* (Oxford: Oxford University Press, 1978)

—— *Criticism and Compliment: The Politics of Literature in the England of Charles I* (Cambridge: Cambridge University Press, 1987)

—— *Politics and Ideas in Early Stuart England* (London: Pinter, 1989)

—— *The Personal Rule of Charles I* (New Haven and London: Yale University Press, 1992)

—— 'The King's Writ: Royal Authors and Royal Authority in Early Modern England', in Sharpe and Lake (eds), *Culture and Politics*, pp. 117–38

—— *Reading Revolutions: The Politics of Reading in Early Modern England* (New Haven and London: Yale University Press, 2000)

—— *Remapping Early Modern England: The Culture of Seventeenth-Century Politics* (Cambridge: Cambridge University Press, 2000)

—— 'Reading Revelations: Prophecy, Hermeneutics and Politics in Early Modern Britain', in Sharpe and Zwicker (eds), *Reading, Society and Politics*, pp. 122–63

—— and Peter Lake (eds), *Culture and Politics in Early Stuart England* (Stanford: Stanford University Press, 1993)

—— and Stephen N. Zwicker (eds), *Politics of Discourse: The Literature and History of Seventeenth-Century England* (Berkeley, Los Angeles, and London: University of California Press, 1987)

—— and Stephen N. Zwicker (eds), *Reading, Society and Politics in Early Modern England* (Cambridge: Cambridge University Press, 2003)

Silcox, Mary, Helen Ostovich, and Graham Roebuck (eds), *Other Voices, Other Views: Expanding the Canon in English Renaissance Studies* (Newark: University of Delaware Press, 1999)

Simpson, Grant G., 'The Personal Letters of James VI: A Short Commentary', in Goodare and Lynch (eds), *Reign of James VI and I*, pp. 141–53

Sinfield, Alan, *Faultlines: Cultural Materialism and the Politics of Dissident Reading* (Oxford: Oxford University Press, 1992)

Skinner, Quentin, *The Foundations of Modern Political Thought*, 2 vols (Cambridge: Cambridge University Press, 1978)

Smuts, R. Malcolm, 'Cultural Diversity and Cultural Change at the Court of James I', in Peck (ed.), *Mental World*, pp. 99–112

—— (ed.), *The Stuart Court and Europe: Essays in Politics and Political Culture* (Cambridge: Cambridge University Press, 1996)

—— 'Art and the Material Culture of Majesty in Early Stuart England', in Smuts (ed.), *The Stuart Court and Europe*, pp. 86–112

—— 'The Making of *Rex Pacificus*: James VI and I and the Problem of Peace in an Age of Religious War', in Fischlin and Fortier (eds), *Royal Subjects*, pp. 371–87

Sommerville, Johann P., 'James I and the Divine Right of Kings: English Politics and Continental Theory', in Peck (ed.), *Mental World*, pp. 55–70

—— 'King James VI and I and John Selden: Two Voices on History and the Constitution', in Fischlin and Fortier (eds), *Royal Subjects*, pp. 290–322

Spiller, Michael R. G., 'The Scottish Court and the Scottish Sonnet at the Union of the Crowns', in Mapstone and Wood (eds), *The Rose and the Thistle*, pp. 101–15

Stern, Virginia F., *Gabriel Harvey: His Life, Marginalia and Library* (Oxford: Oxford University Press, 1979)

Stevenson, David, *Scotland's Last Royal Wedding* (Edinburgh: John Donald, 1997)

Stevenson, W. H. (ed.), *King James Bible: A Selection* (London and New York: Longman, 1994)

Stone, Lawrence, *The Crisis of the Aristocracy* (Oxford: Oxford University Press, 1965)

Strong, Roy, *Portraits of Queen Elizabeth I* (Oxford: Oxford University Press, 1963)

—— *Art and Power: Renaissance Festivals 1450–1650* (Woodbridge: Boydell, 1984)

—— *Henry, Prince of Wales and England's Lost Renaissance* (London: Thames and Hudson, 1986)

—— *Gloriana: The Portraits of Queen Elizabeth I* (London: Thames and Hudson, 1987)

Summers, Claude J., and Ted-Larry Pebworth (eds), *Classic and Cavalier: Essays on Jonson and the Sons of Ben* (Pittsburgh: University of Pittsburgh Press, 1982)

Thrush, Andrew, 'The Personal Rule of James I, 1611–1620', in Thomas Cogswell, Richard Cust, and Peter Lake (eds), *Politics, Religion and Popularity in Early Stuart Britain: Essays in Honour of Conrad Russell* (Cambridge: Cambridge University Press, 2002), pp. 84–101

Tribble, Evelyn B., *Margins and Marginality: The Printed Page in Early Modern England* (Charlottesville and London: University Press of Virginia, 1993)

Velz, John, 'From Authorisation to Authorship, Orality to Literature: The Case of Medieval and Renaissance Drama', *Text: An Interdisciplinary Annual of Textual Studies*, 6 (1994), 197–211

Wakeley, Maria, and Graham Rees, 'Folios Fit for a King: James I, John Bill, and the King's Printers, 1616–1620', *Huntington Library Quarterly*, 68 (2005), 467–95

Wall, Wendy, *The Imprint of Gender: Authorship and Publication in the English Renaissance* (Ithaca and New York: Cornell University Press, 1993)

Weimann, Robert, *Authority and Representation in Early Modern Discourse*, ed. David Hillman (Baltimore and London: Johns Hopkins University Press, 1996)

Weldon, Sir Anthony, *The Court and Character of King James* (London, 1650)

—— *The Court and Character of King James* (London: G. Smeeton, 1817)

Willson, D. H., 'James I and His Literary Assistants', *Huntington Library Quarterly*, 8 (1944–5), 35–57

—— *King James VI and I*, second edition (London: Jonathan Cape, 1963)

Wilson, Arthur, *The History of Great Britain, Being the Life and Reign of King James the First* (London, 1653)

Wilson, Jean, *Entertainments for Elizabeth I* (Woodbridge: Brewer, 1980)

Wormald, Jenny, *Court, Kirk and Community: Scotland 1470–1625* (Edinburgh: Edinburgh University Press, 1981)

—— 'James VI and I: Two Kings or One?', *History*, 68 (1983), 187–209

—— Review of Jonathan Goldberg, *James I and the Politics of Literature*, *History*, 70 (1985), 128–30

—— 'James VI and I, *Basilikon Doron* and *The Trew Law of Free Monarchies:* The Scottish Context and the English Translation', in Peck (ed.), *Mental World*, pp. 36–54

Wortham, Simon, ' "Pairt of My Taill Is Yet Untolde": James VI and I, the *Phoenix*, and the Royal Gift', in Fischlin and Fortier (eds), *Royal Subjects*, pp. 182–204

Woudhuysen, Henry, *Sir Philip Sidney and the Circulation of Manuscripts, 1558–1640* (Oxford: Oxford University Press, 1996)

Zaret, David, *Origins of Democratic Culture: Printing, Petitions, and the Public Sphere in Early-Modern England* (Princeton: Princeton University Press, 2000)

Zwicker, Steven N., *Lines of Authority: Politics and English Literary Culture, 1649–1689* (Ithaca and London: Cornell University Press, 1993)

# Index

Note: 'n.' after a page reference indicates the number of a note on that page: numbers in *italics* refer to illustrations.